Teach Yourself® Microsoft® Word 2000

Teach Yourself®
Microsoft®
Word 2000

Keith Underdahl

IDG Books Worldwide, Inc.
An International Data Group Company

Foster City, CA • Chicago, IL • Indianapolis, IN • New York, NY

Teach Yourself® Microsoft® Word 2000

Published by
IDG Books Worldwide, Inc.
An International Data Group Company
919 E. Hillsdale Blvd., Suite 400
Foster City, CA 94404
`www.idgbooks.com` (IDG Books Worldwide Web site)

ISBN: 0-7645-3284-7

Printed in the United States of America

10 9 8 7 6 5 4 3 2 1

1P/SR/QU/ZZ/IN

Distributed in the United States by IDG Books Worldwide, Inc.

Distributed by CDG Books Canada Inc. for Canada; by Transworld Publishers Limited in the United Kingdom; by IDG Norge Books for Norway; by IDG Sweden Books for Sweden; by IDG Books Australia Publishing Corporation Pty. Ltd. for Australia and New Zealand; by TransQuest Publishers Pte Ltd. for Singapore, Malaysia, Thailand, Indonesia, and Hong Kong; by Gotop Information Inc. for Taiwan; by ICG Muse, Inc. for Japan; by Norma Comunicaciones S.A. for Colombia; by Intersoft for South Africa; by Le Monde en Tique for France; by International Thomson Publishing for Germany, Austria and Switzerland; by Distribuidora Cuspide for Argentina; by Livraria Cultura for Brazil; by Ediciones ZETA S.C.R. Ltda. for Peru; by WS Computer Publishing Corporation, Inc., for the Philippines; by Contemporanea de Ediciones for Venezuela; by Express Computer Distributors for the Caribbean and West Indies; by Micronesia Media Distributor, Inc. for Micronesia; by Grupo Editorial Norma S.A. for Guatemala; by Chips Computadoras S.A. de C.V. for Mexico; by Editorial Norma de Panama S.A. for Panama; by American Bookshops for Finland. Authorized Sales Agent: Anthony Rudkin Associates for the Middle East and North Africa.

For general information on IDG Books Worldwide's books in the U.S., please call our Consumer Customer Service department at 800-762-2974. For reseller information, including discounts and premium sales, please call our Reseller Customer Service department at 800-434-3422.

For information on where to purchase IDG Books Worldwide's books outside the U.S., please contact our International Sales department at 317-596-5530 or fax 317-596-5692.

For consumer information on foreign language translations, please contact our Customer Service department at 800-434-3422, fax 317-596-5692, or e-mail rights@idgbooks.com.

For information on licensing foreign or domestic rights, please phone +1-650-655-3109.

For sales inquiries and special prices for bulk quantities, please contact our Sales department at 650-655-3200 or write to the address above.

For information on using IDG Books Worldwide's books in the classroom or for ordering examination copies, please contact our Educational Sales department at 800-434-2086 or fax 317-596-5499.

For press review copies, author interviews, or other publicity information, please contact our Public Relations department at 650-655-3000 or fax 650-655-3299.

For authorization to photocopy items for corporate, personal, or educational use, please contact Copyright Clearance Center, 222 Rosewood Drive, Danvers, MA 01923, or fax 978-750-4470.

Library of Congress Cataloging-in-Publication Data
Underdahl, Keith.
    Teach Yourself Microsoft Word 2000 / Keith Underdahl.
        p.   cm.
    Includes index.
    ISBN 0-7645-3284-7 (alk. paper)
    1. Microsoft Word.   2. Word processing.   I. Title.
Z52.5.M52U54 1999
652.5'5369--dc21   98–10960
                                                                              CIP

is a registered trademark or trademark under exclusive license to IDG Books Worldwide, Inc., from International Data Group, Inc. in the United States and/or other countries.

ABOUT IDG BOOKS WORLDWIDE

Welcome to the world of IDG Books Worldwide.

IDG Books Worldwide, Inc., is a subsidiary of International Data Group, the world's largest publisher of computer-related information and the leading global provider of information services on information technology. IDG was founded more than 30 years ago by Patrick J. McGovern and now employs more than 9,000 people worldwide. IDG publishes more than 290 computer publications in over 75 countries. More than 90 million people read one or more IDG publications each month.

Launched in 1990, IDG Books Worldwide is today the #1 publisher of best-selling computer books in the United States. We are proud to have received eight awards from the Computer Press Association in recognition of editorial excellence and three from Computer Currents' First Annual Readers' Choice Awards. Our best-selling ...For Dummies® series has more than 50 million copies in print with translations in 31 languages. IDG Books Worldwide, through a joint venture with IDG's Hi-Tech Beijing, became the first U.S. publisher to publish a computer book in the People's Republic of China. In record time, IDG Books Worldwide has become the first choice for millions of readers around the world who want to learn how to better manage their businesses.

Our mission is simple: Every one of our books is designed to bring extra value and skill-building instructions to the reader. Our books are written by experts who understand and care about our readers. The knowledge base of our editorial staff comes from years of experience in publishing, education, and journalism — experience we use to produce books to carry us into the new millennium. In short, we care about books, so we attract the best people. We devote special attention to details such as audience, interior design, use of icons, and illustrations. And because we use an efficient process of authoring, editing, and desktop publishing our books electronically, we can spend more time ensuring superior content and less time on the technicalities of making books.

You can count on our commitment to deliver high-quality books at competitive prices on topics you want to read about. At IDG Books Worldwide, we continue in the IDG tradition of delivering quality for more than 30 years. You'll find no better book on a subject than one from IDG Books Worldwide.

John Kilcullen
Chairman and CEO
IDG Books Worldwide, Inc.

Steven Berkowitz
President and Publisher
IDG Books Worldwide, Inc.

*Eighth Annual
Computer Press
Awards 1992*

*Ninth Annual
Computer Press
Awards 1993*

*Tenth Annual
Computer Press
Awards 1994*

*Eleventh Annual
Computer Press
Awards 1995*

Credits

Acquisitions Editor
Andy Cummings

Development Editors
Tracy Brown
Elizabeth Collins
Ken Brown

Technical Editor
David Haskin

Copy Editor
Ami Knox

Project Coordinator
Regina Snyder

Book Designers
Daniel Ziegler Design
Cátálin Dulfu
Kurt Krames

Graphics and Production Specialists
Linda Boyer
Angie Hunckler
Brent Savage
Janet Seib
Kathie Schutte
Kate Snell
Michael A. Sullivan

Proofreaders
Christine Berman
Kelli Botta
Jennifer Mahern
Rebecca Senninger
Rob Springer
Ethel M. Winslow

Indexer
York Publishing Services

About the Author

Keith Underdahl is an author and electronic publishing specialist who lives in Albany, Oregon. Keith specializes in the publication of historic texts on CD-ROM for a variety of computer platforms. He uses Microsoft Word as his primary editing tool when preparing documents for reading by third-party software.

Keith has served as both a writer and a technical editor on dozens of computer titles from IDG Books Worldwide. When he is not goofing off with computers, Keith works as the Pacific Northwest editor for *Street Bike Magazine*, a motorcycle magazine serving the western United States.

To my sons, Soren and Cole: My wishes for the brightest future.

Welcome to
Teach Yourself

Welcome to Teach Yourself, a series read and trusted by millions for nearly a decade. Although you may have seen the Teach Yourself name on other books, ours is the original. In addition, no Teach Yourself series has ever delivered more on the promise of its name than this series. That's because IDG Books Worldwide recently transformed Teach Yourself into a new cutting-edge format that gives you all the information you need to learn quickly and easily.

Readers told us that they want to learn by doing and that they want to learn as much as they can in as short a time as possible. We listened to you and believe that our new task-by-task format and suite of learning tools deliver the book you need to successfully teach yourself any technology topic. Features such as our Personal Workbook, which lets you practice and reinforce the skills you've just learned, help ensure that you get full value out of the time you invest in your learning. Handy cross-references to related topics and online sites broaden your knowledge and give you control over the kind of information you want, when you want it.

More Answers...

In designing the latest incarnation of this series, we started with the premise that people like you, who are beginning to intermediate computer users, want to take control of their own learning. To do this, you need the proper tools to find answers to questions so you can solve problems now.

In designing a series of books that provide such tools, we created a unique and concise visual format. The added bonus: Teach Yourself books pack more information into their pages than other books written on the same subjects. Skill for skill, you typically get much more information in a Teach Yourself book. In fact, Teach Yourself books, on average, cover twice the skills covered by other computer books — as many as 125 skills per book — so they're more likely to address your specific needs.

...In Less Time

We know you don't want to spend twice the time to get all this great information, so we provide lots of time-saving features:

▶ A modular task-by-task organization of information: Any task you want to perform is easy to find and includes simple-to-follow steps.

▶ A larger size than standard makes the book easy to read and convenient to use at a computer workstation. The large format also enables us to include many more illustrations — 500 screen illustrations show you how to get everything done!

▶ A Personal Workbook at the end of each chapter reinforces learning with extra practice, real-world applications for your learning, and questions and answers to test your knowledge.

▶ Cross-references appearing at the bottom of each task page refer you to related information, providing a path through the book for learning particular aspects of the software thoroughly.

▶ A Find It Online feature offers valuable ideas on where to go on the Internet to get more information or to download useful files.

▶ Take Note sidebars provide added-value information from our expert authors for more in-depth learning.

▶ An attractive, consistent organization of information helps you quickly find and learn the skills you need.

These Teach Yourself features are designed to help you learn the essential skills about a technology in the least amount of time, with the most benefit. We've placed these features consistently throughout the book, so you quickly learn where to go to find just the information you need — whether you work through the book from cover to cover or use it later to solve a new problem.

You will find a Teach Yourself book on almost any technology subject — from the Internet to Windows to Microsoft Office. Take control of your learning today, with IDG Books Worldwide's Teach Yourself series.

Teach Yourself
More Answers in Less Time

Go to this area if you want special tips, cautions, and notes that provide added insight into the current task.

Search through the task headings to find the topic you want right away. To learn a new skill, search the contents, chapter opener, or the extensive index to find what you need. Then find — at a glance — the clear task heading that matches it.

Creating a Fax Cover Sheet

Of the many different kinds of documents you will create using Word, few if any are as mundane as a facsimile cover sheet. This simple piece of paper contains basic information that the recipient probably knows already and will more often than not ignore completely.

Nevertheless, a cover sheet is an important thing to include with most outgoing faxes. Without it, the recipient might not know what is being sent or who is sending it. This is especially important if you are faxing to a company fax machine, where many different people might use the same machine. Furthermore, your fax cover sheets usually need a professional appearance, and they should be laid out in a way that is easy to read.

Creating a document from scratch that meets these goals can take quite a bit of time. Even if you're fast, you may need at least ten minutes to create the document, insert the required text, format it, and print it out. Why spend all this effort for a document that will probably be ignored and thrown in the garbage only minutes after you send it?

A much better solution is to use one of the many fax cover sheet templates offered by Word. These templates turn what would otherwise be a monotonous and time-consuming chore into a simple one- or two-minute affair. With the fax cover sheet templates, all you have to do is open the document, enter a few lines of simple information, and click Print.

You don't even have to save the document to your disk if you don't want to, because as soon as you send the fax, the document will be obsolete anyway.

The figures on the facing page show you how to create a fax cover sheet using one of the fax templates in Word. The first two figures show you how to use the New dialog box to create the cover sheet, and the last two figures demonstrate how to actually enter text into the sheet.

Learn the concepts behind the task at hand and, more important, learn how the task is relevant in the real world. Time-saving suggestions and advice show you how to make the most of each skill.

TAKE NOTE

USING THE FAX WIZARD

Another way to create a fax cover sheet is to use the Fax Wizard, also available in the New dialog box. If you choose the Fax Wizard, you will be taken through a variety of dialog boxes that ask for information about yourself and the intended recipient. The Fax Wizard — and wizards in general — are discussed extensively in Chapter 4 under "Using Wizards."

SENDING THE FAX WITH WINDOWS MESSAGING OR OUTLOOK

If you are sending your fax using Microsoft's Windows Messaging, Exchange, or Outlook, you will be asked by the program if you wish to send a cover letter. Choose No because you have already created a cover sheet in Word. Send the cover sheet as the first page of your fax, and be sure to include the number of pages you sent.

After you learn the task at hand, you may have more questions, or you may want to read about other tasks related to the topic. Use the cross-references to find different tasks to make your learning more efficient.

CROSS-REFERENCE
You might be able to enter some information onto the cover sheet using AutoText. See Chapter 12.

102

FIND IT ONLINE
GFI Fax, at http://www.gfifax.com/, offers software for handling facsimiles on a computer.

Use the Find It Online element to locate Internet resources that provide more background, take you on interesting side trips, and offer additional tools for mastering and using the skills you need. (Occasionally you'll find a handy shortcut here.)

The current chapter name and number always appear in the top right-hand corner of every task spread, so you always know exactly where you are in the book.

Who This Book Is For

This book is written for you, a beginning to intermediate PC user who isn't afraid to take charge of his or her own learning experience. You don't want a lot of technical jargon; you *do* want to learn as much about PC technology as you can in a limited amount of time. You need a book that is straightforward, easy to follow, and logically organized, so you can find answers to your questions easily. And, you appreciate simple-to-use tools such as handy cross-references and visual step-by-step procedures that help you make the most of your learning. We have created the unique Teach Yourself format specifically to meet your needs.

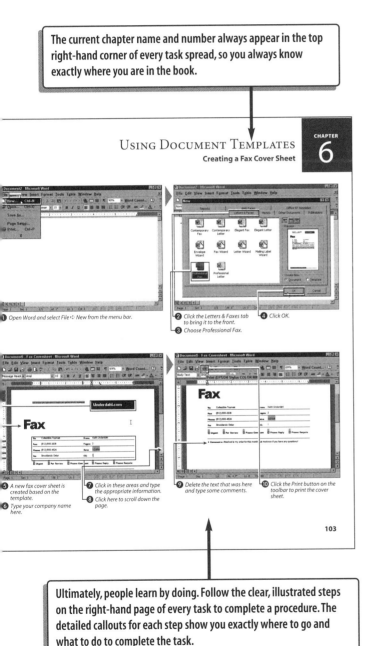

USING DOCUMENT TEMPLATES
Creating a Fax Cover Sheet

CHAPTER 6

① Open Word and select File ❖ New from the menu bar.

② Click the Letters & Faxes tab to bring it to the front.
③ Choose Professional Fax.

④ Click OK.

⑤ A new fax cover sheet is created based on the template.
⑥ Type your company name here.

⑦ Click in these areas and type the appropriate information.
⑧ Click here to scroll down the page.

⑨ Delete the text that was here and type some comments.

⑩ Click the Print button on the toolbar to print the cover sheet.

103

Ultimately, people learn by doing. Follow the clear, illustrated steps on the right-hand page of every task to complete a procedure. The detailed callouts for each step show you exactly where to go and what to do to complete the task.

Personal Workbook

It's a well-known fact that much of what we learn is lost soon after we learn it if we don't reinforce our newly acquired skills with practice and repetition. That's why each Teach Yourself chapter ends with your own Personal Workbook. Here's where you can get extra practice, test your knowledge, and discover ideas for using what you've learned in the real world. There's even a Visual Quiz to help you remember your way around the topic's software environment.

Feedback

Please let us know what you think about this book, and whether you have any suggestions for improvements. You can send questions and comments to the Teach Yourself editors on the IDG Books Worldwide Web site at **www.idgbooks.com**.

Personal Workbook

Q&A

❶ How do you begin creating a new document using a template?

❷ Will only those templates actually installed on your computer be displayed in the New dialog box?

❸ Can you use templates from older versions of Word with Word 2000?

❹ What kind of information can be stored in a template?

❺ Why is using a template to create a new document often preferable to simply copying an existing document?

❻ Can you create your own templates?

❼ What kinds of text should you include in templates?

❽ Can you modify templates that come with Word?

ANSWERS: PAGE 365

112

After working through the tasks in each chapter, you can test your progress and reinforce your learning by answering the questions in the Q&A section. Then check your answers in the Personal Workbook Answers appendix at the back of the book.

Another practical way to reinforce your skills is to do additional exercises on the same skills you just learned without the benefit of the chapter's visual steps. If you struggle with any of these exercises, it's a good idea to refer to the chapter's tasks to be sure you've mastered them.

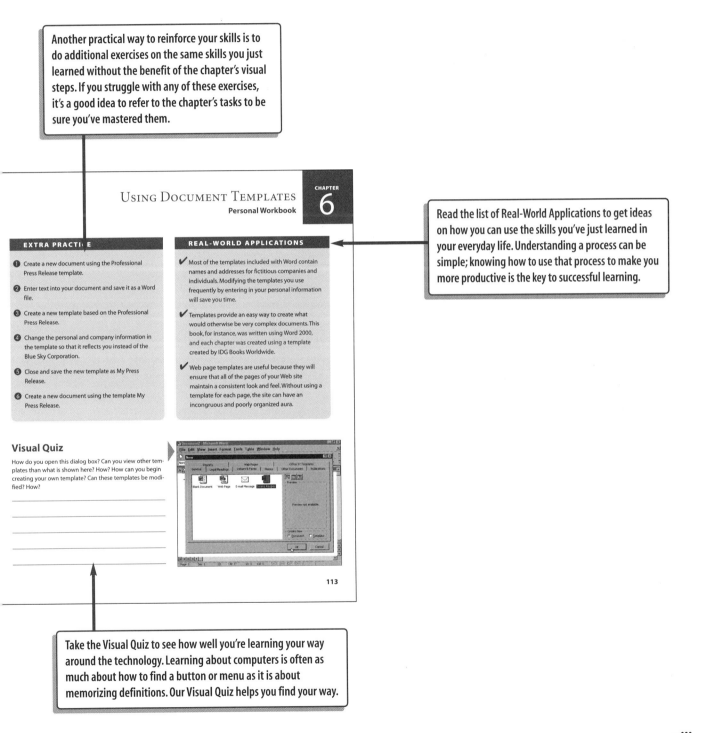

USING DOCUMENT TEMPLATES
Personal Workbook

CHAPTER 6

Read the list of Real-World Applications to get ideas on how you can use the skills you've just learned in your everyday life. Understanding a process can be simple; knowing how to use that process to make you more productive is the key to successful learning.

EXTRA PRACTICE

1. Create a new document using the Professional Press Release template.

2. Enter text into your document and save it as a Word file.

3. Create a new template based on the Professional Press Release.

4. Change the personal and company information in the template so that it reflects you instead of the Blue Sky Corporation.

5. Close and save the new template as My Press Release.

6. Create a new document using the template My Press Release.

REAL-WORLD APPLICATIONS

✔ Most of the templates included with Word contain names and addresses for fictitious companies and individuals. Modifying the templates you use frequently by entering in your personal information will save you time.

✔ Templates provide an easy way to create what would otherwise be very complex documents. This book, for instance, was written using Word 2000, and each chapter was created using a template created by IDG Books Worldwide.

✔ Web page templates are useful because they will ensure that all of the pages of your Web site maintain a consistent look and feel. Without using a template for each page, the site can have an incongruous and poorly organized aura.

Visual Quiz

How do you open this dialog box? Can you view other templates than what is shown here? How? How can you begin creating your own template? Can these templates be modified? How?

113

Take the Visual Quiz to see how well you're learning your way around the technology. Learning about computers is often as much about how to find a button or menu as it is about memorizing definitions. Our Visual Quiz helps you find your way.

Acknowledgments

Although it's my name that appears on the cover, *Teach Yourself® Microsoft® Word 2000* could not have been produced without the efforts of the excellent team at IDG Books Worldwide. I want to thank my acquisitions editor, Andy Cummings, for giving me the opportunity to write this book. I hope that I have justified your faith.

The real credit for this project goes to my outstanding editorial team. Development editor Tracy Brown had the difficult task of making sense out of my submissions and ensuring they were on time. I also wish to thank the technical editor, Dave Haskin, for checking the accuracy of the text. My greatest appreciation goes to development editor Elizabeth Collins, whose efforts ensured the high quality of this book. *Teach Yourself Microsoft Word 2000* would not be the fine work that it is without her assistance.

Finally, I want to thank my family for humoring me throughout this endeavor. My wife, Christa, along with my sons, Soren and Cole, have put up with my working three or four different full-time jobs for the last few months, and they are due for some much needed "daddy time." I also wish to thank my father, Brian Underdahl, for helping me realize my potential as a writer, and for taking time out of his own busy schedule to provide a steady stream of much needed encouragement.

Contents

CONTENTS

CONTENTS

CONTENTS

CONTENTS

PART

I

Learning Common Word Tasks

Word 2000 is a word processing program. It enables you to create letters, memos, reports, or even an entire book. Word is versatile, allowing you to customize these documents and add graphic and multimedia elements to spruce them up. You can even use Word to create and publish Web pages on the Internet.

Before you create documents with Word, you must master the basics. Even if you have used older versions of Word, Word 2000 has a number of new and modified features that will affect the way you use it. In this first part of *Teach* *Yourself Microsoft Word 2000*, you learn how to perform some basic Word tasks.

You begin by learning how to control the program itself by opening and closing it, and how to operate the tools and controls that the program uses to perform its job. Next, you learn a bit about tailoring Word to suit your individual needs, because every user has different expectations. You also discover how to work with the files that store information about the documents you create. Finally, you see how to take advantage of the help system, which can answer many of your toughest questions.

CHAPTER 1

Understanding Word Basics

What do you use your computer for? Everyone has a different answer to that question; and if you are brand new to personal computers, you might not yet have an answer. But whatever you use the computer for, there is a good chance that you will eventually have to type some kind of letter, memorandum, manifesto, advertisement, or other document that contains a lot of words on a page. If so, you will probably end up using a word processing program to accomplish the task. Word processing programs give you a single place on your computer to compose text, change the way it looks, modify the layout on the page, and more. Microsoft Word is one of the most popular word processing programs around.

Ironically, although word processing programs are so common in personal computers, few users make a conscious effort to master the tools these programs have to offer. Thus, many people never learn just how powerful a program such as Word is. Word 2000 has many advanced features that you can use to create stunning documents with minimal effort. *Teach Yourself Microsoft Word 2000* introduces you to the very best that Word has to offer, and provides real examples to make this program work effectively for you.

Before you can jump feet first into Word's most advanced features, you need to master a few basic skills. Understanding the basics of how Word 2000 works is fundamental to completing every task described in this book. Even if you have used previous versions of Word and are simply upgrading, it is a good idea to take this opportunity to brush up on your skills. Some elements of the Word interface — the menu structure, for example — have changed in this version. You will find that following through the tasks in this first chapter will prove beneficial later on.

You begin your experience with Word 2000 by performing the most obvious first step — opening the program. You then move on to learn more about using the Word 2000 interface. Tasks address menus, toolbars, dialog boxes, and the Word program window itself. Finally, you will learn how to move around in a Word document with standard navigation tools and the Document Map.

Opening and Closing Word

As you know, the first thing you have to do for most of the tasks described in *Teach Yourself Microsoft Word 2000* is open the program. For instance, if you plan to type a memo, you must open Word before you can begin typing. Likewise, if you want to edit a document that you created earlier or one that was created by someone else, Word must be open.

To accommodate the needs of different users, Word can be opened or closed in a number of ways. Back in the days before Windows, you had to type an executable filename at a DOS prompt to open a program. Today, the Windows interface makes this initial task much simpler. Using the mouse, you click buttons (also called icons) on a toolbar or select from menus instead of working with cryptic, DOS-style command lines.

Inevitably, the time will come for you to close Word. Just as when you open the program, you can shut down Word 2000 in a variety of ways. Usually, when you close the program, you will be prompted to save your work first. Follow the onscreen commands to save your work before continuing.

The first two figures on the facing page show the two most common methods used to open Word. These techniques apply to virtually all Windows-based programs. You may find that you tend to prefer one method over the other or that you use each one in different situations. The last two figures show different methods for closing Word.

Spend some time experimenting with each method for opening and closing Word. You may find that you really like using the Windows Start menu, for instance, or you may prefer using the Word shortcut on the desktop.

TAKE NOTE

▶ **CLOSE UNNEEDED WINDOWS**

Although Windows lets you have multiple programs and documents open simultaneously, it's a good idea to close ones you don't plan to use any time soon. This will free up your computer's memory so that the documents you *do* need will run more efficiently.

▶ **ONE CLICK OR TWO?**

In the past, you opened a shortcut on the desktop by double-clicking the icon. This is called *classic-style* navigation. But if you have Windows 98, you may be using a type of navigation called *Web style*, which uses underlined icon names. In this case, you click only once on an icon to perform a task. If you have Windows 98 set up for classic-style navigation, though, or if you have Windows 95, Windows NT 4.0, or an older version, you need to double-click shortcut icons. The tasks in this book simply tell you to open icons, so it will be up to you to decide how many clicks you should use.

CROSS-REFERENCE

You can open Word by simply opening a document. Learn how in "Opening and Closing Files" in Chapter 3.

FIND IT ONLINE

See **http://www.microsoft.com/word/default.htm** for up-to-date Word news.

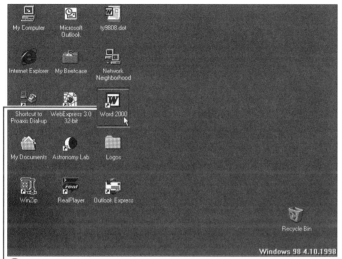

① On your Windows desktop, open the Word 2000 icon.

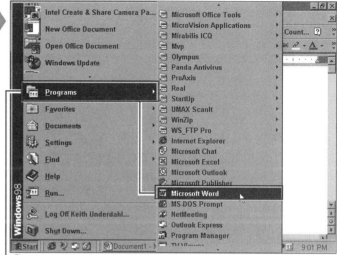

② On the Windows taskbar, click the Start button and choose Programs ➪ Microsoft Word.

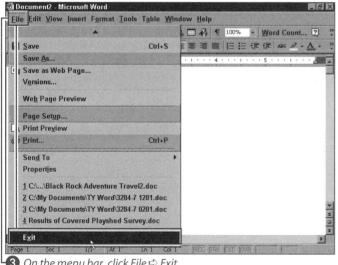

③ On the menu bar, click File ➪ Exit.

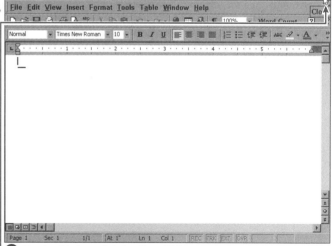

④ On the title bar, click the Close (X) button.

7

Using the Menu Bar

The power of Word comes from the many special features that are available within the program. Word contains tools to help you improve your spelling, create a table, insert graphics, change the way your text looks, search for specific words or phrases, and much more. Whatever feature of Word you want to take advantage of, you can access it through one of Word's many menus. These menus provide a list of tools and functions for your selection. In this respect, a Word menu is similar to one you might see in a restaurant. And, as in a restaurant, once you've made your choice from the list, the menu disappears.

Menus appear in a variety of locations in Word. The program has a *menu bar* at the top of the program window to provide quick access to important functions. Some of these menus contain submenus, indicated by a right arrow next to the item. You may also see ellipses (. . .) next to menu items. This element indicates that selecting the menu item opens a dialog box instead of performing an action, such as cutting or inserting. Another type of menu you are likely to encounter is a drop-down menu, which enables you to pick an item from a list, such as a font or style for some text. To select an item in a menu, click it with the mouse pointer. If you are using the keyboard, use arrow keys to locate the appropriate menu item and press Enter to choose it.

The figures on the facing page show how to access several types of menus. The first three figures demonstrate how to navigate the menu bar, which has been redesigned for Word 2000. The last figure shows a typical drop-down menu that you are likely to encounter while using Word.

TAKE NOTE

A NEW LOOK FOR MENUS IN WORD 2000

Menus account for the most significant change in the Word 2000 interface from previous versions of Word. When you click a menu title on the Word 2000 menu bar, an abbreviated menu appears displaying only the most commonly used items from that menu. With this new design, the menus take up less space on the page, and you should find it easier to locate common items. If you don't see a menu item you need, click the down arrow at the bottom of a menu to see more menu items.

CLOSING MENUS WITHOUT MAKING A SELECTION

If you don't need any of the choices in a menu you just opened, click outside the menu to close it. Just be careful not to click a toolbar button or other element, which could have an undesired result. Alternatively, press the Esc key on your keyboard.

CROSS-REFERENCE
You can move the menu around the window as you would a toolbar. See "Using Toolbars" later in this chapter.

FIND IT ONLINE
Access Microsoft's online resources quickly by clicking Help ⇨ Office on the Web on the Word menu bar.

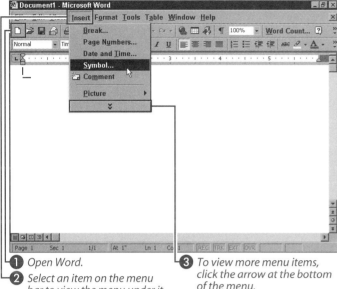

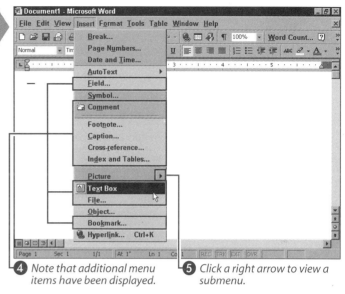

① Open Word.

② Select an item on the menu bar to view the menu under it. For now, select Insert.

③ To view more menu items, click the arrow at the bottom of the menu.

④ Note that additional menu items have been displayed.

⑤ Click a right arrow to view a submenu.

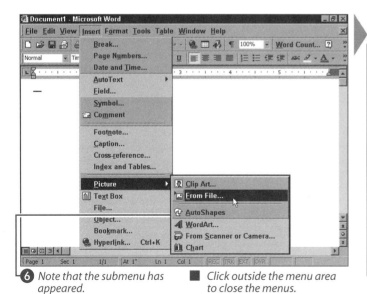

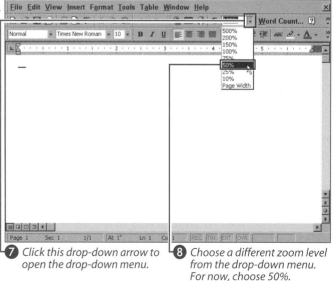

⑥ Note that the submenu has appeared.

■ Click outside the menu area to close the menus.

⑦ Click this drop-down arrow to open the drop-down menu.

⑧ Choose a different zoom level from the drop-down menu. For now, choose 50%.

Using Toolbars

As you have already seen, you can access Word's features via the numerous menus found on the menu bar and elsewhere. Menus simplify Word by enabling you to use the mouse to navigate through an intuitive series of choices to complete various tasks.

However, there is often an even easier way to do your work. In addition to menus, Word 2000 offers *toolbars* to further simplify the completion of certain tasks. Toolbars are bars that usually reside at the top of the Word program window, although they can also be moved around or they can float independently on the desktop. A toolbar contains tool buttons you can click to quickly perform a task. For instance, rather than choosing File ⇨ Open on the menu bar, you could simply click the Open button on the standard toolbar.

Which toolbars — if any — are displayed when Word is first installed will vary. If you are upgrading from a previous version of Word, the installation program analyzes how you had the desktop set up before and sets up Word 2000 in a similar way. In any case, at a minimum you should have the standard toolbar displayed. The standard toolbar has buttons for opening and saving files, printing, cutting, copying, pasting, and more.

In addition to the standard toolbar, Word has 15 other toolbars you can choose to have displayed at any given time. It's not practical to display all the toolbars at once, so you should learn how to open and close the toolbars as you need them. I recommend displaying the formatting toolbar all the time, because it contains a number of tools that you will use almost constantly. Many tasks in this book assume that you have the formatting toolbar on your desktop.

The figures on the facing page show you how to open a toolbar and position it around your desktop. The figures use the formatting toolbar as the example, but these techniques work with all toolbars. To use an item on a toolbar, simply click it with the mouse.

TAKE NOTE

▶ **GETTING HELP ON MYSTERY BUTTONS**

If you're unsure about a button's purpose, pause the mouse pointer over it but don't click. In a moment, a small help bubble appears next to the button that explains the button's purpose.

▶ **AVOID TOO MANY TOOLBARS**

Although toolbars can be quite handy, take a look at your programs from time to time and get rid of toolbars or buttons you never use. This will clean up the program window and give you more room for your work. For instance, you might want to display the Web toolbar when you are viewing Web documents with Word; but you might want to hide it when you are typing a memo.

CROSS-REFERENCE

Toolbars can be customized. See "Adding New Toolbar Buttons" in Chapter 2 to learn more.

FIND IT ONLINE

Visit **http://www.winability.com/** to learn about the custom toolbar add-on software FM Toolbar.

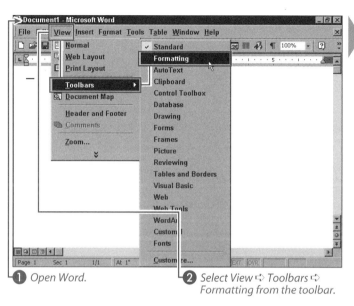

1 Open Word.

2 Select View ➪ Toolbars ➪ Formatting from the toolbar.

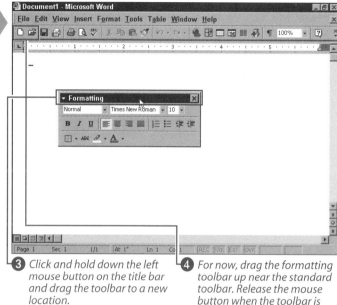

3 Click and hold down the left mouse button on the title bar and drag the toolbar to a new location.

4 For now, drag the formatting toolbar up near the standard toolbar. Release the mouse button when the toolbar is where you want it.

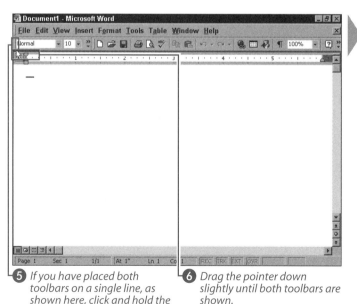

5 If you have placed both toolbars on a single line, as shown here, click and hold the left mouse button on this line.

6 Drag the pointer down slightly until both toolbars are shown.

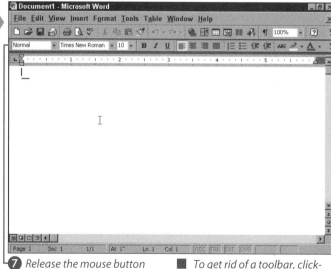

7 Release the mouse button when the toolbar is where you want it.

■ To get rid of a toolbar, click-and-drag it onto the desktop and then click the toolbar's Close (X) button.

Using Shortcut Menus

One of the great strengths of Windows-based programs such as Word 2000 is that they usually have many ways to perform a given task. For instance, if you want to copy a paragraph of text that you have selected, you can either select Copy from the Edit menu, or you can click the Copy button on the standard toolbar. There is yet another way to handle this task, and it involves using a special kind of menu called a *shortcut menu*.

You open a shortcut menu by clicking an item with the right mouse button. Each shortcut menu is unique. Like other menus — such as those that drop down from the menu bar — shortcut menus can be almost any size. But what makes the shortcut menu unique is that it only contains menu commands that apply to the item on which the mouse pointer is located. For instance, if you right-click a selected word, you will see menu options to move the word, change its formatting, turn it into a hyperlink, or even look up synonyms using the Word thesaurus.

Shortcut menus offer a great way to speed up many repetitive tasks. For instance, if you find that you need to change the font used in various parts of a document, you can highlight a block of text with the mouse and right-click. From the shortcut menu, you can open the Font dialog box much more quickly than you could by using the menu bar.

Common commands such as Cut, Copy, and Paste are usually included on shortcut menus. You can also access these commands from the toolbar. For a single operation, using the shortcut menu may not seem to save much time over clicking a toolbar button. However, if you are doing numerous cut-and-paste or copy-and-paste tasks, you may find that those few seconds saved here and there turn into many minutes in the long run.

The figures on the facing page show how to open and use several shortcut menus that you are likely to see in Word 2000. Each one is different, so you should practice on your own to become familiar with the shortcut menus that will help you work more efficiently.

TAKE NOTE

▶ SHORTCUT MENUS ELSEWHERE ON YOUR COMPUTER

Word 2000 isn't the only program that uses shortcut menus. In fact, you can usually pop open a shortcut menu almost anywhere within the Windows environment. Shortcut menus in other programs may have some of the same options as those in Word alongside items that are unique to that program.

▶ WHY ARE SOME MENU ITEMS DISABLED?

Some shortcut menu items may be disabled in certain situations. For instance, if you right-click a word without selecting it, the Cut and Copy commands will be disabled. However if you select the word and right-click it again, the commands will be enabled.

CROSS-REFERENCE

To learn how to select an area of text, see "Selecting Text" in Chapter 5.

FIND IT ONLINE

For more on shortcut menus and other Word features, visit **http://www.microsoft.com/word/**.

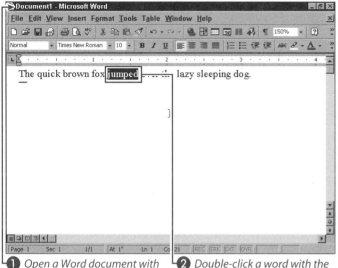

1 Open a Word document with some text in it, or type a couple of sentences in a new Word document.

2 Double-click a word with the left mouse button to select it.

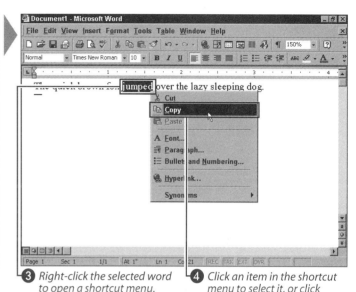

3 Right-click the selected word to open a shortcut menu.

4 Click an item in the shortcut menu to select it, or click outside the menu to close it.

5 Right-click the Word title bar to see some basic controls for the Word window.

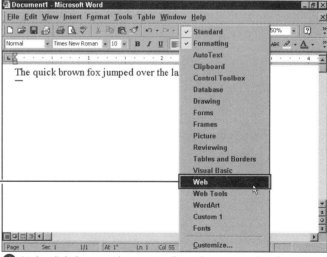

6 Right-click the menu bar or a toolbar. Choose a toolbar from this list to display it.

13

Using Dialog Boxes

As described in previous tasks, you can use menus and toolbar buttons to perform most operations in Word 2000. You make selections from a menu or click a button to accomplish tasks through the course of your work.

For many tasks, such as printing, a selection you make from a menu will open a dialog box in which you make additional choices before performing the task. You can tell which menu items will open a dialog box by watching out for ellipses (. . .) on the menu. You use dialog boxes to adjust settings, manipulate data, or perform many other tasks.

Dialog boxes are used for both simple and complex tasks. For instance, when you choose to open a document or save a file, you will see a dialog box that is virtually identical in all Windows-based applications. Other dialog boxes are more complex. If you want to change settings for your printer, you will see a relatively large dialog box with many different tabs and other elements. These choices could involve selecting a printer, telling Word how many copies to print, and so forth. Changes you make in dialog boxes may involve typing text into text boxes, placing check marks next to options you want, or making selections from drop-down menus.

Sometimes, you may make selections in a dialog box and then change your mind. But if you have made a lot of changes, you might not remember what all of them were. In this case, just click Cancel to close the dialog box without incorporating any of the choices you have made. Pressing the Esc key on your keyboard has the same effect as clicking Cancel in a dialog box.

You will also see another type of dialog box, called a *message box,* in Word. Message boxes open to warn you of a problem or provide a simple reminder. Often you won't have any choice except to click OK after reading a warning in one of these small boxes.

The first figure on the facing page shows how to open one of the most common dialog boxes in Word. The second and third figures describe some of the options and controls you can select in most dialog boxes. The last figure shows a typical message box.

TAKE NOTE

▶ COPYING DATA INTO DIALOG BOXES

You may find that it is easier to copy certain types of data into dialog boxes, rather than type it in. For instance, you can copy an e-mail address from an e-mail message into a dialog box (such as Word's Hyperlink dialog box) to ensure that a simple typo doesn't cause problems later on.

▶ GETTING HELP IN DIALOG BOXES

Help is available for most items in a dialog box. Just right-click an item you are curious about and choose "What's This?" from the small shortcut menu that appears.

CROSS-REFERENCE

See the Mother of all Word dialog boxes in "Setting Key Options" in Chapter 2.

FIND IT ONLINE

Learn more about dialog boxes at **http://webopedia. internet.com/TERM/d/dialog_box.html**.

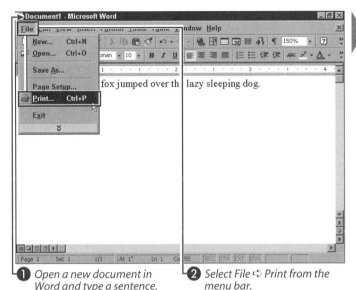

① Open a new document in Word and type a sentence.

② Select File ➪ Print from the menu bar.

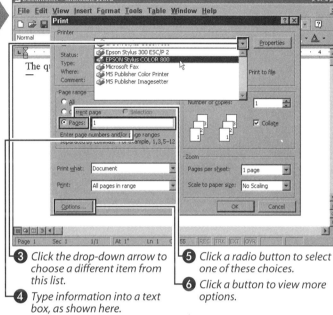

③ Click the drop-down arrow to choose a different item from this list.

④ Type information into a text box, as shown here.

⑤ Click a radio button to select one of these choices.

⑥ Click a button to view more options.

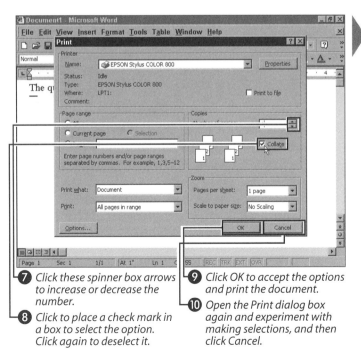

⑦ Click these spinner box arrows to increase or decrease the number.

⑧ Click to place a check mark in a box to select the option. Click again to deselect it.

⑨ Click OK to accept the options and print the document.

⑩ Open the Print dialog box again and experiment with making selections, and then click Cancel.

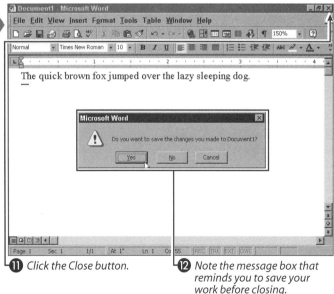

⑪ Click the Close button.

⑫ Note the message box that reminds you to save your work before closing.

Controlling the Word Window

Windows is more than just a catchy product name for the operating system on most personal computers used today. Back in the old days (actually just a little over ten years ago), PC users opened programs by typing command lines at a DOS prompt. These command lines were cryptic and intimidating to many new users. Since then, numerous technological advances have allowed the process to become much easier.

Perhaps the most important advance has been the invention of computer processors that enable you to run more than one program at once. Having multiple programs open at once is called *multitasking*. In modern operating systems, running programs are viewed in boxes called *windows*. This concept is behind the name of Microsoft's very popular operating systems (although it is interesting to note that the original product name was "Interface Manager" until the Microsoft marketing department intervened).

Anyway, when you run Word 2000, the program opens in one of these windows on the screen. You can run other programs at the same time, as well as other sessions of Word. The programs run simultaneously, but in separate windows. You can control Word's window in a number of ways. The first time you open Word, it probably takes up the whole screen, but it doesn't have to. You can resize the window so it uses only a portion of the Windows desktop. You can also move it around so it's not in your way if you are performing another task. Finally, you can minimize the Word window without actually closing the program.

The figures on the facing page show you how to move, resize, minimize, and maximize the Word window. In general, these techniques apply not just to Word but to virtually all Windows applications. If you are already familiar with Windows programs, many of these tools will be familiar. Once you have mastered the skills described here, you will be a true Windows pro!

TAKE NOTE

OPENING MULTIPLE WORD SESSIONS

Another big change in the way Word 2000 operates compared to older versions of Word is that each document you have open in Word has its own session in Windows and its own window on the Windows desktop. Previous versions of Word kept multiple open documents within a single Word window. Users switched between the open documents by clicking the document title in the Window menu.

TAKING ADVANTAGE OF MULTIPLE DISPLAY SUPPORT

If you have Windows 98, Windows NT 5.0, or higher, and a computer that supports more than one monitor, you might consider using separate monitors for separate programs. You could maximize Word on one monitor and continue working, while another program (such as an e-mail client) runs in the other monitor. This way, you can check both programs simultaneously.

CROSS-REFERENCE

See "Switching Between Open Documents" in Chapter 3 to learn how to move between open windows.

FIND IT ONLINE

Get tips from other users at **http://www.wordinfo. com/how_to/UserTips/default.htm**.

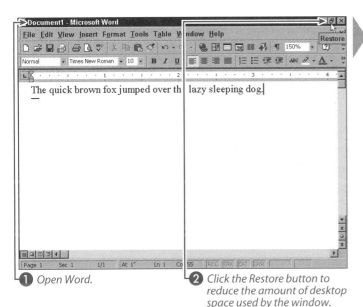

① Open Word.

② Click the Restore button to reduce the amount of desktop space used by the window.

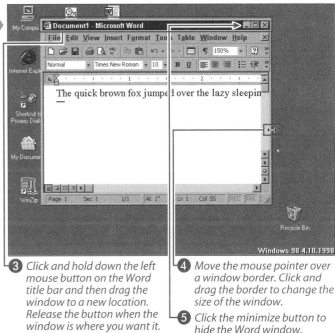

③ Click and hold down the left mouse button on the Word title bar and then drag the window to a new location. Release the button when the window is where you want it.

④ Move the mouse pointer over a window border. Click and drag the border to change the size of the window.

⑤ Click the minimize button to hide the Word window.

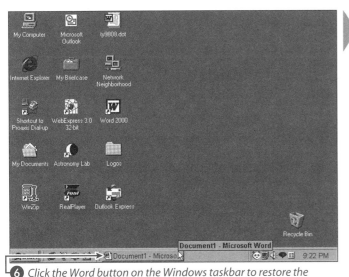

⑥ Click the Word button on the Windows taskbar to restore the window.

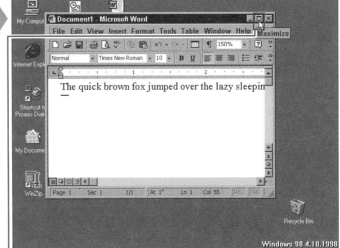

⑦ Click the Maximize button to make Word fill the whole screen again.

Moving Around in Your Documents

As you may have noticed by now, your monitor can display only about one page of information at a time. It is therefore important to know how to move around in your documents once they get too big to fit on a single screen. There are many different methods for moving around within a document, with some more efficient than others in different kinds of documents. For instance, moving around in a single-page memorandum is pretty easy, but displaying page 512 in a 1,000 page document is a little more challenging.

The simplest way to move around in a Word document is to use the arrow keys on your keyboard. You can scroll up and down in the document using these keys, though this method is not efficient in large files. The best navigation tool that Word provides is the scroll bar that resides on the right-hand side of the program window. You can use it to scroll around the document in a variety of ways, as demonstrated in the figures on the facing page.

You can also use a new feature in Word 2000 to move around the document. This is the Browse by Object tool, which is located at the bottom of the Word scroll bar. With this tool, you can choose the kind of document element, such as graphics, edits, pages, or sections, by which you want to browse your document. For instance, if you choose to browse by graphics, clicking the up or down arrow on the

Browse by Object tool will move you to the previous or next graphic in the document, respectively. If you choose to browse by page, the Browse by Object tool will scroll up or down one complete print page.

The figures on the facing page show you several methods for moving around in a document. The first two figures demonstrate how to use the scroll bar, and the last two figures introduce you to the Browse by Object tool.

TAKE NOTE

PAGING UP AND DOWN WITH THE KEYBOARD

Your keyboard has keys on it called Page Up and Page Down. If you press one of them, Word scrolls up or down one entire screen page of the document. A screen page differs from a print page in that a screen page consists of everything that will fit in one screen on your monitor. A print page is everything that will fit on a printed piece of paper. Depending on the size of your monitor, a print page is usually about two screen pages.

BROWSE BY HEADINGS

If you are creating a large document, you probably have headings at the beginnings of major topic points. If so, set the Browse by Object tool to browse by headings; this makes it easier to move around based on your major topics.

CROSS-REFERENCE
You can also move to a specific location using Find. Learn more in "Using Find" in Chapter 13.

FIND IT ONLINE
Find a slew of Word-related links at **http://swschool. com/word.htm**.

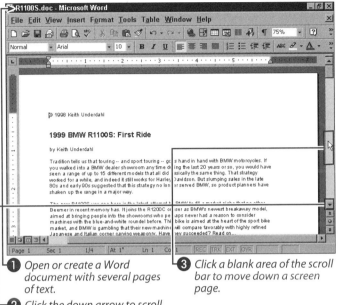

1 Open or create a Word document with several pages of text.

2 Click the down arrow to scroll down one line.

3 Click a blank area of the scroll bar to move down a screen page.

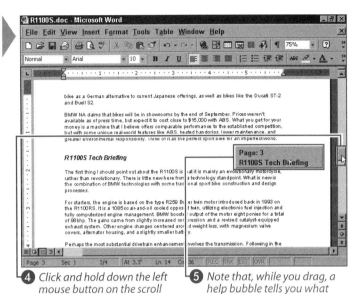

4 Click and hold down the left mouse button on the scroll slider and drag up or down in the document. Release the mouse button when you are near the location you want.

5 Note that, while you drag, a help bubble tells you what page and heading (if applicable) the slider is on.

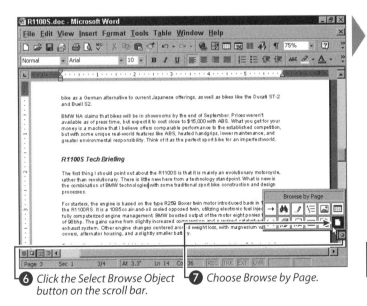

6 Click the Select Browse Object button on the scroll bar.

7 Choose Browse by Page.

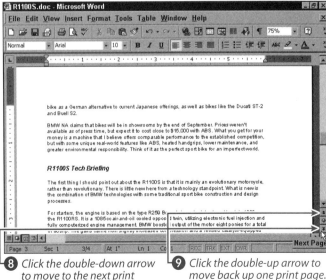

8 Click the double-down arrow to move to the next print page.

9 Click the double-up arrow to move back up one print page.

Using the Document Map

As you learned in the previous task, Word gives you several options for moving around in a document. Perhaps one of the most useful is the innovative new Browse by Object tool, which lets you custom-tailor the way you move around in Word. Another tool you can use in Word is called the Document Map. This tool serves the purpose suggested by its name: It is a virtual roadmap of your document, which you can use to make it easier to move around in that document.

The Document Map looks a lot like an outline. In fact, if you began your document by first outlining the contents, the Document Map may be identical to your original outline. As such, the Document Map does more than simply allow you to jump from one heading to another in the document. You can also use the Document Map to review the general construction of your document.

If you have created a document that is many pages long, you can easily lose sight of the document's overall organization. Did you stick to a central theme throughout the document, and have your points been arranged in a logical order? A quick review of the Document Map can help you answer these important but easy to overlook questions.

The Document Map does have a few limitations. Because it can use up a lot of desktop space, the Document Map is usually hidden from view. To use it, you must manually open it from the View menu on the Word menu bar. Also, the Document Map only shows items that are styled as headings in the document. This includes the Heading 1, 2, and 3 styles that are included with Word, as well as any style that looks like those heading styles. If your document has no headings, the Document Map will be empty.

The Document Map can prove useful in many situations. The figures on the facing page show you how to open and use the Document Map in a larger document. The last figure shows you how to close the Document Map when you are done using it.

TAKE NOTE

▶ CHANGING THE HEADING LEVELS DISPLAYED BY DOCUMENT MAP

Document Map lets you change which headings are shown. If you want only the major headings to be displayed, right-click the Map entries and choose Show Heading 1 from the shortcut menu that appears. You can also click Expand or Collapse in this menu to reduce or expand the number of headings that are shown.

▶ USING DESCRIPTIVE HEADINGS

Some of the headings you may select, such as "Chapter 1," may not be very descriptive of the text that follows them. In this case, the Document Map will not be valuable for reviewing the outline of your document. Consider providing subheadings that are a bit more descriptive.

CROSS-REFERENCE

The Document Map relies on styles for its headings. To learn more about styles, see "Applying Styles" in Chapter 7.

FIND IT ONLINE

Want to learn more about desktop publishing? Visit the newsgroup **news:comp.text.desktop**.

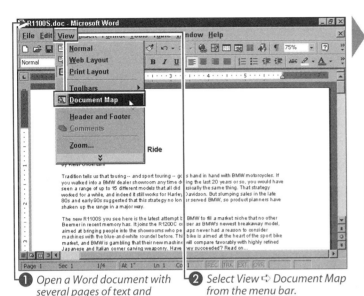

1 Open a Word document with several pages of text and headings.

2 Select View ➪ Document Map from the menu bar.

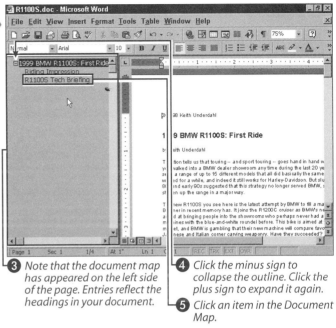

3 Note that the document map has appeared on the left side of the page. Entries reflect the headings in your document.

4 Click the minus sign to collapse the outline. Click the plus sign to expand it again.

5 Click an item in the Document Map.

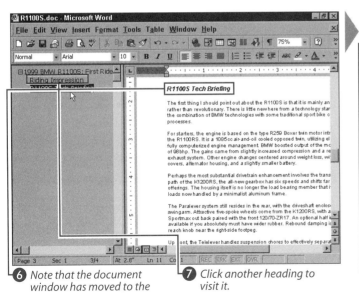

6 Note that the document window has moved to the heading you clicked.

7 Click another heading to visit it.

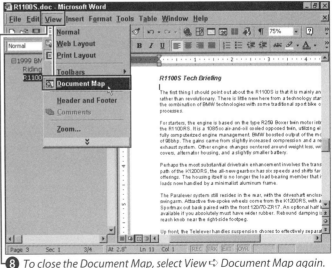

8 To close the Document Map, select View ➪ Document Map again.

Personal Workbook

Q&A

1 How do you open Word without using a desktop icon?

_____

_____

_____

_____

2 Why do menus show only the most commonly used items at first?

_____

_____

_____

3 How can you view additional menu items?

_____

_____

_____

_____

4 When does a shortcut menu appear?

_____

_____

5 How can you tell whether selecting a menu item will open a dialog box?

_____

_____

6 Can you hide or minimize the Word window without closing the program? How?

_____

_____

_____

7 What is the difference between a screen page and a print page?

_____

_____

_____

_____

8 What kind of information does the Document Map display?

_____

_____

_____

ANSWERS: PAGE 360

EXTRA PRACTICE

1 Open Word.

2 Type a paragraph of text.

3 Right-click the paragraph and choose Paragraph from the shortcut menu.

4 Click the spinner box arrow next to Left Indentation to indent the paragraph .5″.

5 Click the drop-down arrow under line spacing and choose Double.

6 Click OK to accept your changes and close the dialog box.

REAL-WORLD APPLICATIONS

✔ Knowing how to control the Word window is important in helping you take full advantage of your computer. For instance, you can adjust the size of the window so that Word is visible on the left side of your screen, and open an e-mail program in the right-hand side of the screen. This makes it easier to copy information between the two programs.

✔ Different toolbars are used at different times. If you are using Word to create a Web page, you might want to have the Web and Web Tools toolbars displayed. When you are done composing the Web page, you can close the toolbars again to get them out of the way.

Visual Quiz

Does the Document Map shown here reflect all the headings in the document? How can you tell? What are two ways to scroll down to the end of this document? How can you quickly view some commands for an area of text?

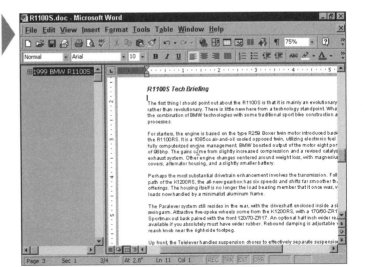

_____

_____

_____

_____

CHAPTER 2

MASTER THESE SKILLS

▶ Choosing Custom Setup Options

▶ Setting Key Options

▶ Changing the View

▶ Adding New Toolbar Buttons

▶ Creating New Toolbar Buttons

▶ Creating Shortcut Keys

Customizing Word

Word is many things to many people. For some, it is simply a tool for composing memos and brief letters around the home and office. Others create Web pages for the Internet with Word, and still others use it to publish entire books. In fact, this entire book was written using Word 2000. The ways in which Word can be used are as varied as the people using it.

Word offers a great deal of flexibility to make the program useful to a wide variety of users. This flexibility is first noticeable when you install Word 2000, and it continues throughout the course of your work. When you install the program, you will have the opportunity to customize the setup procedure and pick and choose which Word components you want installed. You can also modify Word setup options at any time during your work to ensure you maintain the best balance of features and disk space.

As you continue to use Word, you will find that you can tailor many other features to your individual needs. Word has a number of basic settings and options you can choose, and the default settings may or may not be to your liking. Word makes it easy to modify these settings, especially because most of them are controlled from one dialog box.

You can make many other changes to Word as well. Perhaps one of the most useful options is the capability to change the way your documents are displayed on the screen. Word offers a couple of alternative views for you to choose from, and each one contains different kinds of information.

Even some of the most fundamental Word elements can be modified. You have already learned how to display or hide toolbars at the top of the Word 2000 program window. You can also create more toolbar buttons and add them to an existing toolbar. You can even create your own custom toolbars, which can be useful when working on certain kinds of documents. Finally, Word lets you create custom shortcut keys that help you perform complicated actions with the quick press of a key or two on the keyboard. This chapter describes how to make these modifications to Word to customize the program to your individual needs.

Choosing Custom Setup Options

When you first installed Word 2000 on your computer, you probably weren't given too many options for setting up the program. Microsoft has streamlined the setup process to make it quicker and easier. Many of the changes are also designed to reduce the amount of hard disk space needed for Word program files. To this end, many features of Word are not installed initially. Instead, many features are installed the first time you use them. In theory, this approach will result in your installing only the features you use.

Still, you can select some setup options yourself. To do so, you use the Word setup utility, which you usually run from the program disk that you received when you purchased the program. If you have Office 2000 rather than just Word 2000, the setup utility covers all the programs that come with Office. Also notice that if you have Office 2000, many of the options you may want to change are not necessarily listed under the Word category. Check also under Office Tools, which contains many important options that apply to Word. The Converters and Filters category also contains file converters and graphics filters that Word might use from time to time.

You can use the setup utility to save space on your hard drive. As mentioned earlier, many Word features are installed when you use them for the first time. This means that the first time you try to use the feature, you are prompted to insert the Word CD into the disk drive so that it can be installed. Some features, however, you may use once and not expect to ever use again. To free up space, you should consider going back through the setup utility and disabling these features. To uninstall an item, click the item once and choose Not Available from the shortcut menu that opens.

The figures on the facing page show you how to open the setup utility and change installed features.

TAKE NOTE

REPAIRING WORD

If certain Word 2000 features don't seem to work properly, the program crashes frequently, or Word won't even open, open the setup utility and click the Repair Word (or Repair Office) button on the first screen that appears. The utility checks the Word 2000 program files and replaces those that appear missing or corrupted.

INSTALLING UNAVAILABLE FEATURES

Most Word 2000 features install the first time you use them, but some might be disabled in the setup utility. Search through the options in the utility and make sure that the
you want doesn't have a red X in front of it. If it does, click the item and choose "Run from My Computer" from the shortcut menu that appears.

CROSS-REFERENCE

Not sure if you need text converters installed? See "Working with Other File Formats" in Chapter 3.

FIND IT ONLINE

If you appreciate using Word, make a pilgrimage to http://www.brodietech.com/rbrodie/.

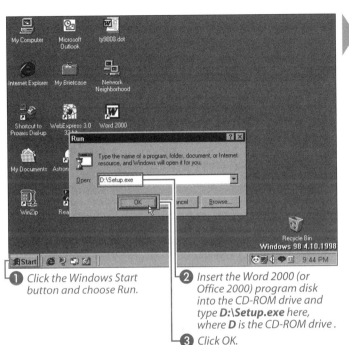

1 Click the Windows Start button and choose Run.

2 Insert the Word 2000 (or Office 2000) program disk into the CD-ROM drive and type *D:\Setup.exe* here, where *D* is the CD-ROM drive .

3 Click OK.

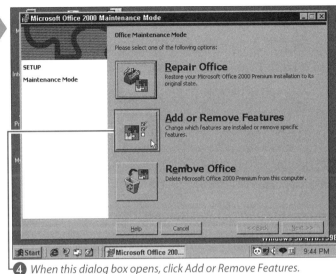

4 When this dialog box opens, click Add or Remove Features.

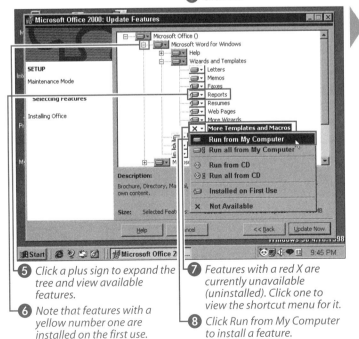

5 Click a plus sign to expand the tree and view available features.

6 Note that features with a yellow number one are installed on the first use.

7 Features with a red X are currently unavailable (uninstalled). Click one to view the shortcut menu for it.

8 Click Run from My Computer to install a feature.

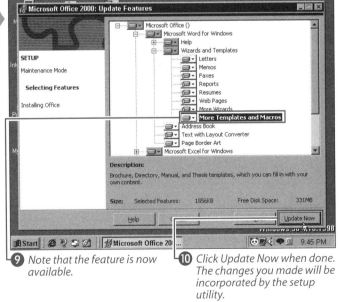

9 Note that the feature is now available.

10 Click Update Now when done. The changes you made will be incorporated by the setup utility.

Setting Key Options

In the previous task, you learned how to change some setup options for Word. These changes affect which features and elements of Word are installed on your computer, but installation is only the first step in tailoring Word to work better for you. In fact, you will probably change setup options no more than once during the time you use Word 2000, whereas you will change other options quite regularly, depending on the task you are performing.

Once you have finished installation, you should check certain key options within the program itself. These options impact virtually every aspect of Word, from what default text looks like to where your files are saved.

Most of the options discussed here are available in one dialog box. The Options dialog box contains ten tabs, each with a separate category of information. It is a good idea to open this dialog box and see what options Word enables you to set. Often, if you don't like something about the program, you can change it here. Take a few minutes to browse the tabs and see what changes can be made.

The figures on the facing page show you how to open the Options dialog box. Once you have the dialog box open, you are taken through some of the tabs to choose key options. Remember, every user has different needs and expectations for Word, so take some time to look over everything. After you have reviewed the Options tabs shown here, turn the next page, where additional options are discussed in greater detail.

Continued

TAKE NOTE

▶ SETTING KEY VIEW OPTIONS

The Options dialog box has a number of view options for you to check. Some of the common screen elements, such as the status bar and scroll bars, can be hidden. Hiding these elements might be a good idea if you have a very small screen, such as on a laptop. You can also customize which non-printing characters (spaces, tab characters, paragraph marks, and so on) are displayed on the screen.

▶ DEALING WITH AUTORECOVER

By default, Word automatically saves your work every ten minutes to an AutoRecover file, which will be used only if your computer crashes or loses power unexpectedly. This feature can save you a lot of trouble in an emergency, but it can also cause some problems if you are taxing your system resources. For instance, if you are running a large, memory-intensive macro, or have some other program running in the background that is using a lot of memory and slowing the computer down, AutoRecover can cause your system to crash when it starts to save the file in the background. If you have this type of problem, disable the AutoRecover feature on the Save tab of the Options dialog box.

CROSS-REFERENCE

Learn more about modifying Word's look later in this chapter in "Changing the View."

FIND IT ONLINE

See **http://www.wordinfo.com/** for an excellent online source of help and Word-related humor.

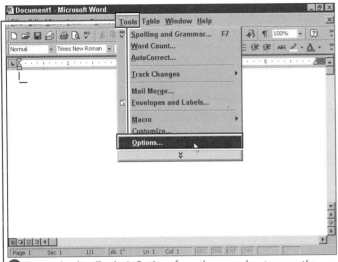

1 In Word, select Tools ⇨ Options from the menu bar to open the Options dialog box.

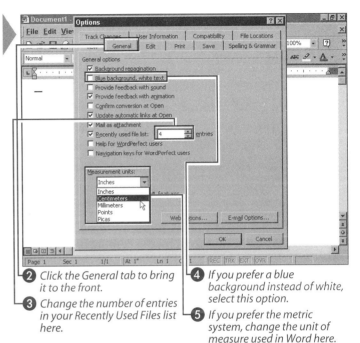

2 Click the General tab to bring it to the front.

3 Change the number of entries in your Recently Used Files list here.

4 If you prefer a blue background instead of white, select this option.

5 If you prefer the metric system, change the unit of measure used in Word here.

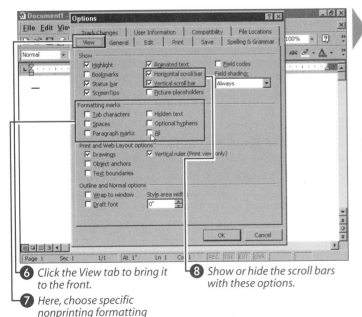

6 Click the View tab to bring it to the front.

7 Here, choose specific nonprinting formatting marks you would like displayed.

8 Show or hide the scroll bars with these options.

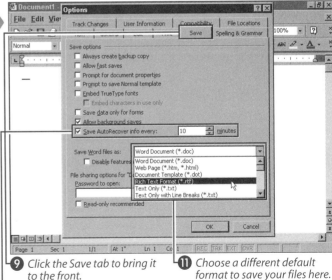

9 Click the Save tab to bring it to the front.

10 Enable or disable Auto-Recover here, or change how often an AutoRecover file is saved.

11 Choose a different default format to save your files here.

Setting Key Options

Continued

As you browse through the Options dialog box in Word, you should find numerous options that can help you make Word suit your needs more effectively. Perhaps one of the first things you should check are the spelling and grammar options. Notice that many of the options that you can set on this tab tell Word to ignore certain things when performing a spelling check. These include Internet and file addresses, words in uppercase letters, words with numbers in them, and so on. You can also disable the spelling and grammar checkers here if you like.

Another tab you should review is the User Information tab. This tab contains information about you, which is sometimes determined automatically by the setup program. Check here to make sure your name, initials, and address are correct. This information, which is incorporated in the properties of documents you create or edit, is especially important if more than one person works on those documents.

Selecting a location for your files is an important part of the saving process, and you can simplify this process by changing some settings in the Options dialog box. When you click the Save button on the toolbar or select File ➪ Save from the menu bar, the default folder that opens is usually the My Documents folder on the desktop. You can change this default if you like. If you have a My Documents folder on your hard drive (left over from a previous program or operating system), for example, you might want to use that instead.

The first figure on the facing page shows you some of the spelling and grammar options you might want to change. The second figure shows what your user information should look like, and the last two figures show you how to choose a new default location for your document files.

TAKE NOTE

CLOSING THE OPTIONS DIALOG BOX

When you are done making all the changes you want in the Options dialog box, click OK. All the changes you have made are incorporated and the dialog box closes. If you change your mind about making any changes, however, remember that you can just click Cancel or press the Esc key on your keyboard to close the dialog box and reject all your changes.

DISABLE AUTOMATIC SPELL CHECKING FOR SOME DOCUMENTS

In most documents, Word automatically checks spelling and puts a red wavy line under suspect words. But if you are working on a document with a lot of acronyms, names, or unusual words, the automatic spell-checking feature can be a nuisance. If your documents look like a sea of red wavy lines, you might be better off deselecting the "Check spelling as you type" option.

CROSS-REFERENCE

Learn more about spelling and grammar in Chapter 11.

FIND IT ONLINE

Discuss various Word-related topics in the newsgroup **news:bit.mailserv.word-pc.**

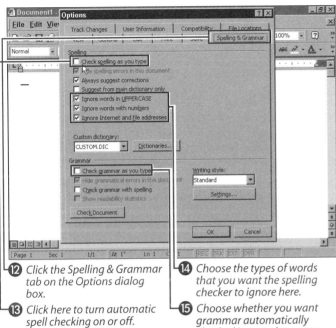

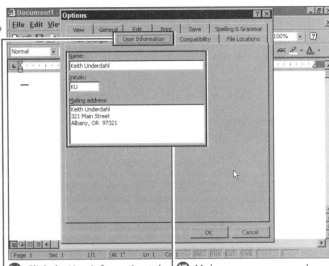

⓬ Click the Spelling & Grammar tab on the Options dialog box.

⓭ Click here to turn automatic spell checking on or off.

⓮ Choose the types of words that you want the spelling checker to ignore here.

⓯ Choose whether you want grammar automatically checked in your document.

⓰ Click the User Information tab to bring it to the front.

⓱ Make sure your personal information is shown correctly here.

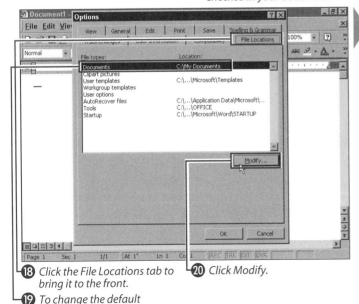

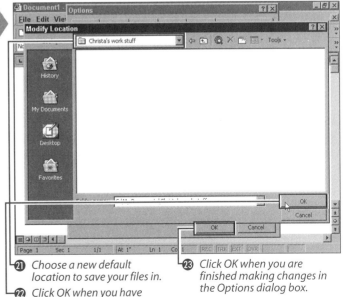

⓲ Click the File Locations tab to bring it to the front.

⓳ To change the default location for your document files, click Documents.

⓴ Click Modify.

㉑ Choose a new default location to save your files in.

㉒ Click OK when you have opened the folder serving as the new location. (You must actually open the folder.)

㉓ Click OK when you are finished making changes in the Options dialog box.

Changing the View

The view of your Word documents can be changed significantly, depending on what kind of information you need to see. When viewing a document, Word has four primary view modes that you can choose from. The primary mode, which is called *Normal View*, provides the most essential document information. In Normal View, the entire document window is white, and such elements as page breaks and section breaks are shown as lines across the page. Many people prefer Normal View, but it does not give a completely accurate representation of what the pages will look like when they are printed on paper.

For a better idea of what your printed document will look like, you might prefer to work in Print Layout View. Print Layout View changes the shape of your document pages onscreen to more accurately reflect the finished, printed pages. Elements such as page and section breaks aren't shown because the breaks are represented onscreen by the pages themselves.

A third view mode is *Outline View*, which tends to be somewhat less useful for most people. This mode lays out the contents of your document in one giant outline. This view may be helpful if you are trying to create an outline or review the general organization of your document.

The fourth mode is *Web Layout View*, which was new in Word 97. Web Layout View shows you what your page would look like when viewed as an HTML document in a Web browser such as Netscape Navigator or Internet Explorer. This view is valuable if you are using Word to create a Web document. Like Outline View, you will use it only in a few limited circumstances. It is not of much use for non-Web documents.

The figures on the facing page show you how to change the view of your documents. In addition to demonstrating three of the views just described, you also learn how to adjust the zoom level of a document. The zoom level lets you zoom in or out, thus changing the amount of the document you can see in the window at once.

TAKE NOTE

WHAT HAPPENED TO PAGE LAYOUT VIEW?

If you have used previous versions of Word, you might remember a view mode called Page Layout View. In Word 2000, that mode has been renamed as Print Layout View. This name change avoids confusion with other uses of the word *page* that have become common lately, such as a Web page on the Internet.

VIEWING HEADERS AND FOOTERS

To see what headers and footers will look like on your page relative to the rest of the text, put the document in Print Layout View. These elements will then appear as light gray text in the appropriate positions on the page.

CROSS-REFERENCE
To learn more about previewing your printed document, see "Using Print Preview" in Chapter 14.

FIND IT ONLINE
Jumbo, at **http://www.jumbo.com/**, offers a variety of shareware for Word.

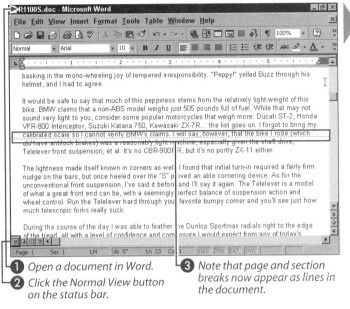

❶ *Open a document in Word.*

❷ *Click the Normal View button on the status bar.*

❸ *Note that page and section breaks now appear as lines in the document.*

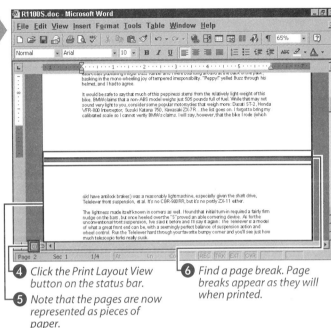

❹ *Click the Print Layout View button on the status bar.*

❺ *Note that the pages are now represented as pieces of paper.*

❻ *Find a page break. Page breaks appear as they will when printed.*

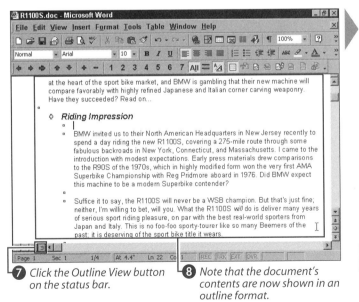

❼ *Click the Outline View button on the status bar.*

❽ *Note that the document's contents are now shown in an outline format.*

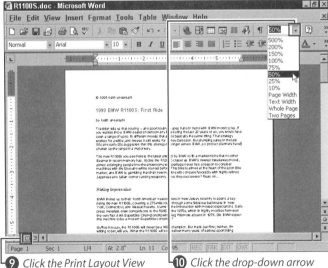

❾ *Click the Print Layout View button again.*

❿ *Click the drop-down arrow here to choose a different zoom level. Experiment with the zoom level to see what works best for you.*

Adding New Toolbar Buttons

Like nearly all Windows applications, Word contains numerous toolbars that can help control various program functions. Often you can avoid making myriad menu selections and choices in dialog boxes with the simple click of a toolbar button. Word provides 16 different toolbars, with buttons for virtually every feature available.

Even with all these toolbars available, there may still be tasks you perform regularly that are not represented by a toolbar button. And even if a toolbar does contain buttons you use, it may contain other buttons you don't use at all. Why clutter your desktop with toolbar buttons you don't use?

Word lets you add buttons to and delete buttons from toolbars. You can add a toolbar button for any Word feature that you can access through one of the menus. Do you need to count the words in your document frequently? Rather than searching through menus for that tool all the time, create a Word Count button on the toolbar.

In addition to menu commands, you can also create toolbar buttons for items such as fonts, styles, AutoText items, and macros. This makes a lot of sense, especially for something like a macro that would otherwise be complicated to start. If you have to run a macro dozens of times in the same document, it just makes more sense to create a toolbar button for it.

You can remove unwanted buttons from toolbars just as easily as you can add them. To remove a toolbar button, open the Customize dialog box just as if you were going to add a button. Click on the button you want to get rid of (you might have to move the dialog box out of the way) to select it. Now, just click and hold down the left mouse button and drag the button off the toolbar. Notice that whenever the Customize dialog box is open, toolbar buttons won't work. Clicking them simply places a black border around the button so that it can be moved around if desired.

The figures on the facing page show you how to open the Customize dialog box and add a button to the toolbar. The last figure demonstrates how to change the way that button looks by replacing the button text with a graphic.

TAKE NOTE

CHANGING THE LOOK OF YOUR BUTTONS

When you create a new toolbar button, by default it will be labeled with text describing the name of the function it serves. But you can give your buttons a more attractive look by assigning graphics to them instead of text. After dragging a new button to the toolbar, click Modify Selection in the Customize dialog box and choose Change Button Image from the shortcut menu. You can choose other options from that menu to further modify the button.

CROSS-REFERENCE

What's a macro? Find out in "Creating New Macros" in Chapter 20.

FIND IT ONLINE

See more customization info at http://www.currents.net/magazine/national/1517/puba1517.html.

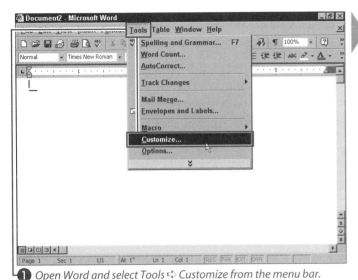

1 Open Word and select Tools ⇨ Customize from the menu bar.

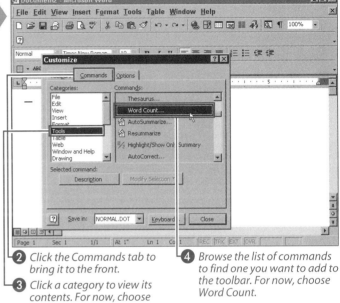

2 Click the Commands tab to bring it to the front.

3 Click a category to view its contents. For now, choose Tools.

4 Browse the list of commands to find one you want to add to the toolbar. For now, choose Word Count.

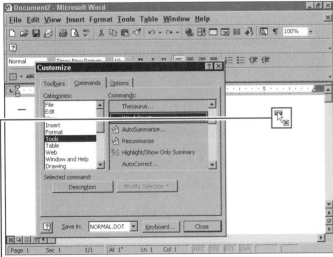

5 Click and hold down the left mouse button on Word Count and drag it out of the Customize dialog box.

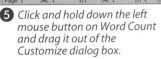 The X under the mouse pointer changes to a plus sign when you are over a place where you can drop the button. Drop the new button on one of the toolbars.

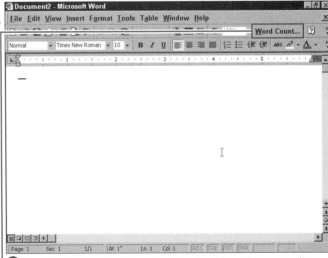

6 Close the Customize dialog box. You should see the new toolbar button you created.

Creating New Toolbars

Being able to place your own buttons on toolbars is terrific and provides a truly innovative way for you to speed up your work. Another solution to tailoring Word to your needs is to create entirely new toolbars. Just as you can create your own toolbar buttons, you can also create the toolbars themselves. As with other toolbars, you can hide and display any toolbar you create.

One reason to create your own toolbars is it makes various functions accessible if you work on different kinds of documents that require different kinds of editing. Adding a single button to an existing toolbar works well if you use that function all the time. If you use different sets of features for different documents, however, you may want to set up a custom toolbar for each document type.

For instance, if you work on a company newsletter once a month, you might want to create a custom toolbar to handle some of the graphics and layout issues associated with the newsletter. When you get ready to work on the newsletter, just open the newsletter toolbar. When you are done working on the newsletter for the month, hide the toolbar again so that it is out of the way. You could also create a custom toolbar that you use all the time. For instance, if you don't like using the menus on the formatting toolbar for applying styles or fonts, you might want to create toolbars for those items instead.

The figures on the facing page show you how to create a custom toolbar. This particular example creates a toolbar for some fonts, but you can create a toolbar containing almost anything you want.

TAKE NOTE

▶ POSITIONING TOOLBARS

It is easy to forget that toolbars don't necessarily have to remain at the top of the Word program window. For your custom toolbars in specialized documents, you might find it useful to place a toolbar alongside or even at the bottom of the Word window. You might even prefer to let them "float" in the document window itself, although this might cause the toolbar to cover some of your text. This positioning might reduce the distance you have to move the mouse to click the buttons, ultimately saving wear and tear on both the mouse and your hand.

▶ CREATE YOUR OWN MENUS

In addition to toolbars, you can also create your own custom menus on the menu bar. On the Commands tab of the Customize dialog box, scroll to the last category, *New Menu*. Select it, click Modify Selection to create a new name, and — voilà! — you have started your own custom menu. You can add items to it just as you would add buttons to a toolbar by dragging and dropping them to the menu in question.

CROSS-REFERENCE

If you haven't yet learned how to add buttons to a toolbar, see "Adding New Toolbar buttons" earlier.

FIND IT ONLINE

Learn more about custom toolbars at http://www.zdjournals.com/msw/9611/msw96b1.htm.

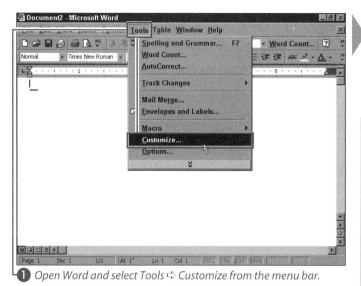

1 Open Word and select Tools ⇨ Customize from the menu bar.

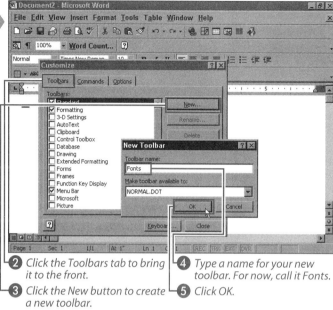

2 Click the Toolbars tab to bring it to the front.

3 Click the New button to create a new toolbar.

4 Type a name for your new toolbar. For now, call it Fonts.

5 Click OK.

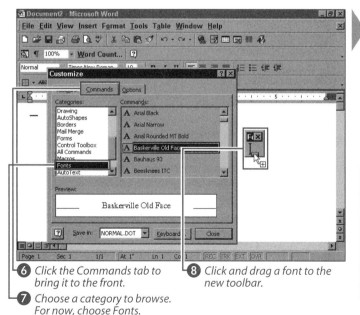

6 Click the Commands tab to bring it to the front.

7 Choose a category to browse. For now, choose Fonts.

8 Click and drag a font to the new toolbar.

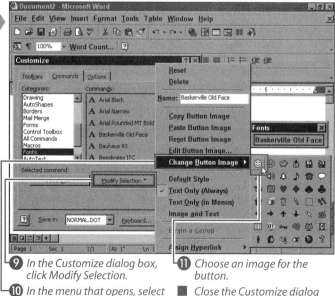

9 In the Customize dialog box, click Modify Selection.

10 In the menu that opens, select Change Button Image.

11 Choose an image for the button.

■ Close the Customize dialog box. You can drag the Fonts toolbar up to the top of the window, or click Close (X) to close it.

Creating Shortcut Keys

Another feature in Word that helps make your work more efficient is the capability to use and create shortcut keys. *Shortcut keys* are keyboard combinations that, when pressed, quickly perform functions that would otherwise require you to click through several menu items. For instance, if you press and hold down the Ctrl key on your keyboard and then press P, the Print dialog box will open. Likewise, if you select some text and press Ctrl+I, the selection will appear in italics.

You can create your own keyboard shortcuts in Word. This task is quite simple. You use the same Customize dialog box that you use for creating new toolbar buttons. You can create a shortcut key for virtually any command, and you can use a wide variety of key combinations. Typically, you select the control (Ctrl), Alternate (Alt), or Shift keys and some other key for your combination. You can even use three or more keys, as in Ctrl+Alt+B.

You can create shortcut keys for existing features, fonts, styles, special characters, and even macros that you record. With just the press of a button or two, you can perform even very complex operations.

As you work with shortcuts, remember that many key combinations are already taken. When you choose the item you want to create a shortcut for, check to see whether a key combination is already assigned to it. If there is, you probably want to stick with that. If not, assign a combination that you will

remember. At this point, Word notifies you if that combination is already assigned to something else. If it is, you should choose a different combination, unless it is assigned to a feature you never use.

The figures on the facing page show you how to assign a shortcut key to an action. In this case, you assign a shortcut to a specific font. Again, just as with toolbar buttons, shortcut keys can be assigned to virtually any function or element in Word, including those you create on your own.

TAKE NOTE

▶ KEYBOARD SHORTCUTS FOR COMMON WORD TASKS

Many common Word tasks already have shortcut keys assigned to them. When you open a menu on the menu bar, assigned shortcut keys are displayed next to items in the menus.

▶ RESETTING SHORTCUT KEYS

You might find after a while that you do not like some of the shortcut keys you have created. Or worse yet, you might have "inherited" your computer from someone else at work who was perhaps a little too enthusiastic about creating shortcut keys. You'll be happy to know that you can undo all custom shortcut keys and restore Windows defaults by clicking Reset All in the Customize Keyboard dialog box.

CROSS-REFERENCE
See shortcut keys in action in "Moving and Copying Text and Objects" in Chapter 10.

FIND IT ONLINE
Looking for a quick tip? Find 2,001 of them at **http://www.winmag.com/library/1996/1496/tip8g.htm.**

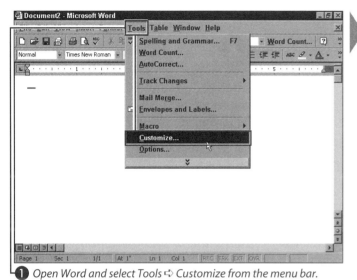

❶ *Open Word and select Tools ➪ Customize from the menu bar.*

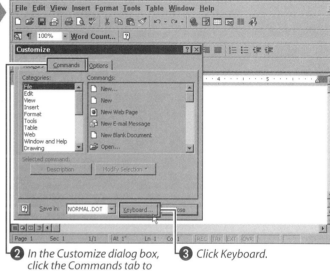

❷ *In the Customize dialog box, click the Commands tab to bring it to the front.*

❸ *Click Keyboard.*

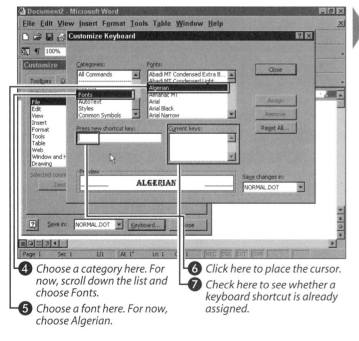

❹ *Choose a category here. For now, scroll down the list and choose Fonts.*

❺ *Choose a font here. For now, choose Algerian.*

❻ *Click here to place the cursor.*

❼ *Check here to see whether a keyboard shortcut is already assigned.*

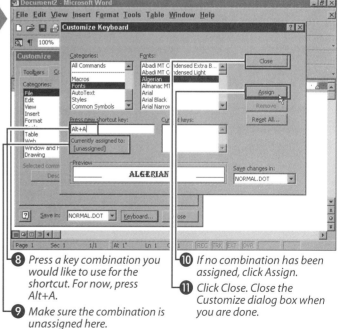

❽ *Press a key combination you would like to use for the shortcut. For now, press Alt+A.*

❾ *Make sure the combination is unassigned here.*

❿ *If no combination has been assigned, click Assign.*

⓫ *Click Close. Close the Customize dialog box when you are done.*

Personal Workbook

Q&A

1 What should you do if a Word feature you want to use is unavailable?

_____

_____

_____

2 How do you change the default location for saving your documents?

_____

_____

_____

3 Can the automatic spelling checker be disabled? How?

_____

_____

_____

4 What does Print Layout View represent?

_____

_____

_____

5 What do page breaks look like in Normal View?

_____

_____

_____

6 Can you add a single button to an existing toolbar?

_____

_____

7 What dialog box must you open to create custom toolbars, toolbar buttons, or shortcut keys?

_____

_____

_____

_____

8 When creating a new shortcut key, how do you know if the key combination is not already assigned?

_____

_____

_____

ANSWERS: PAGE 361

EXTRA PRACTICE

1 Open a Word document and view it in Print Layout View.

2 Change the zoom level to 25 percent, and then change the zoom level to 200 percent.

3 Create a toolbar and call it Custom4.

4 Add a button to your toolbar for the Thesaurus.

5 Change the appearance of the Thesaurus button so that it looks like a pencil.

6 Create a keyboard shortcut for the Verdana font.

7 Change the unit of measure used in Word to points.

REAL-WORLD APPLICATIONS

✔ Speed up routine macros by assigning a keyboard shortcut to them. This will save you the trouble of having to open a dialog box and select the same options over and over again.

✔ As you compose documents you probably apply similar text formatting to certain pieces of text. Consider creating styles (see Chapter 7) for those formats, and then create a custom toolbar that contains buttons for those styles. That way, you can apply your favorite styles with a single mouse click.

✔ If you are using Word on a laptop or older computer with a small hard drive, you can save some disk space by disabling some of the features you don't use in the Word setup utility.

Visual Quiz

What view mode is this document currently being viewed in? Why does the document appear so small? What is the free-floating object on the right side of the screen? How was it created?

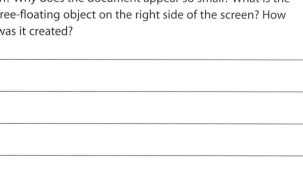

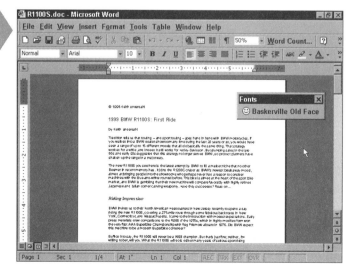

CHAPTER 3

MASTER THESE SKILLS

▶ Opening and Closing Files

▶ Saving Files

▶ Creating New Folders

▶ Renaming Files

▶ Switching Between Open Documents

▶ Working with Other File Formats

Managing Files

One of the most important concepts to understand as you use Word is the relationship between the program itself and the documents you use the program to create and edit. These documents exist on your hard drive as files separate from the program itself; if you think of Word 2000 as a typewriter (albeit a very advanced typewriter), document files are simply the pieces of paper that pass through it.

As you work on these documents, you must learn many skills. This includes the most basic tasks, such as opening and closing the files, which is usually the first thing you do after launching Word itself. If you are familiar with previous versions of Word, or other Windows-based programs, the techniques for opening and closing documents should be familiar. Still, Word 2000 offers some specialized methods for opening and closing files that you should learn.

Before you can open a document, there needs to be something to open. Word lets you save your work on disk, enabling you to open it again at some time in the future. Saving also prevents accidental loss of work due to power outages, operating system crashes, and other unforeseen mishaps.

When you save your work, you need to choose where you want to save it. You can save work on floppy disks, your hard drive, or even locations over your company's network. You can create your own locations for your documents, which are called *folders*. Folders help you keep track of your work, and Word allows you to create and manage folders as part of a complete storage system. Filenames are also an important part of the file management process, and Word lets you change filenames whenever you see fit.

When it comes to working with multiple documents, Word has you covered. Word lets you work with many different documents at once, and some of the techniques for dealing with multiple files have changed with Word 2000. Understanding how to work with multiple documents simultaneously will ultimately help you work more effectively.

This chapter discusses these issues, enabling you to better manage the documents you create with Word.

Opening and Closing Files

You may remember that the very first task in Chapter 1 described how to open and close Word. Once you have opened the program itself, you can begin typing to create a new document from scratch. But if you want to edit a document that was created and saved earlier, the next step is to open the document you want to work on. You can create an infinite number of document files with Word; each one can be opened or closed as needed, and independently of each other.

The files you create are generally small enough to fit on a removable disk, making it possible to move the file between computers. For example, if you write a memo or report on your laptop while flying across the country, you can quickly transfer it to your desktop computer back at the office by simply saving it on a removable disk. You can use this method to share files between computers that aren't connected by a network, or you can transfer a file over the Internet by attaching it to an e-mail message.

Of course, saving a file is only one small part of the picture. Because you save files so that they can be used again later, being able to open and close them is an important skill for any Word 2000 user. You can use one of several techniques for opening a file, whether Word is already open or not. You should also know how to close an individual file without also

closing Word, because sometimes you may want to continue using the program to edit other documents.

The first figure on the facing page demonstrates how to open a file before you open Word by using the Windows Documents menu. The second and third figures show how to open a file from within Word. The last figure demonstrates how to close a file without also closing Word.

TAKE NOTE

▶ WHY IS THE DOCUMENT CLOSE BUTTON NOT ALWAYS THERE?

In previous versions of Word, multiple open files existed within a single Word program window. Each file had its own document Close (X) button separate from the button that closes Word altogether, along with Minimize and Restore buttons. But with Word 2000, the document Close button appears if just one Word document is open. If more than one document is open, each one is displayed in its own separate program window.

▶ USING THE RECENTLY USED FILES LIST

Word keeps a list of recently used files in the File menu. You can quickly open one of these files by opening the File menu and clicking the name of the file you want to open. You can change the number of entries shown in this list on the General tab of the Options dialog box.

CROSS-REFERENCE
Don't have any files to open? See the next task, "Saving Files."

FIND IT ONLINE
See **http://mann.library.cornell.edu/workshops/ word/open** for online tutorials of functions of Word.

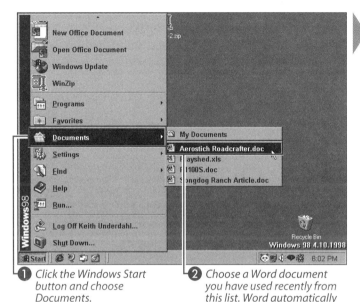

① *Click the Windows Start button and choose Documents.*

② *Choose a Word document you have used recently from this list. Word automatically launches with the selected document open.*

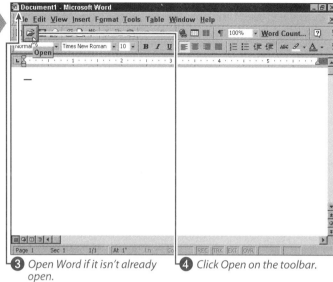

③ *Open Word if it isn't already open.*

④ *Click Open on the toolbar.*

⑤ *Note that the Open dialog box appears.*

⑥ *Choose a folder that contains the file you want to open here.*

⑦ *Click the file to select it.*

⑧ *Click Open.*

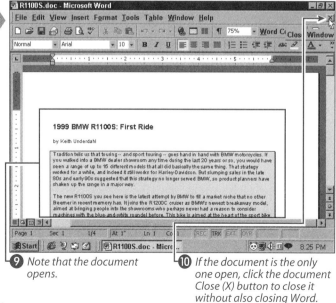

⑨ *Note that the document opens.*

⑩ *If the document is the only one open, click the document Close (X) button to close it without also closing Word.*

Saving Files

One of the most important advances that the personal computer has brought to the home and office is the capability of saving files on disk so they can be worked on again on another day. Without this capability, all of your hours spent slaving over a hot keyboard would blink out of existence every time you flipped off the power switch.

Besides being able to work on your files at a later date, the ability to save files on disk enables you to use those files on other computers as well. For instance, suppose you are creating a cookbook for your family's best recipes. You might spend some time working on the recipes on your laptop because it is easy to carry with you and use it whenever you have spare time. But when it comes time to print the cookbook, you probably want to use the high-quality printer connected to your desktop computer. The easiest way to get your cookbook files to the desktop would be to copy them to a floppy disk, and then use that disk to copy them to the other computer.

Saving files also enables you to keep a running record of your work, a bit like keeping a photocopy of every memo you send out. You can retain copies of old files to create an archive of past projects. That way, if you begin a similar project sometime in the future, you can refer back to the old files to see what you did before. A saved file can be reused after lunch

or ten years from now. One handy tool that Word uses is a warning dialog box that reminds you to save your work before closing a program. This helps to ensure that your valuable work is not lost simply because you forgot to save before clicking the Close (X) button.

The first three figures on the facing page demonstrate how to save a file in Word, and show you how to choose a location for the file. The last figure shows you how to save your file from time to time as you work.

TAKE NOTE

▶ DELETING FILES

Eventually, you will end up with a lot of old files you don't need anymore. The easiest way to delete them is through Windows Explorer or My Computer, but you can also do it right from within Word. Just launch the Open dialog box, click a file to select it, and press the Delete key on your keyboard.

▶ SAVE YOUR WORK FREQUENTLY

It's a good idea to save your files often; every ten minutes is a good rule of thumb. This precaution will help to ensure that a problem such as a locked-up computer or power outage doesn't result in many hours of lost labor.

CROSS-REFERENCE

See "Using Dialog Boxes" in Chapter 1 to learn more about working with this and other dialog boxes.

FIND IT ONLINE

Read top tips at **http://www.pcworld.com/software/ word_processing/articles/nov97/1511tips.html**.

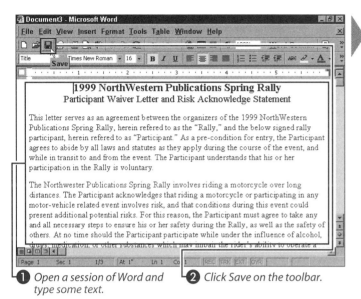

① Open a session of Word and type some text.

② Click Save on the toolbar.

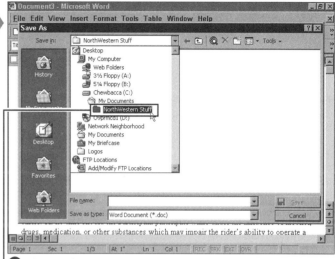

③ Choose a location to save the document in here. You can use any folder you want, but don't forget where you saved it.

④ Type a name for the document.

⑤ Choose a file type to save it as here. If you aren't sure what to pick, just use Word Document.

⑥ Click Save.

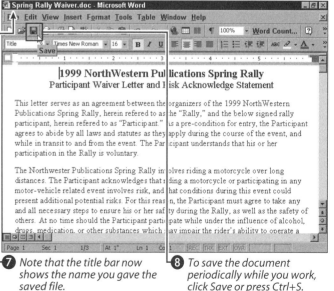

⑦ Note that the title bar now shows the name you gave the saved file.

⑧ To save the document periodically while you work, click Save or press Ctrl+S.

Creating New Folders

The hard drive of your computer is capable of holding many, many files. In fact, it already does. Because you have so many files on your hard drive, they must be organized in a way that enables you to find and use the ones you actually need.

A good way to think of your hard drive is as a drawer in a file cabinet. Each file you work with is a piece of paper that must be stored in that drawer. If you simply throw each piece of paper into the drawer, you will soon be unable to find the things you really need. You will have a large drawer filled with an ugly, chaotic pile of papers. A more effective approach would be to organize the papers by putting them in labeled folders within the drawer.

This is, in essence, the system that is used to organize files on your hard drive. Files reside in virtual folders on the hard drive, and each folder has a descriptive name. In many cases, folders exist within folders to further catalog and organize the files on the drive. These folders-within-folders are called *subfolders*, and are a key piece of the organizational puzzle on your computer. This system also works on removable disks, by the way, so you can organize your files there in a similar manner.

To provide your own custom touch to this process, you can create your own folders and subfolders as you see fit. For instance, if you save most of your work in a folder on your hard drive called *My Documents*, you may want to create subfolders within the My Documents folder for different projects, clients, and so on.

As with most other file management procedures, you can create folders either within Word, or in Windows Explorer and My Computer. In the latter two programs, select the file in which you want to create a subfolder. Then select File ⇨ New ⇨ Folder on the menu bar to create a new folder inside that folder. Be sure to type a new name for the new folder. The figures on the opposite page demonstrate a technique for creating new folders from within Word. Follow along to create new folders in which to store your own work.

TAKE NOTE

▶ HOW MANY FOLDERS FIT IN A DIRECTORY?

If you have spent any time working on a computer with an older operating system such as DOS or Windows 3.1, you may remember the term *directories*. Folders are exactly the same thing as directories, but with a new and improved name.

▶ NAMING FOLDERS

Folders can have long, descriptive names, just like files. Remember that subfolders within a single folder must each have a unique name.

CROSS-REFERENCE

Folder naming is similar to file naming. See the next task, "Renaming Files," to learn more.

FIND IT ONLINE

Learn about folders and directories at **http://www.pcguide.com/ref/hdd/file/index.htm**.

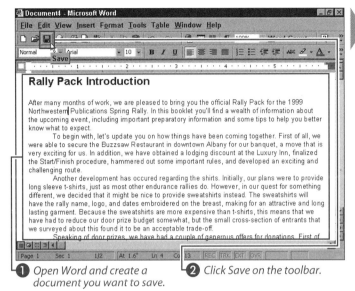

❶ Open Word and create a document you want to save.

❷ Click Save on the toolbar.

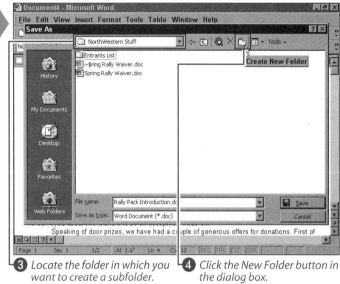

❸ Locate the folder in which you want to create a subfolder.

❹ Click the New Folder button in the dialog box.

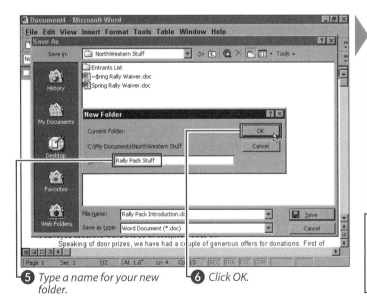

❺ Type a name for your new folder.

❻ Click OK.

❼ Open your new folder here.

❽ Type a name for your document.

❾ Click Save to save your document in this new folder.

Renaming Files

You have learned that giving a file a name is an important part of the file-saving process. Ideally, a filename should be descriptive enough that you can easily remember what it is the next time you need to find it. Fortunately, giving a file a descriptive name is much easier now than it used to be. Modern operating systems permit filenames that are as many as 256 characters long. In the past you could use only 8 characters. An old-style filename may have looked something like this:

▶ kthltr2

But with long filename support, you can give the file a somewhat less cryptic name, such as this:

▶ Letter to Keith on 25 September 1998

Which file would you have an easier time identifying?

Whether or not you use descriptive names, there will come a time when you will need to rename a file. Sometimes you simply need to rename an existing file, which is simple. At other times, you may need to make a copy of a file using a different name. Perhaps you need to make a second draft of a document, for example, or you are creating a document based on one you made previously. In this case, you would be using the old document as a kind of template.

Renaming a file is straightforward. You can handle this task from within Word or by using one of the operating system tools such as Windows Explorer or My Computer. In these Windows applets, the easiest way to rename a file is to right-click it and choose Rename from the shortcut menu. Just keep in mind that files must have unique names if they will be stored in the same folder.

The figures on the facing page demonstrate ways to rename a file from within Word using the Open dialog box. This technique also works in the Save dialog box. The first two figures demonstrate how to save a copy of a file under a new name, and the last two figures show how to rename an existing file.

TAKE NOTE

▶ HOW LONG SHOULD FILENAMES BE?

Older operating systems such as DOS and Windows 3.1 do not support long filenames, nor does the Internet. If you plan to use any of your documents on these systems or online, you should give files names with eight or fewer characters.

▶ ILLEGAL CHARACTERS IN FILENAMES

Windows lets you use a variety of characters, spaces, and punctuation in your filenames. However, you cannot use any of the following characters when naming your files: / \ : < > | " * or ?. If you get an error message when you try to save a file, check to see whether you accidentally used one of these illegal characters.

CROSS-REFERENCE

See "Opening and Closing Files," earlier in this chapter, to learn how to open the dialog box shown here.

FIND IT ONLINE

See a list of filename extensions and what they mean at **http://stekt.oulu.fi/~jon/jouninfo/extension. html**.

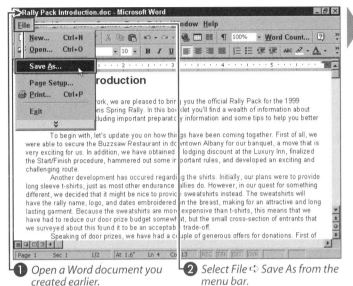

1 Open a Word document you created earlier.

2 Select File ⇨ Save As from the menu bar.

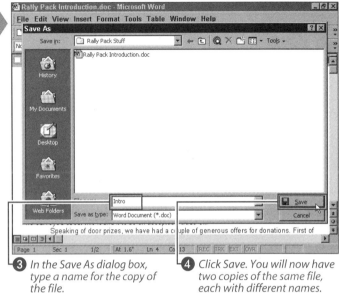

3 In the Save As dialog box, type a name for the copy of the file.

4 Click Save. You will now have two copies of the same file, each with different names.

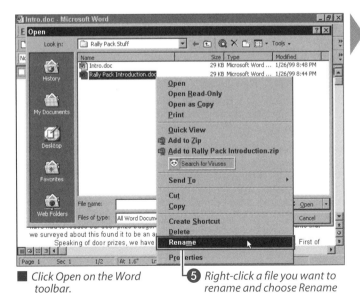

■ Click Open on the Word toolbar.

5 Right-click a file you want to rename and choose Rename from the shortcut menu.

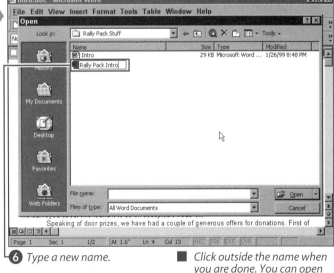

6 Type a new name.

■ Click outside the name when you are done. You can open the file if you want or simply close the dialog box.

Switching Between Open Documents

Word 2000 is designed to work with an operating system, such as Windows, that allows multitasking. This means that you can run more than one program simultaneously. You can, for instance, work on a document in Word while an e-mail client downloads mail in the background and a multimedia applet plays music from a CD. In addition to allowing multiple programs to run simultaneously, you can also have several different Word documents open at the same time.

The way in which multiple open documents are handled by Word has changed dramatically with Word 2000. Before, all documents opened within a single session of Word. So, even if you had ten different Word documents open at once, there would be one button for Microsoft Word on the Windows taskbar. This arrangement made switching from one open Word document to another a pain, because you either had to work with separate document windows inside the one Word window, or you had to find the document you wanted in the Window menu on the Word menu bar.

With Word 2000, each separate document you open launches into its own separate Word program window. This design makes switching between documents easier because each one has its own button on the Windows taskbar. Switching between the documents is a simple matter of clicking the taskbar button for the document you want.

Presumably, this design also provides greater flexibility for arranging document windows in very large

desktops. Windows 98 and NT 5.0 have built-in multiple monitor support, which means you could have two or more monitors side by side (or stacked on one another) to create one giant Windows desktop. Because your Word documents are not constrained to a single program window, they should be easier to organize in this situation.

The figures on the facing page show you how to open and switch between multiple Word documents. Notice here that three separate documents are open; these techniques work in the same way whether you have two or two dozen documents open. The last figure shows you how to switch documents using the shortcut discussed below.

TAKE NOTE

▶ SHOWING AND HIDING THE TASKBAR

If you routinely need to switch between open documents, you will probably find it easier to keep the Windows taskbar in view. You can choose whether you want the taskbar displayed or hidden by right-clicking a blank space on it and choosing Properties from the Shortcut menu. Select or deselect the Auto Hide option as desired.

▶ USING THE WINDOW MENU

You can still use the Window menu to switch between open Word documents. To do so, open the menu and select the filename you want from the list of documents that appears. You might prefer this method if you normally keep your Windows taskbar hidden.

CROSS-REFERENCE

Learn how to open documents in the first task in this chapter, "Opening and Closing Files."

FIND IT ONLINE

The University of Newcastle online tutorial site is located at **http://www.newcastle.edu.au/ department/ cc/helpdesk/tutorial-index.html**.

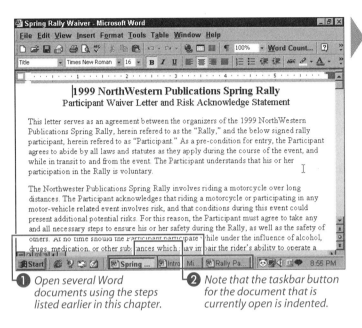

❶ Open several Word documents using the steps listed earlier in this chapter.

❷ Note that the taskbar button for the document that is currently open is indented.

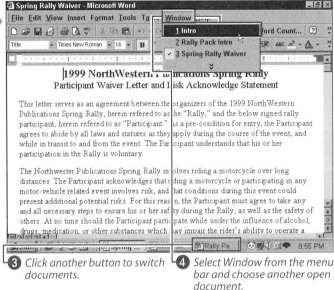

❸ Click another button to switch documents.

❹ Select Window from the menu bar and choose another open document.

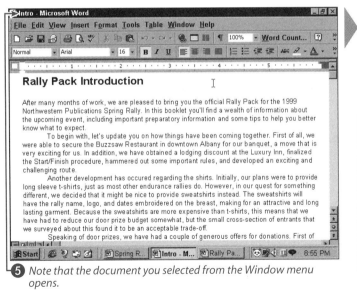

❺ Note that the document you selected from the Window menu opens.

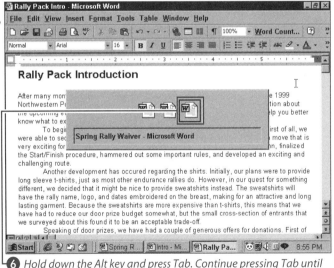

❻ Hold down the Alt key and press Tab. Continue pressing Tab until the document you want to open is selected. Release the Alt key to complete the switch.

Working with Other File Formats

Virtually every aspect of personal computers has improved dramatically over the years, and one of the most significant areas of improvement is the ability for computers to exchange information between a wide variety of platforms. Although significant efforts have been made to standardize personal computer technology, many different platforms are still being used.

PC-style computers running a Microsoft Windows operating system are most common, but many other PCs run alternative operating systems such as UNIX, Linux, OS/2, and others. There is also a large and dedicated contingent of Macintosh owners, and even an occasional Amiga user.

Although there is nothing inherently wrong with this variety, it can present some interesting challenges to people who need to share files — such as word processing documents — across the varying platforms. Even Windows users, working with the same operating system, may use different word processing programs. Is file sharing possible?

To an extent, yes. Word includes a number of file converters designed to read and interpret documents created using different software on a variety of computer types. For instance, suppose someone wrote an article for the club newsletter you edit, and they composed the article using WordPerfect on an old DOS machine. You should still be able to use it. Word 2000 automatically converts the file to the proper format and generally retains the formatting from the original document. Of course, sometimes the conversion is not perfect, but the basic text should still be there.

The first two figures on the facing page show you how to open a document that was created using other software, such as WordPerfect. As you can see, most of the work happens in the background. The last two figures show you how to save a document so it can be opened by older versions of Word.

Continued

Continued

TAKE NOTE

SAVING FILES FOR OLDER VERSIONS OF WORD

If you need to give a file to someone who is using an older version of Word, you have to save the file using the format for that version. A file saved in the standard Word 2000 format will be unreadable in Word 95 or older. A commonly used format for older Word versions is "Word 6.0/95 Windows&Macintosh." Choose the correct file format from the Save as type drop down list in the Save dialog box.

USING RICH TEXT FORMAT FILES

One of the available file formats that can be used across a wide variety of platforms is Rich Text Format (RTF). RTF files support more formatting than plain (ASCII) text files, which means you won't lose elements such as tables, italics, and fonts when you save your files to RTF. RTF files also work well as a "last resort" when you are having problems sharing files with Macintosh users.

CROSS-REFERENCE

Learn more about character formatting in Chapter 7 beginning with "Working with Fonts."

FIND IT ONLINE

Learn more about Word file formats at **http://www.wbs.cs.tu-berlin.de/~schwartz/pmh/laola.html**.

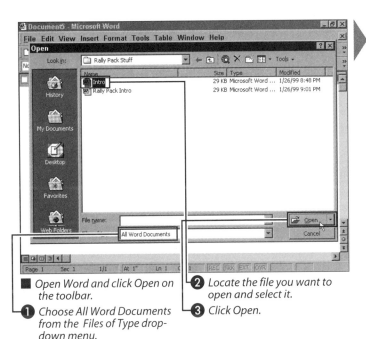

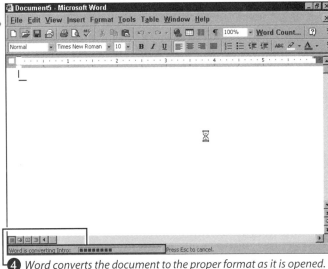

■ Open Word and click Open on the toolbar.

① Choose All Word Documents from the Files of Type drop-down menu.

② Locate the file you want to open and select it.

③ Click Open.

④ Word converts the document to the proper format as it is opened. You might be prompted to insert the Word 2000 program disk into your CD-ROM drive to install the appropriate file converter.

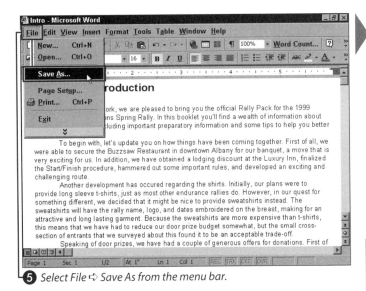

⑤ Select File ➪ Save As from the menu bar.

⑥ Type a name for the file.

⑦ To save the file so it can be used with older versions of Word, choose the proper format here.

⑧ Click Save.

Working with Other File Formats

On the previous two pages, you learned how to open files that were created on non-Windows platforms and from other word processing programs such as WordPerfect. Word 2000's file converters make sharing work between different programs and computer types much simpler. Working with others will therefore become far easier and more efficient.

Unfortunately, the file conversion process doesn't always work exactly as planned. For various reasons, some shared files become unusable, or at best they contain extraneous garbage. This has long been a problem among computer users. As a result, many people save their text documents as *text files*. Text files (also sometimes called *ASCII files*) contain nothing but plain text—no italics, colors, graphics, or special fonts. A text file contains nothing but the text itself, and it can be read on the greatest variety of platforms.

This lack of formatting is at the root of what makes text files the "foolproof" solution for many users. First, you are all but guaranteed that the recipient of a text file you send will be able to read it, and vice versa. Also, text files do not require a large, complex program such as Word 2000 to be read (although you certainly can read text files in Word if you want!). Numerous light text readers are available. In Windows, the text reader is called Notepad. You can open Notepad by clicking the Windows Start button and choosing Programs ⇨ Accessories ⇨ Notepad. There are also a number of shareware text readers available that you can download from the Internet. If you want to try something other than Notepad, visit http://dir.yahoo.com/Computers_ and_Internet/Software/Text_Editors/.

The first two figures on the facing page show you how to open and read a text document in Word. The last two figures show you how to save a file as text only. Remember, any formatting you might have applied to a document will be lost when you save it as a text-only file.

TAKE NOTE

▶ VIEWING README FILES

Most programs come with at least one text file that provides important information about installation, potential conflicts, licensing agreements, and even how to use the software itself. Whenever you prepare to install new software, look for one of these text files. It will almost certainly be called README.TXT. Some software might have many text files; for instance, the README.TXT file that comes with Windows is nothing more than a list of other text files that pertain to various aspects of the software.

▶ PROGRAMMING IN TEXT

Some programmers use text editors such as Notepad and Word to write program code. Many Web pages, for instance, are still created using Notepad. In fact, if you choose to view the source code of an HTML document (usually a Web page), it will probably open with Notepad.

CROSS-REFERENCE
Learn how to enter text into a document in Chapter 5 beginning with "Entering Text."

FIND IT ONLINE
Learn more about text files and ASCII text at
http://www.jimprice.com/jim-asc.htm.

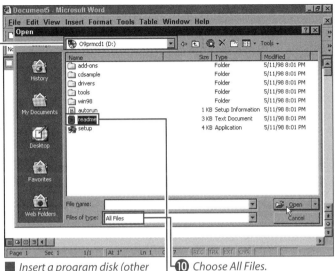

■ Insert a program disk (other than Word/Office 2000) into the drive, open Word, and click Open on the toolbar.

9 Locate the appropriate disk drive.

10 Choose All Files.

11 Double-click a file called Readme.txt to open it.

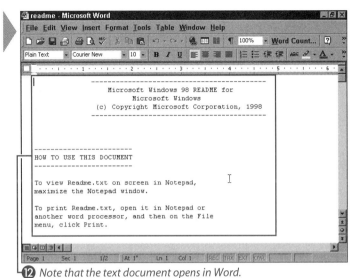

12 Note that the text document opens in Word.

13 Open another document in Word that you have created yourself.

14 Select File ➪ Save As from the menu bar.

15 In the Save As Type list, choose Text Only.

16 Click Save.

■ You will probably see a dialog box that warns you about lost formatting. Click Yes to acknowledge the warning.

Personal Workbook

Q&A

1 Can you close a Word document without also closing Word?

_____

_____

2 How do you know if more than one Word document is open?

_____

_____

_____

3 What are two ways to switch between open Word documents?

_____

_____

_____

_____

4 Should you do anything different when saving a file that will need to be used in Word 6.0 later?

_____

_____

5 Can Word read document files that were created with WordPerfect?

_____

_____

_____

6 What kind of formatting can you include in text files?

_____

_____

_____

7 What are text files often used for on program disks?

_____

_____

_____

8 What are two ways to change the name of a document file?

_____

_____

_____

ANSWERS: PAGE 361

EXTRA PRACTICE

1. Create a short document in Word.

2. Save the document and call it Test1.

3. Create a new folder and call it Test Stuff.

4. Save a text-only version of Test1 in the Test Stuff folder.

5. Open both versions of document.

6. Switch between the documents using only the keyboard.

7. Copy some text from one of the documents and paste it into the other.

8. Save the changed document to a new location.

REAL-WORLD APPLICATIONS

✔ If you have to create a monthly training report for your office but most of it remains the same each month, just use last month's document as a template. Simply open last month's document, and use File ➪ Save as to rename it for this month.

✔ You probably create a lot of memos through the course of your work. Use folders to keep those memos organized on your hard drive. For instance, you could create a separate folder for each client you have.

✔ If you are publishing software, images, or other items on disk, you can save your customers a lot of trouble by including a text-only "Readme" file on the disk that contains important setup information or a list of frequently asked questions (FAQs).

Visual Quiz

Are there any text-only documents shown here? How was the folder named "Rally Pack Stuff" created? Can you rename the file shown here? How?

_____

_____

_____

_____

_____

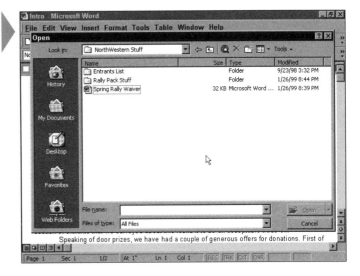

CHAPTER 4

MASTER THESE SKILLS

▶ Using the Office Assistant

▶ Using the Help Contents and Index

▶ Using the Answer Wizard

▶ Using Wizards

▶ Using Microsoft's Online Resources

Getting Help

When it comes to using computer software, even jaded experts occasionally find themselves struggling for an answer, unable to remember the procedure that will help get the job done. Thankfully, Word 2000 is ready to offer a helping hand when the answer seems just beyond your grasp. Word has a useful Help system that provides solutions to almost any problem you are likely to encounter. Can't remember how to format mailing labels? What were those steps for recording a macro? Do not worry; quick solutions are a mouse click away.

Help systems within programs are nothing new. As in many other Windows-based applications, the Word 2000 Help system provides a searchable index of topics. You can browse through the topics or search for a keyword to find specific instructions to help you complete your task.

In addition to the basic Help system, Word offers a number of other innovative elements to help you get your job done quicker and more efficiently. The most obvious element, and probably one of the first things to catch your eye when you start to use Word, is the Office Assistant. The Office Assistant is the little animated paper clip named Clippit who hangs out at the top or the bottom of your screen. The Office Assistant reviews what you are doing and provides timely and interactive advice and tips to help you speed up your work.

Word's wizards can also help you simplify many common tasks. A *wizard* is basically a glorified dialog box that asks you a series of questions as you begin certain kinds of documents. The questions ask you for basic information about what you plan to do. The wizard then automatically creates a document based on the information you provided. Finally, Microsoft provides extensive online help for Word 2000 users. If you have Internet access, you can use online help to receive up-to-the-minute product news, tips, free software plug-ins and updates, or even technical support.

This chapter describes how to use the many help tools offered by Word. Each one can prove helpful in different situations, and the practice here will help you become familiar with each.

Using the Office Assistant

One of the most innovative help features offered by Word is the interactive Office Assistant. The Office Assistant is represented as a cartoonish paper clip character named Clippit who lives on your screen, off to one side. From time to time he winks, wiggles, or acts out little scenes that are somehow related to something you are doing in the program.

The Office Assistant differs from other forms of help in that it doesn't always wait for you to go looking for help; help comes to you. The Office Assistant continually monitors your progress and offers timely advice as you work. You can also ask the Assistant questions by clicking it to open a dialog box. The Office Assistant is shared with other Microsoft Office programs, so if you have Office 2000, you will see Clippit in the other programs as well.

By default, the Assistant provides a Tip of the Day every time you open Word. You can turn this feature off by clicking the Options button in the Assistant dialog bubble. Most of the time, the Assistant remains discreet but close at hand for you to call on as needed. Furthermore, if you do not use the Office Assistant for several minutes, the Assistant actually shrinks so that it takes up less of your screen.

Help comes in many different forms from the Office Assistant. The first figure on the next page shows a typical Tip of the Day from the Office Assistant that appears when a program is first opened. The second and third figures show you how to use the Office Assistant to answer questions you may have, and the last figure demonstrates how to disable the Assistant.

TAKE NOTE

TURNING OFF THE OFFICE ASSISTANT

Useful though the Office Assistant may be, you may not always want its help, and you may actually find it distracting. You can set options to change when and how the Assistant helps you by clicking the Assistant and choosing Options from the menu that appears. On the Options tab of the Office Assistant dialog box, remove the check mark next to the option Use the Office Assistant to disable it and use the more traditional Help system. You can also choose to disable certain Assistant features here, such as sounds or animations.

HIRING A NEW ASSISTANT

Some people think the paper clip is cute, but if you are not one of those people, Word offers several other Assistants from which you can choose. In the Office Assistant Options dialog box, click the Gallery tab. Click the Back or Forward button to browse the Assistants that are available. These include The Dot, F1 (a robot), The Genius, the Office Logo, Mother Nature, Links the Cat, and Rocky the Dog.

CROSS-REFERENCE

Learn more about using online help resources later in this chapter in "Using Microsoft's Online Resources."

FIND IT ONLINE

Download additional Office Assistants from the Microsoft Web site by clicking Help ⇨ Office on the Web.

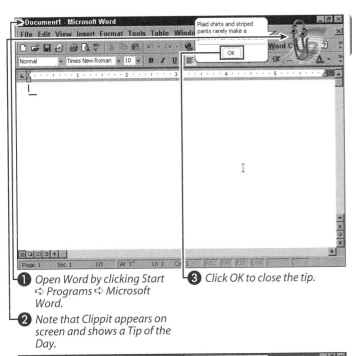

1 Open Word by clicking Start
⇨ Programs ⇨ Microsoft
Word.

2 Note that Clippit appears on
screen and shows a Tip of the
Day.

3 Click OK to close the tip.

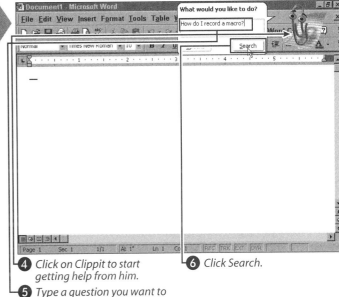

4 Click on Clippit to start
getting help from him.

5 Type a question you want to
ask.

6 Click Search.

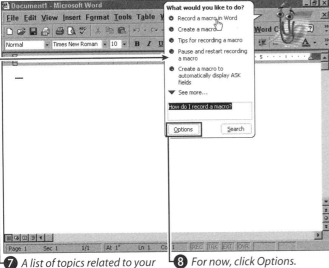

7 A list of topics related to your
question appears. You can
click one to view it.

8 For now, click Options.

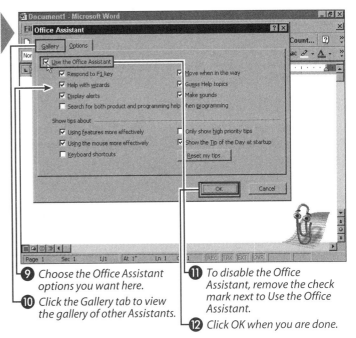

9 Choose the Office Assistant
options you want here.

10 Click the Gallery tab to view
the gallery of other Assistants.

11 To disable the Office
Assistant, remove the check
mark next to Use the Office
Assistant.

12 Click OK when you are done.

Using the Help Contents and Index

The Office Assistant can be extremely helpful, but many users find it intrusive or distracting. After you have been using Word for a while and are more comfortable with it, you may want to turn the Assistant off. If the Assistant is disabled, you can still obtain help through the more traditional Help system. This system consists of a table of contents, an index, and an Answer Wizard. These appear in a Help window that functions much like a Web browser, complete with Back and Forward buttons.

You can take advantage of the help contents and index in a number of ways. If you seek help from the Office Assistant, the Assistant will help you select a topic or list of topics in Help. Likewise, if you look for help in one of the wizards or any dialog box, a topic from Help should appear.

In addition to these methods, you can also access the Help contents and index directly. To do so, you must first disable the Office Assistant. Once in Help, you may find that it is arranged in much the same way as this book. A contents list provides an outline of the major topic areas covered by Word Help, and there is also an alphabetical index of all topic areas. The window itself is divided into a left and right pane. The left pane has the contents list, index, or Answer Wizard, depending on which tab is selected.

The right-hand pane show the text of help topics. Some help text is linked to other topics, as indicated by blue or purple letters and underlining.

The first figure on the facing page shows how to open the Help contents and index from within Word. The next figure demonstrates how to use the features on the Contents tab of the Help system, and the third figure demonstrates items on the Index tab. The last figure shows you how to open and read help topics.

TAKE NOTE

▶ PRINTING A HARD COPY OF HELP

You can print a hard copy of a help topic that you expect to refer back to again in the future. To print the topic, click the Print button near the top of the Help window.

▶ WHY DOES HELP PROMPT FOR AN INTERNET CONNECTION?

Usually, when you prepare to read a help topic in the Help system, you will be prompted to connect to the Internet. If you do, Word will double-check the Microsoft Web site to make sure the help topic has the latest and greatest information. However, you do not need to make the online connection just to read help topics if you do not want to or if you simply cannot connect at that time.

CROSS-REFERENCE

See the next task in this chapter, "Using the Answer Wizard," to learn how to perform searches in Help.

FIND IT ONLINE

Office Toys, at **http://www.officetoys.com/**, provides some excellent and helpful Word add-ins.

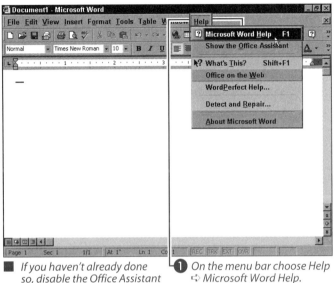

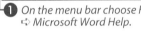

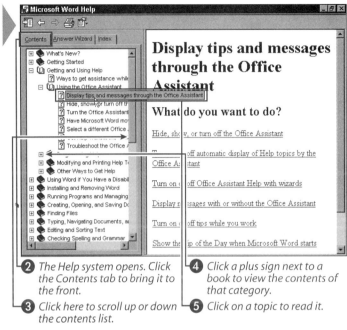

■ *If you haven't already done so, disable the Office Assistant as described in the previous task.*

① *On the menu bar choose Help ⇨ Microsoft Word Help.*

② *The Help system opens. Click the Contents tab to bring it to the front.*

③ *Click here to scroll up or down the contents list.*

④ *Click a plus sign next to a book to view the contents of that category.*

⑤ *Click on a topic to read it.*

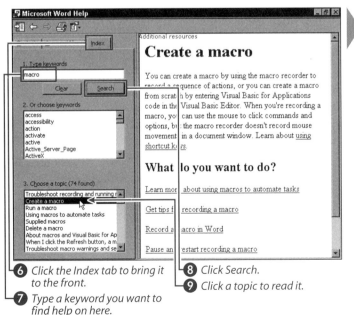

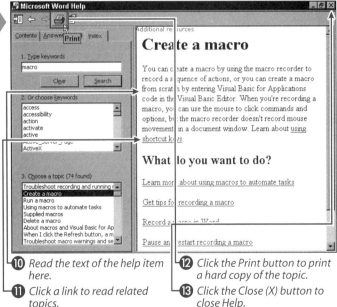

⑥ *Click the Index tab to bring it to the front.*

⑦ *Type a keyword you want to find help on here.*

⑧ *Click Search.*

⑨ *Click a topic to read it.*

⑩ *Read the text of the help item here.*

⑪ *Click a link to read related topics.*

⑫ *Click the Print button to print a hard copy of the topic.*

⑬ *Click the Close (X) button to close Help.*

Using the Answer Wizard

If you're like most people, your work involves an almost constant stream of questions. Often your questions are answered by someone or something (a book, for example) around the office, or by calling or e-mailing an expert. But when your questions involve using Word, answers are even easier to find than you may think. A great place to look for those answers (besides in this book, of course) is in the Answer Wizard.

The Answer Wizard does just what the name implies: It provides answers to many of your tough questions. It asks, "What would you like to do?" Beneath this simple yet ominous question is a text box in which you can type a sentence in plain English, just as you would respond to a human expert sitting by your side. For instance, typing something like "I want to print to a file" causes dozens of topics on the subject of printing to be displayed. You can then select, read, and print the topics just as you would when using the Help contents and index.

The Answer Wizard works by looking for keywords in the sentence you type. For instance, in the example of needing help on printing a file, the wizard extracts the keyword *print* and displays all printing-related topics. It does not immediately narrow your search to the topic on printing to a file, which is the topic you need. As you can see, the Answer Wizard points you in the right direction, but you still have to do some digging to find specific answers.

You can reach the Answer Wizard as you would the Help contents or index: It only works when the Office Assistant is disabled. If you haven't disabled the Assistant, return to the first task in this chapter to learn how to do that. The figures on the facing page show you how to search for help using the Answer Wizard.

CROSS-REFERENCE
You can also perform searches using the Office Assistant. See "Using the Office Assistant" earlier in this chapter.

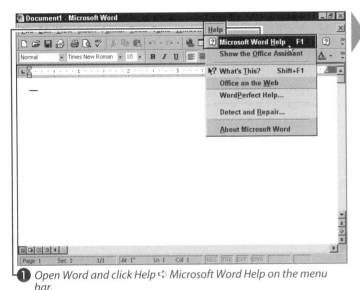

① Open Word and click Help ➪ Microsoft Word Help on the menu bar.

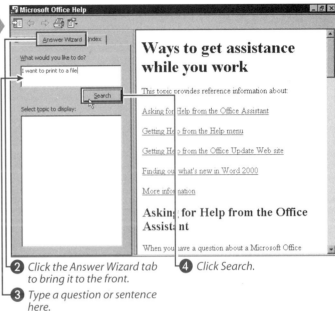

② Click the Answer Wizard tab to bring it to the front.

③ Type a question or sentence here.

④ Click Search.

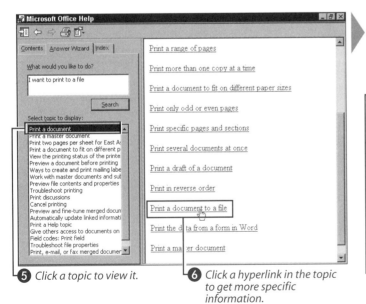

⑤ Click a topic to view it.

⑥ Click a hyperlink in the topic to get more specific information.

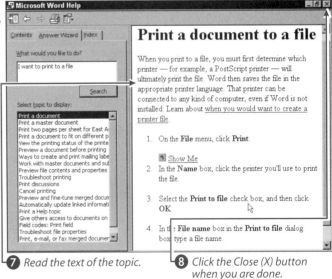

⑦ Read the text of the topic.

⑧ Click the Close (X) button when you are done.

Using Wizards

Creating a new document with a certain look and feel can be a complicated task. For instance, suppose you want to use Word to create a fax cover sheet. Professionals have expectations regarding fax cover sheets, and yours should contain the specific pieces of information they expect. Above all, the cover should be easy to read so that the recipient can glean pertinent information from it quickly.

Creating a good fax cover letter in Word could take a fair amount of time. First you have to figure out exactly which information to include, such as a page count for the fax, phone numbers, addresses, and other contact information. Then there are layout issues, such as where to set margins, graphical elements, and the like. Before you know it, you've just blown thirty minutes on a simple cover letter that the recipient is probably going to look at for five seconds and then throw away. Wouldn't it be nice if there was a way to speed up these monotonous-yet-crucial tasks?

With Word 2000, help is just a mouse click away, so to speak. Word provides special tools called *wizards* to guide you through otherwise time-consuming and complicated tasks. These wizards offer step-by-step procedures to simplify the creation of new documents and save you many headaches. A wizard asks you simple questions about what you want a document to look like and what information you want it to contain.

The wizard then takes your information and automatically creates a document, preformatted with much of your information already filled in. There will still be areas of the document that you need to complete yourself. Like templates, most wizards contain placeholder text in areas where you need to type something. This text usually has a gray background. To enter your own information, click in the space to start typing.

The figures on the facing page demonstrate how to use the Fax Wizard to create a cover letter. This particular wizard demonstrates how Word makes the task of creating a cover letter like this a matter of only a minute or two, and the finished product is professional looking as well as attractive.

TAKE NOTE

OTHER WIZARDS

Word provides wizards for many kinds of documents. There are wizards for letters, faxes, Web pages, legal pleadings, résumés, and more. Browse through the various tabs of the New dialog to see what is available.

CUSTOMIZE THE DOCUMENT FURTHER

Although wizards provide an attractive and easy format to use, you may want to make some minor changes to customize the cover letter to your own tastes. Once you have completed the wizard steps, you can edit the document just as you would any other, and you can change anything you want.

CROSS-REFERENCE

See "Using a Template to Create a New Document" in Chapter 6 to learn more about templates.

FIND IT ONLINE

Microsoft offers extra wizards and templates on its Web site. Click Help ⇨ Office on the Web. On the Internet, look for a link to Enhancements and Assistance.

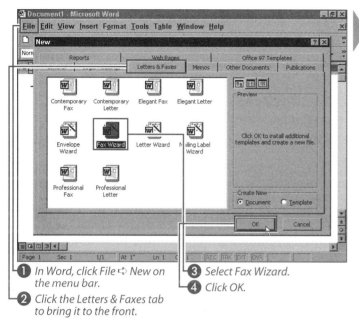

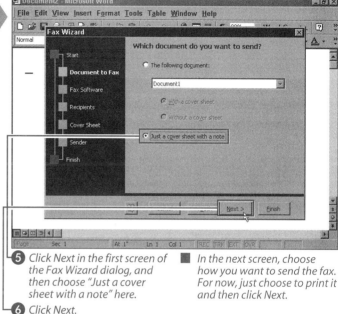

① *In Word, click File ➪ New on the menu bar.*

② *Click the Letters & Faxes tab to bring it to the front.*

③ *Select Fax Wizard.*

④ *Click OK.*

⑤ *Click Next in the first screen of the Fax Wizard dialog, and then choose "Just a cover sheet with a note" here.*

⑥ *Click Next.*

■ *In the next screen, choose how you want to send the fax. For now, just choose to print it and then click Next.*

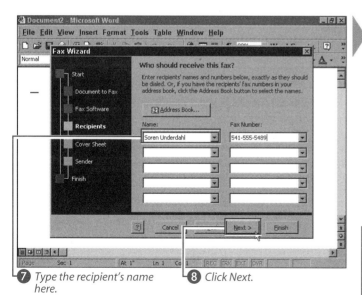

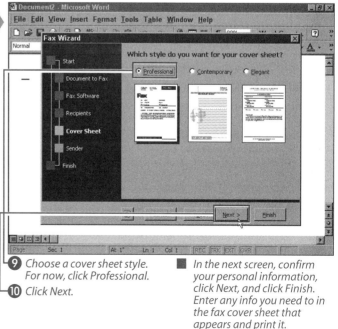

⑦ *Type the recipient's name here.*

⑧ *Click Next.*

⑨ *Choose a cover sheet style. For now, click Professional.*

⑩ *Click Next.*

■ *In the next screen, confirm your personal information, click Next, and click Finish. Enter any info you need to in the fax cover sheet that appears and print it.*

Using Microsoft's Online Resources

In this chapter, you've learned that Word has a plethora of help features. Each resource fits a specific need, and you may find each one useful at different times and in different applications. But the resources covered up to this point — the Office Assistant, Help contents and index, the Answer Wizard, and wizards — are generally static in nature. Although you can update them over the Internet, for the most part they remain fixtures of Word for the entire time you use it.

Software development is always an ongoing process, and the people who created Word want to be able to offer you the most up-to-date assistance they can. To make this possible, Word 2000 incorporates an innovative online support network, whereby you can use your Internet connection to get up-to-the-minute help and support directly from Microsoft. All you need is a modem and an account with an Internet service provider (ISP) to get online.

When you access online resources for Word, you are taken to Microsoft's Web site. Many services are available, including online technical support, a forum for providing Microsoft with user feedback, and general product information. But perhaps the most important resource available to you is the free software add-ins and updates that can be downloaded from the Web site. This software may simply fix or improve the way Word performs certain tasks or may provide enhancements that change the look and feel of Word.

The figures on the facing page demonstrate how to find and download a template for a new kind of document that wasn't included with Word when you purchased it. Microsoft frequently develops and publishes new templates that you can use with Word, and the figures here show you how to download them.

Continued

TAKE NOTE

KEEPING UP WITH CHANGES

The ever-changing nature of the Internet means that the Microsoft Web pages you see may be different from what is shown here. However, no matter how it looks, the link you click in the Word Help menu will always lead to Microsoft's online support resources. Check back from time to time to see if the look and available features have changed.

INSTALLING TEMPLATES AND ADD-INS

Software add-ins that you download from Microsoft — such as Office Assistants, clipart, and templates — are very easy to install. Usually, after the download process is complete, you can just use Start ⇨ Run to run a self-installer. For instance, with the Office Assistant called Kairu the Dolphin, you simply download and then run a program called Dolphin.exe. In any case, make sure you read the instructions provided on the Web site before you leave. You may want to print the instructions out to ensure you have them when it's time to install.

CROSS-REFERENCE

See the first task in this chapter, "Using the Office Assistant," to learn more about using it.

FIND IT ONLINE

If you have trouble using the online help links, check the Microsoft Office Web site at **http://office. microsoft.com/** and look for Products information.

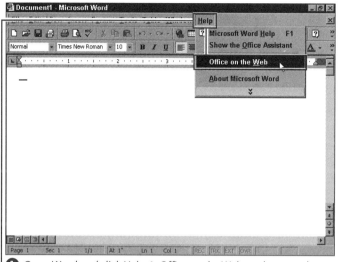

1 Open Word and click Help ⇨ Office on the Web on the menu bar.

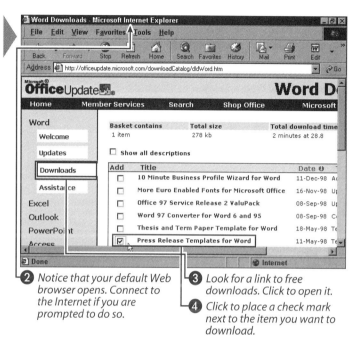

2 Notice that your default Web browser opens. Connect to the Internet if you are prompted to do so.

3 Look for a link to free downloads. Click to open it.

4 Click to place a check mark next to the item you want to download.

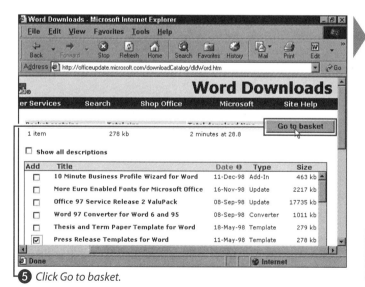

5 Click Go to basket.

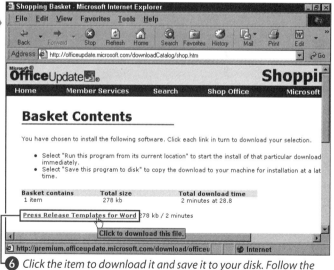

6 Click the item to download it and save it to your disk. Follow the onscreen instructions to complete installation.

Using Microsoft's Online Resources *Continued*

Software engineers put years of work into making programs such as Word 2000 the best they can be, but inevitably there will be something that doesn't work exactly as planned under all conditions. Because of this, software publishers like Microsoft often provide free updates and upgrades for their products as a service to customers.

The Internet has revolutionized how this support is provided. In the past, free upgrades were limited, simply because the expense of producing and mailing thousands of floppy disks with software updates to registered users was too great. But with the Internet, all the publisher has to do is put the upgrade files on a Web server where users can download them with a modem. The cost of distributing software in this manner is minimal, meaning that upgrades are offered on a more regular basis.

So what does this mean for you, the savvy Word user? First of all, it means that if any bugs or glitches occur in the software, Microsoft should be able to provide fixes on the Office Update Web site. In the previous version of Word (Word 97), for example, a file converter flaw prevented users from saving files in Word 95/6.0 format. Microsoft was quick to offer a fix for this problem, in the form of a simple add-in that took less than two minutes to download and ten seconds to install.

In addition to bug fixes, you may also find upgrades and improved support for emerging technologies on the Office Update site. If a new technology becomes available in the near future that Word users would want to take advantage of, Microsoft could offer a plug-in that allows Word to support the technology. For instance, as the World Wide Web grew in popularity, Microsoft offered plug-ins that allowed previous versions of Word to compose and edit Web documents.

The figures on the facing page show you how to access the Office Update Web site and how to download files from it. As with other downloads from the Microsoft Web site, these patches and plug-ins are usually simple and straightforward to install.

TAKE NOTE

CHECK OFFICE UPDATE OFTEN

To make sure you have the most current software technologies available, you should check the Office Update Web site on a regular basis. Consider visiting the site on the first day of every month, and look through all the downloads that are offered. Even older downloads are updated from time to time, so make sure you have the most current version.

GET INTERACTIVE HELP FROM NEWSGROUPS

Microsoft hosts numerous newsgroups for Word users. Click the Newsgroups link on the Office Update site to see whether any may be useful for you. In newsgroups, you can converse with other users, as well as Microsoft experts, to ask and answer tough questions about Word.

CROSS-REFERENCE
For an overview of how to view Web pages, see "Viewing Web Pages" in Chapter 16.

FIND IT ONLINE
If you can't get the Help menu links to work, visit the Office Update site directly at **http://officeupdate. microsoft.com/**.

1 On the Word menu bar, click Help ⇨ Office on the Web.

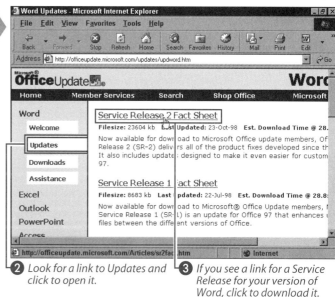

2 Look for a link to Updates and click to open it.

3 If you see a link for a Service Release for your version of Word, click to download it.

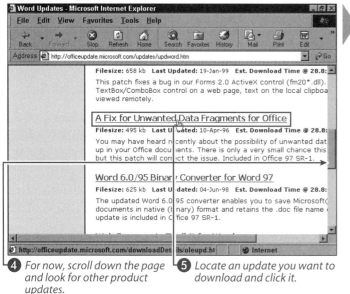

4 For now, scroll down the page and look for other product updates.

5 Locate an update you want to download and click it.

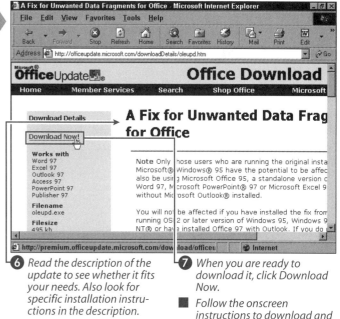

6 Read the description of the update to see whether it fits your needs. Also look for specific installation instructions in the description.

7 When you are ready to download it, click Download Now.

■ Follow the onscreen instructions to download and install the software.

Personal Workbook

Q&A

1 What does the Office Assistant usually look like?

_____

_____

_____

2 By default, what does the Office Assistant do every time you open Word?

_____

_____

_____

3 How do you use the Assistant to obtain help on a particular topic?

_____

_____

_____

4 How do you disable the Assistant?

_____

_____

_____

5 Can you produce a printed copy of help topics? How?

_____

_____

_____

6 What is the quickest way to search for help in the Microsoft Word Help window?

_____

_____

_____

7 Where are most wizards located?

_____

_____

_____

8 What kind of information does Microsoft provide for you on the Internet?

_____

_____

_____

ANSWERS: PAGE 362

EXTRA PRACTICE

1 Open Word and enable the Office Assistant.

2 Ask the Office Assistant how to create a form letter.

3 Open the topic on Form letters, envelopes, and labels.

4 Print the topic, and then close Help.

5 Access Microsoft's online resources, and download an Office Assistant called Kairu the Dolphin.

6 Change the Office Assistant to Kairu.

7 Go to the Office Update Web site and check to see if there are any updates to your software.

REAL-WORLD APPLICATIONS

✔ If you are traveling and forgot how to print a document to a file, there is a remote chance that you will have forgotten to bring *Teach Yourself Microsoft Word 2000* with you on the plane. If that is the case, just ask the Office Assistant, "How do I print to a file?"

✔ The Office Assistant can make the task of teaching your children how to use Word much easier. The Assistant is fun to use, and kids will like the fact that they can ask questions of it using the same words and sentence structure they would use to ask you.

✔ If you encounter a problem that you believe is a software bug, check the Office Update Web site to see if Microsoft has produced a fix for it. If so, the file should only take a few minutes to download and install, allowing you to get on with your work.

Visual Quiz

What is the quickest way to produce a fax cover sheet, as shown here? What does the cartoon dog in the lower-right corner represent? What will happen if you click on some of the text in the dialog bubble coming from the dog? Can you disable this feature? How?

_____

_____

_____

_____

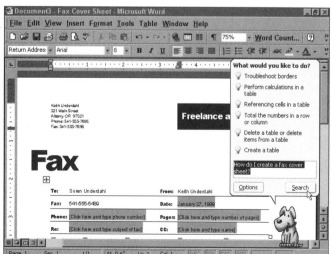

PART

II

Contents of 'Desktop'

Name

My Computer

Network Neigh

Internet Explore

Microsoft Outloo

Recycle Bin

My Briefcase

3252-9

3259-6

3261-8

3262-6

3281-2

3286-3

DE Phone List

Device Manager

In

Iomega Tools

Creating Documents

Your first step in creating a document in Word will usually be to enter some text. There is more to this than simply pressing keys on the keyboard, so the first chapter in Part 2 — "Creating Your First Document" — introduces you to some important document creation concepts. This includes entering text, of course, but you also learn how to change the layout of your pages, separate and select areas of text, use special characters or symbols not normally found on the keyboard, and add page numbers.

In addition to these document basics, you also discover how to use document templates. Templates act as patterns for common types of documents, and you learn not only how to use existing templates but also how to create your own. You see how to apply formatting to virtually every aspect of your document, from single words of text to entire paragraphs. You also learn what tables are and how to use them, as well as how to insert and use graphics to spruce up the appearance of your documents.

CHAPTER 5

MASTER THESE SKILLS

▶ **Entering Text**

▶ **Setting Up the Page**

▶ **Selecting Text**

▶ **Inserting Breaks**

▶ **Using Special Characters and Symbols**

▶ **Numbering Your Pages**

Creating Your First Document

Microsoft Word 2000 is promoted primarily as a word processing program, which as a definition is too limiting. In theory, a word processing program turns your computer into what is essentially an electronic typewriter, but suffice it to say your PC is light years ahead of even the most advanced typewriters. Word lets you create a vast assortment of documents, from simple lost dog flyers to multimedia-rich pages for the World Wide Web.

Realistically, your computer is not only more capable but also more difficult to use than the typical typewriter. Word 2000 is intended to be user friendly, but if you have never created a document using a computer, this task can seem intimidating, to say the least. This chapter starts at square one by showing you how to create a new document with Word. This simple process will be your first step almost every time you use Word, so it's a good idea to take a few minutes and master the basics here.

Once you have created your first document, you go on to discovering a bit more about that document and how to begin changing it. First you see how to change the setup of the actual page by adjusting margins and changing the size of the page itself. You then learn how to select an area of text, which is a critical step in accomplishing many of the editing features described elsewhere in this book. This includes copying, moving, formatting, and virtually any editing task that Word can do.

Next, you see how to work with page breaks and other kinds of breaks in your documents, and how to insert some unusual characters and symbols. You even learn a trick to make inserting symbols you use all the time even quicker. Finally, you are shown how to number the pages of your document and control where and how those numbers appear, an important thing to do if your document contains many pages.

The tasks in this chapter give you some excellent blocks of knowledge on which to build in future tasks. Mastering these skills now will help you achieve greater success later on.

Entering Text

As the name suggests, Microsoft Word is designed primarily to help you work with (surprise) words. It is a word processing program, which means that you probably purchased it for the purpose of writing letters, composing memos, writing books, or any of a thousand other possibilities. Whatever your plans for this program, your first step in completing almost any task is to type some text.

Entering text is straightforward, easily the simplest task in Word to complete. For the most part, you enter text by typing with the keyboard, just as you would on an old typewriter. Of course, there are many, many differences between a typewriter and a computer, but generally speaking, anything a typewriter can do, Word can do better.

If you have used a typewriter in the past, one of the first differences you will notice is that you do not need to hit the carriage return at the end of every line. Pages in your Word documents have margins, and when you reach a margin, the words you type are automatically entered on the next line. You can end a line whenever you want to, however, by pressing the Enter key on your keyboard. The Enter key is the PC equivalent to a typewriter's carriage return. You always press the Enter key — or a combination of the Enter key and something else — at the end of a paragraph.

The figures on the facing page show you some of the basics of entering text. You begin by typing some basic text, and then you practice using the Enter key on your keyboard. You also experiment with viewing certain breaks.

TAKE NOTE

HARD VS. SOFT RETURNS

Pressing Enter on the keyboard ends the current paragraph and creates what is called a *paragraph break* (also referred to as a *hard return*). If you do not want to end the current paragraph but need the cursor on the next line, hold down the Shift key as you press Enter. This creates a *line break* (also called a *soft return*), which means you ended the line, but not the paragraph. This concept will be important when you begin to work with Styles and other tools that apply to entire paragraphs.

USING THE CURSOR

An important concept to understand is the cursor. The *cursor* is the flashing point on the screen, also sometimes referred to as the *insertion point*. When you type a letter or other character on the keyboard, it appears where the cursor is. In this respect, the cursor is like the type head or ball on a typewriter. You can move the cursor around your documents using the arrow keys on the keyboard, or you can place it in a new location by clicking there with the mouse.

CROSS-REFERENCE

See "Inserting Breaks" later in this chapter to learn about other kinds of document breaks.

FIND IT ONLINE

Improve your typing skills with the typing tutor available at **http://www.letterchase.com/**.

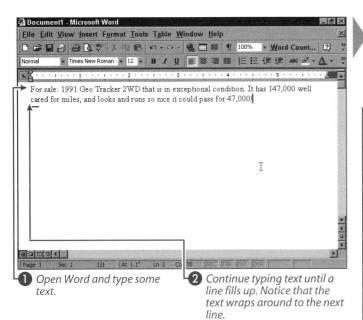

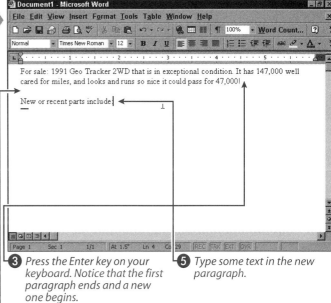

1 Open Word and type some text.

2 Continue typing text until a line fills up. Notice that the text wraps around to the next line.

3 Press the Enter key on your keyboard. Notice that the first paragraph ends and a new one begins.

4 Press Enter again to make a blank line.

5 Type some text in the new paragraph.

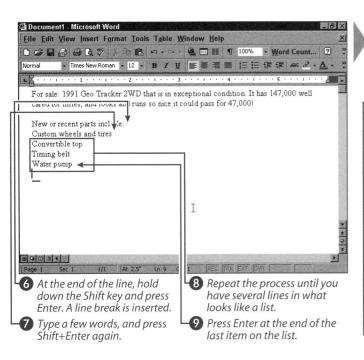

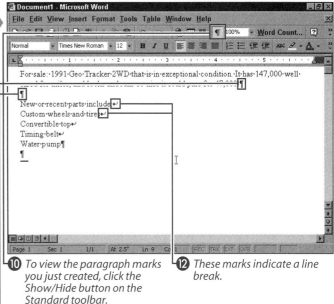

6 At the end of the line, hold down the Shift key and press Enter. A line break is inserted.

7 Type a few words, and press Shift+Enter again.

8 Repeat the process until you have several lines in what looks like a list.

9 Press Enter at the end of the last item on the list.

10 To view the paragraph marks you just created, click the Show/Hide button on the Standard toolbar.

11 These marks indicate a paragraph break.

12 These marks indicate a line break.

Setting Up the Page

In the previous task, you learned how to begin entering text in a document and how to work with line and paragraph breaks. Typing some text is an important first step when you create a document, but it is only one of several things you must do. Another very important task you must take care of early on is setting up the page you will be working on.

When you think of a page in Word, think of the format in which you plan to publish the document. Usually this "plan" will involve printing a document on paper and, more often than not, the paper will be standard 8.5" by 11" sheets. In fact, depending on your individual needs, you may never use anything else.

When you create a new document, Word assumes that you intend to print it on 8.5" by 11" paper. But if you are using another size, you need to give Word new parameters for the page. These parameters include the physical size of the paper, as well as how you would like your document oriented on the page.

Even if you are using standard-sized paper, you may want to make some adjustments to the page itself. You can adjust the margins, which are the areas left blank towards the edges of the paper. Without margins, the text would print right to the edge of the paper, and perhaps even beyond that. Margins are important to have, but you may want to adjust the margins slightly to make your document fit better. By default, Word uses a 1" margin at the top and bottom of the page, and a 1.25" margin along the sides.

The figures on the following page show you how to adjust the margins for your page. You also learn how to apply your changes to an entire document or just to one page.

Continued

TAKE NOTE

▶ SAVE PAPER BY ADJUSTING MARGINS

If your document is very large — say, 100 pages or more — you may want to fiddle around with the margins a bit. A simple reduction of one tenth of an inch on all margins for each page would have a negligible impact on your document's appearance, yet over the course of many pages the space savings may be considerable.

▶ WHAT IS THE PRINTABLE AREA?

If you reduce the margins too much, you may see a warning dialog box that says you have set the margins outside the printable area. Depending on your printer, this could mean that some text near the edges won't print properly, or everything may work out fine anyway. If you see this message, be sure to test print a page before printing the final draft.

CROSS-REFERENCE
To learn how to create a template for unusual page sizes, see "Creating a New Template" in Chapter 6.

FIND IT ONLINE
Get free layout advice online from Microsoft by clicking Help ⇨ Office on the Web on the Word menu bar.

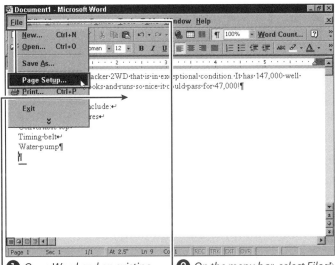

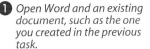

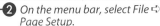

① Open Word and an existing document, such as the one you created in the previous task.

② On the menu bar, select File ➪ Page Setup.

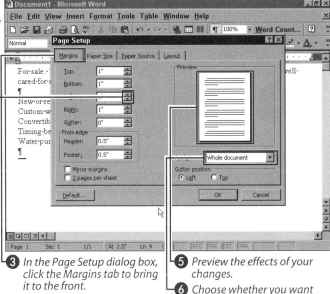

③ In the Page Setup dialog box, click the Margins tab to bring it to the front.

④ Click the spinner box arrows to increase or decrease your margins.

⑤ Preview the effects of your changes.

⑥ Choose whether you want your changes applied to the whole document.

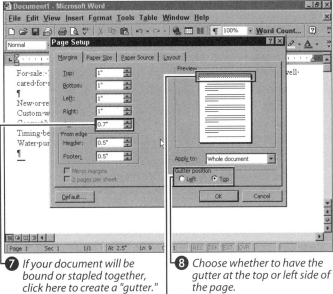

⑦ If your document will be bound or stapled together, click here to create a "gutter." This offsets the margin to keep text from being hidden by staples.

⑧ Choose whether to have the gutter at the top or left side of the page.

⑨ Preview the gutter.

■ Get rid of the gutter for now.

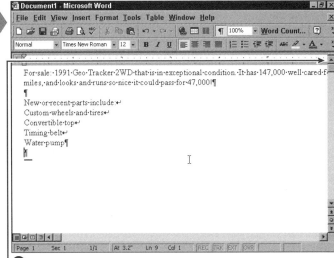

⑩ Click OK to accept your changes and close the dialog box. You can view the changes to the margins of your document here.

Setting Up the Page

Continued

Besides adjusting margins, there are a number of page layout options you can change. One that has already been mentioned is paper size. The standard paper size in the United States for most documents is 8.5" by 11" letter-sized paper. This paper size is used for memos, in-house publications, and a virtually limitless number of other uses.

Other sizes and shapes of paper exist, and you might need to adjust the page size during the course of your work. A common alternative size is legal paper, which measures 8.5" by 14". This size is often used for important legal documents, such as real estate and loan contracts. If you routinely work with an unusual-sized paper, you will need to know how to set up Word to properly handle that unusual size. You might also want to create a new template for documents that use unusual paper sizes. See Chapter 6 to learn more about templates.

Another important consideration when setting up the page is how you would like text oriented on the paper. By default, documents you create in Word will be printed so that the text reads across the narrow (8.5") side of a standard sheet of paper, with the long (11") side running vertically. This type of orientation is commonly referred to as portrait, because the paper is oriented the way it usually is in portrait paintings. But you can turn the text of your document so that the lines run along the long side of the page and the short side of the paper is vertical. This orientation is called landscape, because it is how most photographs of a landscape are taken.

The figures on the facing page show you how to create different-sized pages using the Page Setup dialog box. You also learn how to change the orientation of your page so that it is landscape instead of the default, portrait.

TAKE NOTE

▶ PRINTING ENVELOPES

When you select a different page size, you may notice that some envelope sizes are available. Although you can certainly print an address on an envelope by creating a page of the correct size, this really isn't the easiest way to do it. For better results, use the Envelopes and Labels option in the Tools menu, as discussed in detail in Chapter 15.

▶ SETTING UP A PAGE WITH TABLES

If you are creating a document that is basically just a giant table, you may achieve better results by using landscape orientation. It is difficult to fit many columns of a table on a standard portrait page, but you can fit far more with landscape orientation. Also, you can usually get away with reducing the margins more when tables are involved. Learn more about tables in Chapter 8.

CROSS-REFERENCE

See "Using Print Preview" in Chapter 14 to make sure the page looks right before you print.

FIND IT ONLINE

Make page setup easier with legal templates, available at **http://www.microsoft.com/**.

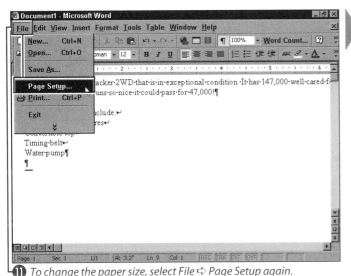

⑪ To change the paper size, select File ➩ Page Setup again.

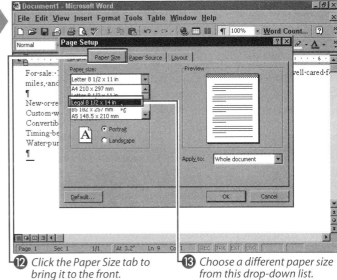

⑫ Click the Paper Size tab to bring it to the front.

⑬ Choose a different paper size from this drop-down list.

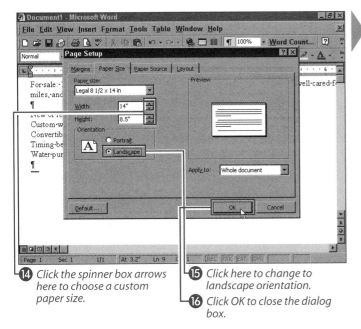

⑭ Click the spinner box arrows here to choose a custom paper size.

⑮ Click here to change to landscape orientation.

⑯ Click OK to close the dialog box.

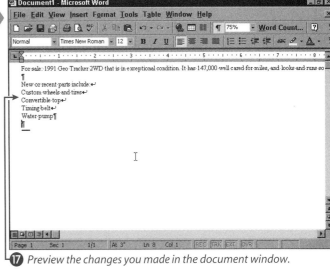

⑰ Preview the changes you made in the document window.

Selecting Text

Usually, when you create a document in Word, much more is involved than simply typing some text and printing it. The vast majority of tasks you perform in Word will require you to select some text. If you want to make a word bold, for instance, you must first tell Word which word you want bold. You do this by *selecting* it.

You can select almost anything on the page, including letters, numbers, words, sentences, paragraphs, and even the whole document. Pictures, tables, and other objects can also be selected. Once you have made a selection, you can do a huge variety of things to that selection. You can delete what you have selected by pressing the Delete key on your keyboard, or you can cut and paste it to a new location. Copying text works in a similar way.

Selecting text in a Word document is easy and can be done in a couple of ways. The easiest way involves using the mouse. Click and hold down the left mouse button wherever you want the selection to begin, and then drag the mouse pointer to the end of your selection. Release the mouse button when you have selected everything you want to. The selection will appear different from the surrounding text, usually as white text on a black background. You can cancel a selection by clicking once outside of it.

You can also make selections using just the keyboard. To do so, first place the cursor at the beginning of the selection. Then hold the Shift key down and use the arrow keys to move the cursor and select everything that the cursor moves over. Release the Shift key when you have selected everything you want.

The figures on the facing page show you several ways to select text. The first two figures show you how to use the mouse to make a selection, and the last two figures utilize the keyboard. Practice using both techniques in a variety of situations to see which works best for you.

TAKE NOTE

▶ **SELECTING WHOLE WORDS AND PARAGRAPHS**

You can quickly select an entire word by double-clicking it with the mouse. If you triple-click something, the entire paragraph will be selected. If you prefer to use the arrow and Shift keys on the keyboard, you can also hold down the Ctrl key as you move the cursor to select entire words or paragraphs.

▶ **USING SHORTCUT MENUS WITH SELECTED TEXT**

You can right-click a selection to open a shortcut menu. The shortcut menu contains the most common items that are used with a text selection, including cut, copy, and paste. You can also choose to reformat the font or paragraph as you see fit.

CROSS-REFERENCE

See "Moving and Copying Text and Objects" in Chapter 10 to learn about moving selected text.

FIND IT ONLINE

A great resource for all flavors of Windows can be found at **http://www.winfiles.com**.

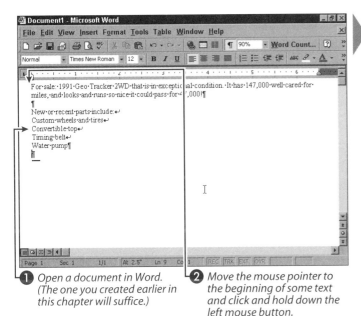

1 Open a document in Word. (The one you created earlier in this chapter will suffice.)

2 Move the mouse pointer to the beginning of some text and click and hold down the left mouse button.

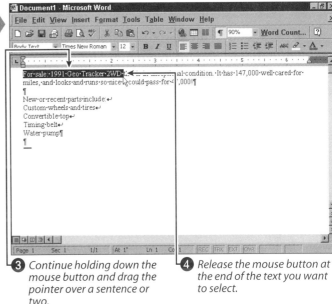

3 Continue holding down the mouse button and drag the pointer over a sentence or two.

4 Release the mouse button at the end of the text you want to select.

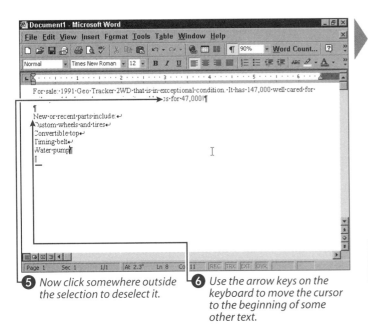

5 Now click somewhere outside the selection to deselect it.

6 Use the arrow keys on the keyboard to move the cursor to the beginning of some other text.

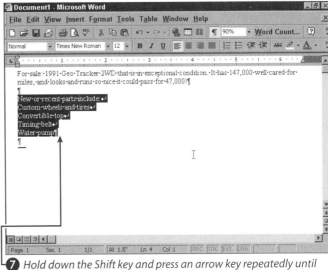

7 Hold down the Shift key and press an arrow key repeatedly until you have reached the end of text you want to select. Release the Shift key when finished.

Inserting Breaks

In the first task of this chapter, you learned how to enter text into a Word document. In addition, you also learned the difference between a paragraph break and a line break, and how to create each within your document. These are the two most common types of breaks you are likely to work with, and they are the easiest to insert.

As the name suggests, a break is a separation between elements within your document. A line break manually separates lines of text but keeps them as part of the same paragraph for styling purposes, and a paragraph break separates text into different paragraphs. Another common type of break you will use from time to time is a page break. A page break splits your text into separate pages.

Less common are column breaks, which separate text into columns. In some documents, you may want to arrange text into columns on the page, kind of like a newspaper. If you want to end the text in one column and move to the next, you can insert a column break. Section breaks are also useful in these kinds of documents. Using columns involves changing the page setup, and if you want to stop using columns and go back to a regular page setup, you will need to insert a section break to separate the two different page formats. You can learn more about columns in Chapter 18.

Line breaks, paragraph breaks, and page breaks can all be entered using simple keyboard combinations. To use column and section breaks, however, you must become familiar with the Break dialog box. This dialog box, which you can open from the Insert menu, contains just a few simple options. The first three figures on the facing page show you how to use the Break dialog box to insert a section break. The last figure shows you how to enter a page break using the keyboard.

TAKE NOTE

▶ APPLYING STYLES OVER BREAKS

Styles apply to entire paragraphs, and are always separated by paragraph breaks. Manual line breaks are different because the same style will always apply on both sides of the break. If you insert a page, column, or section break, however, Word will also automatically insert a paragraph break. You have to apply styles separately on either side of all breaks except line breaks.

▶ VIEWING BREAKS

If you cannot see the breaks that have been entered, try clicking the Show/Hide paragraph mark button on the toolbar. This displays all paragraph breaks as paragraph symbols (¶) and line breaks as carriage return symbols (↵). Viewing page, column, and section breaks is a little trickier. Try switching between Normal View and Print Layout View using the buttons in the lower-left corner of the Word window to view these breaks.

CROSS-REFERENCE
See "Changing the View" in Chapter 2 to learn more about changing the view of your document.

FIND IT ONLINE
Publish RGB, located at **http://www.publish.com/**, is a great site for online layout tips.

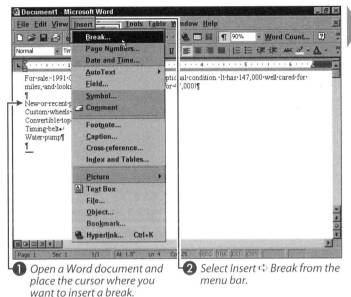

① Open a Word document and place the cursor where you want to insert a break.

② Select Insert ➪ Break from the menu bar.

③ In the Break dialog box, select the type of break you want. For now, choose Continuous section break.

④ Click OK.

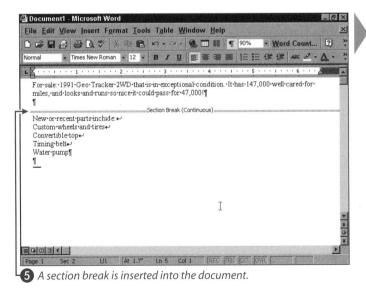

⑤ A section break is inserted into the document.

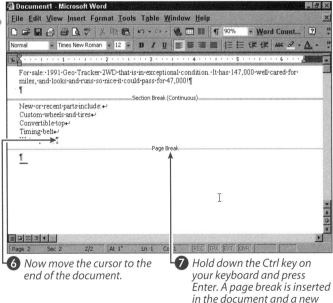

⑥ Now move the cursor to the end of the document.

⑦ Hold down the Ctrl key on your keyboard and press Enter. A page break is inserted in the document and a new page begins after the break.

Using Special Characters and Symbols

One of the biggest drawbacks of typewriters was that you were limited to the character set of the typewriter itself. This meant you could use only a single font at a time, and you usually couldn't use italics or bold text either. Furthermore, if you needed to enter any characters that weren't on the typewriter's keyboard, you were out of luck.

Despite using a keyboard that is roughly based on old typewriters, modern computers have no such limitations. Word comes with a large variety of special characters and symbols built in, ready for you to access. These special characters include trademark and copyright symbols as well as smiley faces, lines, and arrows. Special characters from non-English alphabets are also available.

Word automatically enters many of these special characters when you type or press certain key combinations. For instance, when you type (c), Word automatically inserts the copyright symbol, ©. Such automatic character insertions are based on AutoCorrect entries, and there are many for special symbols. Browse through the AutoCorrect dialog box by clicking Tools ⇨ AutoCorrect on the menu bar to see which key combinations will enter what.

You will find that AutoFormat entries also exist for some common symbols. If you use letters after a number (called ordinals), as in Friday the 13th, Word automatically makes the "th" ordinal superscripted so that it appears closer to how you might have actually written it. The number would look like this: 13th. If you select the right AutoFormat options, you can also format fractions when you type them. So if you type 1/4, it would come out as ¼.

Word contains hundreds, if not thousands, of potential symbols ready for you to use. Your best bet is to browse through them at your leisure. The first three figures on the facing page show you how to use the Symbol dialog box to insert a special character. The last figure demonstrates the use of AutoCorrect for the same purpose.

Continued

TAKE NOTE

▶ GETTING RID OF AUTOCORRECTED SYMBOLS

Sometimes AutoCorrect automatically corrects things that don't need correcting. For instance, if you want the letter *c* inside parentheses instead of a copyright symbol, you may have a problem because AutoCorrect automatically turns (c) into ©. To undo the substitution, type the characters, and then after AutoCorrect enters the symbol, press the Backspace key. This should undo the AutoCorrect without deleting the characters you typed.

▶ USING FONTS FOR SPECIAL CHARACTERS

Most of the special character sets in Word are also available as fonts from the Font drop-down menu on the toolbar. If you need to type a few words or sentences in Greek, for instance, you may have better luck by simply changing to the Symbol font and typing your words.

CROSS-REFERENCE

See "Setting AutoCorrect Options" in Chapter 12 for more on using AutoCorrect.

FIND IT ONLINE

CastleType, at **http://www.castletype.com/**, offers a number of unique fonts.

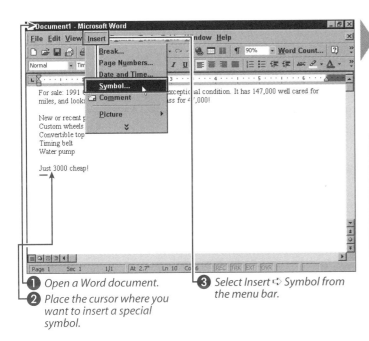

❶ Open a Word document.

❷ Place the cursor where you want to insert a special symbol.

❸ Select Insert ➪ Symbol from the menu bar.

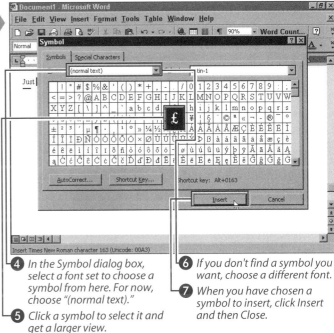

❹ In the Symbol dialog box, select a font set to choose a symbol from here. For now, choose "(normal text)."

❺ Click a symbol to select it and get a larger view.

❻ If you don't find a symbol you want, choose a different font.

❼ When you have chosen a symbol to insert, click Insert and then Close.

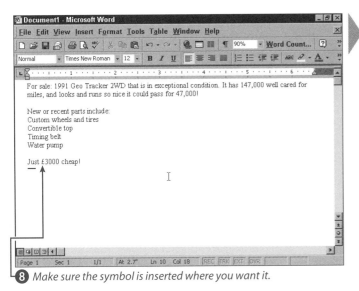

❽ Make sure the symbol is inserted where you want it.

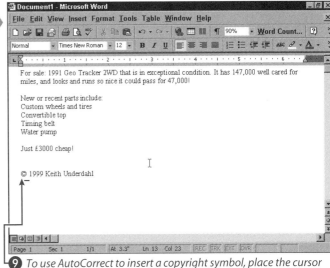

❾ To use AutoCorrect to insert a copyright symbol, place the cursor where you want the symbol to appear and type (c). AutoCorrect automatically changes the characters to the copyright symbol.

Using Special Characters and Symbols *Continued*

On the previous pages, you learned how to enter special characters in your Word documents using both the Symbol dialog box and AutoCorrect. These are the simplest, most straightforward methods for inserting special characters. The Symbol dialog box, in particular, gives you immediate access to any character available in Word.

That said, using the dialog box can also turn into a bulky and time-consuming process if you need to enter the same special character on a regular basis. You can create new AutoCorrect items for some characters, but in many cases that isn't practical either. One time-saving solution may be to create a keyboard shortcut for a commonly used special character. If you are a geometry teacher, for instance, you may want to create a shortcut key for the Greek letter pi (π). Likewise, someone who types in German a lot may want to create a shortcut key for characters that have an umlaut, such as ä.

Creating shortcut keys is a simple affair. You do it by first opening the Symbol dialog box as described previously, selecting the character you want to create the shortcut for, and clicking the Shortcut Key button that is in that dialog box. You can then create a shortcut using virtually any key combination you wish. Most key combinations involve use of the Shift, Alt, or Ctrl keys combined with something on the keyboard that is easy to remember. If you want to create

a shortcut for pi, for instance, you might try Alt and the letter P because that should be easy to remember.

The figures on the facing page show you how to create and use a shortcut key for a common symbol. The first three figures show you how to create the shortcut key, and the last figure demonstrates its use.

TAKE NOTE

▶ AVOID USING EXISTING KEY COMBINATIONS

When you create a shortcut key for a special character, make sure the key combination is not already being used by something else. You can check this from within the Customize Keyboard dialog box. After you press a key combination, look where it says "Currently assigned to." If it says, "Unassigned," the combination you tried should be safe to use. If it is assigned to something else, try another combination. Alternatively, if the combination is currently assigned to something you never use, it might be okay to reassign it.

▶ DON'T FORGET ABOUT AUTOCORRECT

Before you assign a new shortcut key to a symbol or character, check to see whether it already has an AutoCorrect entry. If it does, you might be better off just sticking with that. On the other hand, if you need to delete an AutoCorrect entry for an item, you can always go back and create a shortcut key to replace it.

CROSS-REFERENCE
To learn more about this topic, see "Creating Shortcut Keys" in Chapter 2.

FIND IT ONLINE
A range of artistic fonts are available from Deniart Systems, at **http://www.deniart.com/**.

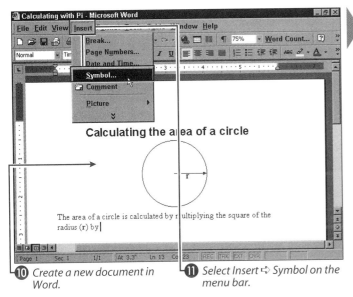

10 Create a new document in Word.

11 Select Insert ⇨ Symbol on the menu bar.

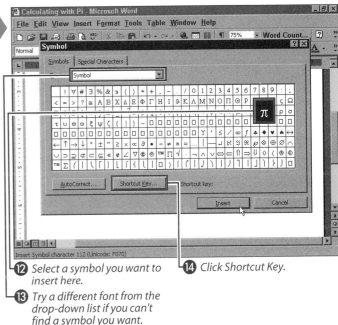

12 Select a symbol you want to insert here.

13 Try a different font from the drop-down list if you can't find a symbol you want.

14 Click Shortcut Key.

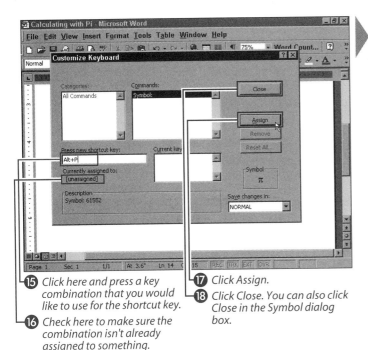

15 Click here and press a key combination that you would like to use for the shortcut key.

16 Check here to make sure the combination isn't already assigned to something.

17 Click Assign.

18 Click Close. You can also click Close in the Symbol dialog box.

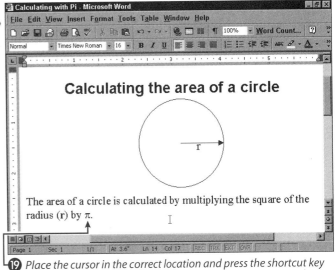

19 Place the cursor in the correct location and press the shortcut key combination you just created. The symbol should be inserted.

Numbering Your Pages

Many documents you create, such as brief memos, letters, sale flyers, and others, consist of only a single page, and other documents may have multiple pages. With Word 2000 you can create documents that are hundreds or even thousands of pages long. If you have created a very large document that you intend to print, sorting through the many pages can become a problem.

The obvious solution is to number your pages. By default, Word does not apply page numbering to documents because most documents created by Word users are only one or two pages anyway. A page number takes up a little bit of margin space, so eliminating it for shorter documents makes sense. Still, if you are creating multipage documents, using numbers is a good idea, if for no other reason than that you will be able to reassemble the printed document if a gust of wind blows it across your office.

Numbering pages is easy, but it is something you must consciously do. When you apply page numbering to a document, you must select a number of options. First, you must decide where on the page you want the numbers to appear. Most people put them at the bottom (footer) of the document, but the top (header) works fine, too.

Besides choosing the top or bottom, you can also choose to have the page numbers centered, placed in the left or right corner, or you can choose to have them placed on the inside or outside of the page. By "outside," Word means the outside corner of the page if all the pages were assembled front-to-back, like in a book. The numbers at the bottom of the page you are reading right now are an example of bottom, outside corner numbering. You could opt to place the numbers on the inside corners, but as you can guess, that choice would create a readability problem in most cases.

The figures on the facing page show you how to apply page numbers to your document, and how to modify the number format.

CROSS-REFERENCE
See "Using Headers and Footers" in Chapter 18 to further customize your page numbers.

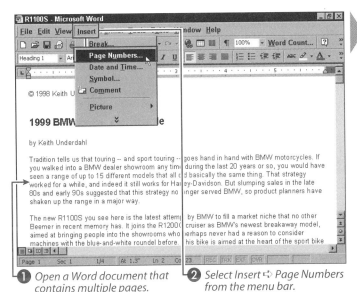

① Open a Word document that contains multiple pages.

② Select Insert ➪ Page Numbers from the menu bar.

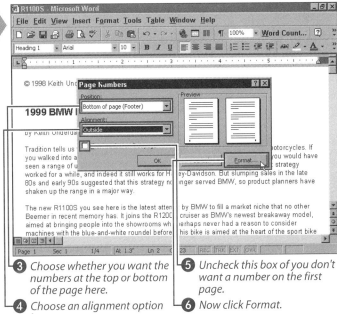

③ Choose whether you want the numbers at the top or bottom of the page here.

④ Choose an alignment option here.

⑤ Uncheck this box of you don't want a number on the first page.

⑥ Now click Format.

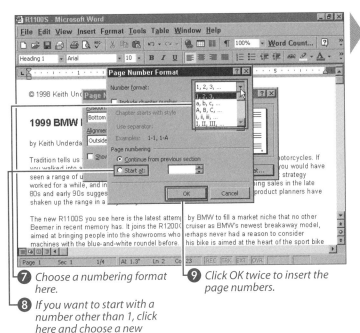

⑦ Choose a numbering format here.

⑧ If you want to start with a number other than 1, click here and choose a new starting number.

⑨ Click OK twice to insert the page numbers.

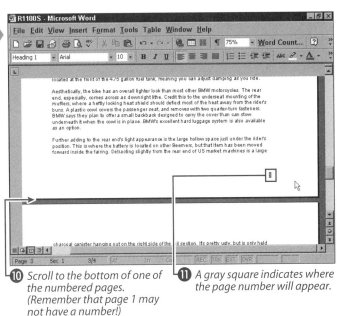

⑩ Scroll to the bottom of one of the numbered pages. (Remember that page 1 may not have a number!)

⑪ A gray square indicates where the page number will appear.

Personal Workbook

Q&A

1 How do you insert a line break?

_____

_____

_____

2 How do you view the exact locations of line and paragraph breaks?

_____

_____

_____

3 What must you do to select text using only the keyboard?

_____

_____

_____

4 What are two ways to insert a page break?

_____

_____

_____

5 How do you adjust margins on the page?

_____

_____

_____

6 What does the term _landscape_ mean when referring to page layout?

_____

_____

_____

7 How do you insert a special character that is not on the keyboard?

_____

_____

_____

8 Does Word automatically number pages in your documents? How do you change page numbering options?

_____

_____

_____

ANSWERS: PAGE 363

EXTRA PRACTICE

① Create a document with directions to your favorite restaurant.

② Make the page the size of an A6 index card, and use landscape orientation.

③ Select the last line of text and press Delete on your keyboard.

④ Insert a page break at the end of the document.

⑤ Place a copyright notice at the top of your document.

⑥ Number the pages so that the first page is page A.

⑦ Create a shortcut key to a foreign currency symbol.

REAL-WORLD APPLICATIONS

✔ When you are entering text for a Web page, you can use line breaks and paragraph breaks to clean up the page's appearance. Web browsers always place a large space under paragraph breaks, which can make things such as addresses kind of funny looking. Use line breaks at the end of each address line instead of paragraph breaks to avoid this problem.

✔ If you are creating a company or club newsletter with Word, there's a good chance that you will use columns in at least part of your layout. Section breaks enable you to use columns in some places, but not in others, depending on your layout needs and tastes.

Visual Quiz

How was the shape and size of this page modified? Is the layout oriented in landscape or portrait? Is the page numbered? How was the special copyright symbol inserted?

_____

_____

_____

_____

_____

CHAPTER  6

MASTER THESE SKILLS

▶ Using a Template to Create a New Document

▶ Creating a Fax Cover Sheet

▶ Creating a Résumé

▶ Using Templates from Old Versions of Word

▶ Creating a New Template

▶ Modifying a Template

Using Document Templates

Chances are, when you create documents with Word, many of them will share a similar appearance or layout. For instance, if you are tasked with creating a weekly work schedule for your company, it probably looks virtually the same every week. Likewise, such documents as fax cover sheets, internal memos, and recurring reports often share a similar or uniform appearance throughout the course of your day-to-day work.

To simplify the task of creating similar documents, Word provides tools called *templates*. A document template contains basic information about the document, such as page setup and paragraph styles, and can even include some text and graphics. The best way to think of a template is as a pattern or mold, similar to a cake pan. Anything you make in a bundt cake pan will always have the same basic shape, but what you pour into that pan is entirely up to you. Likewise, a document created with a specific template will have a specific shape and layout; but once it is created, you can do almost anything with it that you want.

This chapter introduces you to templates and shows you how to create documents using them. Word includes a number of preformatted templates for some common document types, and this chapter shows you how to create a document using two of them. You create documents using both the fax cover sheet and resume templates, and you also learn how to create documents from any of the other templates included with Word. Each version of Word comes with new templates, and if you have upgraded from a previous version of Word, the templates from that version are still available. You learn how to access them here.

Finally, you explore creating new templates yourself. This can be useful if none of the existing templates exactly suit your needs. Once created, you can use the templates you have made to standardize certain documents throughout your company. You also learn how to modify templates, both your own and templates that were delivered with Word. Templates provide a quick way to create what might otherwise be complicated documents, and this chapter provides you with a firm knowledge base to help you work with them more effectively.

Using a Template to Create a New Document

Whenever you create a new document in Word, that document is created from a template. Unless you choose a specific template, Word uses its default template, which is the Normal template. The Normal template includes all the formatting defaults that Word uses in documents, such as 8.5" by 11" letter-sized paper, standard margins, Times New Roman font, blank page, and so on. This template is sufficient for many purposes.

Just because the Normal template is sufficient, however, does not mean that it is ideal for all situations. Setting up templates for documents you create on a regular basis will ultimately save you a great deal of time by eliminating the need for readjusting page formatting, creating new paragraph styles, and many of the other things you do when creating a new document. If you routinely create documents that follow a specific format, it's a good idea to use a template specifically designed for them.

Besides formatting information, a template can also include text and graphics. A good example is the fax cover sheet template discussed in the next task. It already includes some text such as labels for your name, phone number, the number of pages, and usually some simple graphics. All you have to do is type in the addressee and other basic information, and you're ready to print. Without this template, it could take you as much as an hour to create a document from scratch that has the same basic look and content.

Word provides a rather large gallery of templates from which you can choose. You can see these templates in a dialog box you open by selecting File ⇨ New from the menu bar. The various templates are located on tabs, arranged by category. The figures on the facing page show you how to open this dialog box and then show how to use a template to create a new document.

TAKE NOTE

► USING A TEMPLATE FOR THE FIRST TIME

To save space, Word does not install all the templates on your hard drive during installation. A template is not installed on your computer until you choose to use it. The first time you select a template, you will probably be prompted to insert your Word 2000 (or Office 2000) CD into the CD-ROM drive. Follow the onscreen instructions to install the template.

► CREATING TEMPLATE SHORTCUTS

You can create a shortcut to a template on your Windows desktop. Right-click the Windows Start button and choose Explore to open Windows Explorer, and then browse to C:\Program Files\Microsoft Office\Templates. Right-click a template in the right pane and choose Create Shortcut from the shortcut menu. Cut the shortcut and paste it to the desktop. Then, whenever you open that shortcut, Word will open a new document using the template.

CROSS-REFERENCE

See "Choosing Custom Setup Options" in Chapter 2 to learn how to preinstall templates on your hard drive.

FIND IT ONLINE

Select Help ⇨ Office on the Web and check out Template Packs and other free Word enhancements from Microsoft.

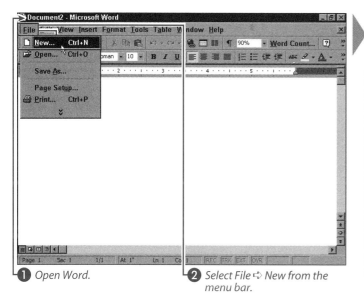

1 Open Word.

2 Select File ➡ New from the menu bar.

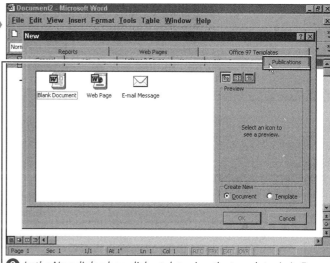

3 In the New dialog box, click a tab to view the templates in it. For this example, choose Publications.

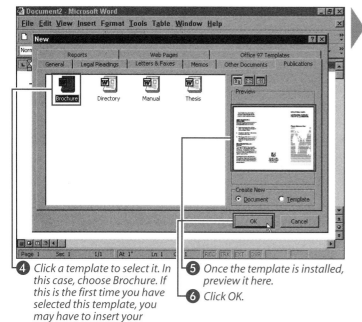

4 Click a template to select it. In this case, choose Brochure. If this is the first time you have selected this template, you may have to insert your program disk to install it.

5 Once the template is installed, preview it here.

6 Click OK.

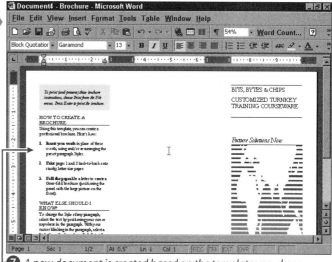

7 A new document is created based on the template you chose. Replace the template text with your own.

Creating a Fax Cover Sheet

Of the many different kinds of documents you will create using Word, few if any are as mundane as a facsimile cover sheet. This simple piece of paper contains basic information that the recipient probably knows already and will more often than not ignore completely.

Nevertheless, a cover sheet is an important thing to include with most outgoing faxes. Without it, the recipient might not know what is being sent or who is sending it. This is especially important if you are faxing to a company fax machine, where many different people might use the same machine. Furthermore, your fax cover sheets usually need a professional appearance, and they should be laid out in a way that is easy to read.

Creating a document from scratch that meets these goals can take quite a bit of time. Even if you're fast, you may need at least ten minutes to create the document, insert the required text, format it, and print it out. Why spend all this effort for a document that will probably be ignored and thrown in the garbage only minutes after you send it?

A much better solution is to use one of the many fax cover sheet templates offered by Word. These templates turn what would otherwise be a monotonous and time-consuming chore into a simple one- or two-minute affair. With the fax cover sheet templates, all you have to do is open the document, enter a few lines of simple information, and click Print.

You don't even have to save the document to your disk if you don't want to, because as soon as you send the fax, the document will be obsolete anyway.

The figures on the facing page show you how to create a fax cover sheet using one of the fax templates in Word. The first two figures show you how to use the New dialog box to create the cover sheet, and the last two figures demonstrate how to actually enter text into the sheet.

TAKE NOTE

▶ USING THE FAX WIZARD

Another way to create a fax cover sheet is to use the Fax Wizard, also available in the New dialog box. If you choose the Fax Wizard, you will be taken through a variety of dialog boxes that ask for information about yourself and the intended recipient. The Fax Wizard — and wizards in general — are discussed extensively in Chapter 4 under "Using Wizards."

▶ SENDING THE FAX WITH WINDOWS MESSAGING OR OUTLOOK

If you are sending your fax using Microsoft's Windows Messaging, Exchange, or Outlook, you will be asked by the program if you wish to send a cover letter. Choose No because you have already created a cover sheet in Word. Send the cover sheet as the first page of your fax, and be sure to include the number of pages you sent.

CROSS-REFERENCE

You might be able to enter some information onto the cover sheet using AutoText. See Chapter 12.

FIND IT ONLINE

GFI Fax, at **http://www.gfifax.com/**, offers software for handling facsimiles on a computer.

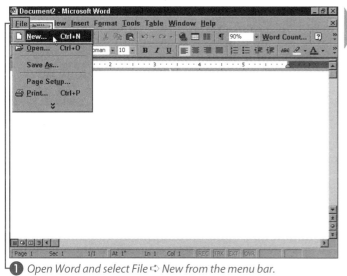

① *Open Word and select File ⇨ New from the menu bar.*

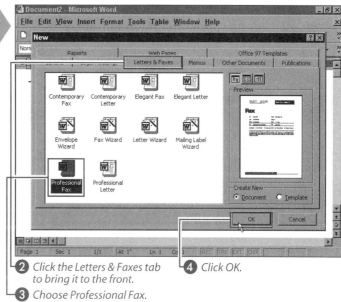

② *Click the Letters & Faxes tab to bring it to the front.*

④ *Click OK.*

③ *Choose Professional Fax.*

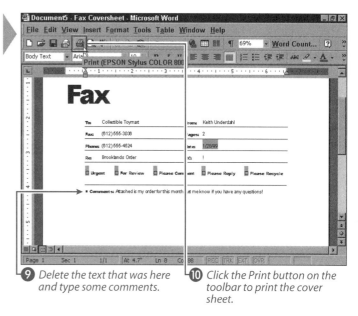

⑤ *A new fax cover sheet is created based on the template.*

⑥ *Type your company name here.*

⑦ *Click in these areas and type the appropriate information.*

⑧ *Click here to scroll down the page.*

⑨ *Delete the text that was here and type some comments.*

⑩ *Click the Print button on the toolbar to print the cover sheet.*

Creating a Résumé

As versatile as Word 2000 can be, the fact is many people produce the same kinds of documents with it. In the previous task, you learned how to use one of Word's fax templates to create a fax cover sheet, easily one of the most common document types that people use. Another frequently used document type is a résumé. The average worker will change jobs seven times during his life, and some of us will switch a lot more often than that!

When you do begin the job-hunting process, it is vitally important that you have a professional-looking résumé to help you through the process. Unfortunately, not everyone knows how to create an effective résumé, so Microsoft has provided a few résumé templates with Word to help make the process a little less gut wrenching.

All three of the résumé templates included with Word use a similar layout, differing only in such details as fonts and graphics. If you have been trained in the art of résumé writing, the templates may look strange to you. You may or may not like the information that is included on these résumés, but you are certainly free to change them as much as you want.

Just keep in mind that there is no "industry standard" for what a résumé should look like. The résumé should be pleasing to the eye, but don't go overboard with visual effects. *Conservative* and *concise* are your keywords in résumé composition. A résumé should simply tell the prospective employer what you want (that would be the job in question), and why you are the most qualified person for that job.

The figures on the facing page show you how to create a résumé with Word. The first screen shows you how to open a new document with the template, and the remaining three guide you through the process of filling in your personal job information.

TAKE NOTE

▶ CREATING AN EFFECTIVE RÉSUMÉ

First and foremost, your résumé should be easy to read and should fit on just one page. Consider what the reviewer wants to know about you: Do you have experience? What *specifically* have you done in the past? Do you meet the specific qualifications for the job? You may also want to demonstrate what a well-rounded person you are, hence the "Interests" section of these résumés. Here you might want to list volunteer work that you have done in the community. Just keep in mind that this comes secondary to job-related information.

▶ WHAT ABOUT THE TIPS?

Notice that there is an item at the bottom of the résumé template called "Tips." That is there for your benefit, not the reviewer's. Once you have read the tip, delete that section before printing the résumé. Alternatively, you could rename it to suit a different purpose.

CROSS-REFERENCE

See "Using Headers and Footers" in Chapter 18 to learn about working with those elements used here.

FIND IT ONLINE

Get résumé tips and other job search advice at
http://www.jobseekersnetwork.com/.

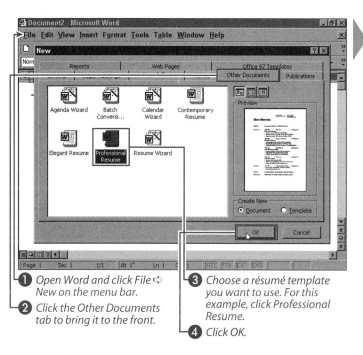

① Open Word and click File ➪ New on the menu bar.

② Click the Other Documents tab to bring it to the front.

③ Choose a résumé template you want to use. For this example, click Professional Résumé.

④ Click OK.

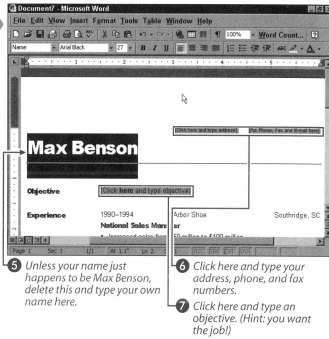

⑤ Unless your name just happens to be Max Benson, delete this and type your own name here.

⑥ Click here and type your address, phone, and fax numbers.

⑦ Click here and type an objective. (Hint: you want the job!)

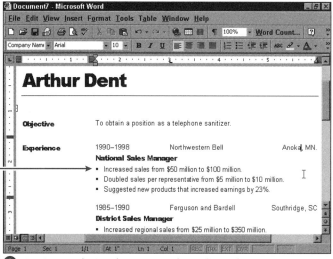

⑧ Continue replacing the preprinted template information with your own. To do so, first select a line of text you want to replace.

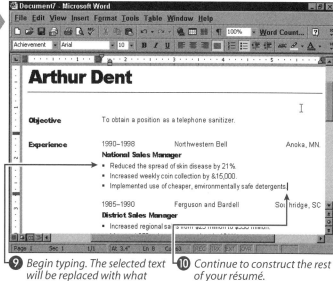

⑨ Begin typing. The selected text will be replaced with what you type.

⑩ Continue to construct the rest of your résumé.

Using Templates from Old Versions of Word

Generally speaking, Microsoft produces a new version of Word every two or two-and-a-half years. With each version comes new templates, often as direct replacements for templates that were offered with older versions of the program. These newer templates are at the very least restyled, and they often also take advantage of some of the new features available.

If you upgraded to Word 2000 from an earlier version of the program, most of the old program files were probably replaced. However, some things — including document templates — were retained in case you still want to use them. Many computer users are creatures of habit, and sticking with your old templates for a while may help ease the stress of a software upgrade. If Word 2000 was installed on your computer when it was new, you probably won't see any old templates.

Templates from any old version of Word you may have had installed on your computer are maintained in their own special folder of the Templates folder. When you open the New dialog box to create a new document, you will see a tab labeled for these older templates. It will be called "Office 97 Templates" or something to that effect. In almost any case you can open and utilize them just as you would any other template that came with Word 2000.

One important thing to note here is that some template features may or may not function properly. In particular, if you are using a template from Word 95 or earlier that contains macros, many or all of those macros may not work, and you will have to create a new template with new macros.

The figures on the facing page show you how to open and use a template left over from a previous version of Word. Old templates that are available on your computer — if any — will look different than the one shown here because it is a custom template used with an older version of Word.

TAKE NOTE

▶ DELETING OLD TEMPLATES

The old templates don't use up very much space on your hard drive. If you want to get rid of them anyway, you can delete them using the Windows Explorer. Right-click the Windows Start button, choose Explore, and then locate the appropriate folder. Which folder they are in will vary depending on how you installed Word 2000, but look in the folder C:\Microsoft Office\Templates\ for a sub-folder of older templates.

▶ WHERE ARE MY OLD CUSTOM TEMPLATES?

If you had templates that were created by you or someone in your company that you used with an older version of Word, they should still be available to you. They should be located in the same folder as other templates from previous versions of Word.

CROSS-REFERENCE
See "Choosing Custom Setup Options" in Chapter 2 to learn more about saving features from older versions.

FIND IT ONLINE
World Language Resources, at **http://www.worldlanguage.com/**, offers foreign language templates.

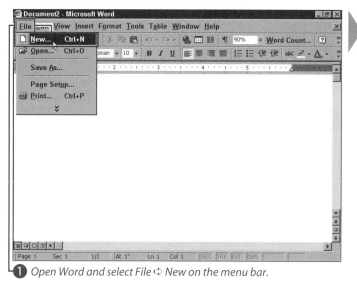

1 *Open Word and select File ⇨ New on the menu bar.*

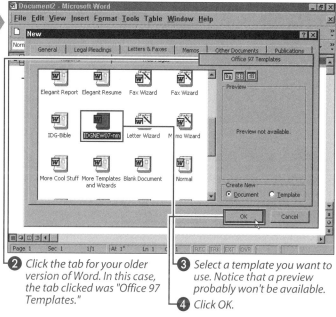

2 *Click the tab for your older version of Word. In this case, the tab clicked was "Office 97 Templates."*

3 *Select a template you want to use. Notice that a preview probably won't be available.*

4 *Click OK.*

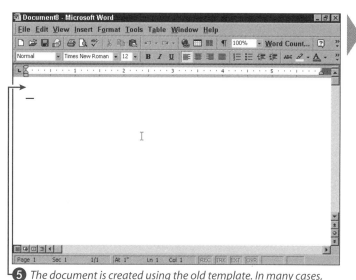

5 *The document is created using the old template. In many cases, the document will appear empty, like this one, because the template contains no text or graphics.*

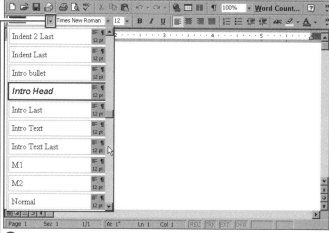

6 *Click the Styles drop-down arrow. Notice that although the page is blank, all the styles from the old template are still available.*

Creating a New Template

Word 2000 comes prepackaged with a number of useful document templates built in. As noted earlier, these templates help you create the most basic kinds of documents, such as fax cover letters, résumés, invoices, financial reports, and more. They can save you time and give many of your documents a more professional look and feel.

As wonderful and varied as the templates that come with Word may be, you will undoubtedly find that they do not suit your every need. You may often want to create documents that do not conform to any of the existing templates. This is no problem; you can create your own templates in Word based solely on your own criteria.

A template you create can contain many different types of information. First, you can determine page setup information such as paper size, margins, orientation, and the like. You can also include information about shortcut keys, AutoCorrect entries, macros, styles, and custom toolbars.

Perhaps most importantly, you can also include text and graphics in your custom templates. By including information such as section titles, headings, and other nonchanging elements in your document, you don't have to add that information every time you use the template.

Finally, you should also consider including instructions in your templates. You may have noticed that many of the existing Word templates include instructions and tips about the templates. You will delete and type over this information when you create a document, but it's still a great idea to include those notes and tips that you might otherwise forget.

The figures on the facing page show you how to create a basic template. The first figure shows you how to begin the template creation process, and the remaining three show you some elements you might want to include in your template.

TAKE NOTE

▶ WHY NOT JUST COPY AN EXISTING DOCUMENT?

You may be wondering why you should create your own template rather than just make a new copy of an older document. First of all, using a template ensures greater consistency among your documents because a "one-time modification" you made last time will not become a normal part of the document. Also, a template may be easier to share with coworkers because you can include specific instructions about what the document is *supposed* to contain. Alternatively, select File ➪ Save As and choose Document Template from the Save As Type drop-down menu.

▶ DON'T FORGET THAT YOU'RE CREATING A TEMPLATE

If you forget that you are creating a template and start to type a lot of text, all of the text you type will appear in every subsequent document you create with it. This could be confusing, especially if other people need to share the template.

CROSS-REFERENCE

Learn more about changing templates in the next task, "Modifying a Template."

FIND IT ONLINE

Law Desq., at **http://www.lawdesq.com/**, offers templates and software for creating legal documents.

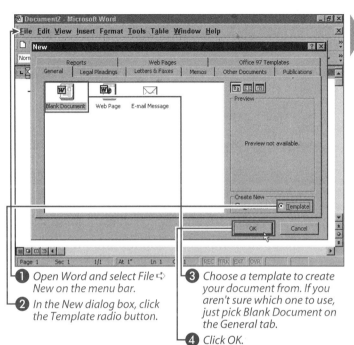

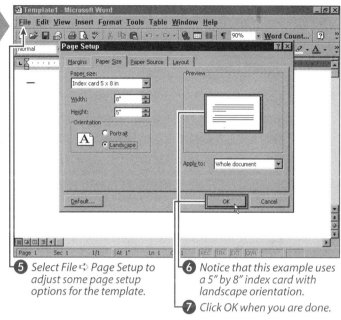

❶ Open Word and select File ➪ New on the menu bar.

❷ In the New dialog box, click the Template radio button.

❸ Choose a template to create your document from. If you aren't sure which one to use, just pick Blank Document on the General tab.

❹ Click OK.

❺ Select File ➪ Page Setup to adjust some page setup options for the template.

❻ Notice that this example uses a 5" by 8" index card with landscape orientation.

❼ Click OK when you are done.

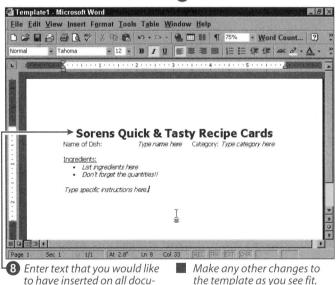

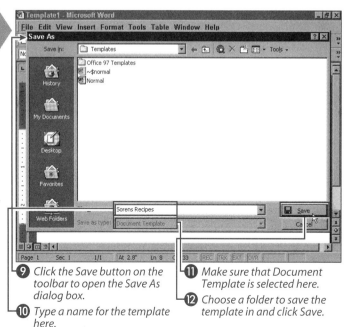

❽ Enter text that you would like to have inserted on all documents created with this template.

■ Make any other changes to the template as you see fit.

❾ Click the Save button on the toolbar to open the Save As dialog box.

❿ Type a name for the template here.

⓫ Make sure that Document Template is selected here.

⓬ Choose a folder to save the template in and click Save.

Modifying a Template

It should come as no surprise that the Word 2000 templates may not fit your needs exactly. Everyone has different needs or preferences concerning a document's appearance, and templates don't need to get in the way of your progress. You can modify a template any time you choose, be it a template you have created yourself or one of the templates that came with Word.

You can open, modify, and subsequently save any template just as you would a regular Word document. When you want to modify an existing template, you have to remember to open it as if it were a regular document. You do this by choosing Document Templates in the Files of type section of the Open dialog box and locating the template you want to modify. You can then make your changes and save the template when you're done.

When modifying a template, consider carefully what you want to modify. For instance, you may want to adjust the page layout to fit a new kind of paper, or you might change the text that is on the page. Consider also what macros and AutoCorrect items you have on the template, and modify them accordingly.

You can also incorporate some kinds of changes to templates without really making a conscious effort to do so. For instance, suppose you create a new document with a template and then make changes to elements such as toolbars or macros. When you save and close the document, you may be asked if you also want

to save changes to the template. If you see a dialog box asking you this, choose Yes or No as you see fit.

The figures on the facing page show you how to make changes to templates. The example shown here describes how to modify a template directly, as opposed to making changes as you work with a document.

TAKE NOTE

WHAT ABOUT DOCUMENTS ALREADY CREATED?

When you modify a template, the changes will be incorporated into the template and any future documents you create using that template. However, any documents you created earlier with that template will not be affected. If you want to change those, you will have to open each individually and modify them one at a time.

ARE ALL YOUR DOCUMENTS SAVING AS TEMPLATES?

Some users have encountered a situation in which every time they save a document, it saves as a template rather than as a regular document file. This problem is indicative of a common Word macro virus. If you encounter this problem, consider running virus-scanning software on your computer. Make sure the software scans *all* files, including those associated with Word. Some virus-scanning programs — such as Norton AntiVirus — ignore Word documents by default, so this virus would not be identified.

CROSS-REFERENCE

To learn more about saving, see "Saving Files" in Chapter 3.

FIND IT ONLINE

Office Toys, at **http://www.officetoys.com/**, is another great source for free Word add-ons!

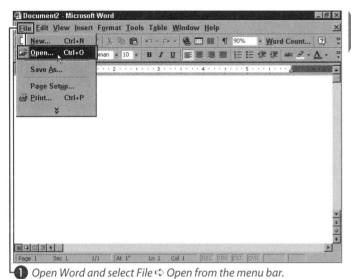

1 *Open Word and select File ⇨ Open from the menu bar.*

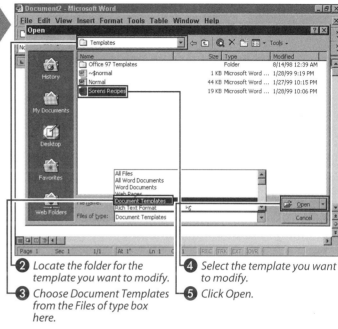

2 *Locate the folder for the template you want to modify.*

3 *Choose Document Templates from the Files of type box here.*

4 *Select the template you want to modify.*

5 *Click Open.*

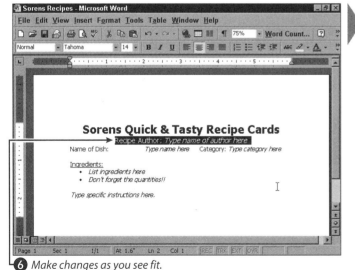

6 *Make changes as you see fit.*

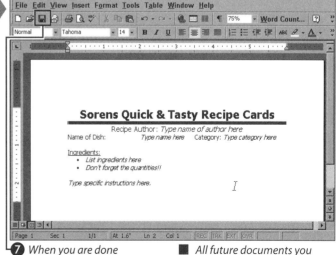

7 *When you are done modifying the template, click Save on the toolbar to save your changes.*

■ *All future documents you create with the template will include your modifications.*

Personal Workbook

Q&A

1 How do you begin creating a new document using a template?

_____

_____

_____

2 Will only those templates actually installed on your computer be displayed in the New dialog box?

_____

_____

_____

3 Can you use templates from older versions of Word with Word 2000?

_____

_____

_____

4 What kind of information can be stored in a template?

_____

_____

_____

5 Why is using a template to create a new document often preferable to simply copying an existing document?

_____

_____

_____

6 Can you create your own templates?

_____

_____

_____

7 What kinds of text should you include in templates?

_____

_____

_____

8 Can you modify templates that come with Word?

_____

_____

_____

ANSWERS: PAGE 364

EXTRA PRACTICE

1 Create a new document using the Professional Press Release template.

2 Enter text into your document and save it as a Word file.

3 Create a new template based on the Professional Press Release.

4 Change the personal and company information in the template so that it reflects you instead of the Blue Sky Corporation.

5 Close and save the new template as My Press Release.

6 Create a new document using the template My Press Release.

REAL-WORLD APPLICATIONS

✔ Most of the templates included with Word contain names and addresses for fictitious companies and individuals. Modifying the templates you use frequently by entering in your personal information will save you time.

✔ Templates provide an easy way to create what would otherwise be very complex documents. This book, for instance, was written using Word 2000, and each chapter was created using a template created by IDG Books Worldwide.

✔ Web page templates are useful because they will ensure that all of the pages of your Web site maintain a consistent look and feel. Without using a template for each page, the site can have an incongruous and poorly organized aura.

Visual Quiz

How do you open this dialog box? Can you view other templates than what is shown here? How? How can you begin creating your own template? Can these templates be modified? How?

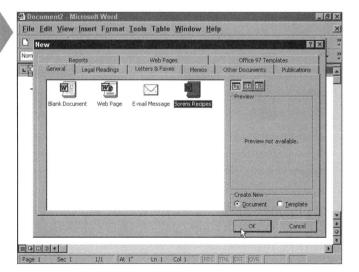

CHAPTER 7

MASTER THESE SKILLS

▶ **Working with Fonts**

▶ **Changing Character Sizes**

▶ **Using Special Character Formatting**

▶ **Formatting Paragraphs**

▶ **Setting Tabs**

▶ **Applying Styles**

▶ **Creating Styles**

Formatting Your Documents

Not so long ago, most word processing programs did little more than put text on a page, with no frills or strings attached. In fact, depending on who you talk to, some would say that modern programs such as Word 2000 have become too bloated, eating up memory and hard disk resources with scores of features that—according to the pundits—most people never use.

On the other hand, Word can be viewed as a powerful desktop publishing tool, placing professional-quality publishing power in virtually anyone's hands. It makes many older programs look positively mundane, with features that today could only be described as archaic.

These programs restricted you to just one character style, with little or no formatting flexibility. But at a time when dot-matrix printers were still within the technological mainstream, this was a practical necessity. Modern printers have no such limitations; they are able to produce virtually anything your computer can conjure up. Change is good.

However you feel about Word's role, chances are you will eventually want to spruce up the appearance and layout of your documents. By utilizing some of those "advanced features that nobody uses," you can create attractive documents that a few years ago could have come only from a professional printing press. Among the many document characteristics you can modify are the typeface and general appearance of the text you use, the size of the text, and positioning of text on the page.

In addition, Word makes applying this advanced formatting easy through the use of handy tools called *styles*. A style can include information about not only text formatting, but also paragraph formatting. Once created, you can use styles to instantly apply special formatting to your text and give the entire document a unique appearance.

This chapter introduces you to these concepts by first showing you how to change the appearance of the characters used in your documents. You then learn about special paragraph formatting, tab stops, and using and creating styles. Once you have mastered these formatting basics, you may want to move on to Chapter 18 to learn about some of the even more advanced formatting features that Word offers.

Working with Fonts

Text used in the English language can be written — or drawn — on a piece of paper with quite a bit of variation. Compare the handwriting of several different people, and you will see that, although each person writes his letters just a bit differently, you can still usually read them all (which, in some cases, is truly remarkable).

Word also enables you to vary the appearance of text in documents by changing the character set that is used. These character sets are called *fonts,* and there is virtually an infinite variety of fonts for you to choose from. As delivered, Word 2000 provides dozens of fonts, and you can also use fonts from a variety of other sources.

Which font you should use depends on how you want the document to look. The default font chosen for normal Word documents is called Times New Roman, a font that is a little plain but very easy to read. You can easily change the fonts used in your documents, and a single document can contain as many different fonts as you like. Just keep in mind that too many fonts in a single document can make the overall appearance busy and unattractive. Also, some fonts might look better onscreen than they do on your printer, so be sure to test print them first.

Fonts can give your document a modern or retro look, provide a festive atmosphere or a note of somberness, or give special emphasis to certain key points. Some fonts contain only characters for foreign languages; if you need to type in Greek or Hebrew, for instance, special fonts are available to help you type them like a pro.

The figures on the facing page show you how to change the font for an area of selected text. You may want to experiment with the fonts a bit more on your own to get a better feel for which ones you like.

TAKE NOTE

USING TRUE TYPE FONTS

Some fonts are called True Type fonts, because they will supposedly print exactly the way they appear on the screen of your monitor. In reality, this may or may not be the case, and ultimately the printer itself is the main limiting factor. Most modern printers are capable of handling almost any font you may choose, so printing shouldn't really be a problem.

INSTALLING NEW FONTS

If you receive a new font from any source, you need to install it before trying to select it. Click the Windows Start button and choose Settings ⇨ Control Panel. Once the Control Panel is open, open the Fonts folder and select File ⇨ Install New Font. Locate the disk or folder where the font file is located and install it. Once installed in the Fonts folder, the font is available not only to Word but also to any Windows application that uses fonts.

CROSS-REFERENCE

See "Applying Styles" later in this chapter to learn about speeding up the process of applying fonts.

FIND IT ONLINE

Internet Type Foundry Index, at **http://www.typeindex.com/**, is perhaps the preeminent font index online.

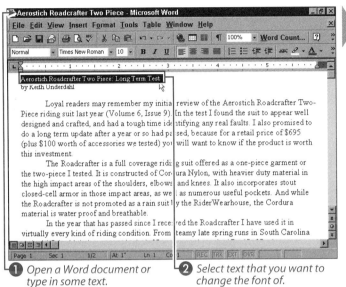

1 Open a Word document or type in some text.

2 Select text that you want to change the font of.

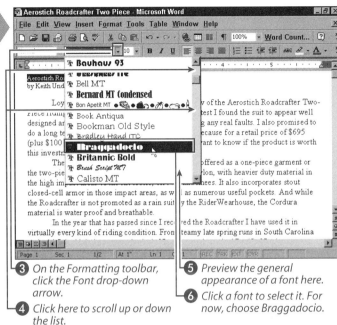

3 On the Formatting toolbar, click the Font drop-down arrow.

4 Click here to scroll up or down the list.

5 Preview the general appearance of a font here.

6 Click a font to select it. For now, choose Braggadocio.

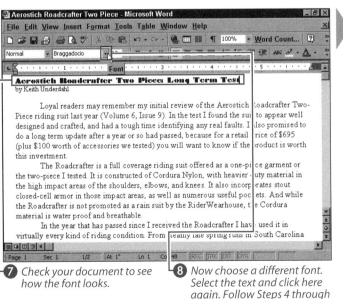

7 Check your document to see how the font looks.

8 Now choose a different font. Select the text and click here again. Follow Steps 4 through 6 to choose the font Verdana.

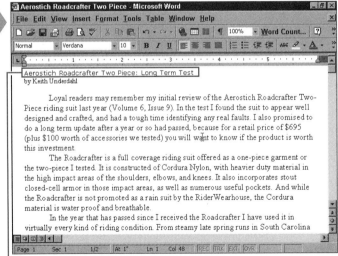

9 Check your document again to see how the font looks.

Changing Character Sizes

As you learned in the previous task, changing the font is a quick way to give your characters a new look. Different fonts can give characters distinct personalities, depending on the kind of document they are used in.

Another, equally important formatting change you can make is to adjust the size of your text. Using different sizes of text can have perhaps the greatest single impact on the overall appearance of your documents and can serve a variety of purposes. Word enables you to select a range of sizes, from huge characters that stand over an inch tall to the tiny "fine print" you may need for your important legal disclaimers. Large characters work especially well in document titles, section headings, and other key introductory elements.

Character sizes in Word are measured according to their point size. A *point* is a traditional unit of measure used by typesetters, dating back to the time when typesetting meant setting blocks of type up in a wooden frame for use on a printing press. The most common character sizes used in Word documents are 10 point and 12 point. Just for a frame of reference, you can fit twelve 10-point characters or ten 12-point characters into an inch. The bigger the point size, the bigger the character, and hence the fewer characters will fit in one inch.

You can change the size of text using a couple of different methods. Perhaps the easiest is to choose a different size from the Font Size drop-down list on the Formatting toolbar. The actual font is previewed in the drop-down list, so you might find it easier to work with different font and size combinations from here. You can also resize characters in the Font dialog box, which makes sense if you have other text formatting changes to make. The figures on the facing page show you how to change the size of text in Word.

TAKE NOTE

HOW BIG IS IT, REALLY?

Be careful when selecting character sizes, because how the words appear on screen might be very different from how they look when printed on paper. Characters that are too small may be difficult to read for some people, and frequent use of large characters would be considered overkill. Try creating a document with words of different sizes to serve as a test pattern for printed text. Include characters that cover a range of sizes and keep the document handy so you have something to refer to later.

USING FONT SIZES WITH WEB DOCUMENTS

Web documents allow only seven different font sizes. When you publish your Web page, Web browsers that read the page will choose whichever size is closest to the size you used when you created the document in Word.

CROSS-REFERENCE
See "Applying Styles" later in this chapter to learn how to speed up this process.

FIND IT ONLINE
Adobe Studios, at **http://www.adobestudios.com/**, is another source for popular fonts.

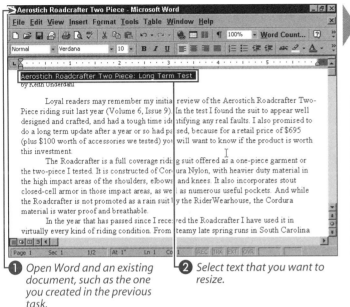

① Open Word and an existing document, such as the one you created in the previous task.

② Select text that you want to resize.

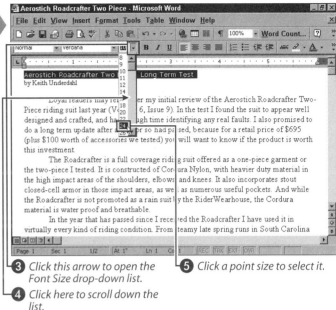

③ Click this arrow to open the Font Size drop-down list.

④ Click here to scroll down the list.

⑤ Click a point size to select it.

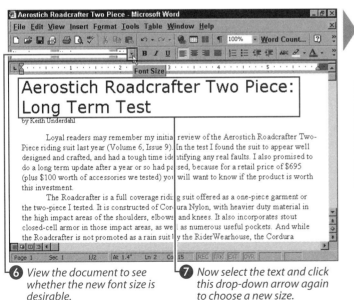

⑥ View the document to see whether the new font size is desirable.

⑦ Now select the text and click this drop-down arrow again to choose a new size.

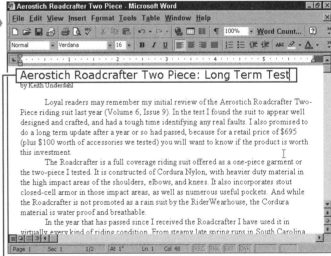

⑧ View the document again to check the font size.

Using Special Character Formatting

Besides using different fonts and font sizes, another way to change the appearance of text on your pages is to use special character formatting. Some of the most common techniques involve making characters bold, italicized, or underlined. These formatting tools have been available since some of the earliest word processing programs and are still quite useful today.

A number of other special formats are available for you to use in Word 2000. They can all be reached through the Font dialog box by selecting Format ➪ Font. Two formats you may use frequently are superscript and subscript. Superscripted text is displayed smaller and raised relative to other text on that line. You might use this format to indicate a footnote or to show an exponential power in a mathematical equation. For instance, in the equation (r^2, the number 2 is superscripted to show that r should be squared. Subscripted text is smaller and lowered on the text line, as in the chemical formula H_2O.

You probably won't use some of the other special formatting options very often. Strikethrough draws a horizontal line over text as if it has been crossed out by an editor. Small caps means that all letters will be capital letters, but letters that would normally be lowercase will still be shorter than uppercase letters. All caps means that all letters will be in uppercase.

Some other effects are available that can give your text an unusual or interesting appearance, including Shadow, Outline, and Emboss. You can experiment with these to see what effect they have on your text.

In addition to the special formats just listed, you can also change the color of text in your documents. You use the Font dialog box for this task, but keep in mind that you won't be able to print colorful text on a black-ink printer. The figures on the facing page show you how to use the Font dialog box to apply special formatting to text. On the following pages you will learn about even more features and effects that can be applied to text.

Continued

TAKE NOTE

USING SPECIAL FORMATTING WITH WEB DOCUMENTS

Bold and italics are the only special formatting you should use in Web documents. Underlining is reserved for hyperlinks, so using underlining elsewhere would result in confusion. You should also be careful about using different colors, because that also is used to indicate a hyperlink.

WORKING WITH HIDDEN TEXT

Another effect you can choose is hidden text. Hidden text does not normally appear in a document, but you can view it by clicking the Show/Hide button on the toolbar. You may want to use hidden text to make notes to yourself in a document. Other people won't see these hidden notes when you print the document.

CROSS-REFERENCE
To learn more about hyperlinks and how they are formatted, see "Creating Links" in Chapter 16.

FIND IT ONLINE
Microsoft has their own online source for type at **http://www.microsoft.com/truetype/**.

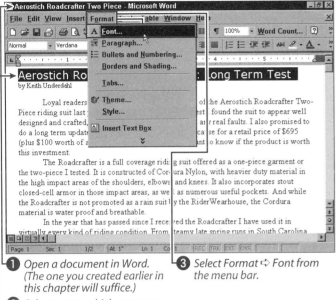

1 Open a document in Word. (The one you created earlier in this chapter will suffice.)

2 Select text to which you want to apply special formatting.

3 Select Format ⇨ Font from the menu bar.

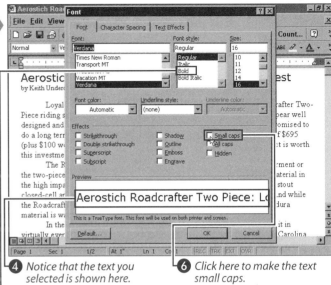

4 Notice that the text you selected is shown here.

5 Click here to make the text bold.

6 Click here to make the text small caps.

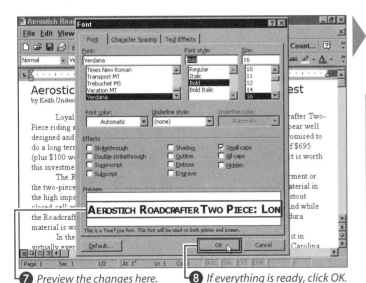

7 Preview the changes here.

8 If everything is ready, click OK.

9 Preview the text in your document. Follow Steps 2 through 8 again to further modify the formatting.

Using Special Character Formatting *Continued*

The preceding two pages showed how to apply special formatting to text. Some of the formatting options discussed — italics, underlining, and bold text, for example — have been around for quite a while. Word processing programs continue to improve, with new features being added all the time. Some even more high-tech features are available with Word 2000 to give you the ability to create truly astounding effects. Many of the newer special effects involve colorful, multimedia-style elements such as flashing lights, blinking text, and animations.

The first of these special features utilizes a blinking background. If the page of your document is white, the area directly behind the text will blink alternately black and white, with the text always a contrasting color to the background. If you want to really get someone's attention, this is the way to do it.

Other special effects place animated borders around text. Las Vegas Lights looks like something you would see in (surprise) Las Vegas, and Marching Red or Black Ants is basically nothing more than a moving dashed border. Shimmer text has an alternating blurred look, and Sparkle Text has colorful sparkles all around it.

One final aspect of formatting you should know involves something less spectacular, namely character spacing. The middle tab of the Font dialog box enables you to adjust the amount of space that is put between characters in your document. This option can be useful in making text fit a fixed area, such as a cell in a table. You can reduce the amount of space that an area of text requires by reducing slightly the amount of space that is put between the characters.

The figures on the facing page show you how to use some of the special character-formatting features. The first two figures show you how to use animations in your text, and the last two figures demonstrate how to reduce character spacing.

TAKE NOTE

PRINTING ANIMATIONS

Printer technology has advanced by great leaps in the last couple of years, but we are still nowhere close to seeing a single piece of paper that can display animations. The animated effects shown here can be useful if you are publishing documents electronically — say, on your company's intranet — but if you are printing to paper, they will not function.

WHY DON'T ANIMATED EFFECTS WORK WITH OLDER DOCUMENTS?

If you are trying to apply animated effects to an older word processing document, they may not work. In particular, any documents that are in Word 95 format or earlier cannot use animated text formatting. To take advantage of this type of formatting, convert the file to a Word 97 or Word 2000 document format.

CROSS-REFERENCE

See "Using Print Preview" in Chapter 14 to see what your text will look like on paper.

FIND IT ONLINE

Click Help ⇨ Office on the Web and look under Free Stuff from time to time for new formatting enhancements.

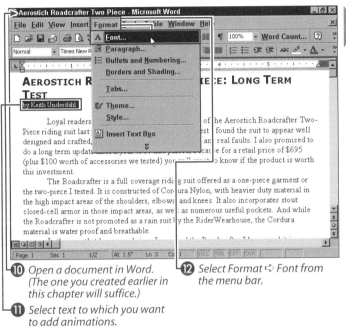

⑩ Open a document in Word. (The one you created earlier in this chapter will suffice.)

⑪ Select text to which you want to add animations.

⑫ Select Format ⇨ Font from the menu bar.

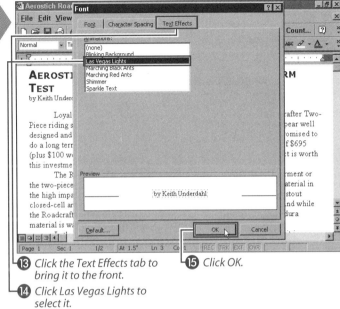

⑬ Click the Text Effects tab to bring it to the front.

⑭ Click Las Vegas Lights to select it.

⑮ Click OK.

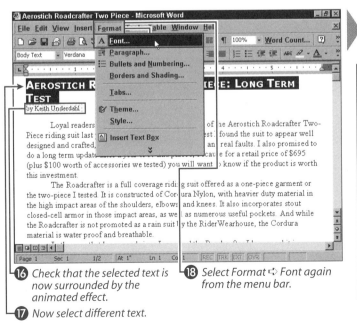

⑯ Check that the selected text is now surrounded by the animated effect.

⑰ Now select different text.

⑱ Select Format ⇨ Font again from the menu bar.

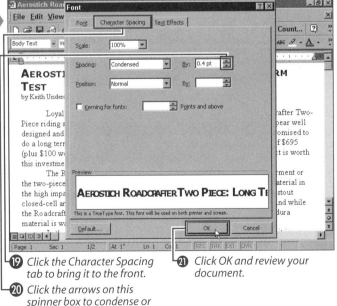

⑲ Click the Character Spacing tab to bring it to the front.

⑳ Click the arrows on this spinner box to condense or expand the text.

㉑ Click OK and review your document.

Formatting Paragraphs

So far in this chapter you have learned how to format text and characters on your page by applying different fonts, sizes, and other special effects. You can make these choices for any character in a Word document, no matter where it is located.

Paragraphs have their own special formatting issues that must be addressed as you create documents. Paragraph formatting always applies to an entire paragraph. This means it applies to everything between paragraph breaks, but it also applies across line breaks. You cannot, for instance, center a single line in the middle of a paragraph.

The most important paragraph formatting issue to consider is alignment. By default, paragraphs are *left*-aligned, which means they line up along the left margin. A right-aligned paragraph would line up along the *right* margin, and a *center*-aligned paragraph would be centered on the page. You may want to use center alignment for titles and other headings.

The final alignment style is *justified* (also sometimes called *full*), which means that the paragraph will line up along both the left and right margins. Word automatically adjusts character spacing to make this work. Text in most books and magazine articles uses justified alignment.

In addition to specifying alignment, you can also indent entire paragraphs. This may be a good choice if you need to offset information that you want to appear as separate from the rest of the document. A good example would be a long quote. If you are quoting several sentences or a paragraph or two from someone, it may make sense to include the quote as a separate, indented paragraph.

The figures on the facing page show how to adjust paragraph formatting. The first two figures demonstrate how to use some common toolbar buttons to adjust paragraph alignment, and the remaining figures show how to use other toolbar buttons to adjust paragraph indenting.

Continued

TAKE NOTE

TABS AND INDENTED PARAGRAPHS

It is not uncommon to indent the first line of a paragraph, and you can easily do that by placing the cursor at the beginning of the first paragraph line and pressing the Tab key. But if you press the Tab key when the cursor is at the beginning of any other line, the entire paragraph will be indented.

TROUBLE WITH PARAGRAPH ALIGNMENT

A common problem that many users have when changing the alignment of a paragraph is that other paragraphs may be affected at the same time. If you notice this problem, the paragraphs are probably not really separate paragraphs. You can confirm your suspicion by clicking the Show/Hide button on the toolbar to see whether paragraph breaks appear where they should. To fix this problem, press Enter to insert a paragraph break where you need it and then realign the paragraphs.

CROSS-REFERENCE

See "Entering Text" in Chapter 5 to learn about working with paragraph breaks.

FIND IT ONLINE

Tips and tutorials are available at **http://mit.edu/isa/ news/msoffice/word/20tips/index.html**.

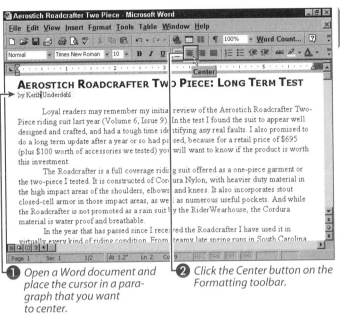

1 Open a Word document and place the cursor in a paragraph that you want to center.

2 Click the Center button on the Formatting toolbar.

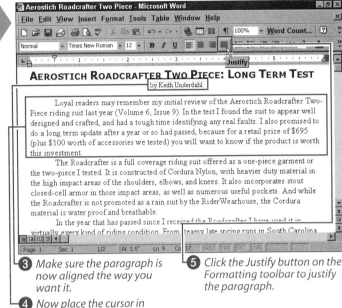

3 Make sure the paragraph is now aligned the way you want it.

4 Now place the cursor in another paragraph.

5 Click the Justify button on the Formatting toolbar to justify the paragraph.

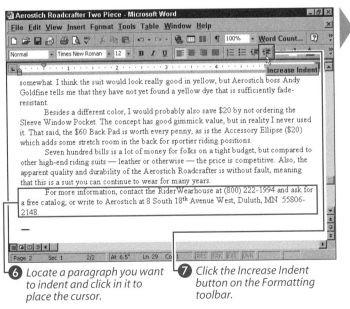

6 Locate a paragraph you want to indent and click in it to place the cursor.

7 Click the Increase Indent button on the Formatting toolbar.

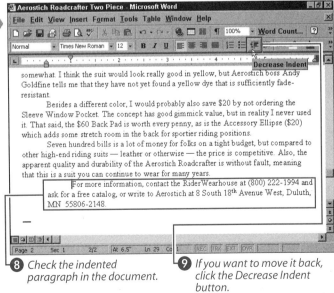

8 Check the indented paragraph in the document.

9 If you want to move it back, click the Decrease Indent button.

Formatting Paragraphs
Continued

Though alignment on the page is probably the most common paragraph formatting adjustment, you have other options as well. You can change spacing within the paragraph, for example, both between lines in the paragraph and between paragraphs themselves.

Line spacing is an issue you have probably dealt with in one form or another before. When you were in school, you probably remember that your teacher asked for typewritten reports to be double-spaced when you turned them in. This left extra room for comments to be written between lines of text, and for every spelling error to be clearly identified. Also, most newspapers and magazines still require that freelance submissions be double-spaced, for basically the same reasons as your teacher's.

Adjusting line spacing in Word is easy if you know what you are doing. By default, paragraphs are single-spaced. You use the Paragraph dialog box to change this default. Double-spacing is one of the available options (of course), or you can specify an interval between lines in terms of point size. Experiment with the various options to see which suits you best.

Besides line spacing, you can also adjust the amount of space that is placed between paragraphs. More specifically, the Paragraph dialog box lets you specify how much space to leave both before and after a paragraph, with zero points being the default. Specifying some paragraph spacing can greatly improve the look and feel of your documents as well as their readability, especially if you do not indent the first line of each paragraph.

With shorter documents in particular, such as memos and letters, adding paragraph spacing provides a more visible break between paragraphs on the page. On the other hand, if your document contains dozens or even hundreds of pages of text, paragraph spacing may add needlessly to the overall page count.

The figures on the facing page show you how to adjust spacing in and around your paragraphs. The first figure shows you how to open the Paragraph dialog box, and the second and third figures show you how to make changes within that dialog box. The final figures display the effects of those changes.

TAKE NOTE

COMBINING LINE AND PARAGRAPH SPACING

If you have specified double-spacing or some other interval between lines in your paragraphs, that same interval will automatically appear between similarly formatted paragraphs. If you want more space between the paragraphs, you can then specify paragraph spacing, but be careful of excess white space on the page.

PARAGRAPH SPACING IN WEB DOCUMENTS

Web documents automatically have some space between paragraphs. Sometimes, as in the case of an address, this is not always desirable. One way around this problem is to use line breaks instead of paragraph breaks, because line breaks do not have this automatic spacing.

CROSS-REFERENCE

See "Tracking Changes" in Chapter 18 to learn a more advanced way to include reviewer comments on a page.

FIND IT ONLINE

If you're a budding writer, get news and info from the National Writers Union at **http://www.nwu.org/nwu/**.

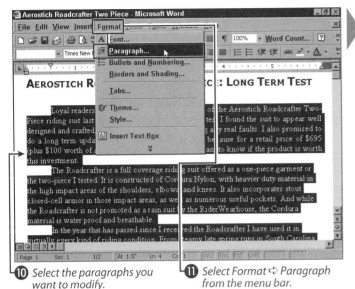

10 Select the paragraphs you want to modify.

11 Select Format ➪ Paragraph from the menu bar.

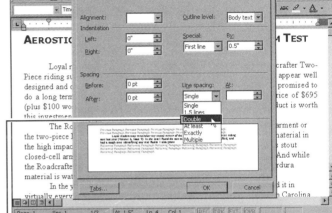

12 In the Paragraph dialog box, open the Line spacing drop-down list and choose Double to use double-spacing between lines.

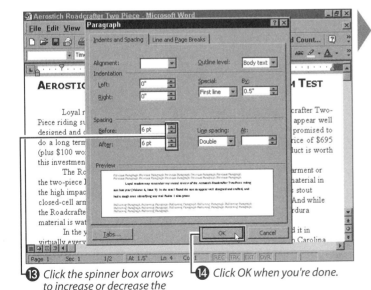

13 Click the spinner box arrows to increase or decrease the spacing before and after the paragraph.

14 Click OK when you're done.

15 Review the changes in your document. Notice that there is a larger space between the paragraphs than there is between lines in the paragraphs.

Setting Tabs

The keyboard on your computer is based roughly on that of a typewriter, and typewriter keyboards have been the same for more than a century. Even the very order of the letters, which are not really in order at all, is a direct result of 19th century typewriter design. That said, many, many new keys and features of your computer keyboard would be foreign to bygone typists. These new keys reflect the countless advances that the modern personal computer represents.

One key that *would* be familiar to classic typists is the Tab key. Most typewriters used tab stops to make moving around the page a bit easier, because all you had to do to jump ahead a number of spaces was to press Tab once. Computers and word processing programs use the Tab key for roughly the same purpose, as well as for a number of other purposes.

Tab stops — or *tabs*, for short — can greatly enhance and simplify your page layout. For instance, if you want to create a list of items, you can use tabs to ensure that all the list items line up properly on the page. Using the spacebar for this task can be imprecise and inefficient. With tabs, you can line things up precisely.

To help with this task, you can set your own tabs in Word documents wherever you wish. By default, Word sets tabs every half an inch on a regular page. In other words, if you press tab twice, the cursor will jump one inch across the page. You can eliminate these default tabs and set your own tabs for the page. You can also adjust the default tab settings using the Tabs dialog box.

The figures on the facing page show you how to set tabs on a page. The first figure shows how to set tabs using the Ruler, and the second and third figures show how to set tabs and tab options with the Tabs dialog box. The final figure shows the results of those changes and demonstrates how to take advantage of the tabs.

TAKE NOTE

▶ USING THE TAB KEY IN TABLES

If your document contains a table, you can use the Tab key to move from cell to cell. This may be more or less useful than simply moving around with arrow keys or the mouse, depending on your situation. This also holds true with Excel worksheets that are copied, linked, or embedded into your Word documents.

▶ GETTING RID OF UNWANTED TABS

If you want to get rid of a tab that you created, just click it with the mouse and drag it off the ruler. You can also use click-and-drag to move tabs around.

CROSS-REFERENCE

If you can't see the ruler, see "Changing the View" in Chapter 2.

FIND IT ONLINE

Visit **http://www.charm.net/~rps/** for some handy setup products for APA-style documents.

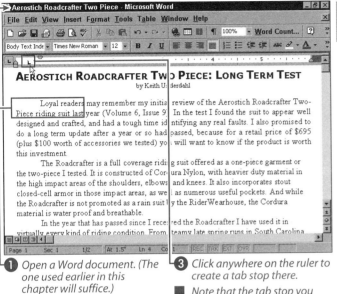

1 Open a Word document. (The one used earlier in this chapter will suffice.)

2 Place the cursor in the paragraph where you want to create a new tab stop.

3 Click anywhere on the ruler to create a tab stop there.

■ Note that the tab stop you create only applies to the current paragraph.

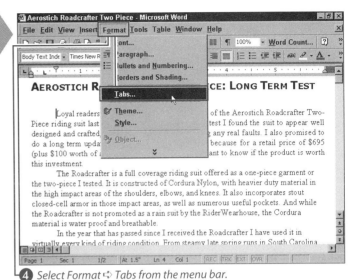

4 Select Format ➪ Tabs from the menu bar.

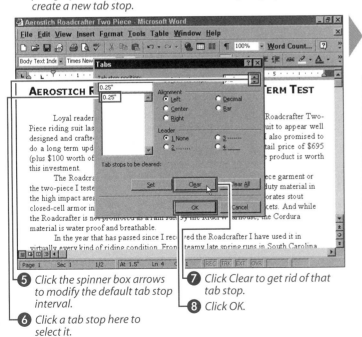

5 Click the spinner box arrows to modify the default tab stop interval.

6 Click a tab stop here to select it.

7 Click Clear to get rid of that tab stop.

8 Click OK.

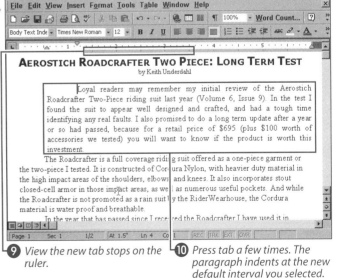

9 View the new tab stops on the ruler.

10 Press tab a few times. The paragraph indents at the new default interval you selected.

Applying Styles

In this chapter you have learned many useful tricks for formatting your text and paragraphs. Understanding these concepts gives you greater control over the final documents you produce and can greatly improve their visual appeal and readability.

Still, if you have a very large document to produce, you might be starting to think that formatting is a pretty time-consuming activity. Before you know it, you've spent half an hour just making the text on one page look pretty, which is time that could have been better spent doing something else. You're probably thinking, "There must be a better way."

Take heart, there is. Word provides tools called *styles* that contain prepackaged formatting for both text and paragraphs. Your copy of Word already has some styles in it ready to go, and using them is easy. All you have to do is place the cursor anywhere in a paragraph and choose a style from a drop-down list on the Formatting toolbar.

Want to quickly format the title of your document? Just type the text and choose the style Heading 1. Voilà! The text is instantly transformed to 16-point, bold Arial font with 12-point spacing above and 3-point spacing below.

Word has five or six different styles that are part of the Normal template, and you can create as many styles of your own as you wish. The figures on the facing page show you how to apply some of those

styles to a document. Once you have mastered these skills, you can move on to creating your own styles in the following task.

CROSS-REFERENCE

If you can't see the Formatting toolbar, learn how to display it in "Changing the View" in Chapter 2.

FIND IT ONLINE

If you're really interested in typography, check out http://www.charm.net/~rps/.

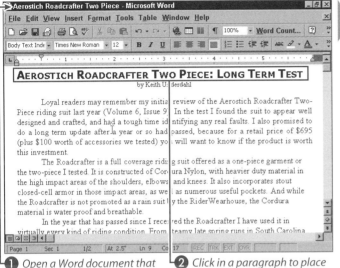

① *Open a Word document that contains several different paragraphs.*

② *Click in a paragraph to place the cursor.*

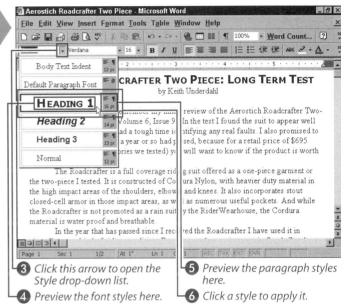

③ *Click this arrow to open the Style drop-down list.*

④ *Preview the font styles here.*

⑤ *Preview the paragraph styles here.*

⑥ *Click a style to apply it.*

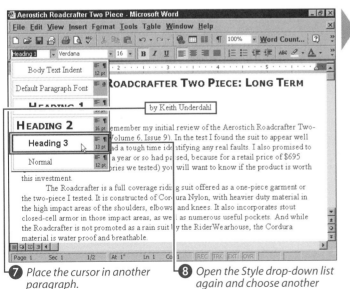

⑦ *Place the cursor in another paragraph.*

⑧ *Open the Style drop-down list again and choose another style.*

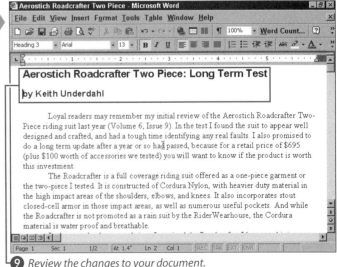

⑨ *Review the changes to your document.*

131

Creating Styles

As you learned in the previous task, styles can be a truly useful and time-saving device with Word. They make short work of applying character and paragraph formatting to your documents by turning what might otherwise take a dozen or more complicated steps into just two or three mouse clicks.

The Normal template contains just a few styles, and they are limited in scope. The various templates that come with Word have many other styles included with them; but if you are creating your own documents from scratch, they will not do you much good. You need to understand how styles are created so that you can create your own and edit already existing styles to suit your individual needs.

Creating a style takes a bit longer than just formatting text the old-fashioned way; but once the style is created, it will save you quite a bit of time. You begin the process of style creation in the Style dialog box, which can be a little intimidating the first time you look at it. Fear not; just take your time and you'll find that the whole process is simpler than you think.

When you create a style, you should begin by formatting the font and paragraph. You can choose other formatting as you see fit. If you are formatting a numbered or bulleted list, specific paragraph formatting is less important because Word automatically applies it for you. You can choose to base your new style on an existing style if you wish to save some time.

The figures on the facing page show you how to create a style. The first figure shows you how to open the Style dialog box and begin the creation process for a new style. The next two figures show you how to create the style, and the last figure demonstrates how to use your new style with the Style drop-down list on the Formatting toolbar.

TAKE NOTE

▶ MODIFYING EXISTING STYLES

You can modify an existing style using basically the same methods shown here to create a new one. Once you have opened the Style dialog box, select the style you want to modify in the Styles list and click Modify. The rest of the process is roughly the same as in the steps shown here.

▶ WHY AREN'T ALL THE STYLES SHOWN?

If you open the Style dialog box and you know that more styles are available than are shown in the Styles list, click the List drop-down arrow. By default this list only displays the styles currently in use in the template you are working in. Select All Styles from this list to display all the styles available to Word. You can also view only styles that you have created by selecting User-defined styles from the list.

CROSS-REFERENCE

Your style will become part of a template. To learn more, see "Modify a Template" in Chapter 6.

FIND IT ONLINE

Add-on software for creating APA-style documents is also available at **http://www.hillysun.com/**.

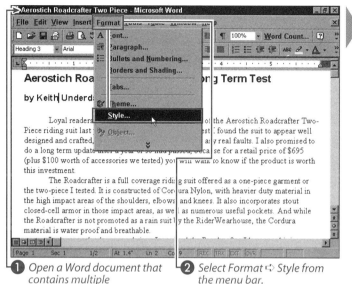

1 Open a Word document that contains multiple paragraphs.

2 Select Format ➭ Style from the menu bar.

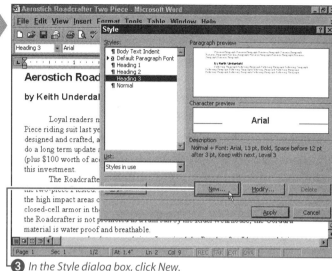

3 In the Style dialog box, click New.

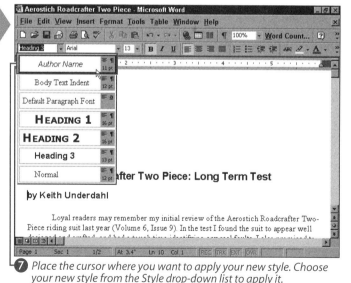

4 Type a name for your new style.

5 Click Format and choose an item to modify. At the very least, format the paragraph and font.

6 When you are done, click OK to close the New Style dialog box and Close to close the Style dialog box.

7 Place the cursor where you want to apply your new style. Choose your new style from the Style drop-down list to apply it.

Personal Workbook

Q&A

1 What is a font?

_____

_____

_____

2 Can you change the size of a font? How?

_____

_____

_____

3 How do you make text bold?

_____

_____

_____

4 Will animated character formatting work for all documents?

_____

_____

_____

5 How do you center a paragraph?

_____

_____

_____

6 What does *justify* mean in relation to paragraph formatting?

_____

_____

_____

7 What kind of information can a style contain?

_____

_____

_____

8 How do you apply a style?

_____

_____

_____

ANSWERS: PAGE 364

EXTRA PRACTICE

1 Create a flyer to advertise something for sale.

2 Make the name of the item for sale bigger and of a different font than the rest of the document.

3 Make the text title bold.

4 Center the item name on the page.

5 Create a style called For Sale.

6 Apply the style to a paragraph on your document.

7 Create a tabbed, two-column list of the item's features under the name of the item.

8 Change the line spacing of the two-column list.

REAL-WORLD APPLICATIONS

✔ If you are making up a flyer for a holiday party at your office, you may want to use a festive yet easy-to-read font for the text. You should also make the title or some key element of the flyer large so that it can be read at a glance by passersby.

✔ When you create a template for a document you generate on a regular basis, you can save yourself some time down the road by also incorporating some styles for the various elements of the document.

✔ Justified paragraphs often look better when used with columns in a document. If you are creating a newsletter, use justified paragraph formatting to clean up the overall appearance of the document.

Visual Quiz

How do you change the font in the title of the document shown here? Based on the style displayed on the Formatting toolbar, where do you suppose the cursor is currently located? How is that paragraph aligned on the page? Is there any other special formatting applied to the characters in that paragraph that you can see?

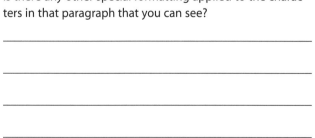

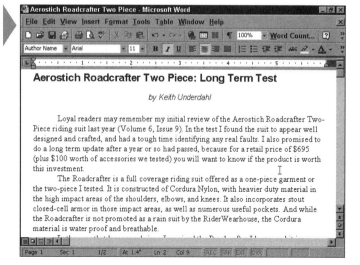

CHAPTER 8

MASTER THESE SKILLS

▶ **Creating a Table**

▶ **Formatting Tables**

▶ **Formatting Cells**

▶ **Selecting Cells**

▶ **Inserting and Deleting Rows and Columns**

▶ **Resizing Cells**

Using Tables

If you have been working through this book from the beginning, you have probably been working with documents that contain words and text. Typing and editing words is the essence of a word processing program, of course, hence the name. Lots of programs enable you to work with words and text, including tools that are simpler than Word (such as the WordPad and Notepad applets, which come with Windows). The big difference between Word 2000 and these other programs is that Word can do so much more than just simple text editing.

The time to learn what else Word can do has arrived. The first of these extras is *tables*. In its simplest form, a table is basically vertical and horizontal lines arranged in a grid on the page. The boxed-in spaces within the grid are called *cells*, and in those cells you can place text, numbers, and even pictures. The lines of the grid can be thick, thin, colorful, or even invisible.

You can use tables for many different purposes. You could use a table to work with numbers, as in an accountant's ledger or a bowling score sheet. Tables can also be used to cross-reference pieces of information by subject, as in a table of contents for a book. Or how about writing a film review and using one side of a table to list what you liked about the movie, and the other side for things you hated? Tables also work well for record keeping; for instance, you could use a table to track batting and pitching statistics for a softball team you coach.

Tables are also growing in popularity among Web publishers. Modern Web browsers can read tables in an HTML document, so Web page builders often use tables to organize elements on otherwise tricky Web pages. You learn more about this specific application of tables in Chapter 16 (see the task "Using Tables in Web Documents"), but you can learn the basics of using tables in Word here first.

The chapter begins by taking you through the process of creating a table. It then shows you how to format tables and the information you put in them. Finally, you learn a few tricks for working with and improving your tables on an ongoing basis.

Creating a Table

If you have ever worked with a spreadsheet program such as Lotus 1-2-3, Quattro Pro, or Excel, you're already familiar with the concept of a table. A table is a grid created by intersecting horizontal and vertical lines, and you can place all kinds of information in the cells created by that grid. A spreadsheet program is essentially a giant table, albeit with a number of advanced features to help you work with large amounts of numerical data.

For pure onscreen number crunching, a table created in Word is really not your best bet. But tables are among the most versatile elements you can use in a document. They provide a logical way to organize data on a page, in a way that is easy for your viewers to read and understand. A table can contain numbers, lists, statistics, cross-reference information, or almost anything else you can dream up. You could also use a blank table to facilitate *off*-screen number crunching when you need to track numbers as you work on something else.

You can also use a table to help organize the layout of your page. Tables have often been used to arrange pictures, vertical text, and other strange elements on a page that would otherwise be challenging to set up. For instance, suppose you want to put a picture on the page and have a caption alongside it. The simplest way to achieve this goal would be to create a one-row, two-column table and put the picture in one cell and the caption in the other. This technique is quite popular in the creation of Web pages, because controlling the page layout in that environment with other methods is difficult.

The figures on the facing page show you how to create a table. The first two figures show how to use the Insert Table dialog box, and the last two figures demonstrate a quicker way to achieve the same task using the toolbar. You may find that each technique works best in different scenarios.

TAKE NOTE

▶ WORKSHEETS VS. TABLES

If you need to make calculations, it would be better to insert an Excel worksheet instead of a table. You can do this by clicking the Insert Microsoft Excel Worksheet button on the toolbar or by linking or embedding a worksheet you have already created with that program. Otherwise, a regular Word table will use less memory and be easier to manipulate.

▶ UNDERSTANDING COLUMNS AND ROWS

When you refer to the cells in a table, you need to understand the difference between a column and row. *Columns* run vertically in a table, which means that all the cells along the right edge of a table could be said to be in the same column. A *row* runs horizontally, so all the cells along the bottom edge of the table are in the bottom row.

CROSS-REFERENCE

To learn how to put an Excel worksheet in your Word document, see "Linking an Excel Worksheet" in Chapter 19.

FIND IT ONLINE

Find user tips, links to free downloads, and more at **http://www.microsoftsoft.miningco.com/msubWord.htm**.

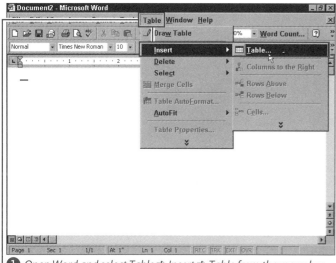

1 *Open Word and select Table ➪ Insert ➪ Table from the menu bar.*

2 *Click here to choose the number of columns you want. For now, choose 4.*

3 *Click here to choose the number of rows you want. For now, choose 3.*

4 *Click OK.*

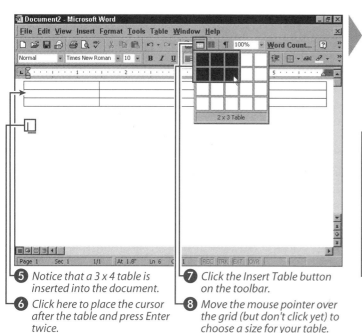

5 *Notice that a 3 x 4 table is inserted into the document.*

6 *Click here to place the cursor after the table and press Enter twice.*

7 *Click the Insert Table button on the toolbar.*

8 *Move the mouse pointer over the grid (but don't click yet) to choose a size for your table. For now, choose 2 x 3.*

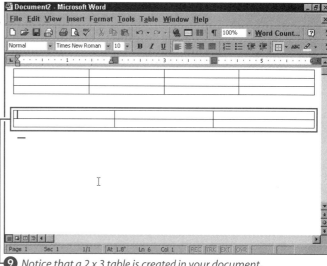

9 *Notice that a 2 x 3 table is created in your document.*

Formatting Tables

In the previous task, you learned how to create basic tables in Word. This is your first step, of course, but far from the last. Now that you have created a table, it's time to decide how that table will look once you publish it. The default appearance for Word tables is pretty plain, so you will probably want to improve on that.

You can spend a great deal of time applying custom formatting to your tables; however, in most cases, this really isn't necessary. With the Table AutoFormat feature, Word provides an outstanding gallery of preformatted table styles for you to choose from. The styles are named according to typical uses, but you can select any you want to use.

You have a number of other formatting issues to consider when creating a table. The table must be aligned on the page, and you will have to decide if you want it aligned to the left side of the page, to the right, or centered. The table can even be indented somewhat. In general, most tables look better when they are indented slightly in relation to other areas of text on the page.

Another option lets you wrap text around the sides of the table rather than just place it on lines above and below. This option works well with smaller tables, but obviously you will have a hard time wrapping text around a very large table. On a standard 8.5-inch-wide page, a table that is more than half the width of the page should not have text wrapped around it.

You can handle many of the formatting issues you will deal with in your tables in the Table AutoFormat dialog box. The figures on the facing page show you how to open and use the Table AutoFormat dialog box to apply basic formatting to your tables.

TAKE NOTE

▶ KEEP YOUR TABLES ON ONE PAGE

If possible, it is visually better to keep your tables on a single page, rather than splitting them with a page break. Using Print Layout View will help you identify where your tables split across pages. If you are having a hard time fitting a table on one page, try condensing the character spacing in the cells. Otherwise, you may want to move the whole table to the next page. An option in the Table Properties dialog box helps you control this automatically, as described on the facing page.

▶ IS YOUR PRINTER UP TO IT?

Using fancy colors and shading to spruce up your tables is often a great idea, but make sure that the final, printed product will be acceptable. It would be a shame to spend hours applying colorful beautification to all your tables, only to learn that your printer is only capable of printing light and dark blurs.

CROSS-REFERENCE

See "Using Special Character Formatting" in Chapter 7 to learn about condensing character spacing.

FIND IT ONLINE

Weston Computing services, at **http://www. webcom.com/weston/**, provides templates for customizing tables.

① *Open Word and a document that contains a table. (The document you created in the previous task will suffice.)*

② *Click in a table to place the cursor there.*

③ *Select Table ⇨ Table AutoFormat from the menu bar.*

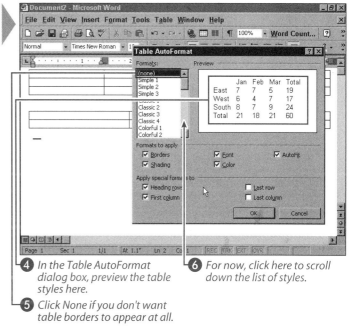

④ *In the Table AutoFormat dialog box, preview the table styles here.*

⑤ *Click None if you don't want table borders to appear at all.*

⑥ *For now, click here to scroll down the list of styles.*

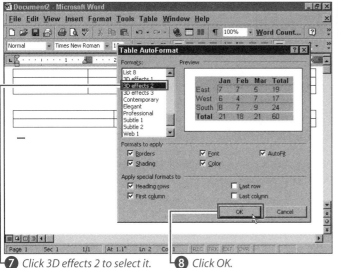

⑦ *Click 3D effects 2 to select it.*

⑧ *Click OK.*

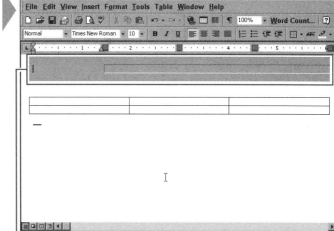

⑨ *See how the table is modified to reflect the style you chose.*

Formatting Cells

As you've learned, you can put almost any kind of information that you wish into a cell in a table. This information can be a single word or an entire paragraph. Pictures are often inserted into cells, and you can even insert another whole table within the cell of a table.

Once information has been entered into the cells of your table, you have to decide how it should be displayed. In the case of text and numbers, you can apply much of the same character formatting that you do to text elsewhere in the document. This includes applying fonts, different character sizes, bold or italics, or anything else you want to use. You can use underlining if you want, but remember that you may not see the underlining if you have selected a table format that includes rules under the cells.

Besides character formatting, cells have their own unique formatting issues associated with them. In some ways, each cell is like its own paragraph; but in other respects, a cell is like a separate page. Formatting a cell in a table is different from formatting anything else in Word, so understanding the basics is critical.

First, you have to decide how information will be vertically aligned in the cell. You can align the cell contents at the top, center, or bottom of the cell, regardless of what the cell contains. You can also set horizontal alignment using the paragraph alignment buttons on the formatting toolbar. An even quicker way to deal with alignment is to make use of the Cell Alignment option in the cell shortcut menu, which combines all the alignment options into one easy-to-use submenu. Just right-click a cell, choose Cell Alignment, and then choose the picture that resembles how you want the alignment set up.

The figures on the facing page show how to change formatting for a cell in a table. Notice that some of these changes are made using the Table Properties dialog box, in which options for table formatting are also available.

TAKE NOTE

► CHANGING THE TEXT DIRECTION

You can easily change the direction of text within a cell without affecting other cells in the table or the document itself. Just select a cell or cells you want to change and select Format ⇨ Text Direction. A Text Direction dialog box opens in which you can choose the direction of text in that cell.

► WORKING IN PADDED CELLS

If information in your table is too close for comfort, you can add margins to cells to "pad" them a bit. Just be careful; margins that are too big will take up a lot more space on your page than you might think. Don't get carried away!

CROSS-REFERENCE
To learn more about character formatting, see "Using Special Character Formatting" in Chapter 7.

FIND IT ONLINE
Look under Solutions and Resources at **http://office.microsoft.com/Word/default.asp** for Word tools and add-ons.

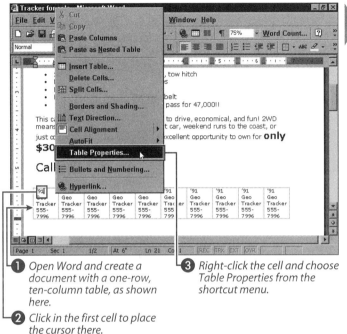

1 Open Word and create a document with a one-row, ten-column table, as shown here.

2 Click in the first cell to place the cursor there.

3 Right-click the cell and choose Table Properties from the shortcut menu.

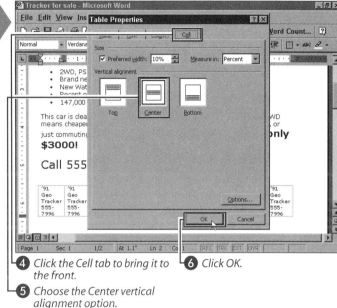

4 Click the Cell tab to bring it to the front.

5 Choose the Center vertical alignment option.

6 Click OK.

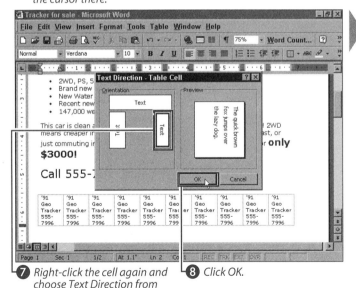

7 Right-click the cell again and choose Text Direction from the shortcut menu. In the Text Direction dialog box, choose a different orientation for your text.

8 Click OK.

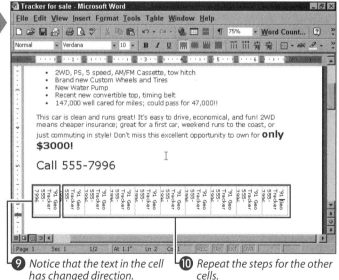

9 Notice that the text in the cell has changed direction.

10 Repeat the steps for the other cells.

Selecting Cells

Tables are extremely versatile, as you have seen in previous tasks in this chapter. Part of that versatility comes from the ability to mold tables to fit even your most unusual needs. You can format them to look the way you want them, and you have quite a bit of flexibility in formatting cells within tables as well.

Many of the things you do with tables will require you to select one or more cells. This should come as no surprise; selecting some text or an object is the first step to accomplishing many editing tasks in Word. Selecting cells in a table is quite simple; and if you have worked at all with a spreadsheet program such as Excel, you probably already know how.

You can make selections using either the keyboard or the mouse. As with text selection, if you use the keyboard, just hold down the Shift key as you move the cursor with the arrow keys. With the mouse, you can use the tried-and-true click-and-drag method over cells you want to select, just as you would with text.

You can also hold the mouse pointer over a table border at the top of a column and click once to instantly select that entire column. This works with rows, too. Just click the border next to a row and — violà! — that row is selected. Try holding the Shift key as you click several rows in this manner. Once selected, a column or row can be resized, copied, or even cut or deleted from its current location.

The figures on the facing page show you how to select cells in a table. In the examples shown here, only the mouse is used to make the selections. You can experiment with the keyboard method on your own to see if that works better for you.

TAKE NOTE

▶ CLICKING TABLE BORDERS

Although the steps here show you how to select an entire row or cell by clicking a border along the edge of the table, you can reach the same goal by clicking any border within the table. Just move the mouse pointer over a border until you see it turn to a small black arrow. Next click the border to select the entire row or column, depending on what border you are pointing at.

▶ NOW WHAT?

You've selected some cells in a table, and now you're wondering what to do with that selection. Where would you like to start? Actually, a lot of the things you do will probably involve formatting. Try right-clicking the selection and see what appears in the shortcut menu. If you want to turn the range of cells you selected into just one large cell, try clicking Merge Cells.

CROSS-REFERENCE

See "Selecting Text" in Chapter 5 to learn more about making selections in Word.

FIND IT ONLINE

See **http://www.tagwrite.com/** for a program that converts tagged programs (including tables) to Word documents.

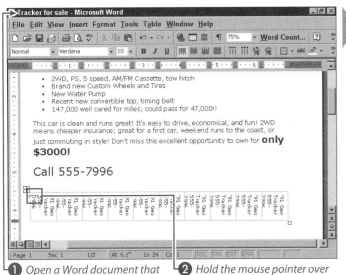

① Open a Word document that contains a table. (The one you created earlier in this chapter will suffice.)

② Hold the mouse pointer over the first cell in the table.

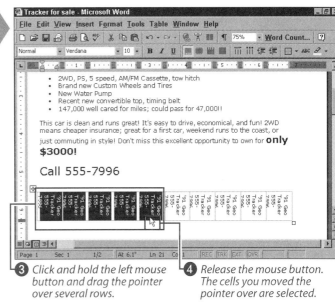

③ Click and hold the left mouse button and drag the pointer over several rows.

④ Release the mouse button. The cells you moved the pointer over are selected.

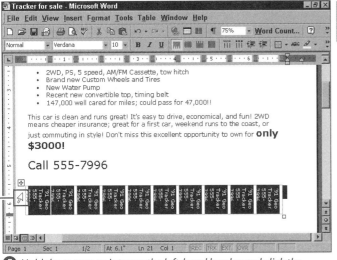

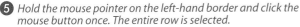

⑤ Hold the mouse pointer on the left-hand border and click the mouse button once. The entire row is selected.

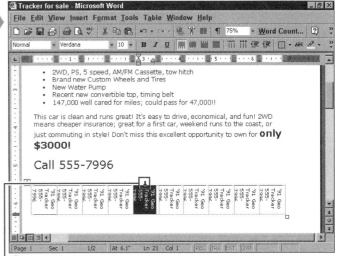

⑥ Hold the mouse pointer on the top border of the table and click the mouse button once. The entire column under the pointer is selected.

Inserting and Deleting Rows and Columns

Although you no doubt pride yourself on being an excellent planner, things happen once in a while that are beyond your control. Tables are not immune to this phenomenon. Compared to regular text, they can present a real challenge if changes or goofs result in the need for rework. Fortunately, Word gives you the ability to make modifications to the layout of your tables. This includes the ability to add or delete rows and columns, just in case your needs change or you created the wrong-size table in the first place.

A major problem that many users face is what to do when the table doesn't have enough rows or columns. Fortunately, the solution is immediately at hand. You can use the Insert Columns or Insert Rows command on the shortcut menu. You could also turn to the Table menu on the menu bar, which has a few more sophisticated options.

If you plan to insert a row or column by following the shortcut menu route, there is just one caveat to bear in mind. If you want to insert a row, you must select the entire row just below where you want the insertion to take place. Likewise, to insert a column, you must select the entire column just to the right of where you want the insertion. The other rows and columns will automatically be shifted to make room for the new column or row.

Deleting rows and columns is just as simple. Select the row or column you want to get rid of, right-click the selection, and choose Delete from the shortcut menu. You can also use the Table menu on the menu bar if you wish.

The figures on the facing page show you how to insert and delete rows and columns. In the first two figures, you will insert a row and a column into a table. In the last two figures, you will delete them again.

TAKE NOTE

▶ WHY NOT JUST USE THE DELETE KEY?

It may seem sensible to select a row or column and just press the Delete key on your keyboard to get rid of the offending selection. Alas, Word does not work this way. These steps will delete any text or data that happens to be in the cells within the selection, but the unwanted row or column will remain.

▶ DELETING CELLS

To delete individual cells, select Delete Cell from the table shortcut menu. A small dialog box opens, prompting you to choose whether you want to shift other cells over or get rid of the entire row (or column). If you delete a single cell, the cells will be shifted over, and your table will no longer have a nice, quadrilateral shape. For best results, delete entire rows or columns at once.

CROSS-REFERENCE

Get the full scoop on shortcut menus in Chapter 1 under "Using Shortcut Menus."

FIND IT ONLINE

Get free Word advice at **http://www.payneconsulting. com/wordtips.htm**.

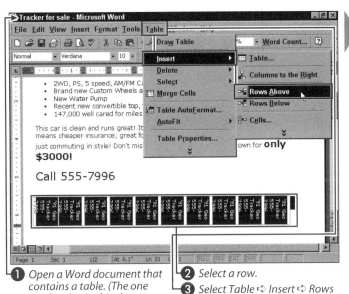

1 Open a Word document that contains a table. (The one used earlier in this chapter will suffice.)

2 Select a row.

3 Select Table ⇨ Insert ⇨ Rows Above.

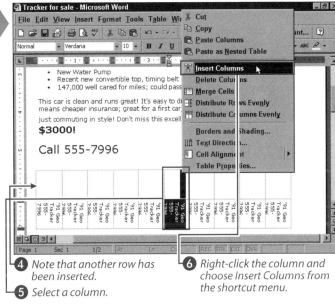

4 Note that another row has been inserted.

5 Select a column.

6 Right-click the column and choose Insert Columns from the shortcut menu.

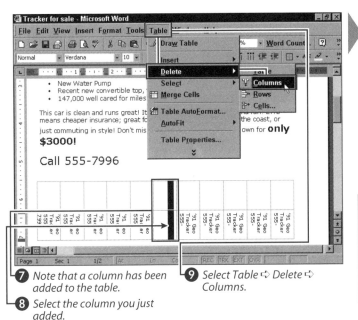

7 Note that a column has been added to the table.

8 Select the column you just added.

9 Select Table ⇨ Delete ⇨ Columns.

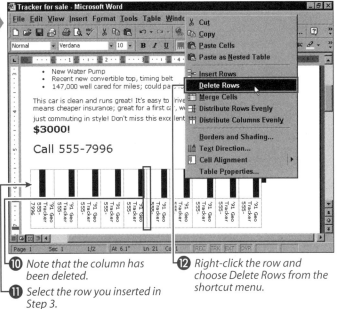

10 Note that the column has been deleted.

11 Select the row you inserted in Step 3.

12 Right-click the row and choose Delete Rows from the shortcut menu.

147

Resizing Cells

One of the final aspects of table setup to consider in your Word documents is the size of cells within a table. By default, Word creates new tables to fill the entire width of your page. Cells are automatically sized evenly and proportionally to the space that is available to them.

Suffice it to say, you do not want to always accept this default. Many tables just don't need to be six inches wide (the width of a default page in Word), and columns in a table rarely need to be of uniform width. Row height is another characteristic that is set automatically, generally to the height of a single line of text.

You have a number of choices for modifying the size of cells in your tables. Sizes can be adjusted manually by clicking and dragging borders, or you can adjust them from within the Table Properties dialog box. Both methods are shown on the facing page.

When you want to resize a cell, keep in mind that you cannot change the size of a single cell. If you make a cell wider, for example, all other cells in that column will be adjusted the same amount. Likewise, any changes made to the vertical height of a given cell will affect all other cells in that row. However, there is no reason why columns within the same table can't have different widths, and that is easy to change.

The figures on the facing page show you how to adjust the size of cells — and thus, rows and columns — in the tables of your Word documents. The first two figures show you how to manually resize a row with the mouse, and the last two figures show you some other available sizing options.

TAKE NOTE

▶ USING AUTOFIT

Word lets you use a feature called AutoFit to automatically adjust the size of cells and tables. Right-click a cell and choose AutoFit from the shortcut menu to see the options that are available. If you use AutoFit to Window, the table will take up the entire width of the page. If you choose AutoFit to Contents, the table size will be based on the information in the tables.

▶ BREAKING ROWS ACROSS PAGES

Even if you allow a table to be broken across two pages, it is almost always a bad idea to allow the contents of a row to break across a page. To prevent this, open the Table Properties dialog box and click the Row tab. Under Options, deselect "Allow row to break across pages" and click OK. This option will keep whole rows on either side of page breaks, even though the table may be allowed to span the break.

CROSS-REFERENCE

Double-check to see if page breaks will mess up your table by reading "Using Print Preview" in Chapter 14.

FIND IT ONLINE

HTML table samples that can also be used in Word are available at **http://www.webeworld.com/ tables.shtml**.

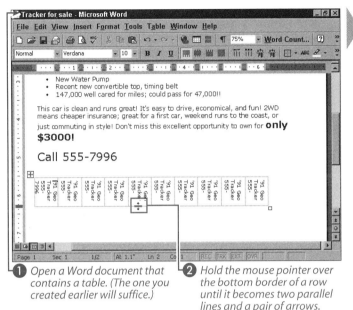

❶ Open a Word document that contains a table. (The one you created earlier will suffice.)

❷ Hold the mouse pointer over the bottom border of a row until it becomes two parallel lines and a pair of arrows.

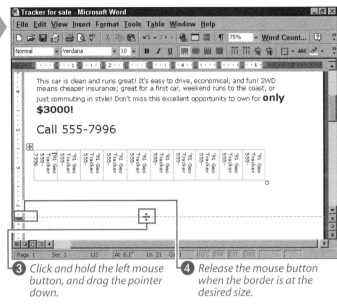

❸ Click and hold the left mouse button, and drag the pointer down.

❹ Release the mouse button when the border is at the desired size.

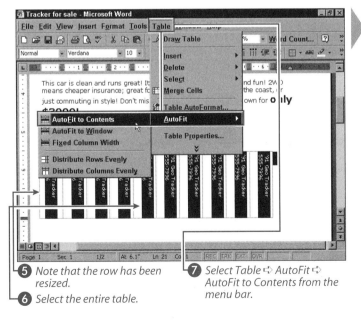

❺ Note that the row has been resized.

❻ Select the entire table.

❼ Select Table ⇨ AutoFit ⇨ AutoFit to Contents from the menu bar.

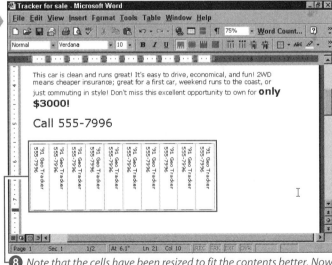

❽ Note that the cells have been resized to fit the contents better. Now you have room to insert more columns!

Personal Workbook

Q&A

1 How do you insert a table?

_____

_____

_____

2 What is the difference between a column and a row?

_____

_____

3 What is the quickest way to format a table?

_____

_____

_____

4 Can you change the size of just one cell in a row without affecting the other cells?

_____

_____

_____

5 How do you change text direction in a cell?

_____

_____

_____

6 What kind of information can you put in a table?

_____

_____

_____

7 Do table borders have to be visible on your printed document?

_____

_____

_____

8 Once a table is created, is it too late to change the number of columns or rows?

_____

_____

_____

ANSWERS: PAGE 365

EXTRA PRACTICE

① Create a document to serve as a daily schedule for everyone in your office or household.

② Use a table and organize names in the rows and parts of the daily routine in the columns.

③ Format the table with the Columns 3 style.

④ Resize the columns to fit the information you have entered.

⑤ Delete a column from the table.

⑥ Insert a row into the table.

⑦ Create column headings and change the text orientation of the headings with respect to the rest of the table.

REAL-WORLD APPLICATIONS

✔ Many managers use Word tables to develop a weekly work schedule. If you do this, make the best possible use of formatting to ensure the schedule is easy to read; this will give your employees fewer excuses for missing work!

✔ A table may provide a more logical way to organize hyperlinks on a Web page. If you have a lot of links to other Web sites on your page, a table can help you organize those links on a more space-efficient manner. If the viewer has to scroll down through a seemingly endless single-column list, the links near the bottom will probably never get visited.

Visual Quiz

This for-sale brochure contains a table. Where is it? Why is it difficult to detect? How is the text in that table oriented? How would you reproduce this effect? If there is room on the page, how could you insert more columns?

_____

_____

_____

_____

_____

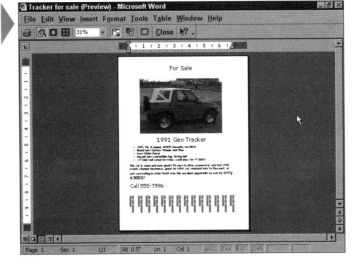

CHAPTER 9

MASTER
THESE
SKILLS

▶ Inserting Graphics

▶ Using Clipart

▶ Using WordArt

▶ Moving and Resizing Graphics

▶ Using Drawing Objects

▶ Formatting Graphics

Working with Graphics

When you think of word processing documents, you probably think primarily of the text that those documents usually include. Obviously, text is the primary emphasis with programs such as Word, along with controlling the formatting and general layout of that text. But when you start to think of all the different kinds of documents you would like to produce with your computer, many of them contain much more than just text. Often you will find a need to produce documents that contain various graphics to spice up the overall appearance of the final product.

Word 2000 enables you to include a wide variety of graphics in the documents you produce. These can include photographs that you or someone else has digitized, or other graphic art and drawings. If you have a scanner or digital camera, you already have a way to get photographs into your computer, and they can then be pasted into the document. But even if you don't have a way to obtain digital versions of your photographs, there are still many kinds of graphics you can use. Word 2000 — along with

Office 2000 — includes an extensive gallery of clipart, which contains literally hundreds of free images for you to use however you see fit.

Another type of graphic you can use in Word documents is WordArt. *WordArt* is a feature that lets you create text with a special graphic appearance. Think of a sales flyer from a local furniture store; it probably has the word *SALE* plastered across the page in a large, cartoonish, colorful typeface. WordArt lets you apply similar styling to your text. WordArt can be curved, bent, twisted, and otherwise manipulated in ways that most other text cannot. You can also create your own graphic effects in Word with drawing objects. Word provides some basic tools to help you draw lines, arrows, circles, boxes, and other objects on the page.

This chapter describes how to place and use graphics in your Word documents to give them a sharper, spicier look. You also learn how to move, manipulate, and control those graphics to ensure you get just the right effect, and you

Inserting Graphics

It has been said that a picture is worth a thousand words. When it comes to the many different kinds of documents you can create in Word, that old axiom still holds true. Graphics can serve an almost unlimited variety of purposes in a Word document, from a simple company logo on a memorandum to photographs of the house you are trying to sell.

Word treats most graphics that you insert into a document in the same way. Graphics are usually a picture of something; but no matter what it is, you will use the same techniques for inserting it and controlling how it looks. There are two basic ways to insert a graphic into a Word document: You can either copy a graphic image from an image-editing program such as Microsoft Paint or Adobe Photoshop, or you can insert an image file. By default, image files are embedded in Word. See "Embedding Objects" in Chapter 19 to learn more about this.

Probably the easiest way to include an image is to insert an image file that has already been created. Word can insert almost any image format supported by Windows. This includes JPEG and GIF format images like those used on the Internet, as well as bitmap (BMP) images such as those you may create in Microsoft Paint.

How you use images in Word documents is limited only by your imagination. In the example shown here, a photograph of a car is used to help sell it. You can also use pictures in publications such as newsletters, brochures, preprinted family albums, and more.

The figures on the facing page show you how to insert an image from a file on your hard drive. You can use the same technique to insert images from floppy disks, CD-ROMs, and other storage media. If you don't have any graphics, download some from the Web site listed below.

TAKE NOTE

USING IMAGES IN WEB DOCUMENTS

If you are using Word to create a Web page, you can only use images that are in JPEG or GIF format. Web browsers generally do not support other kinds of image files. Also, remember that when you put your documents on the Web server, you must also copy over the image files along with the HTML file for the page itself.

CONSIDER YOUR PRINTER'S LIMITATIONS

Unless you spend several thousand dollars on a printer, images you insert into a Word document will almost certainly look better on your monitor than they will on paper. Also, if you only have a black ink printer, keep in mind that multicolor photographs probably won't look very good. Create test files with different kinds of images and print them out to find out what your printer can and cannot do.

CROSS-REFERENCE

See "Inserting Graphics" in Chapter 16 to learn more about using graphics in Web documents.

FIND IT ONLINE

Don't have any images of your own? Visit Free Graphics at http://www.freegraphics.com/ to link to some great sites for free graphics.

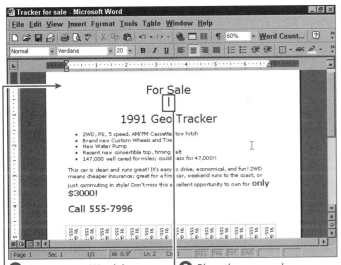

1 Create a new Word document into which you want to insert a graphic.

2 Place the cursor where you want the image to appear.

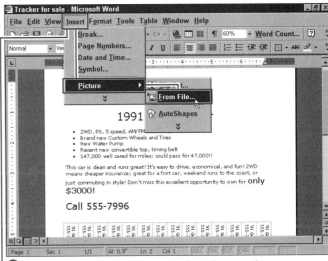

3 Select Insert ➪ Picture ➪ From File from the menu bar.

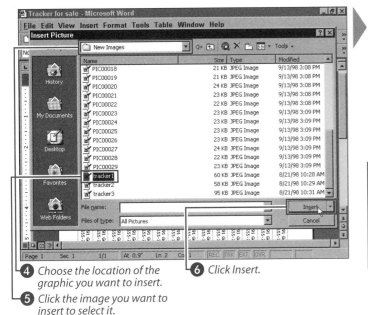

4 Choose the location of the graphic you want to insert.

5 Click the image you want to insert to select it.

6 Click Insert.

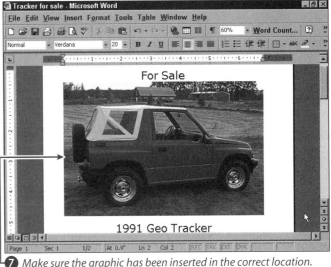

7 Make sure the graphic has been inserted in the correct location.

Using Clipart

Having the ability to insert graphics files is great; but if you don't have any graphics files to insert, having that ability doesn't do you a whole lot of good. Furthermore, you really need not just any graphics, but the right graphics. Because you use graphics to represent a specific concept or subject, it is important that your image fits your subject exactly, both in the message it conveys and how it conveys that message. Otherwise, there really isn't any sense in using the graphic at all.

Microsoft provides an outstanding collection of free artwork that comes with Word and Office 2000. The artwork consists of hundreds of images and icons (generally referred to as *clipart*) that are suitable for a wide variety of occasions. You will find graphics in the clipart gallery that are humorous, professional, casual, traditional, wild, colorful, simple, and complex.

To insert clipart, open the clipart gallery from the Picture submenu in the Insert menu. Notice that the graphics are subdivided into categories based on what they represent. For instance, if you want to find a graphic to put on top of a flyer advertising a summer picnic, try looking in the Seasons category for a sun graphic.

As you insert clipart graphics, remember that you can preview all the images from the gallery, but many of the graphics themselves are not installed on your hard drive. To save disk space, most are stored on the Word 2000 program disk. When you use clipart, therefore, you will probably have to insert the disk into the CD-ROM drive. If you have Office 2000, the clipart files are located on CD1 and CD2.

The figures on the facing page show you how to open the clipart gallery and insert a graphic from it into your document.

TAKE NOTE

▶ WRAPPING TEXT

Most of the clipart you insert will be narrower than the page itself. Normally, Word places a graphic (including clipart) on its own line, and text is placed above and below. But if the graphic is small, you may want it to appear alongside the text and have the text wrap around it. To choose this type of layout, right-click the graphic and choose Format Picture from the shortcut menu. Click the Layout tab and choose a wrapping style that is best for you. A sample of each style is displayed in the dialog box.

▶ DRAGGING IMAGES INTO YOUR DOCUMENTS

In addition to the method shown on the facing page, you can also drag graphics from the clipart gallery into your document. Simply click and hold the left mouse button on the graphic, and then drag the mouse pointer into your document. Release the mouse button when the pointer is where you want to position the graphic.

CROSS-REFERENCE

Once you have inserted the graphic, see "Moving and Resizing Graphics" later in this chapter to learn more about controlling it.

FIND IT ONLINE

Find a great online selection of free clipart at TuDogs, located at **http://www.tudogs.com/**.

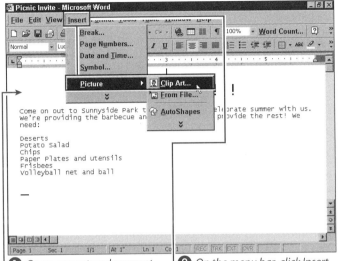

① Open or create a document into which you want to insert clipart.

② On the menu bar, click Insert ➪ Picture ➪ Clip Art.

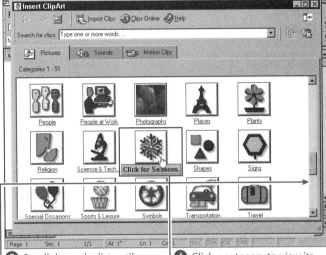

③ Scroll down the list until you see a category you want to look in.

④ Click a category to view its contents.

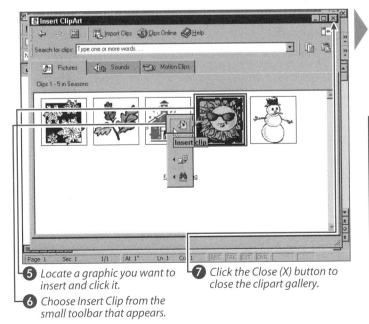

⑤ Locate a graphic you want to insert and click it.

⑥ Choose Insert Clip from the small toolbar that appears.

⑦ Click the Close (X) button to close the clipart gallery.

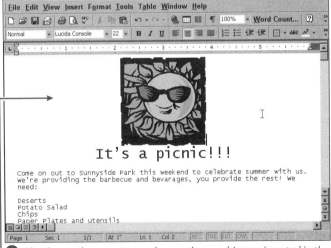

⑧ Check your document to make sure the graphic was inserted in the proper place.

Using WordArt

Chapter 7 discussed how to apply some custom formatting to your text. This formatting includes making letters bold or italicized, applying different colors, adding animations, or creating a number of other effects. Another way to compose text with unique special effects is to use WordArt. Text created using WordArt can have a tremendous visual impact in your document, thanks to its often colorful, almost cartoonish appearance.

Words created with WordArt can have large shadows behind them, be curved or bent, be drawn in three-dimensional perspective, and more. The WordArt dialog box contains representations of how the available styles will look.

The important thing to remember about WordArt is that, once created, it is a true graphic, and not simple text formatting. You cannot apply WordArt "formatting" to existing text as you would many other effects, such as boldface or italics. You create WordArt by first choosing a WordArt style from a number of selections. You then specify the text for it in the Edit WordArt Text dialog box.

WordArt is not something that you would want to use for large pieces of text — such as sentences — because it is too flashy. It works best with one or two words. For instance, if you are creating a spring sales flyer for your store, you could splash a colorful "SALE!" or even "SPRING SALE!" across the top of the page. This treatment can really grab the reader's attention in ways that regular text cannot.

Once you have inserted a WordArt object into your document, you can edit it in a number of ways. It can be moved or resized just like any other graphic (see the next task to learn more), and you can choose other typical graphic options such as text wrapping.

The figures on the facing page show you how to insert WordArt into a document. The first three figures show you how to insert a WordArt object, and the last figure demonstrates how your WordArt should look on the page.

TAKE NOTE

EDITING WORDART TEXT

Once a WordArt object has been inserted into your document, you cannot edit the text by simply clicking it and typing. To modify WordArt text, you must right-click it and choose Edit Text.

CHOOSING A FONT

When you type in the Edit WordArt Text dialog box, you can choose a specific font for the text if you wish. However, most WordArt styles look best when used with one specific font, and that font will be chosen as the default when you first start to create your text. It is usually best to just stick with the default, unless you need to choose a font that contains special characters, such as the Greek letters in the Symbols font.

CROSS-REFERENCE

Unfamiliar with fonts? See "Working with Fonts" in Chapter 7 to learn more.

FIND IT ONLINE

Computer Tips, at **http://www.computertips.com/**, offers many useful Word tips, including how to save a WordArt object as a bitmap for use in other documents.

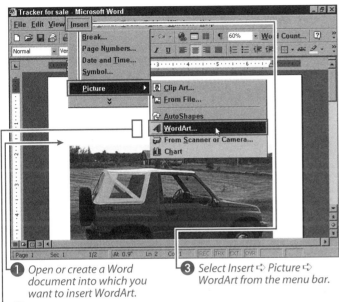

1 Open or create a Word document into which you want to insert WordArt.

2 Place the cursor where you want the WordArt to appear.

3 Select Insert ⇨ Picture ⇨ WordArt from the menu bar.

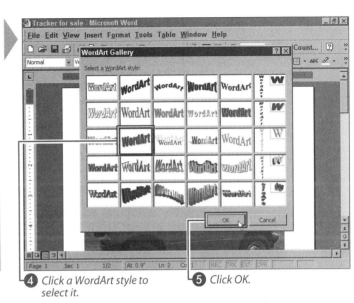

4 Click a WordArt style to select it.

5 Click OK.

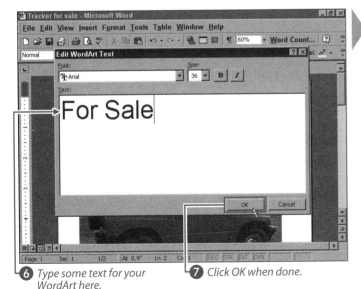

6 Type some text for your WordArt here.

7 Click OK when done.

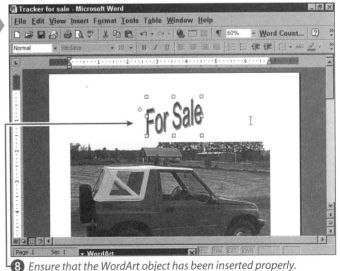

8 Ensure that the WordArt object has been inserted properly.

Using Drawing Objects

When you think of using graphics in your documents, pictures come immediately to mind. You have already seen how you can use pictures in your Word documents, including a wide selection of clipart that Microsoft has provided for your free use. You have also learned how you can create words with wild, attention-getting special effects.

But not all graphics give so stunning an impression. Sometimes, you will have more subtle graphics needs in your documents, such as simple circles and arrows pointing to various things. You can also create boxes, triangles, parallelograms, and almost any other geometric shape you can imagine, all without ever leaving Word. Yet another option is to create shapes with special effects, such as shadows or a three-dimensional appearance.

You can create basic lines and shapes using Word's *drawing objects*. Drawing objects let you do exactly what their name implies: You can use them to draw in your Word documents. This option can be especially useful when you use drawing objects in conjunction with other images, because drawing objects can be placed on top of other graphics. For instance, suppose you are composing a document that provides instructions on how to use a toaster. In the document, you could include a photograph of the toaster, and then use drawing objects to place arrows that point to the toaster's primary controls.

The figures on the facing page show how to open and use Word's drawing objects. You begin by drawing a box on the page and then drawing an arrow that points to it.

Continued

TAKE NOTE

► MAKE DRAWING OBJECTS TRANSPARENT

If you use the rectangle or oval drawing objects to draw a border around existing text, the text might become hidden. To correct this, right-click the shape and choose Format AutoShape from the shortcut menu. On the Colors and Lines tab, choose "No fill" in the Fill Color drop-down menu. This will make the enclosed area of the shape transparent. Alternatively, consider using the Borders and Shading feature instead of drawing objects to make borders around existing text.

► CHOOSING A DIFFERENT LINE STYLE

If you don't like the thin black line used when you first create a graphic with drawing objects, change it using tools on the Drawing toolbar. The Line Color and Fill Color drop-down menus let you choose another color, and the Line Style, Dash Style, and Arrow Style buttons enable you to choose a different size and look for lines. Click these buttons to see the options that are available, and experiment with the choices. Make sure the appropriate line or shape is selected — as evidenced by manipulation handles on the object — before trying to apply these custom styles to lines or shapes.

CROSS-REFERENCE
See "Using Borders and Shading" in Chapter 18 to learn another way of drawing borders around text.

FIND IT ONLINE
Visit RenderMan, at **http://rmr.spinne.com/**, to learn more about 3-D graphic rendering.

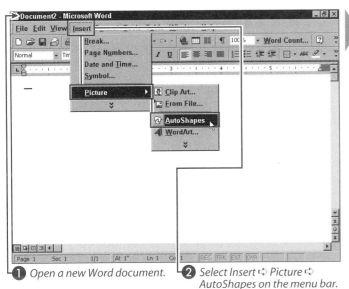

① *Open a new Word document.*

② *Select Insert ➪ Picture ➪ AutoShapes on the menu bar.*

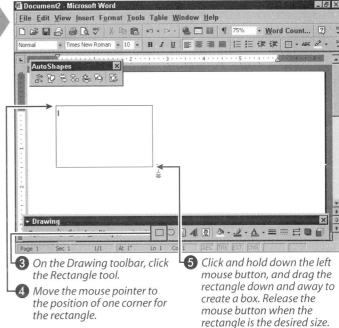

③ *On the Drawing toolbar, click the Rectangle tool.*

④ *Move the mouse pointer to the position of one corner for the rectangle.*

⑤ *Click and hold down the left mouse button, and drag the rectangle down and away to create a box. Release the mouse button when the rectangle is the desired size.*

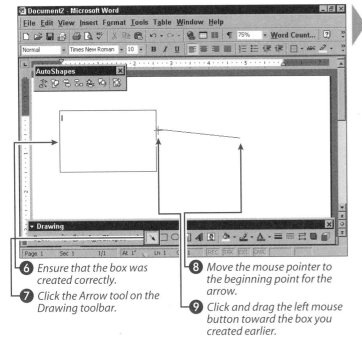

⑥ *Ensure that the box was created correctly.*

⑦ *Click the Arrow tool on the Drawing toolbar.*

⑧ *Move the mouse pointer to the beginning point for the arrow.*

⑨ *Click and drag the left mouse button toward the box you created earlier.*

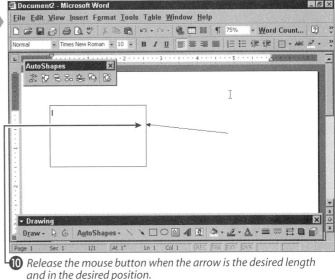

⑩ *Release the mouse button when the arrow is the desired length and in the desired position.*

Using Drawing Objects

Continued

Drawing objects provide you with a simple, yet versatile, tool for drawing shapes in your Word documents. In addition to these basic shapes, you can also produce more sophisticated shapes and objects in Word with AutoShapes. AutoShapes enable you to draw curvy lines, specialty shapes such as stars or hearts, cartoon-style dialog bubbles, flow charts, banners, and more.

You begin inserting AutoShapes just as you do other drawing objects. AutoShapes have their own toolbar, and it opens when you select Insert ➪ Picture ➪ AutoShapes. Usually, the Drawing toolbar appears along the bottom of the Word document window, and the AutoShapes toolbar appears in the upper-left corner.

AutoShapes have many intriguing uses. The Basic Shapes menu contains a number of geometric shapes for you to choose from; open it up by clicking the Basic Shapes button on the AutoShapes toolbar to see what is available. You can also choose from a number of block arrow shapes, which can be especially useful for creating special visual effects.

The AutoShapes toolbar also contains tools for drawing flow chart shapes, which in the past have been used by computer programmers to plan a new program. You can also create callouts with AutoShapes that label various items. Callouts can be used in place of simple arrows when you need to label things on your page. The callout points to a specific item and contains a "bubble" where you can

type text. There are even some cartoon-like callouts that resemble the speech and thought bubbles normally associated with comics.

The figures on the facing page show you how to use one of the callout AutoShapes. You begin by drawing the shape, and then you enter text into it and make the text larger.

TAKE NOTE

▶ PUTTING TEXT INSIDE AUTOSHAPES

The easiest way to place text inside block arrows (or many other AutoShapes) is to use the Text Box tool on the Drawing toolbar. Use it to draw a text box inside the arrow, and then format the text box so that it has no border. You may also have to format the block arrow so that it has no fill color. Callout AutoShapes automatically place a text box in the shape for you.

▶ WHAT IS A FLOW CHART?

A flow chart is a simple planning tool that takes you through some steps and asks basic yes/no questions. For instance, suppose you are planning your morning routine. The first flow chart step might simply say, "Get out of bed." Next it might ask a question like "Is today a work day?" If you answer "Yes," you must follow a series of steps to help you get ready for work. If you answer "No," the steps might concentrate on leisure activities instead.

CROSS-REFERENCE

Text used in callouts and other text boxes can have custom formatting, too. See "Using Special Character Formatting" in Chapter 7.

FIND IT ONLINE

Find some cool fantasy-related clipart at the Clipart Castle, located online at **http://www.clipartcastle. com/**.

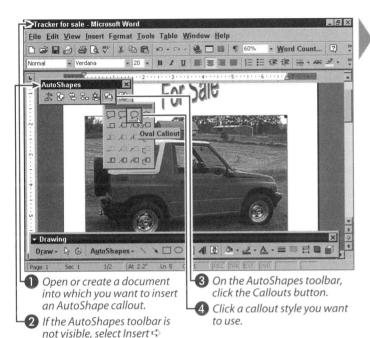

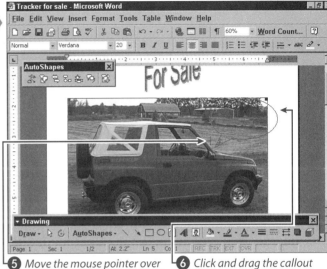

① Open or create a document into which you want to insert an AutoShape callout.

② If the AutoShapes toolbar is not visible, select Insert ⇨ Picture ⇨ AutoShapes.

③ On the AutoShapes toolbar, click the Callouts button.

④ Click a callout style you want to use.

⑤ Move the mouse pointer over where you want one corner of the callout to be.

⑥ Click and drag the callout shape, and release the mouse button when you have achieved the desired size.

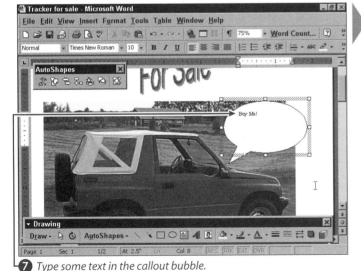

⑦ Type some text in the callout bubble.

⑧ If you want the text to be bigger, select it and choose a different point size here.

⑨ Click outside the callout to hide the manipulation handles and preview the result.

Moving and Resizing Graphics

Graphics that you plan to use in your Word documents can come in many shapes and sizes. Often, such sizes and shapes do not conform exactly to the rest of your document. Fortunately, you can make graphics conform by changing their relative size in the document. You can make them bigger or smaller, or you can stretch graphics horizontally or vertically.

When you resize a graphic, many important things need to be considered. Most graphics on your computer have a relatively limited resolution. Digitized images — that is, any image that has been turned into an electronic file that can be viewed on your computer — usually pale in terms of quality compared to print photographs taken with a camera and film. This means that lines and small details will not be as sharp and clear as they would be on film.

A picture might look okay when you first insert it; but due to low resolution, you may be limited in terms of what you can do to manipulate it. This is especially true if you want to make the image bigger. Enlarging digitized images that you have inserted into a Word document often results in a blocky or pixelated look. On the other hand, reducing the size of a graphic will not have the same result.

Resizing is not the only kind of change you may want to make to your graphics. You'll likely also want to move them around the page. Any graphic can be moved using a simple click-and-drag method, but you must always keep an eye on how moving your graphics affects other items on the page. You can move the graphic whenever the mouse pointer turns into a four-headed arrow.

The figures on the facing page demonstrate how to change the size and position of your graphics. The first two figures demonstrate how to resize a graphic using the manipulation handles, and the last two figures show how to drag and drop the graphic to a new location in the document.

TAKE NOTE

▶ MOVING AND RESIZING OTHER OBJECTS

As you can see in the example shown on the facing page, you can move or resize a graphic whenever the manipulation handles appear around the picture. Many other objects in Word have similar manipulation handles, including embedded objects, sound files, and more. You can move or resize anything in Word that has manipulation handles using the techniques described here.

▶ MAINTAINING IMAGE PROPORTIONS

If you resize graphics using the horizontal or vertical manipulation handles, they can look stretched and unnatural. To avoid this problem, right-click the graphic and choose Format Picture (or Format WordArt) from the shortcut menu. On the Size tab, make sure the option Lock Aspect Ratio has a check mark next to it.

CROSS-REFERENCE

Linked and embedded objects can be manipulated much like graphics. See "Embedded Objects" in Chapter 19 to learn more.

FIND IT ONLINE

Download free icons and Web graphics from The ShockZone at http://www.theshockzone.com/.

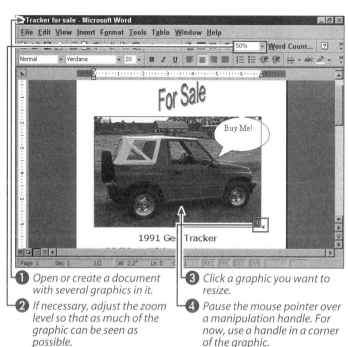

1. Open or create a document with several graphics in it.

2. If necessary, adjust the zoom level so that as much of the graphic can be seen as possible.

3. Click a graphic you want to resize.

4. Pause the mouse pointer over a manipulation handle. For now, use a handle in a corner of the graphic.

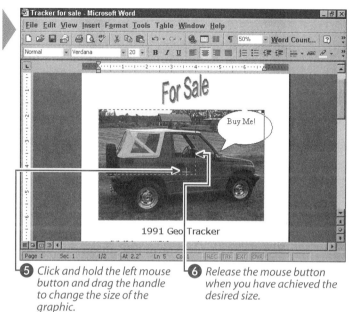

5. Click and hold the left mouse button and drag the handle to change the size of the graphic.

6. Release the mouse button when you have achieved the desired size.

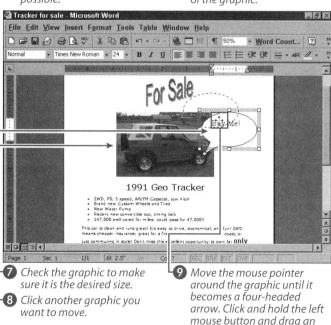

7. Check the graphic to make sure it is the desired size.

8. Click another graphic you want to move.

9. Move the mouse pointer around the graphic until it becomes a four-headed arrow. Click and hold the left mouse button and drag an outline of the graphic to a new location.

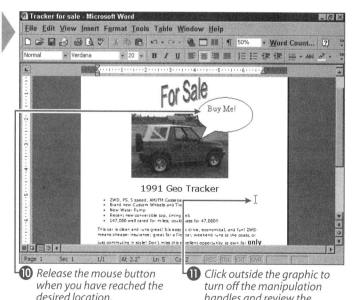

10. Release the mouse button when you have reached the desired location.

11. Click outside the graphic to turn off the manipulation handles and review the results.

Formatting Graphics

The previous task showed how to move graphics around on your page and how to change their size, but there are many other graphics formatting issues to consider. Primarily, you have to deal with how the image is oriented on the page in relation to other text, not to mention other graphics.

As you already know, a page in a Word document has many lines on it. Normally, these lines hold only text. But when you insert a picture into a document, the graphic is inserted on a line of the document. It doesn't matter if the image is much bigger than a single line; with the default graphic formatting settings, the line will become as tall as the graphic.

Most of the time, this really doesn't matter. However, it does make a difference if you want to align text next to the picture. This is a common practice, especially for smaller graphics that only take up about half the width of a page. With the default settings, only one line of text is placed alongside a graphic. This results in a lot of white space and an awkward-looking page layout. You can fix this problem, however, by changing some settings in the Format Picture dialog box.

You open the Format Picture dialog box by using a graphic's shortcut menu. This dialog box contains a number of other useful settings. You can control the size of a graphic here, as well as adjust some basic color and brightness options. Check all the tabs in this dialog box to become familiar with the available options.

The figures on the facing page show you how to adjust some graphics formatting in Word. The example uses one of the files you created earlier in this chapter.

TAKE NOTE

► ALTERNATIVE TEXT FOR WEB DOCUMENTS

If you are creating a Web page, add some descriptive "alternative" text on the Web tab of the Format Picture dialog box. Some viewers of your page may have set their Web browser programs so that graphics are not displayed. Instead of your really cool pictures, they will only see a graphics placeholder and any alternative text you choose to enter. If you enter some alternative text for the picture — such as "A picture of the jackelope that attacked our campsite" — the viewer will at least know what she's missing!

► SETTING ORDERS FOR YOUR GRAPHICS

If you have text and graphics that overlap on the page, one of them will be on top. Likewise, when multiple graphics are overlapped, one will be partially hidden by the other. If you want to change which item is on top, right-click the graphic and choose Order from the shortcut menu. Choose an option from the Order submenu that suits your needs.

CROSS-REFERENCE

To learn more about using graphics in Web pages, see "Inserting Graphics" in Chapter 16.

FIND IT ONLINE

CERN provides a no-frills index of icons you can download, located at **http://www.w3.org/Icons/**.

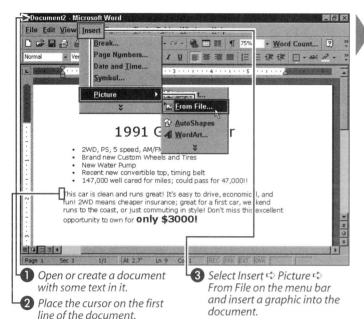

1 Open or create a document with some text in it.

2 Place the cursor on the first line of the document.

3 Select Insert ➪ Picture ➪ From File on the menu bar and insert a graphic into the document.

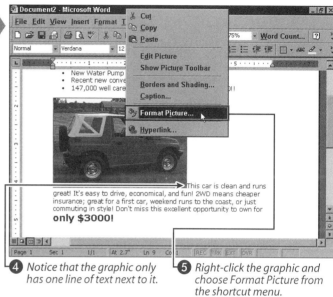

4 Notice that the graphic only has one line of text next to it.

5 Right-click the graphic and choose Format Picture from the shortcut menu.

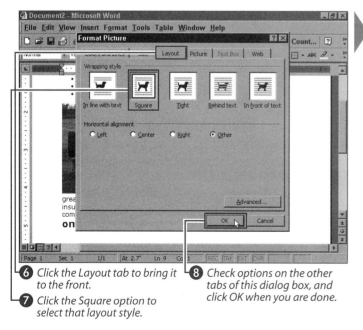

6 Click the Layout tab to bring it to the front.

7 Click the Square option to select that layout style.

8 Check options on the other tabs of this dialog box, and click OK when you are done.

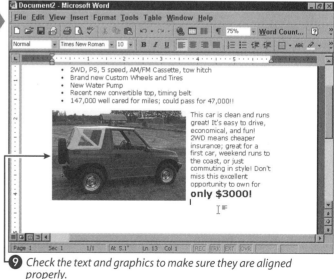

9 Check the text and graphics to make sure they are aligned properly.

Personal Workbook

Q&A

1 How do you insert a graphic into a document?

_____

_____

_____

2 What is the name of the clipart collection Microsoft provides with Word?

_____

_____

_____

3 Is all of this art installed on your hard drive?

_____

_____

_____

4 What is the quickest way to resize a graphic?

_____

_____

5 How can you ensure the proportions of the graphic are not changed when you resize the graphic?

_____

_____

_____

_____

6 How do you begin drawing shapes in your document?

_____

_____

_____

7 Can your shapes be resized after they are created?

_____

_____

_____

8 What wrapping style should you use for a graphic that will serve as a watermark?

_____

_____

ANSWERS: PAGE 366

EXTRA PRACTICE

1. Open a new document and insert a picture of your family.

2. Use AutoShapes to create a thought bubble for one of the people in the picture. Add a remark to the bubble.

3. Move the thought bubble to someone else in the picture.

4. Draw a rectangle around the graphic to make a frame.

5. Change the line on the rectangle to a thicker style, and make the rectangle transparent so that the family photo can be seen.

6. Create a title for the picture using WordArt that says "My Family."

REAL-WORLD APPLICATIONS

✔ Pictures can greatly enhance the effectiveness of documents you create. If your family pet has gone astray, insert a photo of the pet into a document that describes your loss, and how anyone who might find the pet can contact you. Use drawing objects to draw arrows or callouts pointing to distinctive features.

✔ Selling a house by yourself is a daunting task. You can make your job a bit easier by using Word to produce your own advertising. Create flyers that describe the home, and insert lots of pictures of both the interior and exterior. Again, drawing objects and AutoShapes can be used to call attention to key features, such as those solid-oak cabinets in the kitchen!

Visual Quiz

Can the picture shown here be moved? How? If you drag the bottom manipulation handle down, how will the graphic be affected? How was the arrow created? How can you resize it?

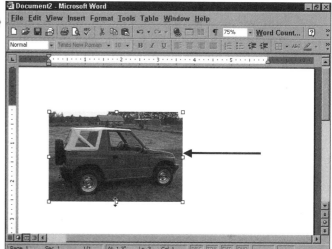

Editing Your Documents

Once you have created documents with Word, you will have to start editing them. No one creates the perfect document the first time around, so editing is just as important a task as creating the document in the first place. This effort includes basic editing tasks, such as changing, deleting, moving, and copying text. You learn how to perform these operations in "Making Basic Corrections," along with how to undo changes you have made.

Another important aspect of creating documents that is discussed in Part 3 is the use of Word's powerful document-proofing tools. Word 2000 helps you out by providing tools to analyze your documents and check for spelling errors and proper grammar. Word also includes a thesaurus, for those times when the right word is just beyond your grasp.

In this part, you see how to use some of Word's automation tools to simplify many editing tasks. Features called AutoCorrect and AutoText simplify the task of entering commonly used words, names, phrases, and special characters, and watch out for common typing errors that most people make. Finally, you learn how to use Word's Find and Replace features to make otherwise time-consuming editing tasks much easier.

CHAPTER **10**

MASTER
THESE
SKILLS

▶ Editing Text

▶ Inserting Text

▶ Deleting Text and Objects

▶ Moving and Copying Text and Objects

▶ Using Undo and Redo

Making Basic Corrections

Wouldn't it be nice if you could do everything perfectly the first time? Here's a little secret: No one ever does. Mistakes are an everyday part of life, especially when it comes to using computers. Creating a document in Word may start with entering text and other kinds of data, but editing and correcting the document are just as important to the process.

You can edit Word 2000 documents in a wide variety of ways. Your simplest option is to delete text using the Backspace and Delete keys on the keyboard, but other tools are available as well. After all, editing does not always involve deleting. You may need to move objects, transpose words, copy text, or insert items. There is almost no aspect of a document that cannot be changed.

Many reasons exist for editing a Word document. You might be correcting a mistake, of course, but you might also be improving text that you or someone else has written. You may also need to modify a document to keep it up to date as time passes. Your Web page, for instance, probably doesn't need to contain the dates and times of say, the family reunion that occurred last month. Some simple editing and corrections are necessary from time to time to keep your page up to the minute.

This chapter discusses how to make basic corrections to your Word documents. It starts with simple editing and moves on to demonstrate inserting, deleting, and moving text and objects. Finally, you learn how to use a tool that saves you when you make the worst mistake of all: You *thought* you were wrong, but it turned out that you were really right. This feature, which is called Undo/Redo, can save you countless headaches and hours of grief. It also gives you greater editing flexibility because you can try edits you are unsure about, and then undo them if you don't like them.

Notice that this chapter places an increased emphasis on using shortcut keys to perform tasks. As useful as the mouse may be at times, many of the editing tasks described here can be done more quickly with keyboard shortcuts. As always, you should practice using several methods to see which ones work best for you.

Editing Text

Soon after you start entering text, you will probably find yourself needing to edit it. In the course of editing, you will change, insert, delete, or otherwise modify what is written on the page.

You don't have to wait until you reach some magical milestone before you start editing. In fact, the vast majority of editing occurs *while* you are entering text. It's not uncommon to accidentally press the wrong key, and a simple press of the Backspace key on your keyboard will help you correct that. Backspace deletes the character just before the cursor. You can then press the correct key and continue typing. Some people have lamented that typing this way has created a generation of lazy typists; but if this means you never again have to buy correction tape or correction fluid, who cares?

Another, more involved way to edit text is to *replace* it. Suppose you need to replace a sentence or even a block of text. The simplest thing to do is to select the material you want to replace, and then type the new text. As soon as you start typing, the material you selected will be automatically deleted and replaced by the new text.

There is another way to replace existing text with new text. Word has two modes for entering text: *type-over* and *insert*. You control the mode by pressing the Insert (or Ins) key on your keyboard. In type-over mode, anything you type replaces the text that is already there. This is a less sophisticated approach to editing than other methods, but it may work well for you in some circumstances. To return to insert mode, press the Insert key again. An indicator on the Word status bar tells you which mode you are in. If OVR is darkened you are in type-over mode; if not, you are in insert mode. The figures on the facing page show you how to edit text using the methods discussed here.

TAKE NOTE

▶ DISABLING THE REPLACE FEATURE

If you don't want Word to replace selected text with whatever you type on the keyboard, open the Options dialog box by selecting Tools ⇨ Options. On the Edit tab, remove the check mark next to "Typing replaces selection" to disable this feature.

▶ DID YOU FORGET THE CAPS LOCK KEY?

It is easy to press the Caps Lock key by mistake as you type. The next words you type will be in the wrong case or mix cases in the wrong way, such as "mISTAKE." Fortunately, Word will immediately recognize what's happening. If you type a word like "mISTAKE" with Caps Lock on, Word automatically fixes the mistake and turns off Caps Lock. If you don't want Word to correct this, disable the feature in the AutoCorrect dialog box.

CROSS-REFERENCE

See "Selecting Text" in Chapter 5 to learn a key skill required during editing.

FIND IT ONLINE

For instructions and guidelines for Windows beginners, go to **http://www.rdg.ac.uk/ITS/Topic/Word/Proc/WoPW7beg01/**.

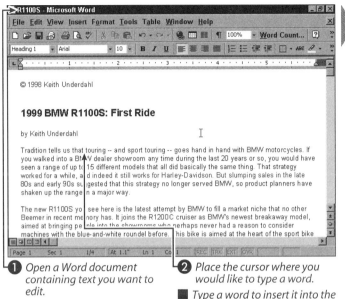

❶ Open a Word document containing text you want to edit.

❷ Place the cursor where you would like to type a word.

■ Type a word to insert it into the text.

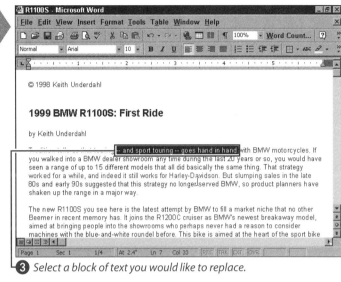

❸ Select a block of text you would like to replace.

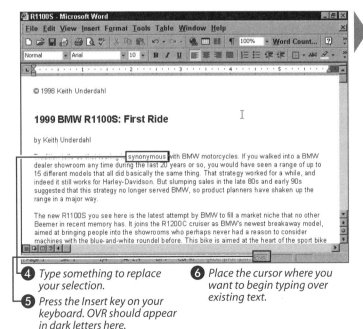

❹ Type something to replace your selection.

❺ Press the Insert key on your keyboard. OVR should appear in dark letters here.

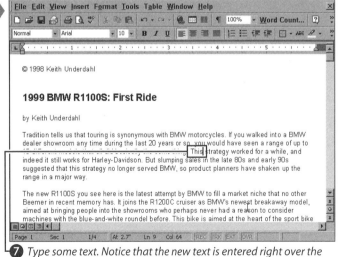

❻ Place the cursor where you want to begin typing over existing text.

❼ Type some text. Notice that the new text is entered right over the old text.

Inserting Text

As I've said before, editing a document often involves inserting text as well as deleting it. Word 2000 provides sophisticated tools for inserting text as well as other elements such as graphics, tables, and the like. You can insert virtually any kind of object into a Word document, and once inserted, you can do a lot with it.

This task focuses on inserting text. Do you feel you need to add a sentence or two into the middle of a paragraph? With an old typewriter, this would have been impossible without retyping the entire page. Now, all you have to do is place the cursor where you want the inserted text and start typing.

Needless to say, this is not the only way to insert text. You can automatically insert a number of specific kinds of data and information using the Insert menu (see Chapter 12). You can also insert large chunks of text that have been removed or copied from other documents. To do so, select Paste from the Edit menu or click the Paste button on the toolbar. (The Paste button looks like a clipboard with a piece of paper in front of it. You see this button in virtually all Windows-based applications.) When you use the Paste command, Word inserts whatever is contained in an area called the *clipboard*. The clipboard can hold text, pictures, sound objects, spreadsheets, or almost any other kind of data that your computer can use. Items are put on the clipboard using the cut or copy commands, so if you haven't cut or copied something, the paste command won't work.

The figures on the facing page show you how to insert text into a document. The first two figures show how to insert by typing from the keyboard, and the last two figures demonstrate how to use Edit ⇨ Paste. Notice that this example uses the Copy command, which is discussed in more detail later in this chapter.

TAKE NOTE

▶ INSERTING OBJECTS

You can insert almost anything you want into a Word document. Pictures, graphics, sound files, and many other objects can be inserted into your documents using roughly the same techniques discussed here. Just check the display properties for the inserted object if you have any problems; most trouble with insertions involves how the object is set to display relative to other items on the page.

▶ WHY DOESN'T THE INSERT FEATURE WORK?

Sometimes when you place your cursor and start typing, you will notice that you are typing over old text rather than inserting new text. If this happens, you are in type-over rather than insert mode. Check to see whether the *OVR* appears in dark letters on the Word status bar. If it does, you need to press Insert on your keyboard to return to insert mode.

CROSS-REFERENCE

To learn more about inserting certain items, see "Using AutoText" in Chapter 12.

FIND IT ONLINE

Check out **http:www.pcworld.com/resources/ hereshow/word_processing_tips.html** for more Windows know-how.

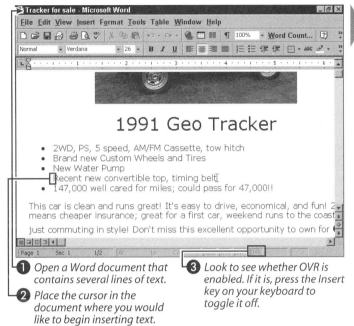

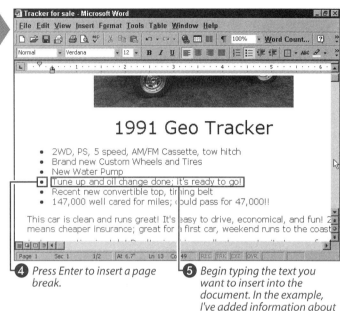

1 Open a Word document that contains several lines of text.

2 Place the cursor in the document where you would like to begin inserting text.

3 Look to see whether OVR is enabled. If it is, press the Insert key on your keyboard to toggle it off.

4 Press Enter to insert a page break.

5 Begin typing the text you want to insert into the document. In the example, I've added information about a tune up and oil change.

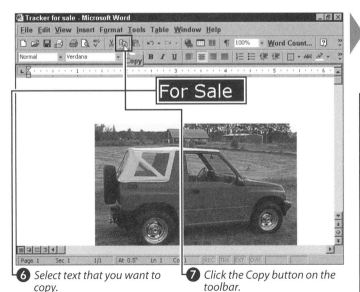

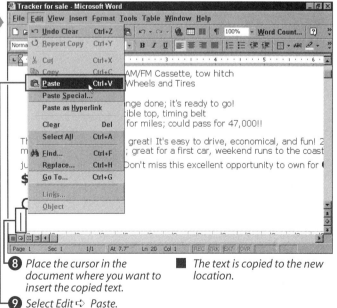

6 Select text that you want to copy.

7 Click the Copy button on the toolbar.

8 Place the cursor in the document where you want to insert the copied text.

9 Select Edit ⇨ Paste.

■ The text is copied to the new location.

Deleting Text and Objects

Whatever kind of document you're working with, you will almost certainly find the need to delete material on a regular basis. Deletion is simply a part of life, like taking out the garbage.

So far, the tasks in this chapter have applied specifically to text. You learned about editing text, and then you saw how to insert text. Now you learn about deleting text, but at the same time you see how to delete other kinds of objects. Word treats any element in your document, including pictures, graphics, sound files, embedded Excel worksheets, and various other items, as *objects*. Inserting and editing objects usually involves performing a specialized series of steps, as described throughout this book.

Deleting an object, however, is quite another matter. Deleting is perhaps the most basic task you can perform, and how you perform that task is virtually the same no matter what you are deleting. Thus, the examples in the figures on the facing page show you not only how to delete text, but how to delete other kinds of objects as well.

The usual way to delete objects in Word is to press the Delete key on the keyboard. You may be familiar with delete buttons on toolbars in other Windows applications, but Word doesn't have one. Likewise, there is no menu command to help you delete something.

The figures on the facing page show you how to delete text and objects, in that order. The first two figures show you how to select and then delete text. The last two figures show how to delete another kind of object — in this case, a picture. This technique works in the same way for virtually any kind of non-text object you might be using in Word, including WordArt.

TAKE NOTE

CUTTING VERSUS DELETING

You may have noticed the Cut feature available in Word. Keep in mind that cutting something is quite different from deleting. When you delete an object, it is gone, permanently dispatched to the electronic ether. But if you cut something, it is simply removed from the current location and stored for future use. You can learn more about cutting in the next task.

GETTING RID OF EXTRA PARAGRAPH MARKS

If you delete a number of paragraphs or objects from a document, you may find that you now have extra space remaining in your document. This excessive space means you probably did not delete all the paragraph marks around the objects you deleted. You have to see paragraph marks to get rid of them, so click the Show/Hide button on the toolbar to display paragraph marks. Then just place the cursor in front of each paragraph mark you want to get rid of, and press Delete.

CROSS-REFERENCE

To learn more about working with object windows, see "Moving and Resizing Graphics" in Chapter 9.

FIND IT ONLINE

For an online tutorial of moving, copying, and deleting blocks of text, go to **http://www.cant. ac.uk/title/Word/Part4/ WordPrt4.htm.**

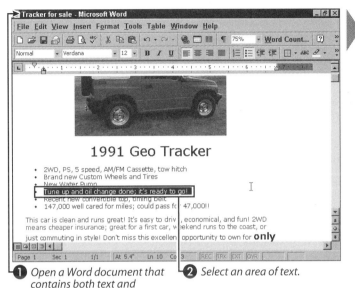

❶ Open a Word document that contains both text and another kind of object, such as a picture.

❷ Select an area of text.

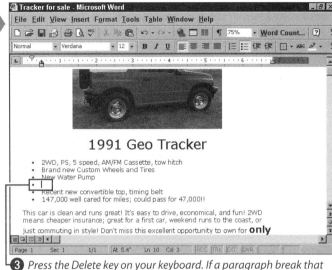

❸ Press the Delete key on your keyboard. If a paragraph break that you don't want still appears on the page, press Delete again.

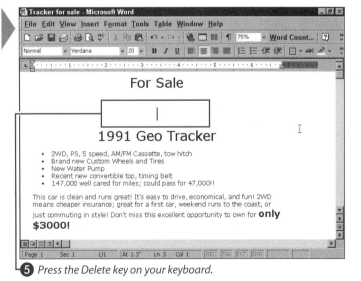

❹ Click the object you want to delete to select it. The object manipulation handles should appear around the borders.

❺ Press the Delete key on your keyboard.

Moving and Copying Text and Objects

As with deleting and inserting text and objects, moving or copying them in Word is a very common task. This feature can save literally hours of typing by letting you simply copy items and move them to new locations.

When you copy text or an object in Word, the program takes advantage of a powerful Windows tool called the *clipboard*. The clipboard can hold almost any kind of copied information, and certainly anything that you might use in a Word document. This copied material can include words and numbers — anything from a single punctuation mark to the text of an entire book. It can also include pictures, various other objects, and even whole files.

Likewise, any material that you cut is placed on the clipboard, so that you can move it and place it elsewhere. Copied text remains in its current position and is also placed on the clipboard. Cut text, on the other hand, is removed from its current position and placed on the clipboard. You can then paste the cut text from the clipboard to a new location in the current document or in any other document.

You can continue to paste material from the clipboard into the document as many times as you want. Traditionally, when you copied something else into the clipboard, whatever was on the clipboard was replaced. This is because the Windows clipboard holds only one item at a time, but a new clipboard enhancement that comes with Office 2000 programs can hold up to twelve different items at once.

Another beauty of the clipboard is that it makes sharing objects between different applications easier. Thanks to a technology called *Object Linking and Embedding* (OLE), almost anything that can be copied to the clipboard can then be pasted into a Word document.

The figures on the facing page show you how to move and copy objects in Word. The first two figures show you how to move a paragraph by cutting it from one location and pasting it to another. The last two figures show you how to copy an object — in this case, a picture — from one location to another. In the example shown here, the picture is being copied into another Word document.

TAKE NOTE

▶ VIEWING THE CLIPBOARD

To see what is in the clipboard, select View ⇨ Toolbars ⇨ Clipboard. This opens the new Office clipboard, which can hold up to twelve items. The Office clipboard works like a toolbar, so you can just place it near your other toolbars and click an item in the clipboard whenever you need it.

▶ USING DOCUMENT SCRAPS

Another way to paste text or objects into different documents is to place them as scraps on your Windows desktop. Select some text and click-and-drag it to the desktop. A scrap icon is created. You can then click-and-drag the scrap into other documents.

CROSS-REFERENCE
To learn more about using OLE, see "Linking Objects" in Chapter 19.

FIND IT ONLINE
Check out ClipTrakker at **http://www.cliptrakker.com/** to learn about this tool for tracking items placed on your clipboard.

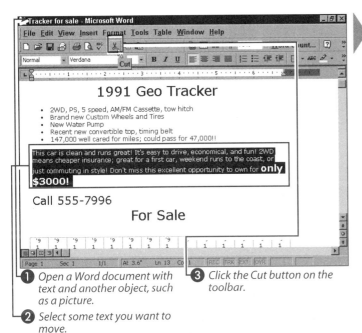

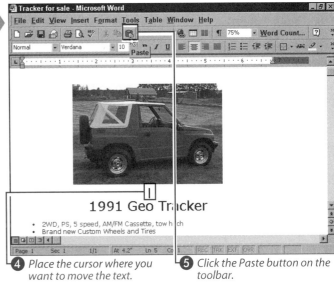

① Open a Word document with text and another object, such as a picture.

② Select some text you want to move.

③ Click the Cut button on the toolbar.

④ Place the cursor where you want to move the text.

⑤ Click the Paste button on the toolbar.

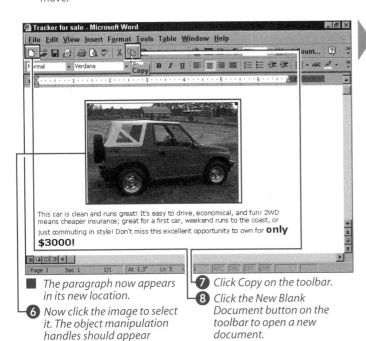

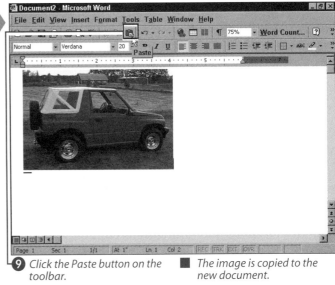

■ The paragraph now appears in its new location.

⑥ Now click the image to select it. The object manipulation handles should appear around the edges.

⑦ Click Copy on the toolbar.

⑧ Click the New Blank Document button on the toolbar to open a new document.

⑨ Click the Paste button on the toolbar.

■ The image is copied to the new document.

Using Undo and Redo

A humorous old saying goes, "I once made a mistake. I thought I was wrong, but it turned out I was right after all." Have you ever second-guessed yourself, only to find that you had it right the first time? This can easily happen when you are using Word. You delete something, only to find that you really should have kept it. Now what?

The Word programmers were smart enough to know that this would happen to you eventually, and they built a safety valve into the program to help you avoid major problems. This safety valve is called *Undo*. As the name implies, this feature can *un*do almost anything you *do* in Word. Your ability to undo is not limited to accidental deletions. For example, you can undo typing, the insertion of a graphic, or the pasting of a paragraph into a new position.

Using Undo is simple: You click the Undo button on the toolbar. Click the button once to undo the last thing you did. Continue clicking the button to undo your editing actions one at a time, from the most recent backward. Instead of clicking the toolbar button, you can also select Undo from the Edit menu.

Serving as a counterpoint to Undo is *Redo*, a button next to Undo on the toolbar. What if you undo something, and then decide you liked the document better before you undid the action? Just click Redo to repeat the action and restore the file.

The figures on the facing page show you how to use these commands. The first two figures show you how to use Undo. The last two figures demonstrate how to redo the actions you undid, just in case you change your mind.

TAKE NOTE

HOW FAR BACK DOES UNDO GO?

Undo commands are common in computer programs these days, but often they enable you to undo only the last action. Word keeps a running memory of tasks, so you can trace back through hundreds of actions if you like. To do this, click the drop-down arrow next to the Undo button on the toolbar. Scroll down until you find the last action you want to undo, and click it. Everything between that action and the most recent action is undone.

ONLY EDITING CAN BE UNDONE

You can't undo everything you do to a file. File commands such as Save or Save As can't be undone, nor can any other command that isn't related directly to editing. You can't undo printing, switching document windows, or even running the spell checker (although actual spelling changes to the document *can* be undone). Undoing macros is a little tricky, because each macro task is listed separately in the Undo list.

CROSS-REFERENCE

To learn another way to edit, see "Tracking Changes" in Chapter 18.

FIND IT ONLINE

Learn more about undoing and redoing actions at **http://www.ag.ndsu.nodak.edu/lessons/word7/l2.moving.htm**.

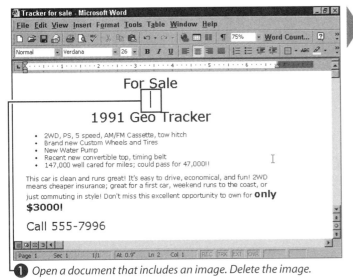

1 Open a document that includes an image. Delete the image.

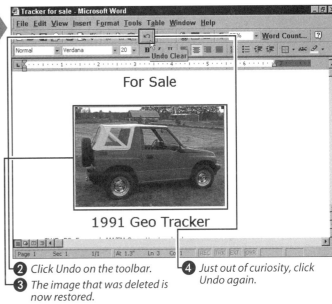

2 Click Undo on the toolbar.

3 The image that was deleted is now restored.

4 Just out of curiosity, click Undo again.

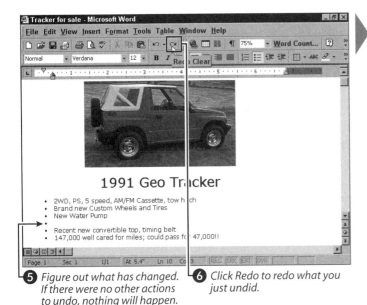

5 Figure out what has changed. If there were no other actions to undo, nothing will happen.

6 Click Redo to redo what you just undid.

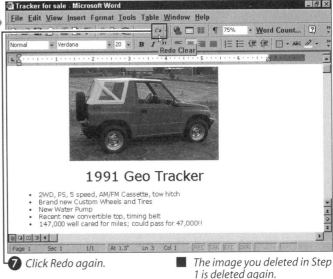

7 Click Redo again.

■ The image you deleted in Step 1 is deleted again.

Personal Workbook

Q&A

1 When should you edit text?

_____

_____

_____

2 What kind of actions are involved in editing?

_____

_____

_____

3 What is the easiest way to replace text in a document?

_____

_____

_____

4 What does OVR on the Word status bar mean?

_____

_____

_____

5 How do you delete an object from Word?

_____

_____

_____

6 What is the difference between deleting text and deleting images?

_____

_____

_____

7 How is moving an object different from copying?

_____

_____

_____

8 How do you restore something you deleted by accident?

_____

_____

_____

ANSWERS: PAGE 367

EXTRA PRACTICE

1 Create a new document that contains several paragraphs of text. Create a title for the document using WordArt.

2 Delete one paragraph.

3 Restore the paragraph you just deleted.

4 Move the WordArt title to the end of the document.

5 Copy the WordArt title and paste it back to the top of the document.

6 Delete the WordArt title at the end of the document.

7 Insert a graphic into the document, and toggle the Undo and Redo buttons to see how the graphic affects the document's appearance.

REAL-WORLD APPLICATIONS

✔ Editing your documents is largely a practice in using basic deletion, insertion, and copying techniques. You can use these techniques to copy similar pieces of information to different documents. For instance, you might want to copy header information from an old letter — your address, the recipient's address, salutation, and so on — into a new letter you are writing.

✔ Windows enables you to copy a variety of objects across many different kinds of applications. For instance, you can copy an image from a Web page and paste it directly into your Word documents, or vice versa. You can even copy a number from a Word document and paste into the Windows calculator to use it in a math problem!

Visual Quiz

The figure shows four copies of the same picture. What is the easiest way to create this effect? Can they be copied to another document? How? Can you insert more text into the middle of the sentence near the bottom? How? How do you delete the images? How can you restore them again after deletion?

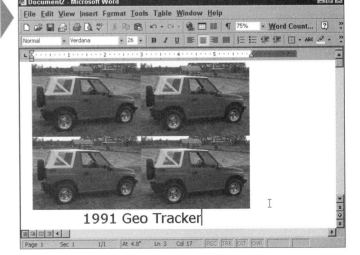

CHAPTER 11

Checking Your Spelling and Grammar

You don't have to work too hard to find some compelling reasons for choosing to use a computer to create your documents instead of a typewriter. When used with a versatile word processing program such as Word 2000, the editing and layout features available on your computer make the typewriter look about as advanced as a chisel and stone tablet.

By far one of the most useful and popular features offered with Word is the spelling checker. Few people have the entire Webster's Collegiate Dictionary committed to memory, and even the best writers need help with their spelling from time to time. Word has a spell-checking feature built in, and you can take advantage of it in either a passive or active way. You can even customize the dictionary so it recognizes special words that you specify. For instance, you can add words such as your name to Word's spelling dictionary to ensure that they are not flagged by the spelling checker when entered.

In addition to the spelling checker, Word has other features to help improve the quality of your writing. One is the grammar checker, which analyzes your documents for various grammatical errors. This feature can help you avoid what could otherwise be embarrassing little errors in grammar and give your writing a much more professional tone.

Word also offers a built-in thesaurus. The thesaurus helps you avoid repetition in your documents by finding synonyms for words you select. The thesaurus suggests alternatives for single words as well as phrases.

All these tools can serve to greatly enhance the quality of your writing, although simply using the thesaurus, grammar, and spelling checkers will not transform you into Ernest Hemingway overnight. These tools only help you avoid making simple grammatical errors.

This chapter shows you how to take advantage of Word's writing tools and also shows you how to turn some of these features off. You may find the spelling and grammar checkers intrusive at times, so being able to disable them at least temporarily is important. You will also learn how to customize the spelling dictionary to add special words such as your name and other unique words.

Using the Spelling Checker

It's no secret that some people are better spellers than others. Even professional writers have trouble from time to time. Many people who read your Word files may not be very good spellers themselves, but proper spelling in a document is still important. Incorrectly spelled words are embarrassing, and such errors make your documents seem less professional. Avoid this pitfall by taking advantage of the tools at hand, such as Word's spelling checker.

The Word spelling checker works both passively and actively. Passively, Word automatically indicates which words might be misspelled by underlining them with a wavy red line. The line appears as soon as you type a problematic word, and it is easy to see. You can fix the word immediately or wait to run the spelling checker on the document. If you right-click on a word underlined with a wavy red line, Word will propose one or more correct spellings. Word also automatically corrects some common spelling errors through the AutoCorrect feature, which is discussed in Chapter 12.

For a more active role in the spell-checking process, open the Spelling and Grammar dialog box from the Tools menu. You can use this dialog box to search your entire document for errors. This is the best approach for making a final check of your document. You may not notice every red wavy line in a document, but the spelling checker will. The tool offers suggestions for correcting each error it finds. You can choose one of the suggestions, make a correction of your own, add the word to the built-in spelling dictionary, or just ignore the word altogether.

The figures on the facing page show you how to check and correct spelling errors using the Spelling and Grammar dialog box. The first figure shows what spelling errors look like in a document, as well as how to open the dialog. The remaining figures demonstrate how to use this tool to correct your document.

TAKE NOTE

CHECKING NON-SPELLING ERRORS

The Word spelling checker checks for more than just spelling errors. If you repeat a word, as in, "This is is fun," the second "is" will be underlined. Also, any errors that AutoCorrect did not fix, such as "mISTAKE" or "COmputer," will be underlined as well.

BE SELECTIVE WHEN ADDING WORDS TO THE DICTIONARY

Once you have added a word to the spell-checking dictionary, Word will no longer flag that word as a spelling error in any other document. Consider using this option for words or names that you use all the time, but don't add too many words to the dictionary. If you do, Word may overlook legitimate spelling errors in another document, because the error just happens to be the same as something you added to the dictionary.

CROSS-REFERENCE
See "Setting AutoCorrect Options" in Chapter 12 to learn how some errors can be fixed automatically.

FIND IT ONLINE
Want to know why you should not rely too heavily on your spell checker? Check out http://www.theslushpile.com/Spell_Checker_Madness.html.

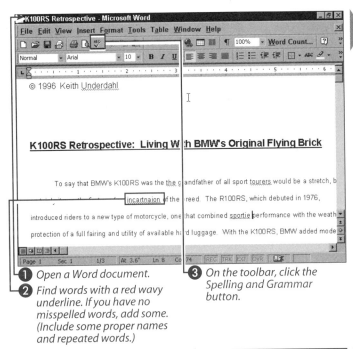

1 Open a Word document.

2 Find words with a red wavy underline. If you have no misspelled words, add some. (Include some proper names and repeated words.)

3 On the toolbar, click the Spelling and Grammar button.

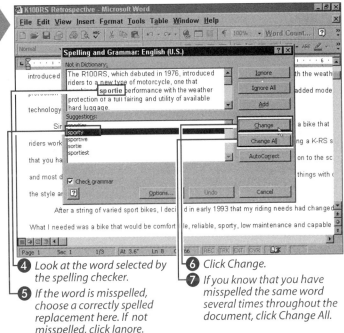

4 Look at the word selected by the spelling checker.

5 If the word is misspelled, choose a correctly spelled replacement here. If not misspelled, click Ignore.

6 Click Change.

7 If you know that you have misspelled the same word several times throughout the document, click Change All.

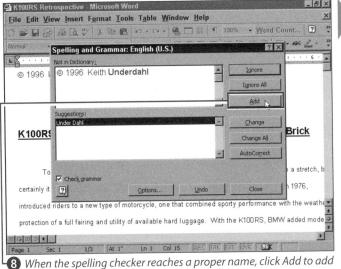

8 When the spelling checker reaches a proper name, click Add to add it to your custom dictionary.

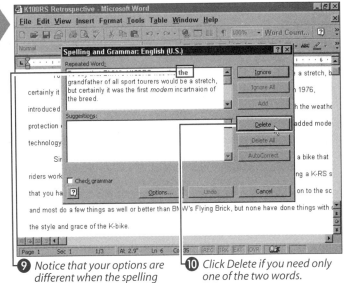

9 Notice that your options are different when the spelling checker finds a repeated word. Ignore All, for example, is disabled.

10 Click Delete if you need only one of the two words.

Customizing the Dictionary

Just because Word puts a wavy red line underneath text doesn't mean the word is spelled incorrectly. Many words, including many personal names, don't appear in any dictionary. Word recognizes common personal names but will put a red underline under many others.

Business names fall in the same category. Many involve combinations of real words or abbreviations, such as MillenniaSoft. If this were the name of your company, you would type it — and get a spelling error — on a regular basis. The same holds true for some industry-specific terms that you might encounter.

Do you want to check the spelling of your own name, or the name of your company, every time you create a document? Probably not. The solution is to add words you use often to Word's spelling dictionary. Once you do so, they will not be highlighted as potential errors in the future. You should use restraint when adding words to the dictionary, however, because too many words can result in legitimate spelling errors being overlooked in the future.

For instance, if you work for a company called, "Colour Brite" and add those words to your dictionary, Word could overlook misspellings of the words "color" and "bright." Adding words from other languages can cause similar problems. If you add the Latin word "accidit" to your dictionary, misspellings of the English "accident" could be missed.

You can open and edit your custom dictionary as a text document whenever you want. You can modify spellings of dictionary words as well as add or delete words. You can also create additional custom dictionaries for different kinds of documents by clicking New in the Custom Dictionaries dialog box. You may want to use an alternative dictionary if a certain type of document requires a lot of custom words. You can continue to use the regular custom dictionary for your other documents.

The Spelling and Grammar tab of the Options dialog box shows you which custom dictionaries are active at a given time. You can select or deselect custom dictionaries from the Custom Dictionaries dialog, or you can disable custom dictionaries altogether. The figures on the facing page show you how to open and edit the custom dictionary.

TAKE NOTE

FORMATTING IN THE DICTIONARY

The custom dictionary is a text file, which means you won't be able to apply character formatting such as italics or boldface to the words. This doesn't matter, however, because the spelling checker ignores formatting when it checks spelling anyway.

DISABLING CUSTOM DICTIONARIES

You might want to disable custom dictionaries for certain kinds of documents that don't have many custom words. Doing so provides a small measure of safety against inadvertent misspellings. To do so, open the Custom Dictionaries dialog box as shown on the facing page, and remove the check mark next to each custom dictionary.

CROSS-REFERENCE
To learn more about using the Options dialog box, see "Setting Key Options" in Chapter 2.

FIND IT ONLINE
Alki Software, at **http://www.alki.com/**, offers foreign-language spelling proofers and more for Microsoft Word.

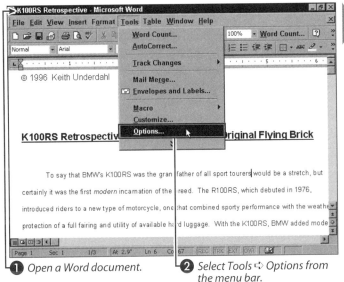

1 Open a Word document.

2 Select Tools ⇨ Options from the menu bar.

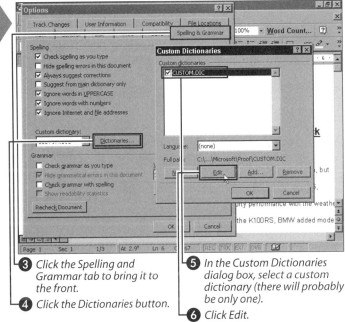

3 Click the Spelling and Grammar tab to bring it to the front.

4 Click the Dictionaries button.

5 In the Custom Dictionaries dialog box, select a custom dictionary (there will probably be only one).

6 Click Edit.

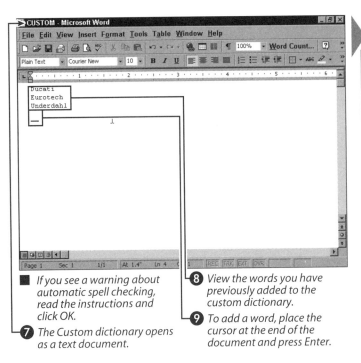

■ If you see a warning about automatic spell checking, read the instructions and click OK.

7 The Custom dictionary opens as a text document.

8 View the words you have previously added to the custom dictionary.

9 To add a word, place the cursor at the end of the document and press Enter.

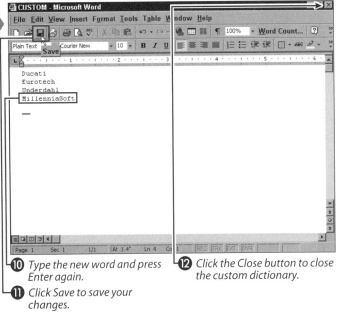

10 Type the new word and press Enter again.

11 Click Save to save your changes.

12 Click the Close button to close the custom dictionary.

Using the Grammar Checker

When you first install Word, certain options are set by default. One of the default setup options in Word is that the spelling checker is automatically enabled. In other words, the first time you start to type something in Word, all misspelled words will have a red wavy line under them.

In addition to the spelling checker, Word has another helpful writing tool that checks your grammar. But unlike spell checking, the grammar checker is turned off by default. This is because people have divergent opinions about the grammar checker. Some users think it greatly improves the quality of their writing by providing useful and timely tips, whereas others feel it just gets in the way of their style.

You should give the feature a try before making up your mind. Once enabled, the grammar checker analyzes your writing and provides feedback when you make errors or when you could improve sentence structure. In earlier versions of Word, the grammar and spelling checkers were separate features, but Word 2000 integrates them more completely. You can still enable the tools separately using the Spelling and Grammar tab of the Options dialog box. If you enable both of them, Word will find spelling and grammar issues in the same pass through the document.

Word's grammar checker looks for a number of different issues. It places a green wavy line under errors such as improper capitalizations, incorrect or missing punctuation, passive sentences, mixed tenses, and other text that breaks the many rules you learned in grade school.

The figures on the facing page show you how to use the grammar checker. The first two figures show you how to enable the grammar checker and set some key options. The remaining figures show you how to put the grammar checker to use.

TAKE NOTE

SETTING YOUR WRITING STYLE

The grammar check feature has five different writing styles you can choose from, depending on the kind of document you are writing. If you plan to use the grammar checker, it is important to set the right style to ensure you receive valuable feedback. If, for instance, you are writing a love letter, the Technical writing style option is probably not the one you want to choose. (Or maybe it is!)

CHANGING GRAMMAR SETTINGS

You can customize the settings of the grammar checker. For instance, suppose you are protesting the arcane system of capitalization used in the English language. You can set the checker so that it does not flag instances in which you have not capitalized the first letter of sentences. To set this and other options, open the Spelling and Grammar tab of the Options dialog box and click the Settings button under Writing Style.

CROSS-REFERENCE
Learn how to avoid repeating yourself by reading "Using the Thesaurus" at the end of this chapter.

FIND IT ONLINE
Visit English Plus+ at **http://englishplus.com/** for online grammar advice and more.

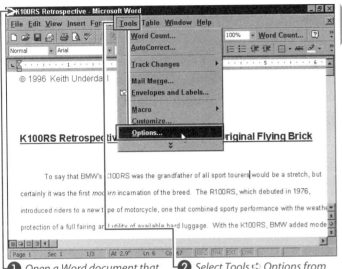

1 Open a Word document that contains several paragraphs of text. Just to be sure the grammar checker has something to find, type in some known errors.

2 Select Tools ⇨ Options from the menu bar.

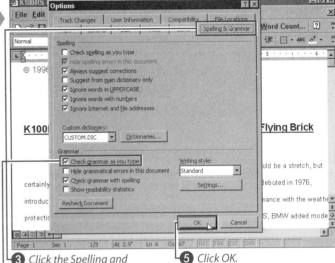

3 Click the Spelling and Grammar tab to bring it to the front.

4 Under Grammar, place a check mark next to "Check grammar as you type."

5 Click OK.

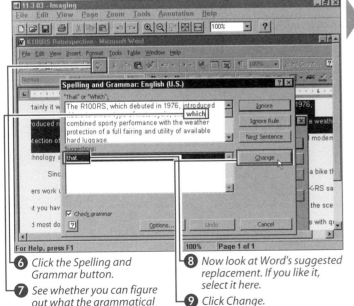

6 Click the Spelling and Grammar button.

7 See whether you can figure out what the grammatical error is before you look at Word's suggestion.

8 Now look at Word's suggested replacement. If you like it, select it here.

9 Click Change.

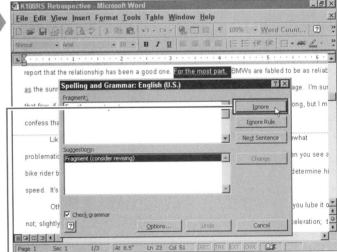

10 Continue through the grammar and spelling check. If you do not like a suggestion, click Ignore. You can also click Ignore Rule to keep the grammar checker from highlighting the same kind of error again.

Turning Off the Spelling and Grammar Checkers

Most of the tasks in this book describe ways to take better advantage of Word's many features and put them to hard use. You bought this program to use, and that includes its most advanced features. Thus, almost all the tasks in *Teach Yourself Microsoft Word 2000* guide you through specific steps to complete a real job.

This is not one of those tasks. You have already learned how to use the spelling and grammar checkers, two of the most powerful features included in this program. But the simple fact is that many users do not like the computer telling them what to fix. This is especially true of the grammar checker, which some people consider to be downright invasive. If you find yourself ignoring the advice of either of these features, you may want to consider turning them off.

Turning off these features is easy, and you can always use them on a temporary basis if you want. You can disable one or both of them using the Options dialog box. Once you have turned them off, you can still run either the spelling or grammar checker by clicking the Spelling and Grammar button on the toolbar. You will not, however, see the wavy red or green lines under words or sentences.

An even quicker way to disable the grammar checker is to uncheck the Check Grammar check box in the Spelling and Grammar dialog box. There is no such check box for the spelling checker, so for this feature you must use the Options dialog.

The figures on the facing page show you how to disable the spelling and grammar checkers and then how to use them manually. The first figure illustrates how to open the Options dialog box to select various options and turn off features. The remaining figures show you how to check spelling and grammar without those features being enabled.

TAKE NOTE

CHECKING YOUR WORK ON THE FLY

You may prefer to compose your documents without turning on the spelling and grammar checkers, but use these features from time to time as necessary. First, turn off both features. Then, as you work, select text you want to check and click the Spelling and Grammar button on the toolbar. If you don't like using the mouse, press F7 on your keyboard. Word checks only the selected text, though you are given the option to check the rest of the document as well.

WORKING WITH INTERNET ADDRESSES

Web page and e-mail addresses are becoming increasingly common in Word documents. One of the options you can select for the spelling checker is to have it ignore such addresses when checking for errors. Word can easily recognize what is and is not an Internet address, making this feature quite useful.

CROSS-REFERENCE

See "Setting Key Options" in Chapter 2 to learn more about using the Options dialog box.

FIND IT ONLINE

It's not quite "Save the Whales," but "Save the Adverb" at **http://www.cs.wisc.edu/~dgarrett/ adverb/ index.html** is a worthy cause. Check it out!

Turning Off the Spelling and Grammar Checkers

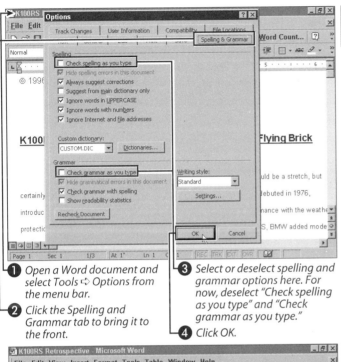

1 Open a Word document and select Tools ⇨ Options from the menu bar.

2 Click the Spelling and Grammar tab to bring it to the front.

3 Select or deselect spelling and grammar options here. For now, deselect "Check spelling as you type" and "Check grammar as you type."

4 Click OK.

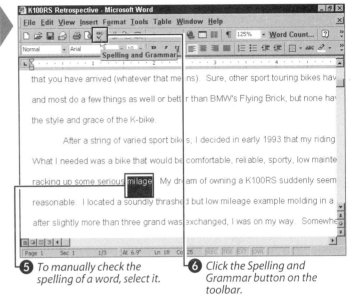

5 To manually check the spelling of a word, select it.

6 Click the Spelling and Grammar button on the toolbar.

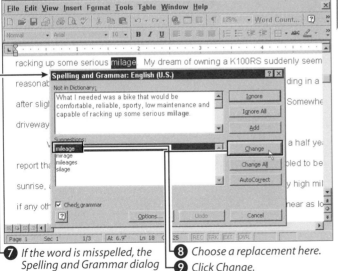

7 If the word is misspelled, the Spelling and Grammar dialog box will open.

8 Choose a replacement here.

9 Click Change.

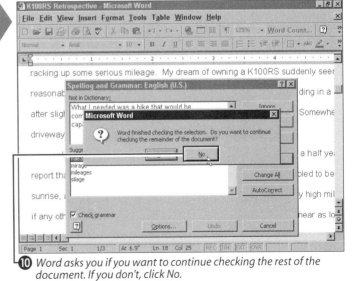

10 Word asks you if you want to continue checking the rest of the document. If you don't, click No.

Using the Thesaurus

A few fortunate people have always been able to use printed words on a page to effectively get their point across. Word has helped to expand that number to a much wider group, thanks to its many excellent editing and writing tools. The final writing tool you need to learn about here is the thesaurus. A thesaurus is basically a cross-reference of synonyms for various words. By using a thesaurus, you can avoid repeating the same words or phrases over and over again in a relatively short document. Word has a built-in thesaurus to make this process even easier.

A common mistake that some writers make is to use suggestions from a thesaurus without really thinking about how the word should be used. You must know what the words shown in the thesaurus really mean; just because a word is synonymous doesn't mean it works in every situation. For instance, in the sentence, "See Jane run," Word's thesaurus offers "perceive" as a synonym for "see." However, "Perceive Jane run" doesn't really mean the same thing as "See Jane run," and sounds weird to boot.

One nice thing that the Word thesaurus can do that a traditional thesaurus cannot is offer synonymous phrases. In addition to highlighting single words, you can highlight a phrase or even an entire sentence and see what Word comes up with. Alternatives may be in the form of slightly modified versions of the phrase, new phrases, or even single words that have the same meaning as the phrase.

Word's thesaurus is very easy to use. The figures on the facing page show you how to select a word and then find a synonym for it with the thesaurus. In the last figure, notice that a phrase has been selected, as opposed to a single word.

TAKE NOTE

▶ WORD THESAURUS COOKIES

Some of the favorite "stupid Word tricks" that Word users have enjoyed for years involve the Word thesaurus. In the past, you could enter a phrase into Word's thesaurus like, "I would like to see you naked," and the thesaurus would respond with, "I'll drink to that." For the most part, these so-called "Word thesaurus cookies" appear to have been eliminated from the Word 2000 thesaurus.

▶ USING LOOKUP

If you are not sure of the meaning of a word in the list of synonyms that Word provides, select it and click Look up. Word will display alternative meanings for that word. Notice also that single-word synonyms are followed by an abbreviation for the part of speech — noun (n.), verb (v.), adjective (adj.), conjunction (cont.), adverb (adv.), and so forth. If you think you might be replacing a word with the wrong kind of alternative, check the sentence with the grammar checker when you're done.

CROSS-REFERENCE

To learn another way to edit, see "Tracking Changes" in Chapter 18.

FIND IT ONLINE

You can also access a fully searchable Merriam-Webster Thesaurus at **http://www.m-w.com/thesaurus.htm**.

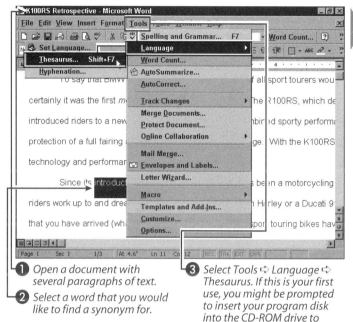

① Open a document with several paragraphs of text.

② Select a word that you would like to find a synonym for.

③ Select Tools ⇨ Language ⇨ Thesaurus. If this is your first use, you might be prompted to insert your program disk into the CD-ROM drive to install the feature.

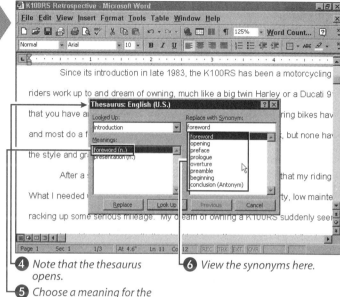

④ Note that the thesaurus opens.

⑤ Choose a meaning for the word here.

⑥ View the synonyms here.

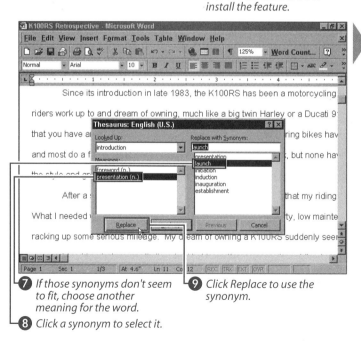

⑦ If those synonyms don't seem to fit, choose another meaning for the word.

⑧ Click a synonym to select it.

⑨ Click Replace to use the synonym.

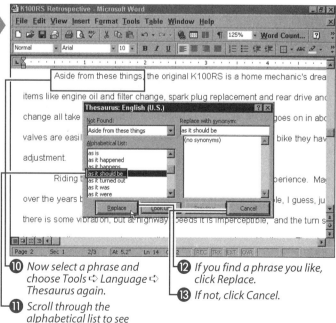

⑩ Now select a phrase and choose Tools ⇨ Language ⇨ Thesaurus again.

⑪ Scroll through the alphabetical list to see suggested phrases.

⑫ If you find a phrase you like, click Replace.

⑬ If not, click Cancel.

Personal Workbook

Q&A

1 How does Word indicate a spelling error?

_____

_____

_____

2 Does this mark always indicate that a word is misspelled?

_____

_____

_____

3 How can you avoid having to always spell check your own name?

_____

_____

_____

4 Can you remove words from your custom dictionary? How?

_____

_____

_____

5 Name three kinds of errors that the grammar checker will identify.

_____

_____

_____

6 How does Word identify grammatical errors in your document?

_____

_____

_____

7 How do you disable the grammar and word checkers?

_____

_____

_____

8 What does the Word thesaurus do?

_____

_____

_____

ANSWERS: PAGE 368

EXTRA PRACTICE

1. Type a document of at least one page in Word. Do not correct any typing errors as you go. Include the name "Underdahl" somewhere in your document.

2. Run the spelling checker and fix any spelling errors that may occur.

3. When you encounter the name "Underdahl" with the spelling checker, add it to your custom dictionary.

4. Check your document for grammatical errors.

5. Open your custom dictionary and remove "Underdahl" from it.

6. Use the thesaurus to find a synonym for the very first word in your document.

REAL-WORLD APPLICATIONS

✔ The grammar checker can be tailored to the type of letter you are writing. To do so, select a different writing style from the Options dialog. Try checking a letter with the Casual style, and then check the same document again using the Technical style.

✔ If your documents use a lot of words from different languages, you should consider disabling the spelling and grammar checker. If you are typing a document exclusively in another language, install support for that language from the Word 2000 CDs.

✔ When writing an article about something like a sporting event, it is hard to make your words match the excitement of that event. The thesaurus can give you other ways to say, "She threw the ball …" and "He ran.…"

Visual Quiz

Is the dialog identifying a spelling or grammar error? Is the word misspelled? Could you tell Word never to call this a spelling error again? How? If it is an error, how would you correct it?

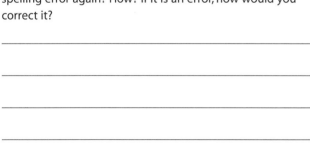

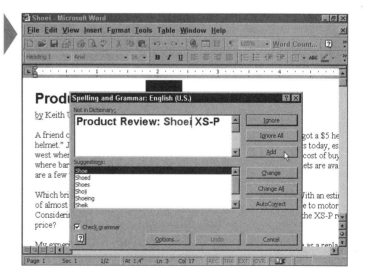

CHAPTER 12

MASTER THESE SKILLS

▶ Setting AutoCorrect Options

▶ Creating AutoCorrect Items

▶ Deleting AutoCorrect Options

▶ Using AutoText

▶ Inserting Dates and Times

▶ Using AutoFormat

Using AutoCorrect and AutoText

When you watch old science fiction movies, it is interesting to see what people predicted for today and the future only a few years ago. One of the most common themes involved automation and the way computers would change our lives. Many of those prophecies have indeed come to pass, as computers have encroached on nearly every aspect of our work and personal lives.

The concept of automation was not lost on the designers of Word 2000, and the program includes many features to make your work more efficient. The best automation features work with little or no user input. One of these is AutoCorrect, an extensive but basically invisible feature that corrects some of your most common mistakes. Most of the errors that AutoCorrect changes are simple typing errors, such as holding down the Shift key too long and capitalizing the first two letters of a word instead of just the first one. It also corrects the error when you forget to capitalize the first word of a sentence, accidentally use the Caps Lock key, or mistype some common words.

AutoCorrect does more than just correct common typing mistakes, however. You can use it to insert special symbols that aren't on the keyboard. You can even create your own AutoCorrect items. This chapter describes how to set some common AutoCorrect options, and how to create or remove your own custom AutoCorrect items.

Another excellent but not as invisible automation feature in Word is AutoText. AutoText simplifies the task of entering common pieces of data such as the date and time, addresses, and other elements you use on a regular basis. AutoText constantly monitors your work and provides automatic text tools based on what you are currently typing.

Finally, Word provides a feature called AutoFormat that automatically formats certain kinds of document elements, such as ordinals, some symbol characters, and bulleted lists. The final task in this chapter describes how to use AutoFormat.

Setting AutoCorrect Options

Word 2000 is nothing if not versatile, and AutoCorrect is among the most versatile features of the program. AutoCorrect covers for you by fixing some simple yet common errors, automating the process of entering certain symbols and special characters and other words or phrases as you specify.

Perhaps most amazing is the fact that AutoCorrect works almost without your even noticing it. AutoCorrect is active behind the scenes, looking for certain key combinations, as you type in a Word document. Every time it recognizes one of these combinations, it replaces it with a correction.

Most AutoCorrect items involve typing errors such as "NOne of them knew the color of the sky." AutoCorrect automatically fixes this and other common mistakes for you. Simple misspellings are also usually the result of typing errors, and AutoCorrect can fix them too. For instance, quick fingers can accidentally type "teh" instead of "the" on a surprisingly regular basis. AutoCorrect fixes this problem so quickly you probably won't even realize you made a mistake. Likewise, AutoCorrect will fix accidental use of incorrect punctuation. This is especially true in contractions such as "I'll" and "shouldn't." The apostrophe and semicolon are next to each other on most keyboards, so errors like "I;ll" and "shouldn;t" are common. AutoCorrect even inserts the apostrophe in such words when you forget to do so.

These AutoCorrect features are helpful in most cases, but at times they can get in your way. If you intentionally type an unusual combination of letters that includes two initial capital letters, for instance, AutoCorrect will still apply its rule and make the change. You need to understand which AutoCorrect options you can change and how to change them. The figures on the facing page show you how to do this.

CROSS-REFERENCE

To learn more about customizing Word, see "Setting Key Options" in Chapter 2.

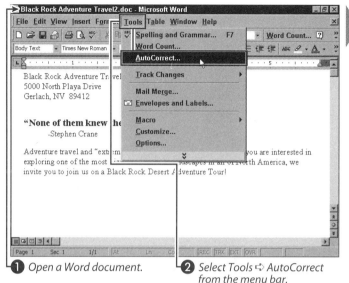

❶ Open a Word document.

❷ Select Tools ⇨ AutoCorrect from the menu bar.

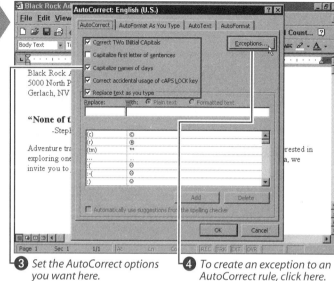

❸ Set the AutoCorrect options you want here.

❹ To create an exception to an AutoCorrect rule, click here.

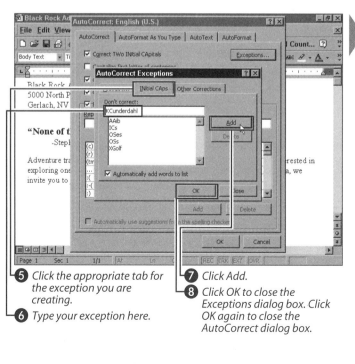

❺ Click the appropriate tab for the exception you are creating.

❻ Type your exception here.

❼ Click Add.

❽ Click OK to close the Exceptions dialog box. Click OK again to close the AutoCorrect dialog box.

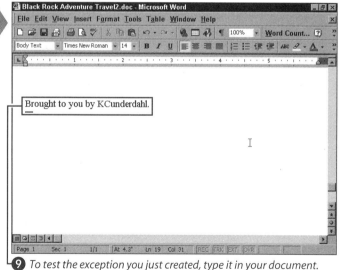

❾ To test the exception you just created, type it in your document. Does AutoCorrect change your spelling?

Creating AutoCorrect Items

By now, you have already seen some of the things that AutoCorrect can do. It can correct common typing mistakes, including some spelling errors, and it can help you enter some special characters into your documents. (Chapter 5 demonstrates the use of AutoCorrect to add some special characters to your documents.)

AutoCorrect comes preset with a large number of items that it will correct. You should take this opportunity to scroll down the list of text combinations that will be replaced with an AutoCorrect item when they are typed. Watch out for any combinations that you may intentionally type from time to time. AutoCorrect may inadvertently replace acronyms that are specific to your company, for example.

One of the best features of AutoCorrect is that you can create your own entries. For instance, suppose you frequently type the full name of your company — Black Rock Adventure Tours, Inc. Typing that entire name will get tiring after many repetitions. You could save yourself a lot of trouble by creating an AutoCorrect entry for your company's name.

One option for this AutoCorrect entry is to use the company's initials as the combination you want the tool to replace with your company's name. In this case, however, the company's initials (BRAT) might cause a minor problem. You might want to use the word "brat" in a sentence without having AutoCorrect insert your company's name. Fortunately, AutoCorrect is case sensitive, so if you use all uppercase letters, as in "BRAT," typing "brat" or even "Brat" won't trigger AutoCorrect.

The figures on the facing page show you how to create and use a new AutoCorrect entry. The first two figures show how to create an AutoCorrect entry, and the last two figures demonstrate how to use this tool.

TAKE NOTE

▶ USING PUNCTUATION IN AUTOCORRECT

You may find it is easier to create an AutoCorrect entry that you will remember if you include punctuation in the entry. For Black Rock Adventure Travels, Inc., for example, you could use (B) as the keystroke combination. It is unlikely that you would ever enclose a capital letter B in parentheses, so any changes AutoCorrect makes for this entry are likely to be appropriate.

▶ CREATE AUTOCORRECT ENTRIES FOR YOUR OWN MISSPELLINGS

AutoCorrect contains many entries that cover common misspellings resulting from hitting the wrong key on the keyboard. These entries are useful, but cannot possibly correct every typist's mistakes. If you consistently find yourself misspelling the same word, consider creating an AutoCorrect entry for it. You can also create an AutoCorrect entry during a spelling check by selecting the correct spelling from the suggestions list and clicking the AutoCorrect button in the Spelling and Grammar dialog box.

CROSS-REFERENCE

See "Using the Spelling Checker" in Chapter 11 to learn more about correcting spelling errors.

FIND IT ONLINE

Have a question about Word? Visit Help Talk Online at **http://helptalk.com/msword/**.

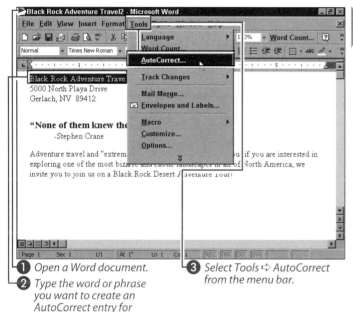

1 Open a Word document.

2 Type the word or phrase you want to create an AutoCorrect entry for and select it.

3 Select Tools ⇨ AutoCorrect from the menu bar.

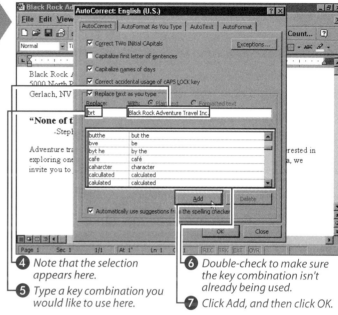

4 Note that the selection appears here.

5 Type a key combination you would like to use here.

6 Double-check to make sure the key combination isn't already being used.

7 Click Add, and then click OK.

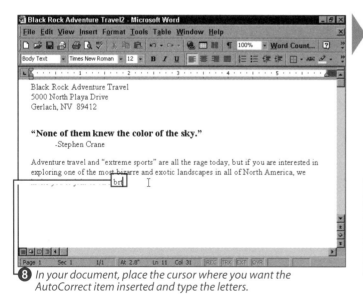

8 In your document, place the cursor where you want the AutoCorrect item inserted and type the letters.

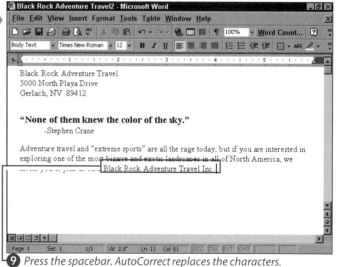

9 Press the spacebar. AutoCorrect replaces the characters.

Deleting AutoCorrect Items

Just as surely as automation can make lives and work easier, it can also get in the way. AutoCorrect is not immune to this limitation. You may find yourself getting frustrated when Word automatically corrects something you didn't want corrected in the first place. What's worse, if you're not paying attention, this mistake could slip through into your final document.

If this is happening to you, you should consider removing the offending AutoCorrect entry or entries. You can delete any entry, even the ones that were put there by Microsoft. Taking this step may be especially important for symbols and special punctuation. Having special symbols automatically inserted into a document can cause problems if your document will later be saved in HTML or text format.

For these special symbols, you should also check the AutoFormat feature discussed later in this chapter. A good example of such a symbol is an em dash (—), which is inserted whenever you type two hyphens (--). Why an ellipsis is replaced by AutoCorrect and an em dash is handled by AutoFormat is anyone's guess.

Before you begin disabling AutoCorrect features, you should realize that you can often undo an AutoCorrect correction by pressing the Backspace key immediately after AutoCorrect makes a replacement. In the case of symbols, this step should undo the AutoCorrect correction without deleting any of the characters you typed. But again, if you have to repeat this step on a very regular basis, it might just be easier to remove the AutoCorrect entry.

The first figure on the facing page shows you how review and delete items from AutoCorrect. In the second figure, you will see how to disable AutoCorrect temporarily, and then how to enable it again. The last two figures show you how to undo an AutoCorrected item after you have typed it.

TAKE NOTE

DISABLING THE REPLACE TEXT FEATURE

You may find that you need to delete a large number of AutoCorrect "Replace text" items just because they are incompatible with one kind of document you work with. But if you delete the entries, they will not be available to other documents that can use them. If this is the case, consider disabling the "Replace text" feature temporarily by removing the check mark next to "Replace text as you type" in the AutoCorrect dialog box.

USING WORD TO COMPOSE E-MAIL MESSAGES

E-mail messages are traditionally text-only documents. If you send a message with a lot of special symbols that text-only e-mail programs can't identify, they will choke on your message. You can use Word to compose and edit e-mails in conjunction with Microsoft Outlook; but to ensure that the greatest number of people can read your messages, you should disable most AutoCorrect features.

CROSS-REFERENCE

See "Using AutoFormat" later in this chapter to learn about a similar feature.

FIND IT ONLINE

Visit another great online discussion forum for Word users at **http://www.zdjournals.com/m_mw9/**.

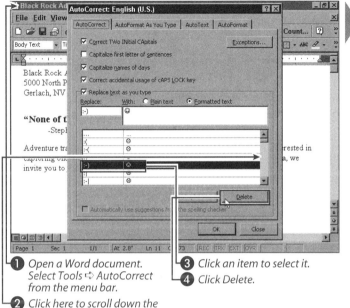

1 Open a Word document. Select Tools ⇨ AutoCorrect from the menu bar.

2 Click here to scroll down the list of text replacement items.

3 Click an item to select it.

4 Click Delete.

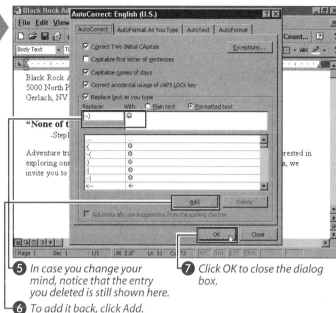

5 In case you change your mind, notice that the entry you deleted is still shown here.

6 To add it back, click Add.

7 Click OK to close the dialog box.

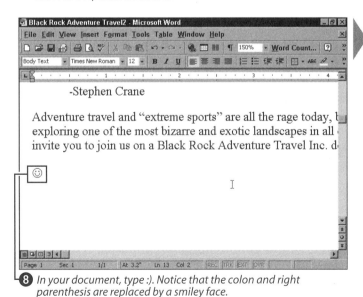

8 In your document, type :). Notice that the colon and right parenthesis are replaced by a smiley face.

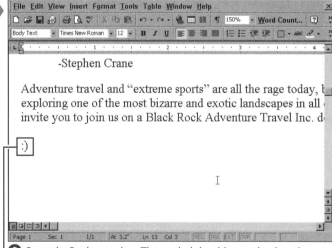

9 Press the Backspace key. The symbol should revert back to the colon and parenthesis.

Using AutoText and AutoComplete

AutoCorrect is an extremely useful tool for accomplishing many tasks, but it does have some limitations. Word offers yet another automation feature called AutoText to help handle those limitations. AutoText differs from AutoCorrect in that its entries tend to be tailored to you personally, or to your current job. They are less general in nature, although they still cover commonly used pieces of data like your address, name, and more.

As you work, Word analyzes the documents you create and remembers certain elements. For instance, when you type a letter, you probably include a salutation near the beginning of it that goes something like, "Dear Mr. Smith...." Word remembers that salutation and places it on a menu. You can retrieve the phrase when you need it again.

You can access AutoText entries from the Insert menu. The AutoText submenu contains various AutoText entries that are categorized into smaller submenus to make them easier to find.

Another way to use AutoText requires a less proactive stance on your part. As you type, Word is constantly looking for familiar words and phrases. If you start to type your name, for instance, Word should recognize this fact after the first few characters. If it does, you may see a help bubble appear just above the cursor position that contains an AutoText entry. If you continue typing as if it weren't there, it will go away. But if the help bubble contains the name or phrase you are typing, you can press the Tab or Enter key to have AutoText automatically fill in the rest of the name or phrase. This feature is actually called AutoComplete, but it uses AutoText entries.

The figures on the facing page show you how to use AutoText. The first two show you how to manually add an item to AutoText, and the third figure shows you how to use the AutoText submenu to insert that item. The last figure shows you how to add the item using the AutoComplete tip bubble.

TAKE NOTE

► TURNING OFF THE AUTOCOMPLETE TIPS

Many Word users never take advantage of AutoText or AutoComplete tips, yet they remain quite content. If you don't like the little AutoComplete tip bubbles showing up from time to time while you type, you can disable them by deselecting the "Show AutoComplete Tip" option in the AutoText dialog box.

► USING THE AUTOTEXT TOOLBAR

Word has a toolbar exclusively devoted to AutoText, but it is typically not displayed. You can open the AutoText toolbar as described in "Using Toolbars" in Chapter 1, or click the Show Toolbar button in the AutoText dialog box. This toolbar contains the submenu structure of the AutoText menu under Insert, as well as a button you can use to manually add words and phrases to AutoText.

CROSS-REFERENCE
Learn how to select text as shown on the facing page in "Selecting Text" in Chapter 5.

FIND IT ONLINE
The Microsoft Word: Consultant's Tutorial is a great reference that can be found at: **http://is.rice.edu/~consult/cross/word/**.

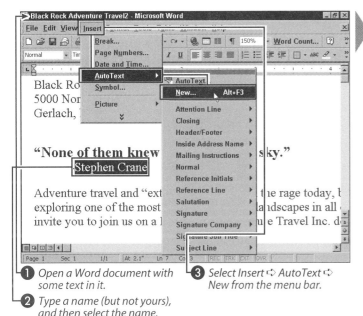

1 Open a Word document with some text in it.

2 Type a name (but not yours), and then select the name.

3 Select Insert ➪ AutoText ➪ New from the menu bar.

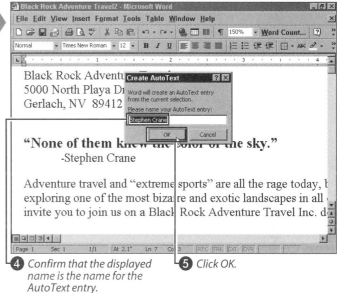

4 Confirm that the displayed name is the name for the AutoText entry.

5 Click OK.

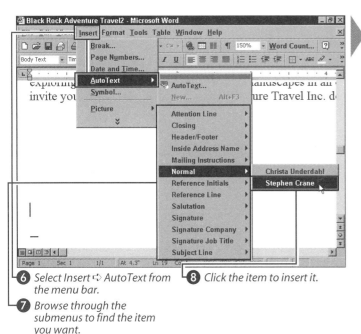

6 Select Insert ➪ AutoText from the menu bar.

7 Browse through the submenus to find the item you want.

8 Click the item to insert it.

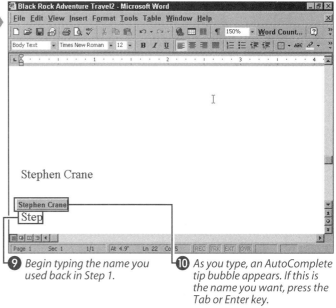

9 Begin typing the name you used back in Step 1.

10 As you type, an AutoComplete tip bubble appears. If this is the name you want, press the Tab or Enter key.

Inserting Dates and Times

So far in this chapter, you have learned how to use some common Word automation tools to help make your work more efficient and accurate. Features such as AutoCorrect, AutoText, and AutoComplete help you enter common pieces of information and fix typical typing errors. Word can also help you quickly enter the current date and time into your documents.

When entering the current date or time, Word takes the information directly from the computer's internal clock and calendar, making the process just that much easier. You can also choose to have the date or time updated automatically whenever you open the document to ensure it always displays the most current data. If you choose this option, the date (or time) will appear in a gray block on your computer screen. Not to worry — it will look normal once printed on paper. To manually update the entry (without closing and reopening the document) just right-click it and choose Update Field from the shortcut menu. This information will also be updated automatically whenever you reopen or print the document and the Update automatically option is selected in the Date and Time dialog box.

You can enter the current date or time using a couple of different methods. The simplest way to enter the date is to start typing it manually. After a few characters, an AutoComplete tip bubble appears. If the tip matches the date format you want, just press Tab (or Enter) to enter the rest of it.

You can also take the approach of opening the Date and Time dialog box from the Insert menu. You must select this method if you want to also enter the current time, or if you want to be able to automatically update the date and time in the document.

The figures on the facing page show you how to enter the date and time into a document. The first figure shows how to enter the date using an AutoComplete tip, and the remaining figures show you how to insert and update the current time using the Date and Time dialog box.

TAKE NOTE

INSERTING THE CORRECT TIME AND DATE

Word relies on the clock and calendar in your computer, so make sure it is accurate if you want to automate this process. Widely distributing a memo dated January 1, 1980, will get you noticed around the office, but not necessarily in a good way.

USING PROPER DATE AND TIME FORMATS

Word recognizes a variety of date and time formats. Which date format you use will probably depend on the country you are in and who will be reading the document. The time can also be varied between a 12- or 24-hour (sometimes called *military style*) clock. Browse the Available formats list in the Date and Time dialog box to find the one that suits you.

CROSS-REFERENCE

See the previous task, "Using AutoText and AutoComplete," to learn more about using AutoComplete.

FIND IT ONLINE

Learn all about date troubles from The Year 2000 Information Center at **http://www.year2000.com/**.

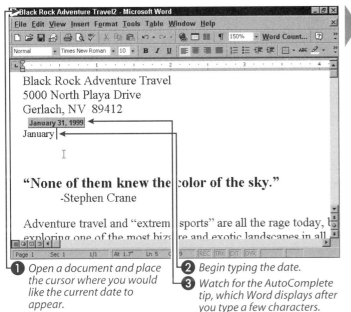

1 Open a document and place the cursor where you would like the current date to appear.

2 Begin typing the date.

3 Watch for the AutoComplete tip, which Word displays after you type a few characters.

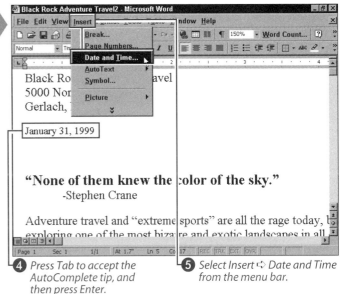

4 Press Tab to accept the AutoComplete tip, and then press Enter.

5 Select Insert ➪ Date and Time from the menu bar.

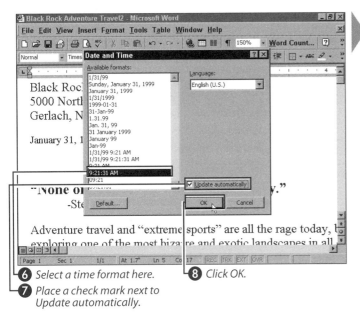

6 Select a time format here.

7 Place a check mark next to Update automatically.

8 Click OK.

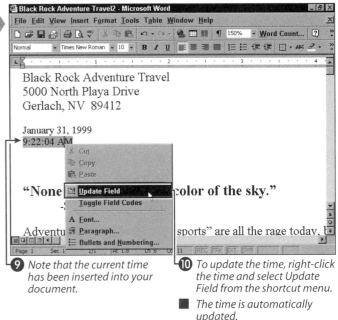

9 Note that the current time has been inserted into your document.

10 To update the time, right-click the time and select Update Field from the shortcut menu.

■ The time is automatically updated.

Using AutoFormat

One more automation feature yet remains in Word that you should learn about. That feature is AutoFormat, which automatically formats certain text and paragraph styles as you type. In general, document elements that are modified by AutoFormat serve to give your document a slicker look. They don't necessarily change the content, as AutoCorrect and AutoText do, but they make existing content look better.

Perhaps one of the most popular ways in which people use AutoFormat is to automatically create and format bulleted and numbered lists. These lists are discussed in greater detail in Chapter 18, but they nevertheless represent one of the most advanced uses of this feature. AutoFormat can also automatically format headings and tables in your document.

Other AutoFormat features stick primarily to character formatting. One of these controls the use of smart quotes. When you type a quotation mark in a text document, Word puts two tiny straight scratch marks where the quotes go. If you have the smart quotes feature turned on, Word converts these straight quotes to nicely curved smart quotes.

AutoFormat also formats ordinals in your document. If you type "1st", for example, Word displays "1st". Notice that the "st" in the ordinal is superscripted. Fractions receive a similar treatment with AutoFormat; 1/2 is displayed as ½.

Setting AutoFormat options is an important part of optimizing Word 2000 to work for you. As with some AutoCorrect items, most AutoFormatting will not work if you plan to convert your document to a text file later on. The first figure on the facing page shows how to set AutoFormat options, and the remaining figures show how to put some of those options to use.

CROSS-REFERENCE

To learn more about character formatting, see "Using Special Character Formatting" in Chapter 7.

FIND IT ONLINE

Get some great AutoFormat tips from Tech Talk at http://www.visser.com/TechTalk.htm.

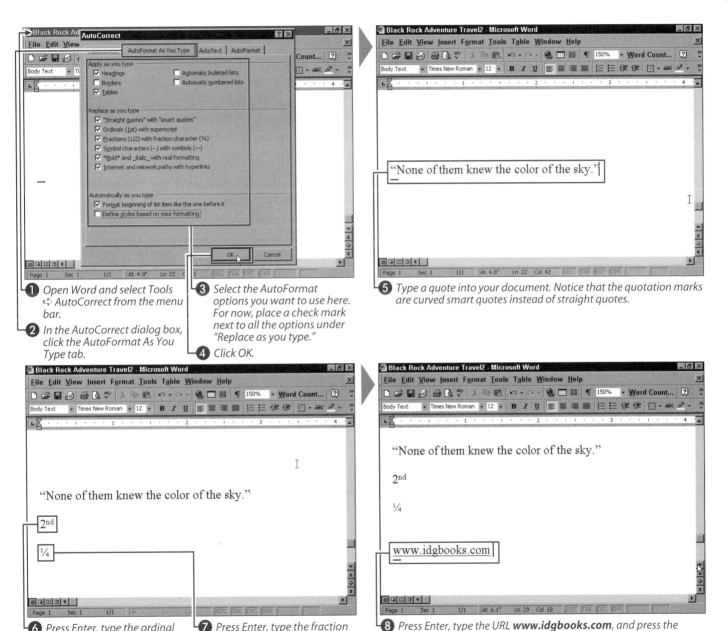

① Open Word and select Tools ⇨ AutoCorrect from the menu bar.

② In the AutoCorrect dialog box, click the AutoFormat As You Type tab.

③ Select the AutoFormat options you want to use here. For now, place a check mark next to all the options under "Replace as you type."

④ Click OK.

⑤ Type a quote into your document. Notice that the quotation marks are curved smart quotes instead of straight quotes.

⑥ Press Enter, type the ordinal **2nd**, and press the spacebar. The "nd" will be superscripted.

⑦ Press Enter, type the fraction **1/4**, and press the spacebar. The characters will be reformatted.

⑧ Press Enter, type the URL **www.idgbooks.com**, and press the spacebar. The URL is automatically formatted as a hyperlink.

Personal Workbook

Q&A

1 If you accidentally type "teh" instead of "the", what do you have to do to correct the error?

_____

_____

_____

2 What is the quickest way to enter a copyright symbol (©) into your document?

_____

_____

_____

3 Can you create a shortcut to enter a long company name? How?

_____

_____

_____

4 How do you delete AutoCorrect entries?

_____

_____

_____

5 What is one way to access AutoText entries?

_____

_____

_____

6 How do you enter text from an AutoComplete tip into your document?

_____

_____

7 If you insert the current date into your document, can it be updated automatically? How?

_____

_____

_____

8 Web site URLs are automatically formatted as hyperlinks. How can you disable this feature?

_____

_____

_____

_____

ANSWERS: PAGE 368

EXTRA PRACTICE

1 In a new Word document, type the story title *The Open Boat*.

2 Create an AutoCorrect entry for the title using "tob" as the shortcut.

3 Use the shortcut to enter the title into your document again.

4 Delete the AutoCorrect entry.

5 Use AutoText to enter your name into the document.

6 Insert the current date and time into your document. Wait a few minutes, and update the time.

REAL-WORLD APPLICATIONS

✔ If you are writing instructions to help someone view your Web page with Netscape Navigator, you will probably have to type the name of that program frequently. To save yourself some time, create an AutoCorrect entry for Netscape Navigator. Use "nn" as the entry for the full program name.

✔ You probably type various memos on an almost-daily basis. These memos often contain the same kinds of information, much of which can be entered quickly by using AutoText. You might even want to display the AutoText toolbar to make the process that much quicker.

✔ If you are working with text-only files, you should disable most or all of the AutoFormat options. None of them work in text files, and some (like the em dash) could actually cause problems later on.

Visual Quiz

Is there a quick way to enter the company name at the top of this document? How can the special formatting used in the fraction and ordinal in the address be applied quickly? What is the quickest way to enter the date shown here? Can it be updated automatically? What about the time? What kind of quotation marks are used around the quote?

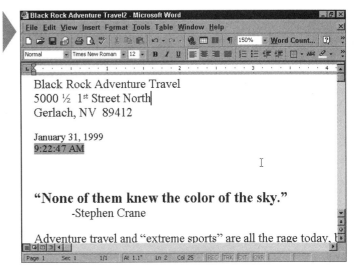

_____

_____

_____

CHAPTER **13**

MASTER
THESE
SKILLS

▶ **Using Find**

▶ **Replacing Text**

▶ **Using Wildcards**

▶ **Using Find and Replace to Change Formatting**

Using Find and Replace

Different people use Word for different tasks. Many users never create anything more complicated than single-page memos, whereas others use the program to compose advanced, multimedia-rich documents. You can even write an entire book using Word, which, depending on the length, could be a very long file. Just keep in mind that very large files can become unmanageable and can cause even a very powerful computer to crash. If possible, break up documents into chunks that are no bigger than about 100 pages each.

Word is a popular tool for creating large documents. In fact, *Teach Yourself Microsoft Word 2000* was written using the program. However, working with chapter-sized files can present some unique and interesting problems for the user. For instance, suppose you have just written a thesis on the life and work of Stephen Crane, author of *The Red Badge of Courage* and other stories. However, on review, you find throughout the document you spelled his name "Steven" instead of "Stephen." What do you do now?

No professor will give you a passing grade on a paper in which the name of the subject is repeatedly misspelled. Now you are faced with having to scroll through the document, finding every instance of the name "Steven," and manually changing it to "Stephen." This process could take a while, and there's a good chance you will blink and miss an occurrence of the misspelling.

But wait! Word simplifies this process with a feature called Find and Replace. This feature can search your document for every occurrence of a word and give you the opportunity to replace that word with something else. Although this feature is reliable and incredibly efficient, many people never take advantage of its possibilities.

You can use Find and Replace for more than just replacing words in your document. Word lets you use "wildcards" to broaden your searches. You can, for instance, look for any character that uses the Verdana font, or for every character that is italicized. You can even change the formatting of text and paragraphs using this feature, or insert different kinds of breaks. Once mastered, Find and Replace could become your best friend in Word.

Using Find

When you type a short memo, it's pretty easy to proofread it once or even several times before you print it and send it along. If you use Word to create more than single-page memos, however, the process of reviewing and editing is much more challenging. To enhance your editing capabilities, Word offers a truly versatile feature called *Find*. Find lets you search a document for every occurrence of a character, word, number, phrase, graphic, break, or any number of other elements used in Word documents.

For instance, suppose you are writing a long paper that discusses the Big Bang Theory. After writing the article, you learn some new information about Edwin Hubble that you want to add to the paper, but you can't remember exactly where you covered this scientist in your article. The solution is simple: Use Find to locate the word "Hubble" in your document. You can use this feature to find every occurrence of that name, if you want. The word you are searching for — "Hubble" in this case — is called the *search string*.

The Find tool can also be useful if you are using Word to read a large technical document. Sometimes software or hardware you buy comes with all of its documentation in electronic files. These are often text files, which means you can use Word as a reader.

In this case, you can use the Find tool to search the document for coverage of a particular topic. For example, if you are reading the electronic documentation for a new modem and want to set up the modem for sending and receiving faxes, use Find to locate every occurrence of the word "fax" in the document. Used in this manner, Find can be a real time-saver.

The figures on the facing page show you how to use Find to locate a specific word in a document. You begin by learning how to launch Find and set a couple of important options. Once you have used Find to locate the word, you continue to use it to find other occurrences of the word.

TAKE NOTE

▶ LEAVE FIND OPEN AS YOU WORK

Unlike most other dialog boxes, Find lets you work in the document without closing the dialog box. Keeping the dialog box in sight is useful if you are using Find to locate and correct small errors that exist throughout the document. You don't have to keep opening and closing the same dialog box.

▶ SETTING KEY OPTIONS

In Find, click More in the dialog box to see available options. If you select Match Case, for example, Find will only locate words that use the case you entered in the Find What field. For instance, if you select Match Case and look for "hubble", Find will overlook occurrences of "Hubble".

CROSS-REFERENCE

See "Moving Around in Your Documents" in Chapter 1 to learn more about moving around in a large file.

FIND IT ONLINE

Learn more about using Find and Replace at http://duff-5.ucs.ualberta.ca/HELP/wordpro/wordint4.html#.

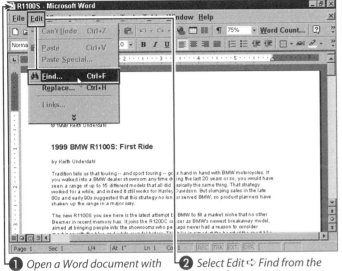

1 *Open a Word document with several pages of text.*

2 *Select Edit ⇨ Find from the menu bar.*

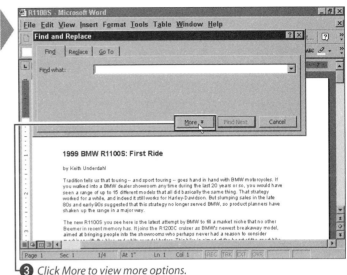

3 *Click More to view more options.*

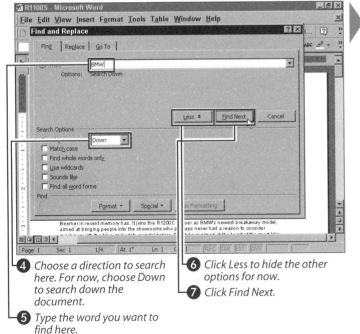

4 *Choose a direction to search here. For now, choose Down to search down the document.*

5 *Type the word you want to find here.*

6 *Click Less to hide the other options for now.*

7 *Click Find Next.*

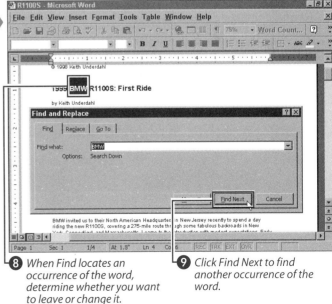

8 *When Find locates an occurrence of the word, determine whether you want to leave or change it.*

9 *Click Find Next to find another occurrence of the word.*

Replacing Text

Find is an excellent tool, but by itself is somewhat limited. You can use it to search a document for words and phrases, but you still have to make changes manually after you find what you are looking for. Find truly shines when you are using Word as a document reader and need to locate a particular topic. For editing documents, however, much more powerful tools are at your disposal.

One of those tools is *Replace*, which is actually an offshoot of Find. Replace—also called *Find and Replace*—searches your document for an occurrence of a word or phrase and replaces it with something else. This capability is extremely useful when you are editing large documents, especially if you learn that you have made a mistake many times throughout the file. To illustrate, imagine that you have just finished writing an article about the aircraft carrier USS Lincoln only to find out the proper name of that ship is USS Abraham Lincoln. Depending on how long the article is, you could spend a lot of time going through and adding "Abraham" to every occurrence of the ship's name.

You don't need to waste your time in this way. Using Find and Replace, you can tell Word to locate every occurrence of "USS Lincoln" and change it to "USS Abraham Lincoln". With the click of a mouse, you can fix every incorrect ship name in the document, whether there be 3 or 3,000 occurrences.

The figures on the facing page show you how to find and replace pieces of text in your document. Notice the use of Replace and Replace All. Replace replaces only the first occurrence of your search string. If you want to continue to the next occurrence in the document, you must click Replace again. If you are already sure that you want to replace every occurrence of the search string in the document, click Replace All. Selecting this button could save you a lot of mouse clicks in a long document, but it can also make a lot of unwanted changes if you are not careful. If there is any doubt, just use Replace.

TAKE NOTE

▶ WATCH OUT FOR UNWANTED KEYSTROKES

Find and Replace look for and replace exact matches of what you type into the dialog box, including blank spaces. If you accidentally press the spacebar after typing something into the "Replace with" field, an extra space will be inserted after each occurrence in your document.

▶ USING THE WHOLE WORD OPTION

If you are finding and replacing a single word, it's a good idea to select the Whole Word option in the dialog box. Otherwise, you may make replacements you aren't intending. For instance, if you are replacing "brat" with "munchkin", a word such as "bratwurst" could be inadvertently changed to "munchkinwurst" unless you replaced only whole words.

CROSS-REFERENCE
Wildcards add even more power to Find and Replace. See the next task, "Using Wildcards," to learn more.

FIND IT ONLINE
Learn more about correcting text at **http://cac.psu.edu/ets/projects/modules/Word/winword97/ww4-1-5.htm#correcting**.

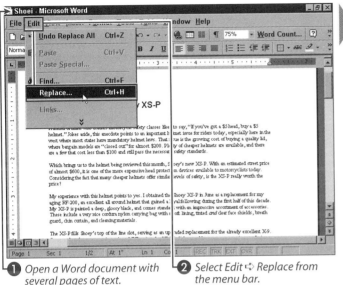

1 Open a Word document with several pages of text.

2 Select Edit ➪ Replace from the menu bar.

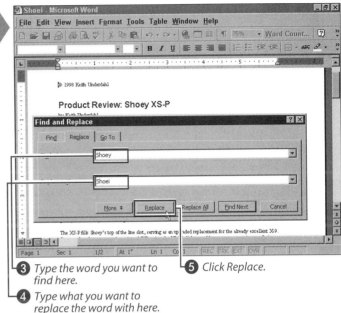

3 Type the word you want to find here.

4 Type what you want to replace the word with here.

5 Click Replace.

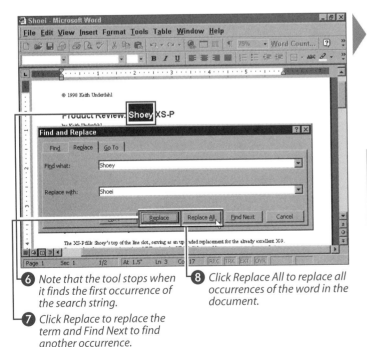

6 Note that the tool stops when it finds the first occurrence of the search string.

7 Click Replace to replace the term and Find Next to find another occurrence.

8 Click Replace All to replace all occurrences of the word in the document.

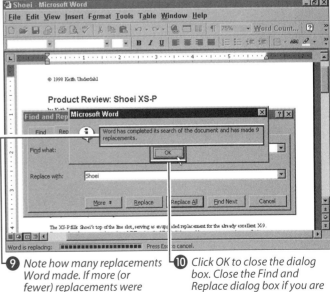

9 Note how many replacements Word made. If more (or fewer) replacements were made than expected, check the search string.

10 Click OK to close the dialog box. Close the Find and Replace dialog box if you are done.

Using Wildcards

The next step in maximizing Find and Replace is to master the use of *wildcards*. A wildcard is a special character that you can use in Find and Replace search strings to make the searches more flexible. A wildcard in this tool is similar to a wildcard in a card game; it can represent almost anything you want.

Word provides a wide selection of wildcards. Whenever you use a wildcard in a search string, it must always be preceded by the caret (^) character. The caret acts as a flag that tells Word that the next character in the search string is a wildcard. For instance, if you want to search for any character, you would enter the wildcard ^?. If you just enter ?, Word will look for question marks in the document.

Other common wildcards represent any digit (^#), or any letter (^$). These differ from any character because ^? can represent a numeric digit, letter, or even punctuation. As you experiment with wildcards, remember that a single wildcard can represent only a single character. If you are looking for a two-digit number (like 42), you must enter ^#^#.

You can use the wildcards I've described so far only in the "Find what" field of the Find and Replace dialog box. You can also use certain wildcards in the "Replace with" field. One of these is the "Find what text," or result, wildcard (^&). This places the result of the search string used in the "Find what" field into the replace string. See the note on using this wildcard below.

The figures on the facing page show how to use wildcards in a Find and Replace action. Notice that the wildcards can be used by themselves, or in conjunction with normal characters and text.

Continued

TAKE NOTE

SEARCHING UP, DOWN, AND AROUND

Find and Replace lets you choose whether you want to search up, down, or the entire document. If you choose down, the search will begin at the cursor and move down to the end of the document. Once the tool reaches the end, you will be prompted to continue searching from the beginning. Searching up works the same way, but in the opposite direction. If you choose All, the tool will search the entire document, regardless of the cursor's location. You can also use Find and Replace in just a small section by selecting the section before launching the dialog box.

USING THE "FIND WHAT TEXT" WILDCARD

The "Find what text" wildcard provides many interesting possibilities. For instance, suppose you want to enclose all two-digit numbers in parentheses. In the "Find what" field, search for ^#^#. In the "Replace with" field, type (^&). This places the result of the find in parentheses and replaces the original text.

CROSS-REFERENCE
To learn to copy items in the "Find what" field, see "Moving and Copying Text and Objects" in Chapter 10.

FIND IT ONLINE
Shareware.com at **http://www.shareware.com/** has dozens of plug-ins and other useful software for Word users.

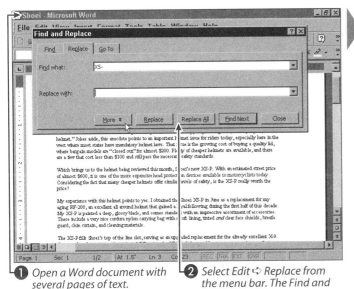

❶ Open a Word document with several pages of text.

❷ Select Edit ➪ Replace from the menu bar. The Find and Replace dialog box appears.

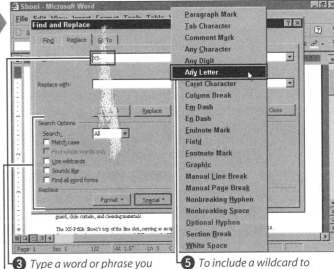

❸ Type a word or phrase you want to search for here.

❹ Click More to view more search options.

❺ To include a wildcard to search for any letter, click Special ➪ Any letter.

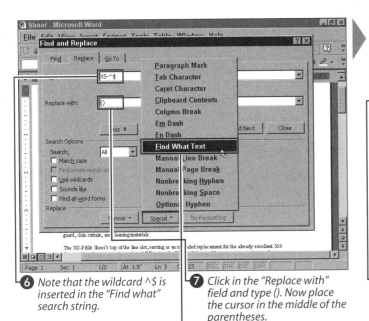

❻ Note that the wildcard ^$ is inserted in the "Find what" search string.

❼ Click in the "Replace with" field and type (). Now place the cursor in the middle of the parentheses.

❽ Click Special ➪ Find What Text.

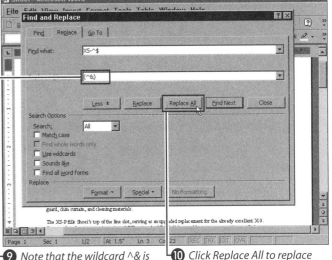

❾ Note that the wildcard ^& is inserted into the "Replace with" field. This will place the results of your search in parentheses.

❿ Click Replace All to replace all occurrences of the search string. Click Close when done.

223

Using Wildcards

Continued

On the previous two pages, you learned how to use wildcards to refer to text and numbers in your documents. As you know, these are not the only kinds of document elements that you must work with. In addition to actual characters, you also deal with breaks of various kinds in your documents.

Word lets you refer to breaks when you are using Find and Replace through the use of special wildcards. Wildcards are available for everything from simple line breaks (^l) and paragraph breaks (^p) to manual page breaks (^m) and column breaks (^n). Unlike other kinds of wildcards, these can be used in both the "Find what" and "Replace with" fields. Many different wildcards are available, and you can review them in the Special drop-down list.

Two of the most common reasons for using break wildcards are to remove unwanted breaks or add new ones. For instance, if you have written a memo and suddenly decide you want to have an extra space between every paragraph, just replace each paragraph mark (^p) with two (^p^p).

Likewise, you can use this technique in reverse to change two paragraph breaks (^p^p) into one (^p). You can even eliminate breaks altogether. Suppose you have just copied the text from an e-mail message into a Word document. In this case, the lines of the e-mail message will probably be separated by line breaks (^l). This causes some layout problems with your Word document, so the breaks need to be deleted. Rather than go through and manually delete

each and every line break, just put ^l in the "Find what" field, and leave the "Replace with" field blank. The tool will then delete all the unwanted line breaks from your text document.

The figures on the facing page show you how to take advantage of the special break wildcards that Find and Replace has to offer. You will begin by adding a second paragraph mark. Then you will use Find and Replace to delete those extra paragraph marks without having to scroll through the document.

TAKE NOTE

WORKING WITH TAB MARKS

To add a tab at the beginning of each paragraph, replace one paragraph mark (^p) with a paragraph mark and a tab character (^p^t). Paragraph marks come at the end of a paragraph, which means that anything that appears after the paragraph mark is actually at the beginning of the next paragraph.

WORKING WITH GRAPHICS

Find and Replace has a wildcard for working with graphics (^g). Although the applications of this wildcard are somewhat limited, you could use the wildcard to delete all graphics in a document, or you could replace each graphic with a placeholder, such as "INSERT GRAPHIC HERE," that would be used later.

CROSS-REFERENCE

See "Inserting Breaks" in Chapter 5 to learn more about working with different kinds of breaks.

FIND IT ONLINE

Still more great shareware titles for Word are available at the ZDNet Software Library at **http://www.hotfiles. com/**.

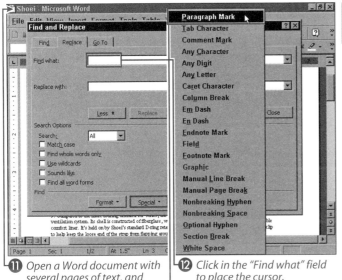

⓫ *Open a Word document with several pages of text, and select Edit ➭ Replace from the menu bar.*

⓬ *Click in the "Find what" field to place the cursor.*

⓭ *Click Special ➭ Paragraph Mark.*

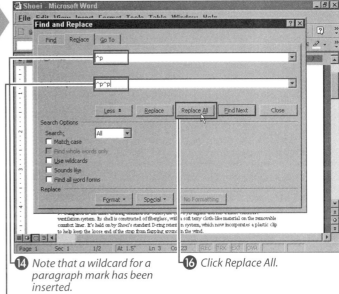

⓮ *Note that a wildcard for a paragraph mark has been inserted.*

⓯ *Type the same wildcard twice in the "Replace with" field.*

⓰ *Click Replace All.*

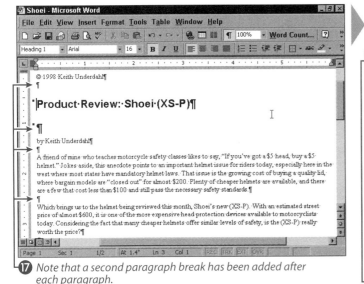

⓱ *Note that a second paragraph break has been added after each paragraph.*

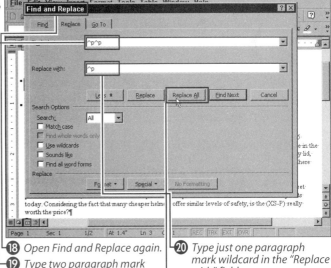

⓲ *Open Find and Replace again.*

⓳ *Type two paragraph mark wildcards in the "Find what" field.*

⓴ *Type just one paragraph mark wildcard in the "Replace with" field.*

㉑ *Click Replace All. The extra paragraph marks you added earlier are removed.*

Using Find and Replace to Change Formatting

Find and Replace is a powerful feature because it lets you perform simultaneous editing throughout a document. And as you learned in the previous task, wildcards make it that much more powerful by adding variables to your searches. So far, you have used Find and Replace to modify text throughout your document, but that is not all you can do.

You can also use Find and Replace to modify formatting, including both character and paragraph formatting. You can choose specific formatting in both the "Find what" and "Replace with" fields. This capability opens up a wide range of possibilities for you to manipulate your documents. You can search for every instance of a boldfaced term, for example, and change the term's formatting to italics. Or you could change every instance of Times New Roman font to Arial.

Formatting has many uses in Find and Replace. To continue with the list of possibilities, suppose you want to get rid of all italicized text in your document. You could have Find and Replace look for any character that is italicized, and replace it with the same nonitalicized text. You can also modify paragraph formatting or apply a new style to a paragraph. You can make centered paragraphs indented, left aligned paragraphs justified, and more. You will probably have to rely heavily on wildcards when you perform many of these formatting tasks.

The figures on the facing page show you how to change some character formatting in a document using Find and Replace. Although this only demonstrates font formatting, you can use this same technique to apply paragraph formatting, styles, and more.

Continued

TAKE NOTE

▶ USING HIGHLIGHTING

If you are creating a document and have a term or phrase you know will need to be replaced later on, highlight it. For instance, if you are writing the minutes from your last PTA meeting but can't remember the school principal's name, just type **name** each time it should appear and highlight the word. When you figure out the name, you can have Find and Replace look only for words that are highlighted — in this case, highlighted occurrences of "name".

▶ WORKING WITH STYLES

When you are creating a document in Word, it might automatically apply some heading styles to headings. To use a different font in those headings (or make any other formatting change), you can use Find and Replace. For example, you could change a title in the Heading 1 style to a new font, or apply any other formatting changes that you see fit. Alternatively, you might want to just create a new style for your own titles, as discussed in Chapter 7.

CROSS-REFERENCE
To learn more about paragraph formatting, see "Formatting Paragraphs" in Chapter 7.

FIND IT ONLINE
Search 300,000 titles for Word plug-ins at Jumbo!, located at **http://www.jumbo.com/**.

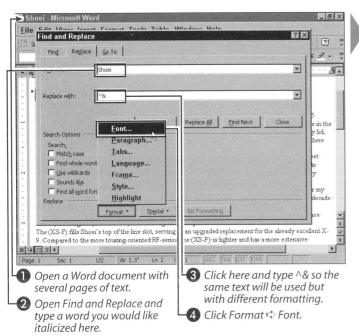

① Open a Word document with several pages of text.

② Open Find and Replace and type a word you would like italicized here.

③ Click here and type ^& so the same text will be used but with different formatting.

④ Click Format ➪ Font.

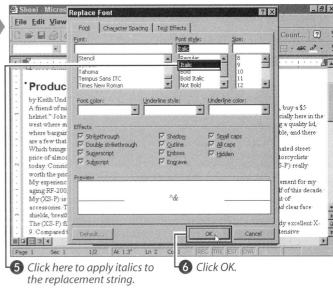

⑤ Click here to apply italics to the replacement string.

⑥ Click OK.

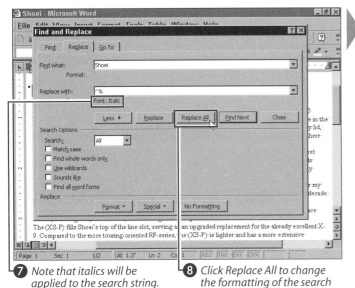

⑦ Note that italics will be applied to the search string.

⑧ Click Replace All to change the formatting of the search string throughout the document.

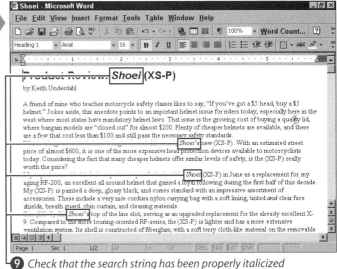

⑨ Check that the search string has been properly italicized in your document.

Using Find and Replace to Change Formatting *Continued*

Using Find and Replace to modify formatting in your documents can be a real time-saver. On the last two pages you learned how to change formatting in your document through the use of this feature.

Modifying formatting with Find and Replace has many possible applications. The example given on the previous two pages was straightforward, but combining formatting with Find and Replace can provide some interesting solutions to other problems. Recall, for example, an illustration provided earlier in this chapter where you enclosed numbers in your document inside parentheses. A problem cropped up because, if you simply have Word find ^# and replace it with (^&), a number such as 309 will end up being (3)(0)(9).

Formatting provides a possible solution to this issue. Start by having Word find all occurrences of three-digit numbers (unless you have numbers in the document with more than three digits) that are not bold. Replace them with (^&), and format the replaced numbers as bold. Then perform the exact same search for two-digit numbers, and then single digits.

In this example, you have gotten around the problem by making Word ignore numbers that you have already enclosed in parentheses. It ignores them because you made them bold at the same time you placed them in parentheses, and you also told Word to specifically ignore any bold numbers. If you don't want the numbers to remain bold when you are

done, just find any number that is bold and replace it with the same number nonbolded.

The figures on the facing page show this example in practice. This concept has virtually limitless possibilities. If you are creative, you can save yourself quite a bit of time when you are editing large documents.

TAKE NOTE

▶ USING FIND AND REPLACE FOR PROGRAMMING

Many programmers use Word to edit their code. If you are entering a lot of repetitive code or tags, you might be able to speed things up a bit with Find and Replace. For instance, suppose you are coding HTML and want to turn every occurrence of the name of your company into a hyperlink. Do this quickly be replacing every occurrence of "YourCompany, Inc." with "<A HREF="http://www.yourcompany.com/">^&</A>". Notice that the appropriate tags will be placed before and after the "Find what" result (^&). For best results, try it with several different variations of the name to make sure that each one gets properly tagged.

▶ CANCELING FIND AND REPLACE

Though most Find and Replace actions happen instantaneously, the tool may need a number of seconds if your document is very long. You can stop Find and Replace in progress by pressing the Esc key on your keyboard. You can also undo any Find and Replace using the Undo button on the toolbar.

CROSS-REFERENCE
To learn more about undoing unwanted actions, see "Using Undo and Redo" in Chapter 10.

FIND IT ONLINE
Learn more about formatting with shortcut keys at http://www.als.uiuc.edu/infotechaccess/win-sc-word7.html.

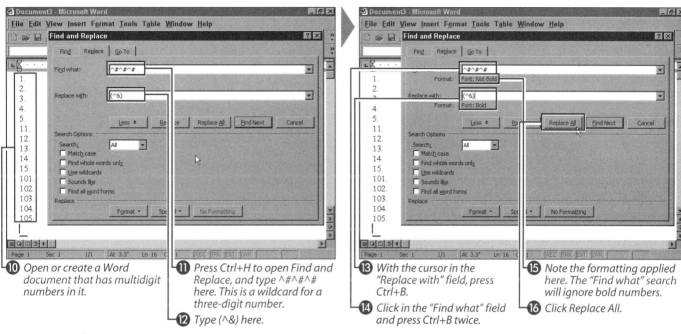

10 Open or create a Word document that has multidigit numbers in it.

11 Press Ctrl+H to open Find and Replace, and type ^#^#^# here. This is a wildcard for a three-digit number.

12 Type (^&) here.

13 With the cursor in the "Replace with" field, press Ctrl+B.

14 Click in the "Find what" field and press Ctrl+B twice.

15 Note the formatting applied here. The "Find what" search will ignore bold numbers.

16 Click Replace All.

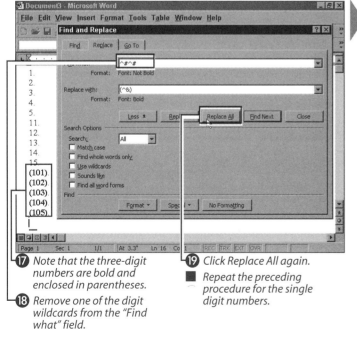

17 Note that the three-digit numbers are bold and enclosed in parentheses.

18 Remove one of the digit wildcards from the "Find what" field.

19 Click Replace All again.

■ Repeat the preceding procedure for the single digit numbers.

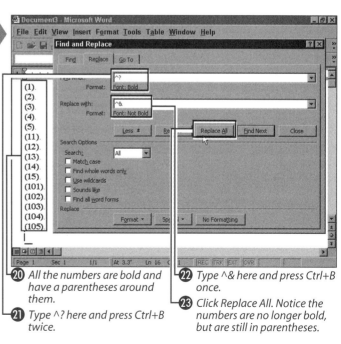

20 All the numbers are bold and have a parentheses around them.

21 Type ^? here and press Ctrl+B twice.

22 Type ^& here and press Ctrl+B once.

23 Click Replace All. Notice the numbers are no longer bold, but are still in parentheses.

229

Personal Workbook

Q&A

1 When you use Find, does Word ignore extra spaces you type at the end of the word?

_____

_____

_____

2 Can you make more than one replacement at a time?

_____

_____

_____

3 What is a wildcard?

_____

_____

_____

4 What is the wildcard for any letter?

_____

_____

_____

5 What is the wildcard for a paragraph mark?

_____

_____

_____

6 What kinds of changes can you make with Find and Replace?

_____

_____

_____

7 Can you edit your document while the Find and Replace dialog box is open?

_____

_____

_____

8 Does Find and Replace have a wildcard for a whole word?

_____

_____

_____

ANSWERS: PAGE 369

EXTRA PRACTICE

1 Type at least two pages worth of your life story.

2 Search for every occurrence of your name and replace it with that of your favorite member of The Beatles.

3 Now format every occurrence of the name of your favorite Beatle so that the text is red and enclosed in brackets.

4 Change all red text in the document to bold-faced black, with the Desdemona font.

5 Replace the name of your favorite Beatle with your own.

6 Add extra paragraph marks between paragraphs to the document.

REAL-WORLD APPLICATIONS

✔ Sometimes when you type the first draft of an important document you don't have all of the information you need right in front of you. If you come to a spot where an unknown name should go, type something that would not be used for anything else, like %%%%. During review, you can update the document by replacing all occurrences of %%%% with the proper name.

✔ Some document elements look similar and may need similar formatting. For instance, if you were quoting verses from a book of the Bible frequently, you could use John ^#:^#^# in your search string. Find and Replace should find many different references in your document because the wildcards were used, such as John 3:16 or even John 1:1.

Visual Quiz

In this Find and Replace dialog box, what is the text that will be replaced? How will it differ from the text that was found? Are more options available? How do you see them? Without using a formatting menu, how was the formatting for this item changed?

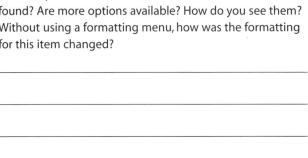

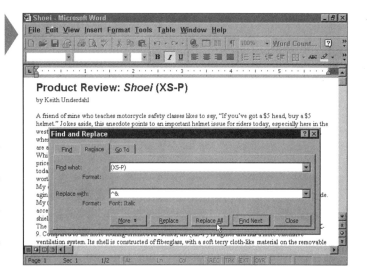

PART

IV

Publishing Documents

Virtually all the documents you create using Word 2000 are meant to be read by others. This means that once you have created and edited your documents, they must be published. Word provides options to help you publish your documents in a variety of ways.

The most common method for publishing a document is to print it out on paper. This is a simple process, but one that must be undertaken with care. Printing a Word document on paper is costly in terms of paper and supplies, so Chapter 14, "Printing a Document," introduces you to ways to control the printing process. The tasks described there help you utilize Word to print your documents in the most efficient and effective way possible.

In addition, you learn how Word can be used to print information on labels and envelopes. These are items you use often around the home and office, and Word makes it easy to produce professional-quality printed materials.

Finally, this part introduces you to the Web publishing capabilities of Word 2000. The Internet is a growing medium for publishing documents of all kinds, and Word has the tools to help you join the online world.

CHAPTER **14**

Printing a Document

What do you use Word for? If you sit down and think about it, you may find that you use Word on an almost-daily basis. And even if you don't use Word that regularly, you are likely to produce a wide range of documents with this tool. Whatever you do in Word 2000, you probably print most of your documents on paper. It is true that electronic document sharing is becoming more common, both on the Internet and on company networks; but for now, printing is still the most popular way to publish a document.

When you are printing documents, many things must be considered. Perhaps one of your greatest concerns should be the amount of paper you are using. Are you printing document drafts that you are then just throwing away? Do you find that your printed documents don't look quite like you thought they would? Do you end up wasting paper because you print an entire document when you really needed only one page?

If you answered yes to any of these questions, consider spending some time mastering the skills described in this chapter. Even if you didn't answer in the affirmative, the tasks described here will help you get off on the right start when printing.

Understanding how Word prints your documents is important, both to ensure your documents look their best and to reduce waste. You should also understand how your printer works, because some settings on it might help you save resources as well. Paper and printer toner aren't getting any cheaper; knowing how to print what you want the way you want it will ultimately save both time and expense.

This chapter helps you achieve these goals. You begin by learning some basic printing techniques, which are common to virtually all Windows-based applications. Next, you learn how to use a feature called Print Preview, which helps you get a better idea of what will be printed *before* you print it. You move on to exploring how to control the features and settings of your printer, and how to print only certain parts of your document. You also learn how to print multiple copies of documents, and how to print to a file instead of to a printer.

Basic Printing Techniques

The vast majority of documents created in Word 2000 will eventually be printed on paper. Even if you use Word primarily to edit Web pages or other electronic documents, there's a high probability that you will eventually have to print something.

Obviously, before you can print, you need a printer. Once it is installed, you are ready to print. Printing in Word is similar to printing in virtually any Windows-based application. In fact, the Print dialog box is shared with other Windows programs; once you master using it, you will know how to print in almost every program you use.

Word gives you two basic options for printing. One is fast, and the other is faster. The first of these options, printing through the Print dialog box, is preferable in most circumstances because you can choose a number of print options in this dialog box. To choose these options, you select Print from the File menu on the menu bar. You can also open the dialog box from other menus, such as some shortcut menus.

The faster printing method is to click the Print button on the toolbar. You may have noticed that many Windows programs have a similar Print button. However, in many of those programs, clicking the Print button opens the Print dialog box. In Word, it doesn't. Instead, the whole document begins printing instantaneously using the default printer settings. If you are absolutely certain that your entire document is ready to print and you need only one copy,

use the toolbar button. Otherwise, use the Print dialog box to double-check options before you print.

The figures on the facing page show you how to open and use the Print dialog box. You should also practice clicking the Print button, which resembles a little printer, on the toolbar.

CROSS-REFERENCE

To learn more about dialog boxes, see "Using Dialog Boxes" in Chapter 1.

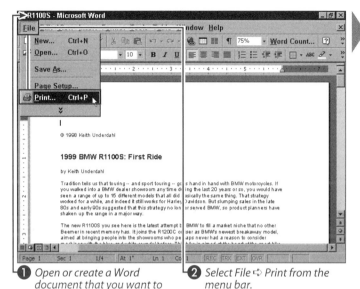

❶ Open or create a Word document that you want to print.

❷ Select File ➪ Print from the menu bar.

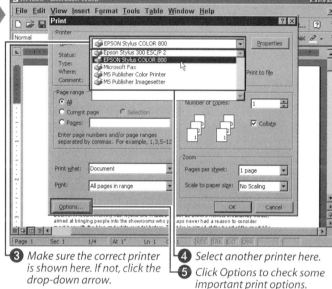

❸ Make sure the correct printer is shown here. If not, click the drop-down arrow.

❹ Select another printer here.

❺ Click Options to check some important print options.

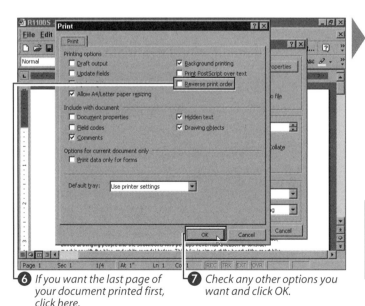

❻ If you want the last page of your document printed first, click here.

❼ Check any other options you want and click OK.

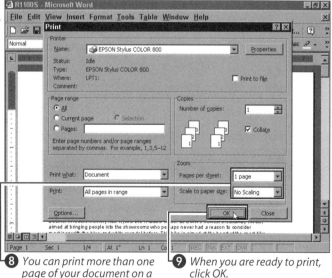

❽ You can print more than one page of your document on a piece of paper. Choose zoom options here.

❾ When you are ready to print, click OK.

Using Print Preview

When you view a document on your computer's screen, it may or may not resemble the final, printed product. Documents on your screen almost always display important information that is not intended to appear on the printed copy, such as rulers, breaks, and other nonprinting characters. This information is important for you to see while you work on a document, but it would have no value printed on paper. Furthermore, the actual layout of the document on your screen may differ drastically from the printed copy; Excel worksheets are infamous for this. Word documents that use columns may be just as confusing.

Word offers a useful tool to help you alleviate much of this confusion as you develop your documents and get them ready for printing. The Print Preview option lets you preview a representation of what your document will look like when it is printed on paper. A number of view options let you change the view and even the document itself. You can zoom in or out in Print Preview, and you can view multiple pages at once. This last feature is useful for viewing facing or adjacent pages, which are also called *spreads*.

The most important result of Print Preview is that it reduces or even eliminates the need to print draft copies of a document. By using this tool, you can avoid printing any pages until your final draft is ready. By getting a better idea of how a document will look before printing it, you will save a great deal of time, not to mention paper and printer toner.

The figures on the facing page show you how to preview a Word document. You begin by learning how to open print preview, and then you practice zooming in and out and changing the view so that several pages are displayed at once.

TAKE NOTE

▶ KNOW YOUR PRINTER'S LIMITATIONS

As wonderful as a document may look in Print Preview, you may still be limited by your printer. For instance, if you only have a black-ink printer, don't expect any items in the document to print in color. Also, some printers can print closer to the edge of the page than others. If you have reduced the margins drastically, some text might get cut off. Print Preview always assumes you have the latest and greatest in printer technology.

▶ REDUCING PAGE COUNT WITH PRINT PREVIEW

Print Preview offers a unique feature that automatically reduces the number of pieces of paper your document requires by one. Click the Shrink to Fit button on the Preview toolbar to see the result. If you don't like it, select Edit ⇨ Undo to undo the change.

CROSS-REFERENCE

To learn about Print Layout View as an alternative to Print Preview, see "Changing the View" in Chapter 2.

FIND IT ONLINE

Have a question about your printer? Take it to Usenet at news:comp.periphs.printers.

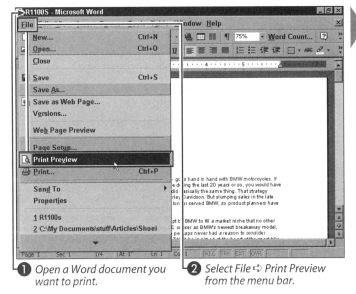

1 Open a Word document you want to print.

2 Select File ⇨ Print Preview from the menu bar.

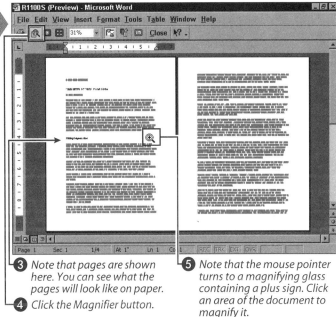

3 Note that pages are shown here. You can see what the pages will look like on paper.

4 Click the Magnifier button.

5 Note that the mouse pointer turns to a magnifying glass containing a plus sign. Click an area of the document to magnify it.

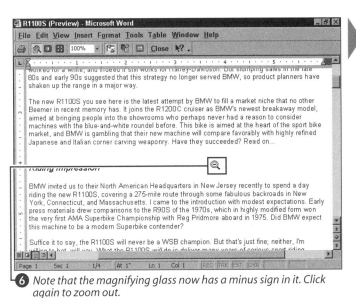

6 Note that the magnifying glass now has a minus sign in it. Click again to zoom out.

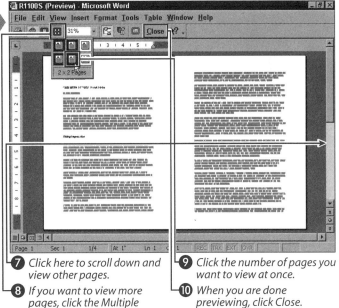

7 Click here to scroll down and view other pages.

8 If you want to view more pages, click the Multiple Pages button.

9 Click the number of pages you want to view at once.

10 When you are done previewing, click Close.

Controlling Your Printer

As noted earlier, the quickest way to print a document is to click the Print button on the toolbar. The document prints instantly, but you have no control over the printing process. This tradeoff is fine in many printing situations; but in some, you need control.

Being able to control the printing process is important to ensure you get the most efficient use out of your printer. The Print dialog box you learned how to open earlier in this chapter enables you to set a wide variety of printing options for your document, a couple of which are detailed in subsequent tasks. Depending on what you are printing and what kind of hardware you have, you may also need to control the printer itself and change some options on it.

Some older printers don't provide many printer control options, though many current products do. You can usually control printer options through special utility software that comes with the printer when you buy it; Windows has drivers for many popular printer models built in, and these drivers enable printers to function on a basic level with Windows programs. However, the utility for the printer may give you more options for controlling how printing occurs and what is printed. The printer may also have its own queue software that manages print jobs and other aspects of printing. Some printers can communicate with your computer, providing ongoing feedback on the printing progress. If your printer came with utility software, you should install it before trying to use the printer.

The figures on the facing page show you how to control a printer from the Print dialog box. The available options vary depending on the printer you have installed. You may not have any printer-specific options at all.

TAKE NOTE

SETTING PRINT QUALITY

Some printers enable you to adjust the quality or resolution of the pages you are printing. It's a good idea to experiment with this feature to get a feel for the highest and lowest quality your printer can produce. The high-quality settings are appropriate for your most important documents, but you can probably get away with lower resolution in most cases. Generally speaking, lower print quality or resolution will result in faster printing and a longer life for your toner cartridge.

PRINTING MULTICOLOR DOCUMENTS

If the document you are printing is multicolored and you have a color printer, the color will print by default. Color ink-jet cartridges are expensive and notoriously short-lived, so if you are printing a draft or something you expect to photocopy on a black ink copier, look for an option to print the document in black only. The document will print, but color items will be printed as grayscale images. This will save your color ink for when you really need it.

CROSS-REFERENCE

See the first task in this chapter, "Basic Printing Techniques," to learn how to select a different printer.

FIND IT ONLINE

Tired of paying a fortune for ink cartridges? See Refill Ink at **http://www.refillink.com/**.

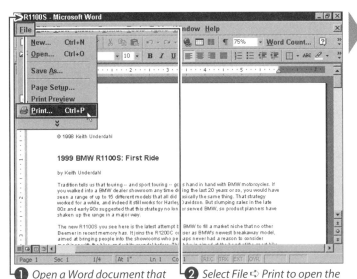

1 Open a Word document that you want to print.

2 Select File ⇨ Print to open the Print dialog box.

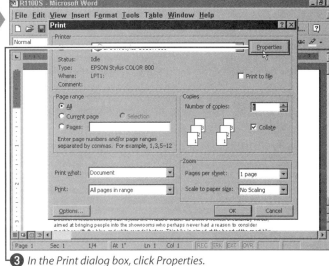

3 In the Print dialog box, click Properties.

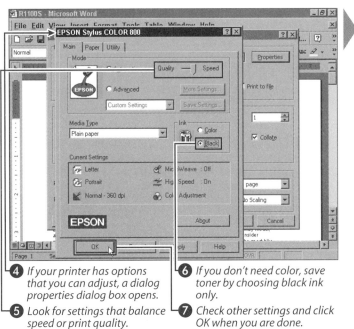

4 If your printer has options that you can adjust, a dialog properties dialog box opens.

5 Look for settings that balance speed or print quality.

6 If you don't need color, save toner by choosing black ink only.

7 Check other settings and click OK when you are done.

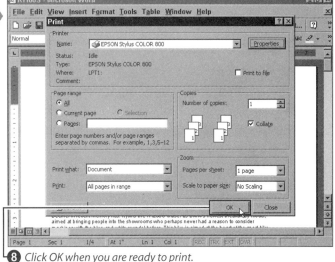

8 Click OK when you are ready to print.

Printing Parts of a Document

As easy as the print button on the toolbar may be to use, this is not always the most desirable way to start a print job. For one thing, it begins printing your document immediately, which means you won't be able to change printers or change any other print options. Furthermore, it prints your *entire* document, no matter how much of the document you actually want or need.

Word gives you a number of options for printing portions of data, text, and other file elements. The simplest way to print portions of a document is to print only specified pages. Options in the Print dialog box enable you to select the entire document, the current page — that is, the page that the cursor is currently on — or a specific page or range of pages. For instance, suppose you print a long document, only to discover that the address was typed incorrectly on the first page. Rather than print another copy of the whole document, you can make the necessary corrections to the document and then print only the page you need.

Another method of printing portions of a document involves selecting portions of text and using options in the Print dialog box to print your selection. This method may be useful if you only need small pieces of information from a document, such as an address, schedule of events, or list of phone numbers.

The first two figures on the facing page demonstrate how to open the Print dialog box and select basic options. The last two figures show you how to select some text and print only that selection.

TAKE NOTE

▶ PRINTING REPLACEMENT PAGES

Users often only reprint one or two pages after they have done some touch-up editing to a document. However, you should be careful to ensure that the seemingly minor changes you have made have not affected other pages you are not reprinting. For instance, if you have added material to a page, lines of text may have been bumped from the bottom of the page you are reprinting to the top of the next page, which you are not reprinting. In this case, you may have to print additional pages to ensure your document is complete.

▶ PRINTING A SELECTION

If you opened the Print dialog box after selecting an area of data or text, you will probably see the Selection option available in the Page Range box, but not selected. Make sure it is selected before trying to print that selection. Also, keep in mind that even if the selection is in the middle of the page onscreen, it will actually print at the top of the paper when you print it. Print Preview will not reflect this.

CROSS-REFERENCE

See "Selecting Text" in Chapter 5 to learn more about making selections.

FIND IT ONLINE

Save money and the environment with recycled toner and ink cartridges. See **http://www.eco-office.com/**.

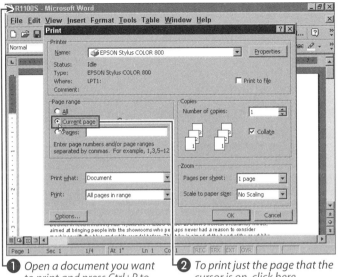

1 Open a document you want to print and press Ctrl+P to open the Print dialog box.

2 To print just the page that the cursor is on, click here.

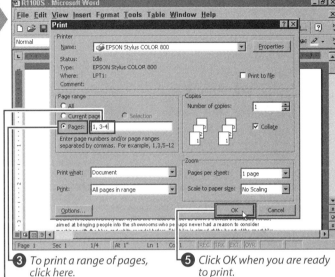

3 To print a range of pages, click here.

4 Enter the numbers of the pages you want to print here.

5 Click OK when you are ready to print.

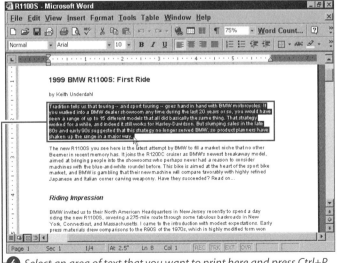

6 Select an area of text that you want to print here and press Ctrl+P to open the Print dialog box.

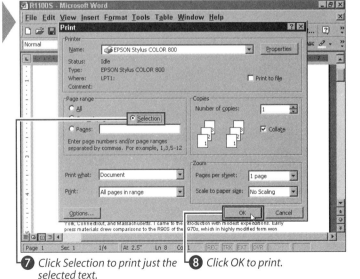

7 Click Selection to print just the selected text.

8 Click OK to print.

Printing Multiple Copies of a Document

Usually, when you print a document with Word, you print only one copy of it. This is because most of the time you won't need more. Still, at times you need more than one copy of a document, and Word lets you print multiple copies efficiently.

Before you run dozens of copies of your memos and charts for a meeting this afternoon, there are a few things you should consider. First of all, is printing multiple copies of a document directly from your computer the most cost-effective way of obtaining copies? If you have a photocopy machine around the office, the answer to that question is probably no. Photocopiers tend to be much more cost effective than ink-jet or laser printers, and they are usually much quicker to boot.

So, your office photocopier has a lot going for it. Still, there will probably be times when you need or want to just use your printer to produce multiple copies. You can make this choice from the Print dialog box. Word places no limit on the number of copies you can make.

When you print multiple copies of a document with two or more pages, you can choose whether you want the printed pages collated. If you print three copies of a three-page document, leave the Collate option selected (the default). Word will print one set, and then print the next set. On the other hand, if you deselect the Collate option, Word will first print three copies of page one, and then three copies of page two, and so on.

The figures on the facing page show you how to print multiple copies of a document. Notice how the diagram in the Print dialog box changes as you toggle the Collate function on and off.

TAKE NOTE

▶ TROUBLES WITH THE WEATHER

The ink used in ink-jet printers and, to a lesser extent, the toner used in laser printers is extremely susceptible to streaking when it gets wet. Even small amounts of moisture can cause documents printed by an ink-jet printer to smear to the point at which they are almost unreadable. If you think your document might be exposed to small amounts of moisture, consider printing it and then making a copy of it with a photocopier. The photocopy will be far more weatherproof than the original.

▶ PRINTING MULTIPLE PAGES ON ONE PIECE OF PAPER

In the Print dialog box, you can choose to have more than one page printed on a single piece of paper. The option is available under "Zoom," and enables you to "shrink" the pages. This can be another good way to preview your page layout without using too much paper, especially if you are producing a newsletter or other document where an attractive page layout is crucial.

CROSS-REFERENCE

See "Setting Up the Page" in Chapter 5 to read more on page setup.

FIND IT ONLINE

Compare 30 different printers at **http://www.zdnet.com/pcmag/features/hardware/1519/_open.htm**.

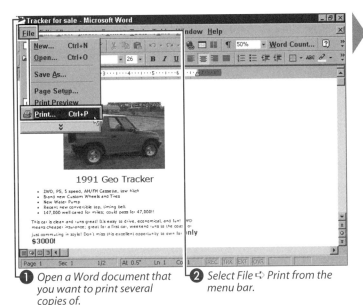

① Open a Word document that you want to print several copies of.

② Select File ⇨ Print from the menu bar.

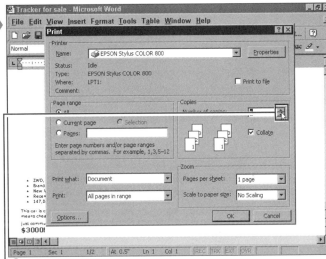

③ Click the spinner box arrows to increase or decrease the number of copies that will be printed.

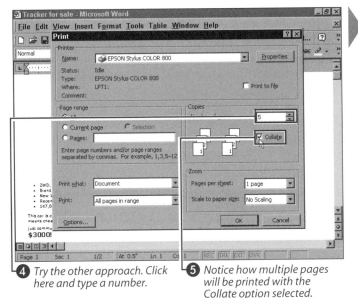

④ Try the other approach. Click here and type a number.

⑤ Notice how multiple pages will be printed with the Collate option selected.

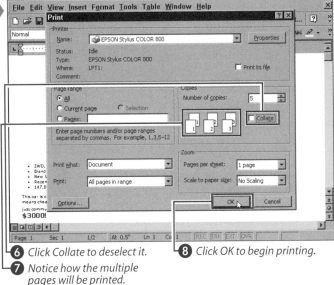

⑥ Click Collate to deselect it.

⑦ Notice how the multiple pages will be printed.

⑧ Click OK to begin printing.

Printing to a File

Generally speaking, when you think of something being printed, you assume that means it will be printed on a piece of paper. For the most part, when you use the term *print* around computers, that is exactly what it means. But what if a printer isn't currently hooked up to the computer you are working on? What if you want to use a printer that is connected to a Macintosh, OS/2, Linux, or UNIX system?

Word gives you a solution to these problems by enabling you to print a document to a file instead of directly to a printer. You can do this with any printable document, and for the most part you even follow the same printing procedures. The only difference is that instead of being sent to the printer, the document is saved as a *print file*. This file is saved in the language format for whatever printer you select. Therefore, the printer driver for the printer you expect to use must be installed on your computer, even if the printer itself is not physically connected to the computer.

Once you have created the print file, that file can then be moved via floppy disk to the computer you want to print from. You can then print the file by copying it to a printer from a DOS prompt. This adds a certain level of complication, but it also has some advantages. For instance, it means that the print file can be transferred to any computer, regardless of the operating system. If you want to print the file using a printer connected to a Macintosh, a Linux machine, or even an ancient IBM PC running DOS, you won't have any trouble doing so.

This method of "remote" printing may or may not suit your needs very well. Nonetheless, it gives you some added capabilities, and can enable you to take better advantage of the resources that might be around you. The figures on the facing page demonstrate how to print a document to a file, and then print it using the MS-DOS prompt available in Windows 95 and 98.

TAKE NOTE

▶ PRINTING ON NON-WINDOWS COMPUTERS

You can use a printer that is connected to virtually any kind of computer running almost any operating system. The exact procedure for copying the print file to the printer will vary for computers running an operating system other than Windows or MS-DOS. Contact your network administrator or tech support specialist to learn the specific commands to use on those other computers.

▶ NAMING YOUR PRINT FILE

Because you will be printing this file in DOS, you will have a problem if you give the print file a long name. To ensure you can use the print file when you need it, do not use more than eight characters in the print file's name.

CROSS-REFERENCE

See "Renaming Files" in Chapter 3 to learn how to work with filenames.

FIND IT ONLINE

Connect multiple printers to your PC with a switching device: see http://www.belkin.com/.

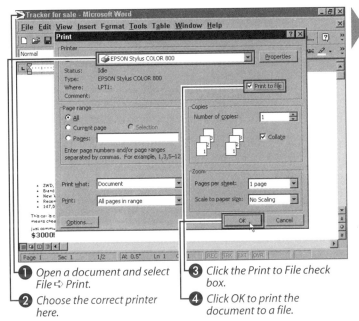

① Open a document and select File ➪ Print.

② Choose the correct printer here.

③ Click the Print to File check box.

④ Click OK to print the document to a file.

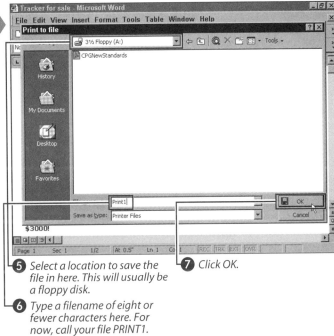

⑤ Select a location to save the file in here. This will usually be a floppy disk.

⑥ Type a filename of eight or fewer characters here. For now, call your file PRINT1.

⑦ Click OK.

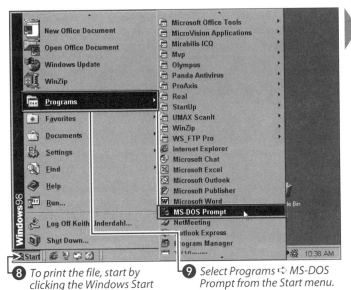

⑧ To print the file, start by clicking the Windows Start button.

⑨ Select Programs ➪ MS-DOS Prompt from the Start menu.

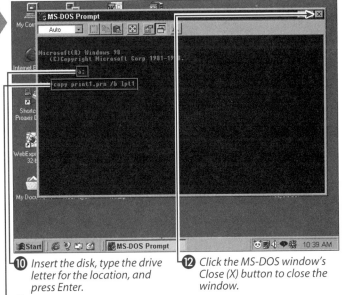

⑩ Insert the disk, type the drive letter for the location, and press Enter.

⑪ Type **COPY PRINT1.PRN /B LPT1**. (PRINT1 is the saved file.) Press Enter to print.

⑫ Click the MS-DOS window's Close (X) button to close the window.

Personal Workbook

Q&A

1 How do you open the Print dialog box?

_____

_____

_____

2 Why would you want to open the Print dialog box before printing?

_____

_____

_____

3 Can you preview more than one page at a time in Print Preview?

_____

_____

_____

4 What are some printer settings you should check before printing?

_____

_____

_____

5 How do you print three pages of a five-page document?

_____

_____

_____

6 How do you print more than one copy of a document at a time?

_____

_____

_____

7 What does the Collate option do?

_____

_____

_____

8 Can you print using a printer that is not connected to your computer?

_____

_____

_____

ANSWERS: PAGE 370

EXTRA PRACTICE

1. Create a multipage document you want to print. Make the first page a title page with your name and address on it.

2. Open the Print dialog box.

3. If your printer has adjustable settings, choose the lowest print quality for now.

4. Print two copies of the first page.

5. Print one copy of the rest of the document.

6. Print the document to a file called PRINT2. Close Word and print the file PRINT1.PRN.

REAL-WORLD APPLICATIONS

✔ Understanding how to operate the Print dialog box is especially important when you start producing multipage documents. If you are producing a newsletter, for instance, it will be useful to know how to print single pages after some minor editing.

✔ Some documents require higher print quality than others. If you are printing documents that will only be used within your office, using a lower print quality setting for the printer will save you a lot of money on printer ink and toner.

✔ Sometimes, the best printer in the office is hooked up to someone else's computer. If that computer is not on your network, or the network is down, but you are in a hurry, you can print your document to a file and transfer it there via a removable disk.

Visual Quiz

The document in the figure is in Print Preview. How do you close the Preview? How can you quickly control the zoom in Preview? How many copies of this document will be printed? Will every page be printed? Will the pages be collated or printed consecutively?

_____

_____

_____

_____

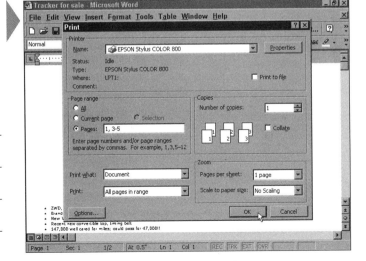

CHAPTER **15**

MASTER
THESE
SKILLS

▶ **Formatting Labels**

▶ **Entering Graphics on Labels**

▶ **Printing Labels**

▶ **Formatting Envelopes**

▶ **Printing an Envelope**

Printing Labels and Envelopes

Word lets you create a wide variety of documents, from simple letters and memos, to Web pages or even an entire book. Oddly, you will often find that it is the smallest, seemingly simple documents that can end up consuming a great deal of your day, simply because a one-page document often requires just as much formatting and setup as a 1,000-page book.

Word contains tools to help you produce many types of documents, including labels. A label is a seemingly simple item, usually with no more than one or two inches of real estate. Labels can serve a variety of uses. You can use them to address envelopes and boxes, create price tags, label file folders in a cabinet, and more.

These sticky and versatile items offer a unique challenge because printing text on them requires considerable page formatting. Many companies produce sheets of labels that can be fed through modern laser and ink-jet printers, with the labels arranged on a standard 8.5" by 11" sheet of backing paper. Even so, you still need to print text on the tiny labels, and setting up the print document properly could take hours. Fortunately, Word gives you a way to turn those hours of formatting into just a minute or two of simple option checking.

Printing addresses on envelopes is another common task that can cause trouble in the printing department. Envelopes are almost never the same size as a normal piece of paper, so printing text and graphics directly onto them can be problematic. Many people simply give up and handwrite their addresses, but if you are going for a professional look, it is better to print the addresses with your computer. Not to worry; Word gives you a quick and easy way to format and print envelopes as well.

This chapter shows you how to print labels and envelopes. You begin by exploring how to format labels, and you learn some quick techniques for entering text for an entire sheet of labels. You then move on to envelopes. First you see how to format some common envelope sizes, and then you print them. Following the techniques shown here will make your mailings appear far more professional without adding a great deal of complication to your work life.

Formatting Labels

Labels are one of the most versatile items you can have around the home or office. Labels are those small, blank decals that you peel off backing paper and stick onto envelopes, boxes, file folders, or virtually anywhere else you see fit. They can serve a huge variety of purposes, limited only by your imagination.

The most obvious use for labels is for addressing things you plan to mail. Printing addresses on labels with your computer rather than using handwriting will give your mailings a far more professional appearance. This approach can also save you time. Handwriting an address on a single label or envelope may take only a few seconds; however, if you need to address dozens or even hundreds of items at a time, using a pen becomes impractical.

Labels don't have to be limited to addressing mail. You can also use very small labels to produce price tags for items in a store or sale you are having. For a garage sale, for example, preprint labels with common garage sale prices (25 cents, 50 cents, and so on). This way, the time-consuming process of pricing everything will go much quicker.

Yet another great use for labels is to identify the content of floppy disks. A number of companies produce labels for both 3.5" floppy disks as well as other common formats such as ZIP disks and CD-ROMs. If you are producing software or other files that you need to share with a large number of people, use preprinted labels to make each disk appear to be a

more finished product. Other labels are available for cassette tapes, file folders, video tapes, name tags, and more. Browse the products list in the Label Options dialog box to see what else is available.

The figures on the facing page show you how to format labels. After you have mastered this task, you can move on to learning about sprucing up those labels with graphics.

TAKE NOTE

▶ WORKING WITH PRODUCT CODES

Word provides a number of preformatted label types. These types are based on label products produced by companies such as Avery-Dennison Office Products and others. Look on the packaging that your labels came in for a four-digit number that should be clearly identified as the product code. You should select the Word label type that matches that code. Word recognizes these codes and automatically formats the labels according to label templates that were built into the program.

▶ USE LABELS FOR YOUR RETURN ADDRESS

The one address you use more than any other is your own. You have to write it as a return address on every envelope and package you mail out. You can save yourself the monotony of writing it over and over by producing labels with your return address already printed on them.

CROSS-REFERENCE

To learn more about page setup, see "Setting Up the Page" in Chapter 5.

FIND IT ONLINE

Learn more about Avery labels by visiting the Avery Web site at **http://www.avery.com/**.

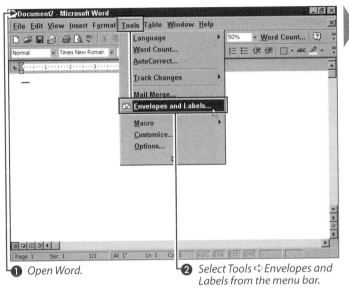

① Open Word.

② Select Tools ⇨ Envelopes and Labels from the menu bar.

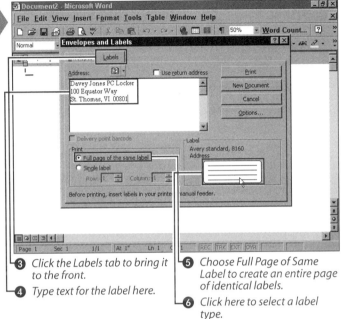

③ Click the Labels tab to bring it to the front.

④ Type text for the label here.

⑤ Choose Full Page of Same Label to create an entire page of identical labels.

⑥ Click here to select a label type.

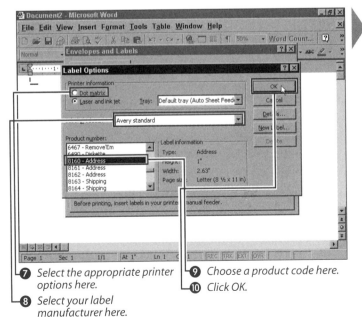

⑦ Select the appropriate printer options here.

⑧ Select your label manufacturer here.

⑨ Choose a product code here.

⑩ Click OK.

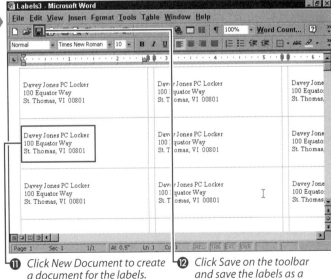

⑪ Click New Document to create a document for the labels.

⑫ Click Save on the toolbar and save the labels as a document.

Entering Graphics on Labels

As discussed in the previous task, labels can serve a variety of purposes. Besides the most obvious use as address labels, you can use labels as price tags, product labels for CDs and floppy disks, and much more. Above all else, preprinted labels give your mailings and products a far more professional look and feel, and they can save you quite a bit of time as well.

Of course, the concept of preprinted labels is nothing new. Individuals and companies have been using them for years, since long before the personal computer revolution. In the past, preprinted labels had to be produced by a professional printer. Although these labels were usually of high quality, having to use a printer also presented a logistical challenge that many people weren't willing to confront. Fortunately, the personal computer revolution has put the production of professional-quality labels within the reach of even the smallest home office.

One way in which you can give your labels an even more advanced look is to add some graphics to them. You may want to include a company logo or other graphical elements to make your labels look more polished. This extra effort is especially important if you are using the labels as product labels, such as for floppy disks or CDs. If your products have a more professional and polished look, your customers will ultimately have more confidence in you to produce a quality product. Using a simple graphic on your labels can go a long way.

The figures on the facing page show you how to put graphics on a label. The figures use new labels that were not created in the task on the previous page, but you can place graphics on virtually any kind of label you want — assuming you have enough room, that is.

TAKE NOTE

▶ CONSIDER THE PRINTER

If you plan to use graphics on your labels, consider the quality of the printer you will be using. Many individuals and companies use dot-matrix printers to produce mailing labels because they are robust and cheap to operate. However, the print quality of even the best dot-matrix printers pales in comparison to even the cheapest ink-jet and laser printers, which means that graphics probably won't turn out very well on labels. If you're not sure, test a couple of labels before you run off several hundred.

▶ AVOID TOO MANY COLORS

Chances are that any graphics you use on a label — even a relatively large label — will be small. If the graphic contains many colors, it could end up looking busy and unintelligible once printed on the label. For best results, use a graphic that has as few colors as possible, ideally only one or two.

CROSS-REFERENCE

See "Inserting Graphics" in Chapter 9 to learn more about inserting and working with graphics.

FIND IT ONLINE

Find a huge selection of clipart graphics online at http://www.clipart.com/.

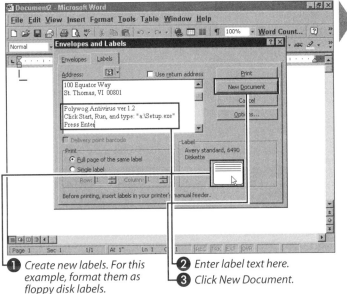

1 Create new labels. For this example, format them as floppy disk labels.

2 Enter label text here.

3 Click New Document.

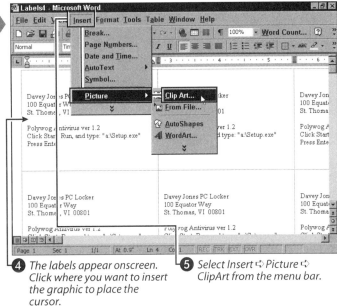

4 The labels appear onscreen. Click where you want to insert the graphic to place the cursor.

5 Select Insert ➪ Picture ➪ ClipArt from the menu bar.

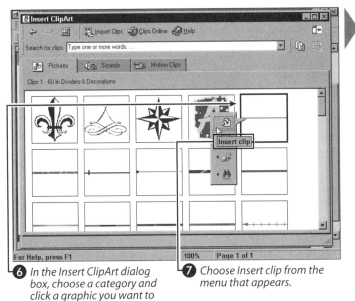

6 In the Insert ClipArt dialog box, choose a category and click a graphic you want to insert.

7 Choose Insert clip from the menu that appears.

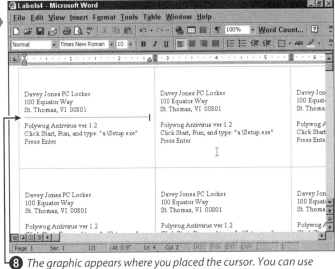

8 The graphic appears where you placed the cursor. You can use copy and paste commands to copy the graphic to other labels as well.

Printing Labels

After your labels are formatted and ready to go, your first step should be to test print the labels on a plain sheet of paper. Minor variances in printer design can cause the print for your labels to be slightly misaligned. A sheet of plain paper is much cheaper than a sheet of labels, so it's better to find out about misalignments *before* your print the actual labels. Print the labels on paper, and then hold the paper over the label sheet in front of a bright light. Check to see how well the label text and graphics fit within the edges of each label.

If you do encounter misalignment, the problem is relatively easy to fix. You can usually make needed adjustments by changing the margins of the page slightly using the Page Setup dialog box. If the labels are misaligned significantly, check to make sure you selected the correct manufacturer and product code when you formatted the labels in the first place. After you have adjusted the alignment, test the labels on regular paper again until everything lines up just right. The figures on the facing page show you how to adjust misaligned labels.

When everything is lined up, you are ready to print your labels. Check the documentation for your printer to see how and if you should load label paper into the printer. Make sure you insert the label sheet with the correct side facing up so that the text is printed on the right side. You may also want to remove regular paper from the feeder tray before you print the labels.

TAKE NOTE

PRINT A SHEET OF LABELS ONLY ONCE

If you need to print a single label, you may be tempted to print it on a sheet of labels and plan to use the rest of the labels another time. Unfortunately, this plan often will not work. When the label sheet passes through your printer, it must turn and curl around rollers inside the printer. This causes the labels to become slightly curled. If you try to pass them through the printer again they may come off inside, causing significant damage to the printer. To be safe, never pass a sheet of labels through your printer more than once.

USE LABELS DESIGNED FOR YOUR PRINTER

Most labeling products are designed specifically for either ink-jet or laser printers. You should make sure that you use only the correct type for your printer, because poor print quality could result. Also, the ink may not adhere properly to the wrong kind of label, causing it to rub off and streak as it is handled. Check the packaging of the labels before you buy them to make sure you're getting the correct type.

CROSS-REFERENCE

See "Printing Multiple Copies of a Document" to learn how to print more than one sheet of labels at a time.

FIND IT ONLINE

Here's a great reference for Word topics: **http://www .com.msu.edu.isa/news/msoffice/word/20tips/ index.html**.

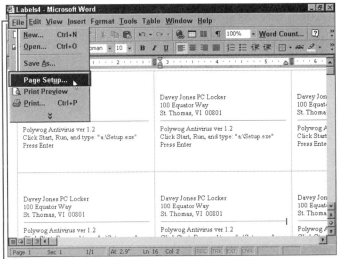

1 *Print a test page of your labels and compare it with the label sheet you plan to use. If they do not line up, select File ⇨ Page Setup from the menu bar.*

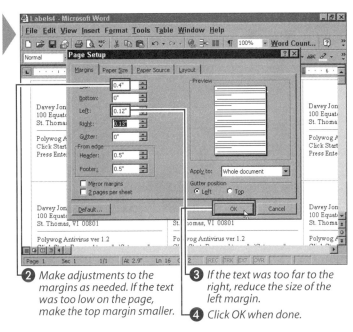

2 *Make adjustments to the margins as needed. If the text was too low on the page, make the top margin smaller.*

3 *If the text was too far to the right, reduce the size of the left margin.*

4 *Click OK when done.*

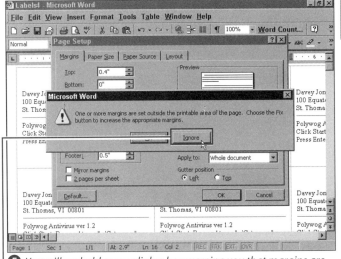

5 *You will probably see a dialog box warning you that margins are set outside the printable area. Click Ignore.*

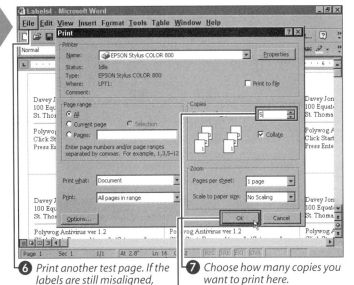

6 *Print another test page. If the labels are still misaligned, repeat Steps 1 through 5. If everything is ready, select File ⇨ Print from the menu bar.*

7 *Choose how many copies you want to print here.*

8 *Insert the label sheets and click OK. If you see a warning box telling you to insert paper, do so and click OK.*

Formatting Envelopes

As you have learned in previous tasks, labels are extremely versatile items to have around the office. They are especially useful when you are producing mass mailings, because they eliminate the need to write addresses over and over by hand. You can also use them for your return address, which you probably use many times each day.

But what happens when you need to mail only one thing? Labels usually come in sheets that can have as many as 80 labels per page, and you have to feed the whole sheet through at once. Because it is inadvisable to feed a sheet of labels through your printer more than once, you can see how wasteful it would be to print a single label at a time.

A solution to this problem is to print your addressing information directly on the envelope you plan to use. Unlike labels, envelopes are not held on sheets, so they can be printed one at a time. Thus, printing addresses on labels is ideally suited to those one-time mailings. Of course, if you need to address items to hundreds of people, feeding in one envelope at a time to your printer would be a waste of time.

As with labels, envelopes come in standard sizes. Unlike labels, however, envelope sizes are more standardized throughout the industry. Whereas when formatting labels you must first choose the label manufacturer and then select a product code, with envelopes you simply need to choose a standard size from a relatively short list. You should be able to find this information on the packaging that your envelopes come in. If not, you can always measure the envelope with a ruler and create a custom envelope size.

The figures on the facing page show you how to format an envelope. If you print envelopes on a regular basis, consider creating a separate file for each envelope size, and title the file by the envelope size. That way, whenever you need to print a Size 10 envelope, just open the file Size10.doc, type a new address, and print it.

TAKE NOTE

ADDRESSING UNUSUAL ENVELOPE SIZES

If you have an unusual envelope size, choose Custom from the Envelope Size drop-down list. You will need to get out a ruler and measure the envelope, and then enter the size in decimal format into Envelope Size dialog box.

USING BARCODES

Word lets you print USA postal (zip) code bar codes on labels and envelopes to help your envelope get to its destination more efficiently. If you select the Deliver Point Barcode option in the Envelope Options dialog box, the correct bar code for whatever zip code you typed on the envelope will automatically be printed. You can learn more about using postal barcodes from the U.S. Postal Service.

CROSS-REFERENCE

You can speed up the address entry procedure using AutoText features. See "Using AutoText" in Chapter 12.

FIND IT ONLINE

Visit the U.S. Postal Service site at **http://www.usps. gov/** to learn more about using postal barcodes.

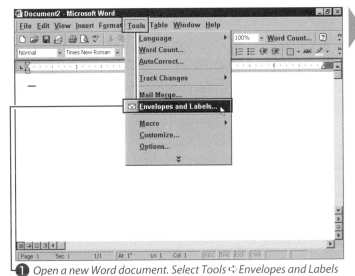

1 Open a new Word document. Select Tools ➪ Envelopes and Labels from the menu bar.

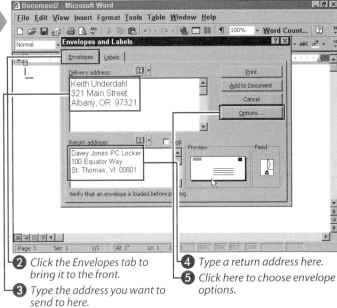

2 Click the Envelopes tab to bring it to the front.

3 Type the address you want to send to here.

4 Type a return address here.

5 Click here to choose envelope options.

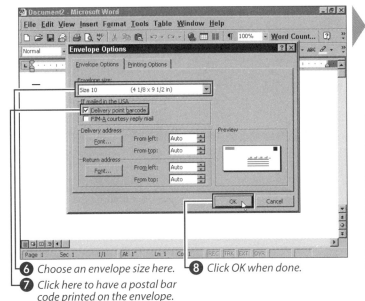

6 Choose an envelope size here.

7 Click here to have a postal bar code printed on the envelope.

8 Click OK when done.

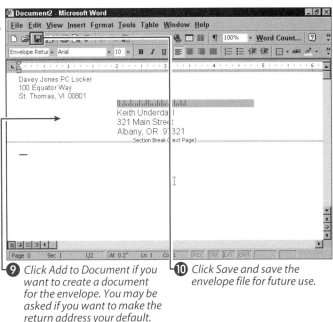

9 Click Add to Document if you want to create a document for the envelope. You may be asked if you want to make the return address your default. Choose Yes or No.

10 Click Save and save the envelope file for future use.

Printing an Envelope

Once you have selected the type of envelope you want to print, you are ready to enter an address and print it. Though this is a relatively simple procedure, it is key to the success of this endeavor. As with labels, printing an envelope has its own unique procedures that must be followed to ensure success.

Entering the address is quite simple. You can manually type the address, or you can import it from your Outlook Address Book. If you selected the option to have a postal barcode printed on the envelope when you formatted it in the previous task, make sure that the zip code on the address is correct. If it's wrong, the bar code will not be correct and your letter will end up in Nome, Alaska.

Once the address is correctly entered, you are ready to print the envelope. Most printers capable of printing envelopes have special procedures for inserting them, and you are usually limited to printing one envelope at a time. Consult your printer's documentation to see how it should be loaded. Just to be on the safe side, try test printing the envelope with a plain piece of paper. This will also help you judge how the envelope itself should be aligned in the printer feeder to ensure that the addresses are printed in the proper locations.

Finally, make sure you insert the envelope with the correct side up. Obviously you don't want the address printed on the sealing side of the envelope, so use your test print with the plain sheet of paper to make sure you're printing on the right side. The figures on the facing page show you how to change the address on your envelope and how to print it.

TAKE NOTE

IS YOUR PRINTER ENVELOPE-COMPATIBLE?

Some printers are better at handling envelopes than others. Envelopes that have clasps — such as legal size envelopes — can cause considerable damage to some printers. Just to be safe, consult the documentation for your printer to see what you can and can't do. Also, you will need to read the printer instructions to find out how envelopes should be loaded for printing.

ENVELOPES AND INK-JET PRINTERS

Unlike labels, most envelopes are not designed specifically for ink-jet or laser printers. This is usually not a big problem when you are using a laser printer; however, if you have an ink jet printer, there may be a problem getting the ink to adhere adequately to the envelope. If you are using an ink-jet printer, test the addresses before you mail the envelope to make sure they don't smudge too severely. If this will be a major problem, try covering the address with a strip of clear packaging tape to protect it from weather and smudging.

CROSS-REFERENCE
You may want to use Print Preview to see how the envelope will look before you print. See "Using Print Preview" in Chapter 14.

FIND IT ONLINE
Find an easier way to address wedding invitations at http://www.weddingsoft.com/.

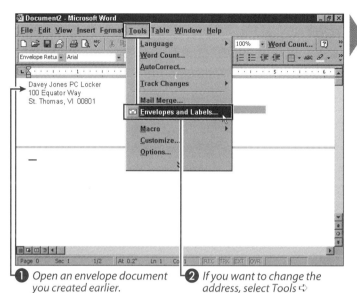

❶ Open an envelope document you created earlier.

❷ If you want to change the address, select Tools ⇨ Envelopes and Labels from the menu bar.

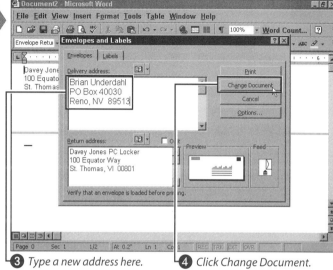

❸ Type a new address here.

❹ Click Change Document.

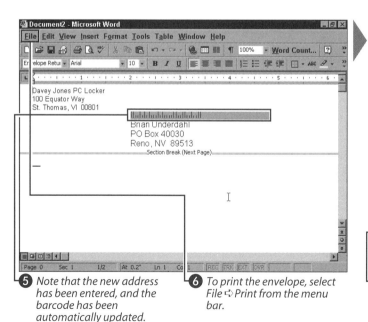

❺ Note that the new address has been entered, and the barcode has been automatically updated.

❻ To print the envelope, select File ⇨ Print from the menu bar.

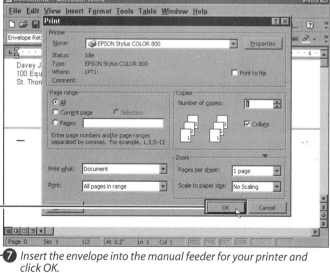

❼ Insert the envelope into the manual feeder for your printer and click OK.

Personal Workbook

Q&A

1 Do you have to manually measure the size of any label you want to print?

_____

_____

_____

2 Can you use any kind of graphic you want on a label?

_____

_____

_____

3 What should you do before printing labels?

_____

_____

_____

4 What should you do if the labels are misaligned?

_____

_____

_____

5 Can you feed a sheet of labels through your printer more than once?

_____

_____

_____

6 What is the best way to address a single item?

_____

_____

_____

7 What additional postal information besides the address can Word print on an envelope?

_____

_____

_____

8 What is the best type of printer to use when printing envelopes?

_____

_____

_____

ANSWERS: PAGE 371

EXTRA PRACTICE

1 Create a sheet of return address labels for yourself.

2 Add a small graphic to the labels.

3 Test print a sheet of your return address labels. Adjust the alignment if necessary.

4 Print a sheet of return address labels for yourself.

5 Format an envelope addressed to your closest friend.

6 Print the envelope.

7 Format an envelope to match your résumé.

REAL-WORLD APPLICATIONS

✔ If you are in charge of publishing a club newsletter, you can create address labels to help you address and mail the newsletters. You can give the labels a more custom touch by adding a small version of the club logo to each address label.

✔ As part of a project at work, you may need to share a file with a number of coworkers. If this is done in conjunction with a meeting at which you present some information, you can hand out floppy disks to each attendee. Preprinted labels on each disk will give the whole affair a polished feel and make you look like the consummate professional that you really are.

Visual Quiz

How were these labels created? What kind of label is this? Does the label format have to be manually created? Why or why not? How was the graphic added to the labels? Will it appear on the printed labels? If you only need to print one address, what would be a more efficient way to do that?

_____

_____

_____

_____

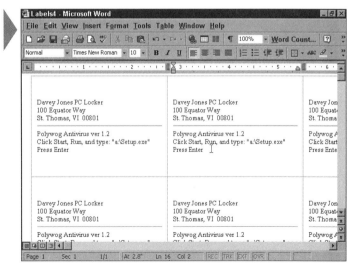

CHAPTER **16**

Creating and Publishing a Web Page

To paraphrase Bob Dylan, it doesn't take a weatherman to know which way the electronic winds are blowing. And these days, the winds are crossing the virtual landscape of the Internet, that fabulously popular global network that offers news, entertainment, information, communication, and education to almost anyone with a computer and a modem. You, too, can connect to the online world and sample its bounty, using Internet software such as Internet Explorer or Netscape Communicator. And if you don't have one of those programs, you can still view some Internet content using Word 2000. Word enables you to view Web pages if you don't have another Web browser on your computer.

Some critics have compared the Internet to television, pointing to the increasing number of hours people spend sitting in front of a monitor absorbing cathode rays without contributing anything useful to society. But discussions of content value aside, this argument ignores the greatest strength of the Internet — interactivity. Unlike television, anyone who can afford access to the Internet can produce content for it as well.

Word makes producing your own online content easy. Specifically, Word includes tools to help you produce pages for the World Wide Web, the graphics-oriented part of the Internet that has become the most popular in recent years. You can create a Web page to contain whatever you want, from your personal political manifesto to a page dedicated to your favorite hobby. A Web page can also prove extremely beneficial for your business, because it provides customers with easy access to information about your products and services. If you have ever dreamed of publishing material for others to view and read, the World Wide Web is perhaps the best opportunity you have ever had.

This chapter describes how to use tools provided by Word 2000 to help you view and create Web pages. You begin by learning some basic Web browsing techniques, and then move on to learning how to create your own Web pages. You also discover how to use graphics in your Web pages, and how to link your page to other pages on the Web. Finally, you learn how to use a shareware program called WS-FTP to publish your page on the Web.

Using the Web Toolbar

Word 2000 is first and foremost a word processor. However, Microsoft and other companies have been blurring the lines between word processors and other kinds of programs in recent years, to the point where a program such as Word can serve as an all-in-one application for many people.

Among the many nontraditional features that have been added to Word in recent years is the capability to view and create documents for the World Wide Web. Being able to create a Web page with Word is not so surprising, because Web pages and word processing documents are really not so different. But being able to view Web pages with Word is quite unusual, and depending on the software you have installed on your computer, this capability might prove quite useful to you.

If you already have a Web browser program installed on your computer, you might find it easier to use instead of Word. Programs such as Internet Explorer, Netscape Communicator, NeoPlanet, and others are designed specifically for this purpose, and they excel at it. In fact, if you have Internet Explorer 4.0 or newer already installed on your system, it will automatically launch when you try to view a Web document in Word. If that is the case, you can skip this task.

Still, if you have nothing else, Word will suffice. In fact, if you are working on a computer on which hard disk space is limited — such as a laptop — you can save some space by uninstalling other Web browsers and just using Word for your Web browsing sessions.

Word provides many of the same browsing tools as dedicated Web browsers through the use of a special toolbar called the Web toolbar. You can open this toolbar as you would any other toolbar. It contains buttons and menus to help you browse the Web. The figures on the facing page show you how to open and use the Web toolbar.

TAKE NOTE

▶ WEB VS. WEB TOOLS

When you open the Web toolbar, you may notice another toolbar called Web Tools. Whereas the Web toolbar contains tools to help you view Web pages, you use the Web Tools toolbar to create Web pages, a process discussed later in this chapter. If you just plan to view Web pages, you don't need the Web Tools toolbar.

▶ HIDE UNNEEDED TOOLBARS

If you are using Word to view Web pages, you probably don't need the Standard and Formatting toolbars displayed on your screen. You can free up more space to view the Web pages if you hide those toolbars temporarily. Doing so is especially important on the smaller screens that are typical of laptop computers. With these computers, limited desktop space can make it difficult to view large images.

CROSS-REFERENCE

To learn more about working with toolbars, see "Using Toolbars" in Chapter 1.

FIND IT ONLINE

Learn history, policy, and other information about the World Wide Web at **http://www.w3.org/**.

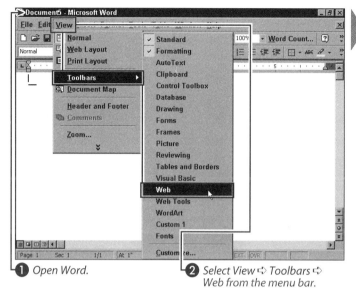

1 Open Word.

2 Select View ⇨ Toolbars ⇨ Web from the menu bar.

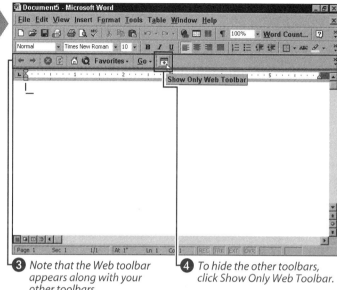

3 Note that the Web toolbar appears along with your other toolbars.

4 To hide the other toolbars, click Show Only Web Toolbar.

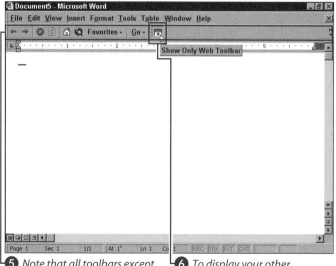

5 Note that all toolbars except the Web toolbar are hidden. This gives you more viewing area on your desktop.

6 To display your other toolbars, click Show Only Web Toolbar again.

7 To close the Web toolbar, right-click the toolbar and click Web to deselect it.

Viewing Web Pages

Once you have opened the Web toolbar as described in the previous task, you are almost ready to start viewing Web pages with Word. However, before you can view pages, you still need to do a couple of things. (Actually, you don't need to do anything if you just want to view Web pages on your hard drive, but where is the fun in that?)

First and foremost, you need to have access to the Internet. This means getting an account with an Internet service provider (ISP). Online accounts are generally available for about $20 per month or less, but rates vary depending on the services provided and your geographic location. You can choose between national providers such as Prodigy or Earthlink, or you can use a local provider that serves your specific area.

In addition to an Internet account, you also need a modem on your computer and TCP/IP software to help your computer facilitate the connection. TCP/IP software comes built into Windows; and if you need any help getting connected, you can contact your ISP.

Once you are prepared, opening a Web document is simple. Just connect to the Internet with your modem, type a Web address in the Address bar, and press Enter. You can also use buttons on the Web toolbar to visit specific sites on the Internet. If you are viewing a Web page on your hard drive (see "Preparing Your Web Pages for Publication" later in this chapter to learn how to do this), simply type the location path (including the drive letter and folders) into the Address bar and press Enter.

The figures on the facing page show you how to open a Web document in Word. Depending on which version of Windows you have, the Web documents may or may not open in Word. If you have Windows 98 or NT 5.0, Internet Explorer will launch (unless it has been uninstalled) and display the page you selected. If you are using Windows 95 or NT 4.0, the Web documents will probably open within Word. Either way, the basic browsing techniques are the same.

TAKE NOTE

AVOIDING LONG DISTANCE PHONE CHARGES

When choosing an ISP, make sure they have a local or toll-free dial-up number for you to use. If you have to pay long distance phone charges to access the Internet, you may find that access gets very expensive after only a short time online.

UNDERSTANDING INTERNET ADDRESSES

The proper name for an Internet address is *Uniform Resource Locator* (URL). URLs usually begin with *http://*, *www.*, or something to that effect. You can type a URL into the Address bar of the Word Web toolbar to visit that page. For instance, to visit the IDG Books Web site, type **http://www.idgbooks.com/**.

CROSS-REFERENCE

See "Preparing Your Web Page for Publication" later in this chapter to learn about opening a page on your hard drive.

FIND IT ONLINE

Not sure which browser to use? Visit **http://www.threetoad.com/main/Browser.html**.

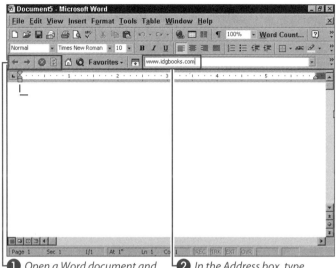

1 Open a Word document and select View ➪ Toolbars ➪ Web to display the Web toolbar.

2 In the Address box, type **www.idgbooks.com** and press Enter.

■ Connect to the Internet if you are prompted to do so.

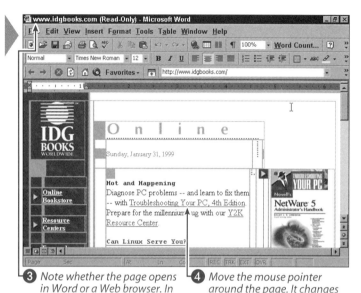

3 Note whether the page opens in Word or a Web browser. In this case, the page opened in Word.

4 Move the mouse pointer around the page. It changes to a hand when it is over a hyperlink. Click a hyperlink.

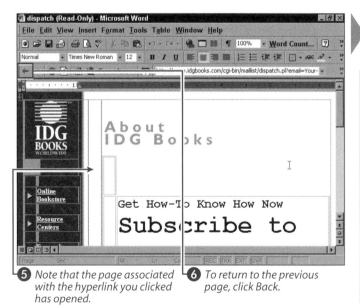

5 Note that the page associated with the hyperlink you clicked has opened.

6 To return to the previous page, click Back.

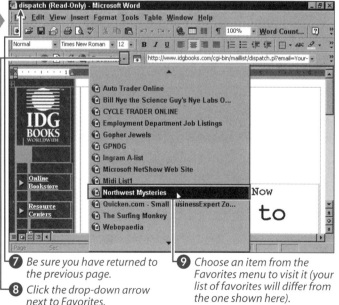

7 Be sure you have returned to the previous page.

8 Click the drop-down arrow next to Favorites.

9 Choose an item from the Favorites menu to visit it (your list of favorites will differ from the one shown here).

Creating a Basic Web Page

The Internet has been around in one form or another since the late 1960s. But it wasn't until 1994, when the World Wide Web came into general use, that the public's attention was captured. The Web is made up of documents called *Web pages* published by anybody and everybody. Web page documents are stored on Web servers that are permanently connected to the Internet, so anyone with an Internet connection can download and view the page. Web pages are interactive, easy-to-use documents that contain text, graphics, links to other pages, and a variety of other elements.

You can create and edit your own Web pages using Word 2000. Web pages are also sometimes called *HTML documents*. HTML stands for *HyperText Markup Language*, which is the programming language used on the Web. Although Word is not the most advanced Web page editor around, it is sufficient for most needs. Besides, you've already paid for it! You can use this capability to create your own page for the World Wide Web, your company's intranet (sort of a microcosm of the Internet that resides solely on your company's network), or even only for your own computer.

The figures on the facing page show you how to create a Web page. You start by creating a basic Web page with some headings and text. In the last two figures you learn how to save the page as an HTML document so that it can be used on the Web. After that, move on to the next page, where you create a second, slightly more sophisticated page that contains a bit more content.

Continued

TAKE NOTE

▶ FILE NAMES ON THE WORLD WIDE WEB

You need to be careful when naming a Web page. Long filenames are not supported on the Internet, so you must use eight or fewer characters for your filenames. Also, you should name the main page of your Web site "Index" or "Home" to ensure that most Internet software will be able to find it quickly.

▶ WHERE TO PUBLISH?

Before anyone on the Internet can view your Web page, it must be published to a Web server. Many ISPs provide free disk space on their servers for your Web pages; check with your ISP to see what you can put there, and also ask them how to transfer your files over to their server. If your ISP does not provide this service, there are many Web sites that offer free or low-cost server space for your pages. Often the only cost to you is that you must include an advertisement for the provider on your own Web page. If you plan to move or change ISPs from time to time, using a free server on the Web will help you keep a consistent Web address no matter where you move.

CROSS-REFERENCE

To learn more about styles, in Chapter 7 see "Applying Styles" in Chapter 7.

FIND IT ONLINE

You can get free and low-cost Web server space from Tripod at **http://www.tripod.com/**.

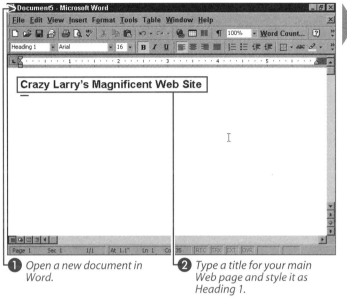

❶ Open a new document in Word.

❷ Type a title for your main Web page and style it as Heading 1.

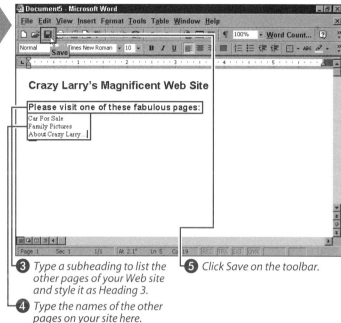

❸ Type a subheading to list the other pages of your Web site and style it as Heading 3.

❹ Type the names of the other pages on your site here.

❺ Click Save on the toolbar.

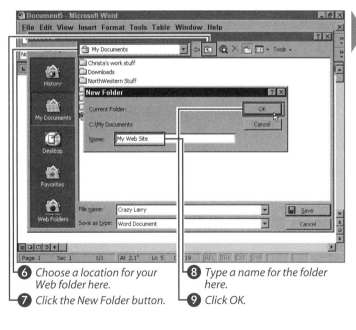

❻ Choose a location for your Web folder here.

❼ Click the New Folder button.

❽ Type a name for the folder here.

❾ Click OK.

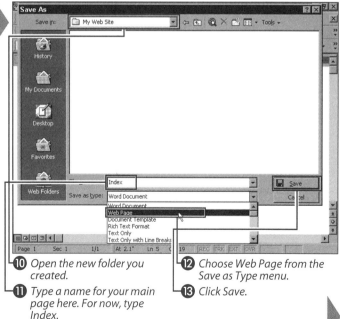

❿ Open the new folder you created.

⓫ Type a name for your main page here. For now, type Index.

⓬ Choose Web Page from the Save as Type menu.

⓭ Click Save.

Creating a Basic Web Page

Continued

A mistake that many new Web publishers make is to heap everything they have onto one page. This causes a number of problems, all of which serve to keep Web surfers from visiting your page more than once. For one thing, even with relatively fast modems, downloading a long file over the Internet can be time consuming. If your page takes several minutes to download, potential readers will get frustrated and just go somewhere else.

The best solution to this problem is to create multiple Web pages, all of which are collectively known as your *Web site*. This way, viewers can choose to download only the information they want to look at. For instance, you could create a separate page for your family pictures, another for information about your hobby, and another page of nothing but links. For best results, keep your opening page as simple as possible. Many Web publishers put nothing but an introductory banner and a site index on this first page. Visitors choose which pages they want to see by clicking hyperlinks that connect your pages. Links are discussed later in this chapter under "Creating Links."

You should also arrange the information on your pages in a logical and attractive format. You can use a number of basic tools to improve the look and feel of your Web pages, thereby enhancing their readability for your viewers. You can use numbered or bulleted lists for some information, and you can apply special formatting to your text to give it a different look. You can also change the color of your background if you wish, but make sure the text remains readable.

The figures on the facing page show you how to create a second page and apply special formatting to it. You begin by creating another Web page and incorporating a bulleted list. Next, you change some text formatting and give your background a different color.

TAKE NOTE

▶ CONSERVE BANDWIDTH

When publishing a Web site, try to avoid making that site a bandwidth hog. *Bandwidth* is a term generally applied to how much time it takes your Web site to download. If you are blessed with an excellent Internet connection, test your Web site with a slower modem to make sure it doesn't load too slowly.

▶ CHOOSE COLOR SCHEMES CAREFULLY

In most Web pages, blue or purple underlined text indicates a hyperlink. To avoid confusing your readers, don't manually apply this formatting to your text. Also, keep these colors in mind when choosing a background color; if you choose a blue background, blue hyperlinks will be invisible. Many professional Web publishers prefer to use a light-colored background with black text. It might look a little plain, but will be easiest to read.

CROSS-REFERENCE

To learn more about working with lists, see "Creating a Numbered or Bulleted List" in Chapter 18.

FIND IT ONLINE

LEARN HOW *NOT* TO CREATE A WEB PAGE AT HTTP://WWW.

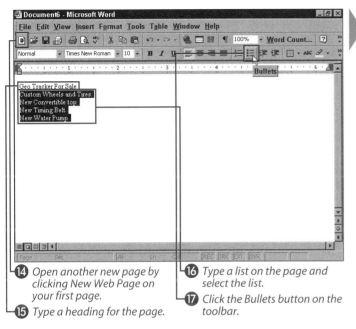

⑭ Open another new page by clicking New Web Page on your first page.

⑮ Type a heading for the page.

⑯ Type a list on the page and select the list.

⑰ Click the Bullets button on the toolbar.

⑱ Select your heading.

⑲ Select Format ➪ Font. The Font dialog box appears.

⑳ Choose a different font, color, and size.

㉑ Click OK.

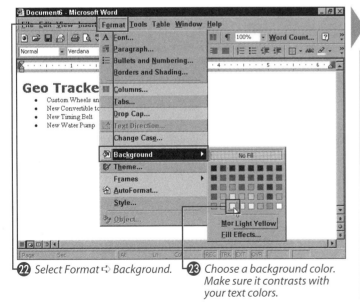

㉒ Select Format ➪ Background.

㉓ Choose a background color. Make sure it contrasts with your text colors.

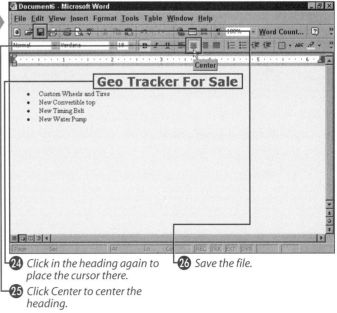

㉔ Click in the heading again to place the cursor there.

㉕ Click Center to center the heading.

㉖ Save the file.

Using Tables in Web Documents

Laying out elements on a Web page presents some challenges above and beyond creating a simple word processing document. HTML — the programming language used by Web pages — provides limited options for fine-tuning the layout of your page. These limitations have been a source of much frustration among new Web publishers from the very beginning. You may find it difficult, for example, to position text exactly where you want it on the page. This problem is exacerbated when you start including graphics on your pages, because text often has to be placed above or below — but not alongside — a picture.

As frustrating as these issues may seem, there is a good reason for the built-in limitations of HTML. Web pages must be viewable on a wide variety of computers. A reader of your Web page could be using a PC, Macintosh, Amiga, or who knows what — and the size of his or her viewing area may be vastly different from what you see on your own monitor. Text that looks indented only slightly on your 19" monitor may be off the page on someone else's laptop.

One very simple way around this layout problem is to use tables, which the latest versions of all Web browsers support. You can use an invisible table to place text and graphics almost anywhere on the page that you want. The most common use of tables is to align text alongside an image so that the page resembles something you might see in a book or magazine.

You can also use tables to align a collection of links across the page rather than down.

The figures on the facing page show you how to insert a table into your Web page, and then demonstrate how to insert some text into a cell in the table. After you have done this, move on to the next task to learn how to insert a graphic into the table.

TAKE NOTE

▶ BE WARY OF READERS' LIMITATIONS

You might have some truly outstanding hardware to work on, including a large, high-resolution monitor. But keep in mind that many of your readers don't. If your goal is to share information with a wide variety of people in a way that they will find appealing, try creating your Web page with your display set at 800 x 600 or 640 x 480 resolution. This setting will ensure proper viewing across the greatest variety of platforms.

▶ MAKE THE BORDERS INVISIBLE

When you use tables to help control the layout of your Web page, you might want to make the borders invisible so that readers don't even know they are there. You will still be able to see the dotted-line borders when you are editing the Web page, but readers will see nothing if you have chosen no border.

CROSS-REFERENCE
To learn more about controlling the table border, see "Formatting Tables" in Chapter 8.

FIND IT ONLINE
Yale offers an excellent Web page style guide at **http://info.med.yale.edu/caim/manual/**.

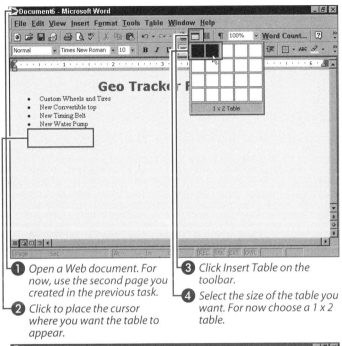

① Open a Web document. For now, use the second page you created in the previous task.

② Click to place the cursor where you want the table to appear.

③ Click Insert Table on the toolbar.

④ Select the size of the table you want. For now choose a 1 x 2 table.

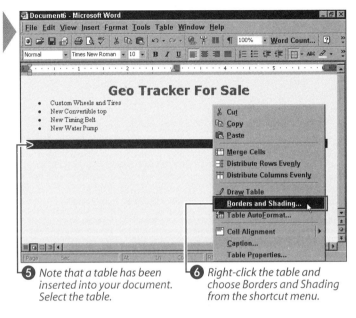

⑤ Note that a table has been inserted into your document. Select the table.

⑥ Right-click the table and choose Borders and Shading from the shortcut menu.

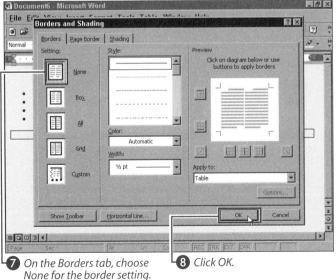

⑦ On the Borders tab, choose None for the border setting.

⑧ Click OK.

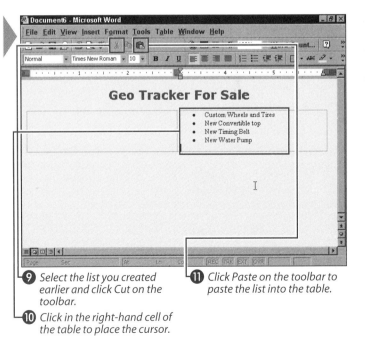

⑨ Select the list you created earlier and click Cut on the toolbar.

⑩ Click in the right-hand cell of the table to place the cursor.

⑪ Click Paste on the toolbar to paste the list into the table.

Inserting Graphics

The Internet has been around for quite a while now, but it didn't used to have the broad-reaching appeal that it now enjoys. Back before the proliferation of the World Wide Web (that would be prior to 1994), almost everything on the Internet was text. There were no compromising photos, spy cams, "under construction" banners, animated soothsaying fowl, or even so much as little green buttons next to links. The Internet was not very interesting to the general public.

Enter the World Wide Web. Web sites are not only capable of containing pictures and graphics, but this level of sophistication is now expected. The text-only pages you have already created may be filled with great information, but you should consider spicing them up with some graphics. Not only can graphics give your Web pages broader visual appeal, but they might also convey additional information that would be difficult to communicate in print. In the case of the Web page you have been creating in this chapter's exercises, a photograph or two of the car you are trying to sell could contribute significantly to the sale. On such a Web page , a picture truly is worth a thousand words.

In terms of bandwidth, a picture may actually be worth *many* thousands of words. Graphics take up a lot more disk space than the HTML file for your Web page. You need to be careful about how many graphics you include. If the graphics are too large or there are too many of them, few viewers will hang around for the time required for those pictures to download.

The figures on the facing page show you how to insert graphics into your Web documents. The first two figures show you how to insert an image into a regular Web page. The last two figures demonstrate inserting an image into a table to illustrate how you can use tables to align text and pictures side by side.

TAKE NOTE

USE THE CORRECT GRAPHIC FILE FORMAT

Generally speaking, only two kinds of graphic file formats are used on the Internet: GIF and JPEG. Web browsers are not designed to view other kinds of image formats. If you have some other kind of graphic, such as a bitmap (BMP) image, you cannot use it. Consider buying some image-editing software such as Adobe PhotoDeluxe so you can convert graphics to the proper format.

CONSERVE BANDWIDTH

To conserve bandwidth, try using relatively small images on your main pages. These smaller pictures are often called thumbnails, and you can turn the thumbnail into a hyperlink to a larger version of the same picture. This enables viewers to download the larger pictures only if they want to.

CROSS-REFERENCE

See "Moving and Resizing Graphics" in Chapter 9 to learn more about dealing with graphics.

FIND IT ONLINE

Get free graphics and more from TuDogs at http://www.tudogs.com/.

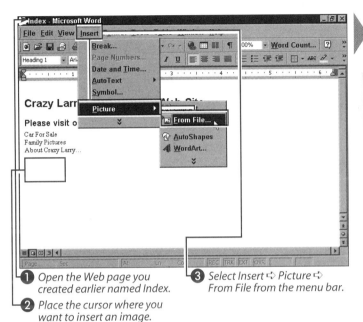

① *Open the Web page you created earlier named Index.*

② *Place the cursor where you want to insert an image.*

③ *Select Insert ⇨ Picture ⇨ From File from the menu bar.*

④ *Open the folder for your Web page here. (Note: You should copy any image files you want to use into this folder before trying to insert an image.)*

⑤ *Click to select an image file.*

⑥ *Click Insert.*

■ *The image is inserted into the document.*

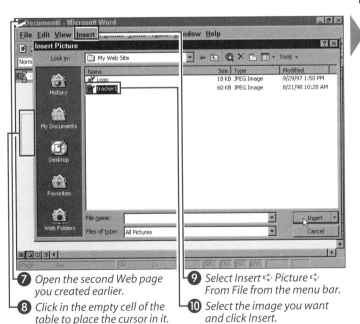

⑦ *Open the second Web page you created earlier.*

⑧ *Click in the empty cell of the table to place the cursor in it.*

⑨ *Select Insert ⇨ Picture ⇨ From File from the menu bar.*

⑩ *Select the image you want and click Insert.*

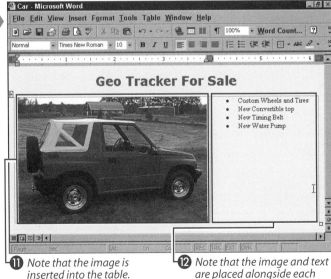

⑪ *Note that the image is inserted into the table.*

⑫ *Note that the image and text are placed alongside each other, thanks to the table.*

Creating Links

A Web page derives its name from the larger entity that it is a part of the World Wide Web. The Web is composed of millions and millions of documents linked together in a giant network that conceptually resembles a spider's web. These documents are linked by tools called *hyperlinks*. When a viewer clicks on a hyperlink with a mouse pointer, whatever file that hyperlink leads to is immediately opened. The file that is being linked to is often called a *target*, because the link has to be aimed at something before it will work.

Earlier in this chapter, you created two Web pages. A viewer who reads one of those pages may also want to read the other. Thus, you should create hyperlinks that connect the two pages to each other. This is easy to do, and brings to the pages a more dynamic element that is the touchstone of the World Wide Web.

Creating hyperlinks between your pages makes your entire Web site a single entity. In addition to linking your own pages, you will probably want to link to other Web sites as well. For instance, suppose you have created a Web page that provides information about your company to potential investors. You may want to provide them with a link to the Web site of the New York Stock Exchange (http://www.nyse.com/) so they can get up-to-the-minute stock pricing for your company. You could also boost sales by include links to retailers who sell your products

online. Links help your Web pages come alive by connecting them to the rest of the world.

The figures on the facing page show you how to create several different kinds of hyperlinks. The first two figures show you how to link the pages you created in the previous task. The third figure demonstrates how to create a link to a different Web site, and the last figure shows how to create an e-mail link.

TAKE NOTE

CREATING E-MAIL LINKS

If you want some feedback from your Web site viewers, you can make it easy by providing an e-mail link on each of your pages. Create the e-mail link just as you would any other, but in the Insert Hyperlink dialog box, type **mailto:** and then your e-mail address. An example would be mailto:kunderdahl@idgbooks.com.

MONITOR YOUR LINKS

The Internet is ever-changing. Although that is certainly one of its main strengths, it can also present a few problems. If you create hyperlinks to other Web sites, check them on a regular basis to ensure they still work. Some Webmasters rename their files frequently, and this renders your hyperlinks to those files obsolete. Broken links frustrate your viewers and gives the impression you haven't updated your information for a while.

CROSS-REFERENCE

To learn how to use the Insert Hyperlink dialog box more effectively, see "Using Dialog Boxes" in Chapter 1.

FIND IT ONLINE

Need a great directory of links? Visit **http://www.yahoo.com/**.

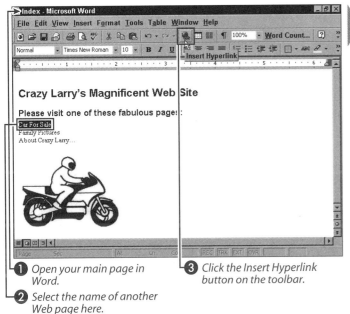

1 Open your main page in Word.

2 Select the name of another Web page here.

3 Click the Insert Hyperlink button on the toolbar.

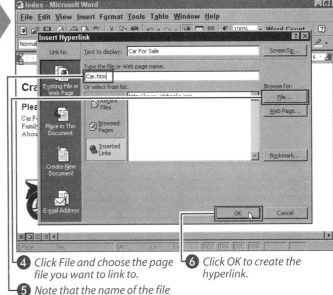

4 Click File and choose the page file you want to link to.

5 Note that the name of the file has been inserted here.

6 Click OK to create the hyperlink.

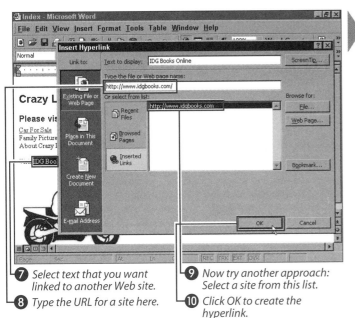

7 Select text that you want linked to another Web site.

8 Type the URL for a site here.

9 Now try another approach: Select a site from this list.

10 Click OK to create the hyperlink.

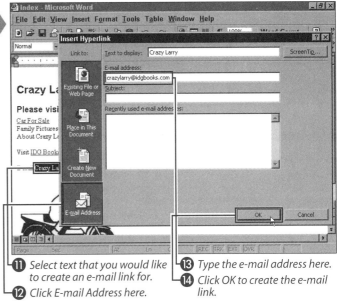

11 Select text that you would like to create an e-mail link for.

12 Click E-mail Address here.

13 Type the e-mail address here.

14 Click OK to create the e-mail link.

Preparing Your Web Pages for Publication

If you have been following the tasks in this chapter, you have created at least two different Web pages. Those pages are connected to each other with hyperlinks, and at least one of them includes an image of some sort. You have created your own Web site, but you are not a Webmaster yet. Your pages are still on your computer and can be viewed only by you. The next step, then, is to publish your pages on the Web.

Before you publish your pages, you should make a few final checks to ensure they are ready for publication. Perhaps the most important thing is to test the pages with a Web browser to make sure they function the way you expect. You can use a Web browser such as Netscape Navigator or Internet Explorer to view a Web document on your hard drive by simply entering the correct drive and folder path into the browser's address bar.

It is also a good idea to put all the files that will be needed for your Web site in one folder. You can call this folder "My Web Site," or something to that effect, and place all HTML and image files in that folder. This organization will give you a better idea of how much disk space your Web files use. Whatever Web server you plan to publish to will probably have a limit on how much disk space you can use.

The figures on the facing page show you some steps you should take before you publish your Web pages. The first two figures demonstrate how to open Windows Explorer and check the amount of space that is used by your Web documents. The last two figures show how to test your Web pages with a Web browser. The browser shown here is NeoPlanet, but Internet Explorer or Netscape Navigator will work just as well.

TAKE NOTE

PUT IMAGE FILES IN THE WEB FOLDER BEFORE INSERTING THEM

For best results, copy image files into your Web documents folder *before* you insert them into the HTML file. If you move the files after they have been inserted, the path for the image will not be correct and the image will not display properly. You can usually fix this by reinserting the images after they have been moved.

TESTING THE WEB SITE

Although you can test your Web pages with Word's built-in Web browsing abilities, it is better to test them with a dedicated Web browser, if possible. You can see in the example here that the pages are being tested with a browser called NeoPlanet. After you have published the pages to a Web server, test them again over your Internet connection.

CROSS-REFERENCE

To learn how to create a folder for your Web documents, see "Creating New Folders" in Chapter 3.

FIND IT ONLINE

Visit **http://www.neoplanet.com/** to learn more about this Web browser from Bigfoot.

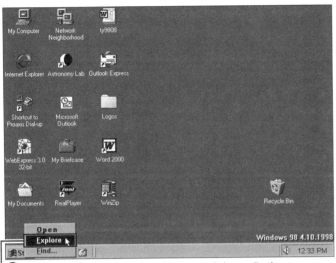

1 Right-click the Windows Start button and choose Explore.

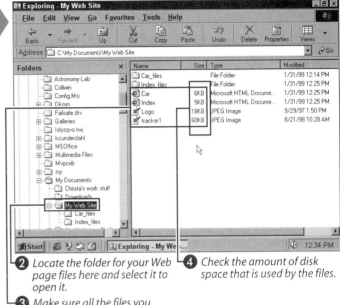

2 Locate the folder for your Web page files here and select it to open it.

3 Make sure all the files you need are shown here, including image files.

4 Check the amount of disk space that is used by the files.

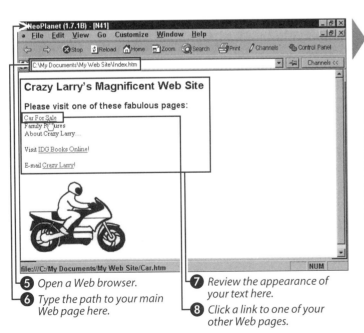

5 Open a Web browser.

6 Type the path to your main Web page here.

7 Review the appearance of your text here.

8 Click a link to one of your other Web pages.

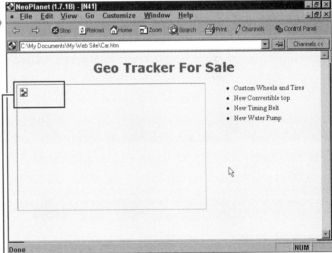

9 If you encounter an error (such as the one shown here), fix it in Word. In this case, the image probably needs to be reinserted or moved into the correct folder.

Using WS-FTP

O nce you have prepared your Web pages for publication, the only task left to do is to physically copy them to a Web server. Many different methods are available for handling this task. When you are ready to publish, you should follow whatever instructions the server provides.

Some ISPs provide special software to help simplify the publication process. Sometimes this software acts like a Wizard or series of dialog boxes in which you answer a few simple questions and click OK a few times. In other instances, the procedures are cryptic and require a degree in software engineering and a fair bit of luck. The publishing wizards that come with many popular Web site editing programs also vary in complexity.

If all else fails, the simplest and most trouble-free way to publish Web documents is through the use of an *FTP server*. FTP stands for *File Transfer Protocol*, and it offers a simple way to transfer any kind of file over the Internet. Most Web servers have an FTP server that you can use, even if other methods are provided.

Now all you need to publish your documents is an FTP client. A popular shareware program called WS-FTP is one such client, and it is generally available from software download sites across the Internet or directly from producer Ipswitch, Inc. WS-FTP is extremely simple to install and use.

The figures on the facing page show you how to open, set up, and use WS-FTP. If you are not already connected to the Internet, you will probably be prompted to connect when you try to log on to the FTP server.

TAKE NOTE

► JUST THE FACTS

If you plan to publish your Web documents using WS-FTP (or any other FTP client), you must obtain a few pieces of information from your Web server. First, you need to know the FTP server or host name, which will probably be something like ftp.servername.com. You also need to know your login name and password. If the Web server is your ISP, this information will probably be shared with your e-mail account. Finally, you need to know the account name, which will be the URL that your Web site will ultimately use. Consult your ISP to obtain this information.

► DOWNLOADING AND INSTALLING WS-FTP

When you download WS-FTP, you must first choose which version to download. If you are a qualified noncommercial user, you can download a nonexpiring, limited edition of the software for free. If you are a professional user, you must download the Pro version. Once it is downloaded, select Start ⇨ Run and run the executable file you received.

CROSS-REFERENCE

Before publishing your Web site with WS-FTP, see the previous task "Preparing Your Web Page for Publication."

FIND IT ONLINE

Learn more about WS-FTP or download a trial version at **http://www.ws-ftp.com/**.

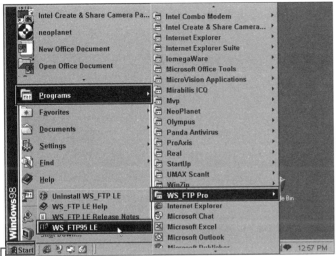

1 After you have installed WS-FTP, click Start ➪ Programs ➪ WS_FTP Pro ➪ WS_FTP95 LE.

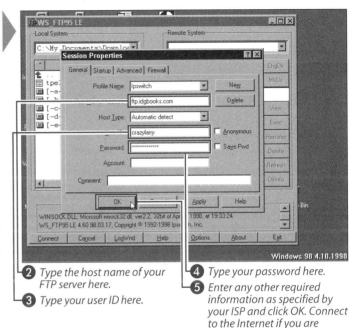

2 Type the host name of your FTP server here.

3 Type your user ID here.

4 Type your password here.

5 Enter any other required information as specified by your ISP and click OK. Connect to the Internet if you are prompted to do so.

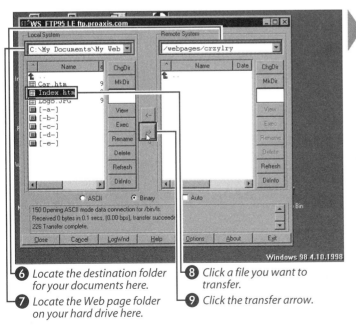

6 Locate the destination folder for your documents here.

7 Locate the Web page folder on your hard drive here.

8 Click a file you want to transfer.

9 Click the transfer arrow.

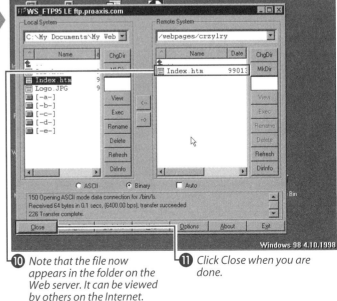

10 Note that the file now appears in the folder on the Web server. It can be viewed by others on the Internet.

11 Click Close when you are done.

Personal Workbook

Q&A

1 What is the difference between the Web toolbar and Web Tools toolbar?

_____

_____

_____

2 If you have a Web browser installed on your computer, will Web documents open in Word?

_____

_____

_____

3 What file format must you use when you save a file as a Web document?

_____

_____

_____

4 What is the easiest way to align a picture and some text alongside each other in a Web document?

_____

_____

5 What is a hyperlink?

_____

_____

_____

6 Can you create a link that makes it easier for people to contact you?

_____

_____

_____

7 What must you do before others can view your Web pages?

_____

_____

_____

8 Where should your Web files be located before your publish?

_____

_____

ANSWERS: PAGE 372

EXTRA PRACTICE

① Create a new Web page that describes yourself.

② Create an outline in your Web page.

③ Insert a picture of yourself into one cell of the table. (Some clip art that resembles you will suffice.)

④ Create a link back to your main Web page.

⑤ Create a link that makes it easy for readers to contact you via e-mail.

⑥ Publish the Web page using WS-FTP.

⑦ Test your Web page, correct any errors in Word, and test it again.

REAL-WORLD APPLICATIONS

✔ Web pages that you create with Word can serve many purposes. If you are trying to sell your home, consider creating a Web page for it. Take many pictures of the home so that Web site viewers can have a "virtual open house" online.

✔ Sharing photographs with distant friends and family can be tough. But with a Web page and either a scanner or digital camera to take pictures, you can post the pictures online and let others view them at their leisure. They can even print the pictures if they have a color printer!

✔ WS-FTP can be used for more than publishing your Web page. Choose a different profile when you start the program to download tax forms, shareware, and more.

Visual Quiz

The Web document shown here has a picture alongside some text. What is an easy way to create this format? Are there any hyperlinks on this page? What does a hyperlink look like?

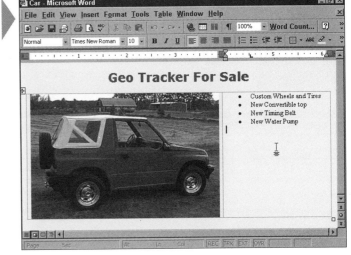

_____

_____

_____

_____

PART

V

Using Advanced Word Features

Word 2000 provides many powerful tools to help you publish attractive, professional-looking documents. One of the advanced features covered in Part 5 is called *Mail Merge*. Mail Merge enables you to manage large amounts of data such as names, addresses, and sales data. You can use this data to create form letters and other mass-produced documents that might otherwise be too time consuming to create.

You also learn about some of the more advanced formatting features that Word has to offer. These features include items often associated with documents created by professional book publishers, such as footnotes, page headers and footers, borders and shading, and more.

Next, you see how easy it is to integrate Word with other programs on your computer. Modern software technology lets you create documents that incorporate elements from seemingly incompatible kinds of software, including word processing programs, spreadsheets, multimedia objects, and others.

Finally, you are introduced to macros. Macros are small programs you can create to run in Word documents and automate otherwise complicated processes. These are normally associated with the most advanced users, but with a few simple steps you, too, can become a Word power user.

CHAPTER **17**

MASTER
THESE
SKILLS

▶ **Creating a Main Document**

▶ **Creating a Data Source**

▶ **Merging Documents**

▶ **Using a Microsoft Access File as Your Data Source**

Using Mail Merge

How you use Word can vary greatly, depending on the type of work you do, your hobbies, and your other personal interests. But whatever your chosen purpose for this program, you are probably using it because you want to take advantage of Word's capability to automate and simplify otherwise complicated tasks. You have already learned how to automate a variety of things with features such as Find and Replace, AutoCorrect, templates, and more. These features can be extremely useful because they help you avoid manually entering the same, repetitive information over and over again.

But what do you do if you need to enter large amounts of nonrepetitive information into documents? For instance, suppose you work in the billing department for a local veterinarian. At the end of every month, you have the unenviable task of preparing and sending past due notices to customers who have not yet paid their bills. You might have, say, 30 notices to send, and the text of each letter will probably be the same. However, each letter needs to include the name and address of the person, as well as the past due amount.

This situation sounds like the ideal candidate for a form letter. A form letter is a letter that you send to many people, with spaces to insert each person's name and other information. In years past, form letters typically included a blank line where you had to handwrite the person's name. However, you probably want to avoid this tactic for several reasons. First, it makes the form letter seem very obvious and impersonal, and recipients are less likely to take it seriously. Furthermore, handwriting all that information can be time-consuming.

Word offers a solution in the form of a feature called *Mail Merge*. Mail Merge enables you to create form letters based on data you have already entered into the computer. Word reads a data source and *merges* it with the form letter, making the merged data look like it was typed in right along with the rest of the text.

This chapter introduces you to Mail Merge by showing you how to create form letters and data sources, and then how to merge the two together. You also learn how to use outside data sources, such as a Microsoft Access database.

Creating a Main Document

Mail Merge provides a virtually limitless stream of possibilities for you, the creative Word 2000 user. By far the most common use for this feature is the creation of form letters, for purposes such as billing notices, sales materials, and contest promotions. Of course, you can use Mail Merge for virtually any kind of mass mailing that you need to distribute.

You can also use Mail Merge for more personal correspondence, although remember that form letters typically have an impersonal tone and feel. For example, it would probably not be a very good idea to mail merge thank-you letters for birthday gifts that your family sent you, but you could very well use it to prepare invitations for a reunion or party.

You have several steps to complete before you can use Mail Merge. A merge requires two main elements: a *data source*, and a *main document*. The data source is the place where Word obtains the data you want merged into the form letter. This is a list of names, addresses, or other information that you want to use in the letter. You can use a variety of data sources, including a Microsoft Access database, a personal address book, or simply a Microsoft Word data source.

For now, concentrate on creating a main document. This is the form letter or other document type that you want to merge data into. The example shown on the facing page shows a letter inviting people to a picnic. This is an excellent use of the merge technique, because it helps you keep track of who is being invited, and provides a more personalized feeling to what would otherwise be an impersonal invitation and map.

The figures on the facing page show you how to create a main document for a mail merge. You can edit the main document before or after you open the Mail Merge dialog box, but in this example, you perform the editing after.

TAKE NOTE

▶ USING THE MAIL MERGE TOOLBAR

Word provides a special Mail Merge toolbar to help you work with your Mail Merge documents, but this toolbar cannot be opened like most other toolbars. To open this toolbar, you must select Tools ⇨ Mail Merge and begin creating a main document and data source as described here.

▶ USE A TEMPLATE

You can give your main documents a more professional look by creating them from a template. Consider creating a template that incorporates standard fonts and other layout options, and perhaps even a company logo near the top. If you do choose to use a template, create it and compose the text of the main document before you open the Mail Merge dialog box.

CROSS-REFERENCE
See "Using a Template to Create a New Document" in Chapter 6 to learn more about working with templates.

FIND IT ONLINE
Check out some great freeform letters at Thomas Blake's One Stop Form Letter Shop at **http://tblake.com/formshop.html**.

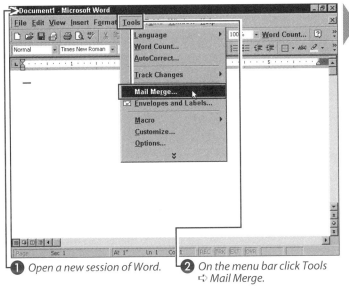

1 Open a new session of Word.

2 On the menu bar click Tools
⇨ Mail Merge.

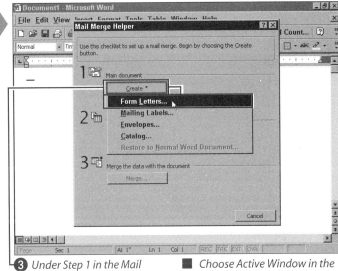

3 Under Step 1 in the Mail
Merge dialog box, click Create
⇨ Form Letters.

■ Choose Active Window in the
next dialog box that appears.

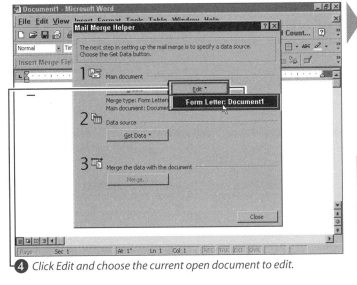

4 Click Edit and choose the current open document to edit.

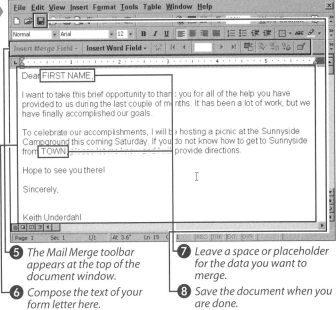

5 The Mail Merge toolbar
appears at the top of the
document window.

6 Compose the text of your
form letter here.

7 Leave a space or placeholder
for the data you want to
merge.

8 Save the document when you
are done.

Creating a Data Source

As discussed in the previous section, a Mail Merge action requires two primary elements. You have already learned how to create the main document, which is the body of your form letters and documents, so now it's time to create a data source. The data source is the list of data that will be merged into the document. This list could contain names, addresses, company names, or various other bits of information. Once created, you can use a data source as many times as you want, in a wide variety of main documents.

Data in a data source is separated into *fields*. A field contains a single piece of information, such as a name, phone number, or favorite color. You can create as many or as few fields as you like, but for best results, you should create separate fields for every piece of information you might collect.

For instance, suppose you work for a software company and are tasked with customer service and marketing. Your customers probably had to register the software they purchased from you, and in doing so, they filled out a form with many different pieces of information. When designing a data source, you should create a separate field for each piece of data. This approach will provide greater flexibility in the future, even as your needs and uses of that data change. In fact, you may end up creating fields of information that are never used, but that is better

than needing a special piece of data later on and not being able to get it from the data source.

The figures on the facing page show you how to create a data source. This example describes how to create a source that includes personal information about some friends or clients. When you are following along, enter names and addresses of people that you need to contact. That way, you are able to continue using this data source in the future.

TAKE NOTE

WHERE DOES THE DATA GO?

When you create a data source, the data is entered into a table. Each piece of data goes into a table cell, and Word organizes the data by field. Make sure that you give a descriptive name to each field so that you remember what it is later.

CREATE SEPARATE FIELDS FOR FIRST AND LAST NAMES

You should consider creating separate fields for first and last names as well as titles, instead of using a single field for a person's entire name. With this approach, you can use the names separately as you see fit. For instance, you might want to use "Mr. Smith" in the salutation, but later in the letter, make use of the person's first name "John."

CROSS-REFERENCE

Learn more about dealing with dialog boxes in Chapter 1 under "Using Dialog Boxes."

FIND IT ONLINE

Visit **http://www-csag.cs.uiuc.edu/individual/ pakin/complaint** for a form letter of a very different kind.

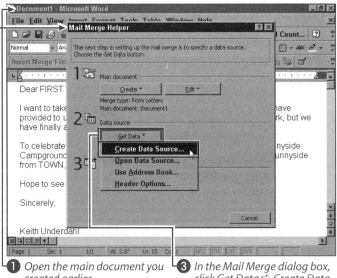

① Open the main document you created earlier.

② Click Tools ➪ Mail Merge. The Mail Merge Helper dialog box appears.

③ In the Mail Merge dialog box, click Get Data ➪ Create Data Source.

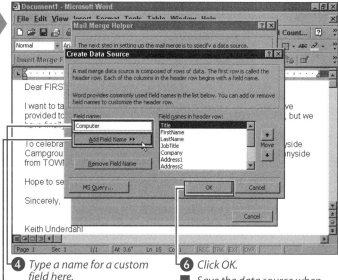

④ Type a name for a custom field here.

⑤ Click Add Field Name to add it to the list of fields.

⑥ Click OK.

■ Save the data source when you are prompted to do so. Make sure you give it a name that is descriptive of the types of records it contains.

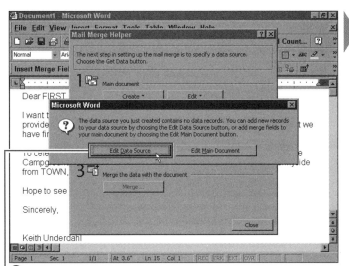

⑦ Click Edit Data Source.

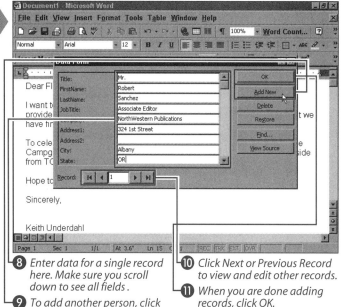

⑧ Enter data for a single record here. Make sure you scroll down to see all fields.

⑨ To add another person, click Add New.

⑩ Click Next or Previous Record to view and edit other records.

⑪ When you are done adding records, click OK.

Merging Documents

Once you have created a main document and a data source document, it is time to merge them. For the most part, this step happens automatically during the print job. So, if there were 30 entries in the data source, you will get 30 copies of the main document, each one containing the unique information from the applicable data record.

You can preview how the merged document looks before you print it. To do so, click the View Merged Data button on the Mail Merge toolbar to display the data in the main document. You can move back and forth to separate copies by clicking the Next or Previous Record buttons.

Another option you might want to choose is to specify which records will be merged. For instance, consider again the example of the software company. One of the pieces of information you collected was the type of computer each person used. If you are composing a letter to promote a new version of software created for a Macintosh, you probably don't need to send that letter to customers with PCs.

To specify the fields you want to use, filter the records from within the Query Options dialog box (click Tools ➪ Mail Merge, and then click the Query Options button). In this example, you filter the records by comparing entries in the Computer field to a standard you specify. So, if you enter "Macintosh" in the Compare To box, only records that have "Macintosh" in that field are chosen.

The figures on the facing page show you how to insert merge fields into a document and merge the fields.

TAKE NOTE

▶ ALLOW FOR VARIANCES WHEN FILTERING

For best results, you should try to keep your entries fairly standard, especially in fields that might be used to filter the records. However, variations can occur, and Word lets you select multiple criteria when comparing records. If you are only looking for records of Macintosh users, for instance, you might want to look for records that have "Macintosh" as well as "Mac" or "Apple". You can do this by using "and" or "or" operators.

▶ CLEARING FILTER SETTINGS

When you choose filtering criteria for your data records, those settings are saved with the main document. This means that if you choose to use the main document again in the future, it will filter out the same records. If you don't want this to happen, clear the filtering criteria in the Query Options dialog box.

CROSS-REFERENCE
You can also preview your merged documents with Print Preview. Learn how in "Using Print Preview" in Chapter 14.

SHORTCUT
Press ALT+Shift+F to quickly insert a merge field.

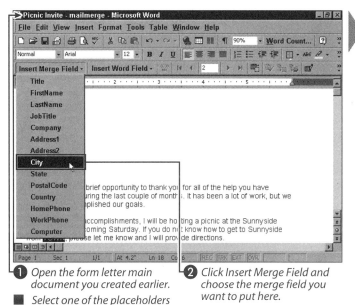

① Open the form letter main document you created earlier.

■ Select one of the placeholders you created earlier.

② Click Insert Merge Field and choose the merge field you want to put here.

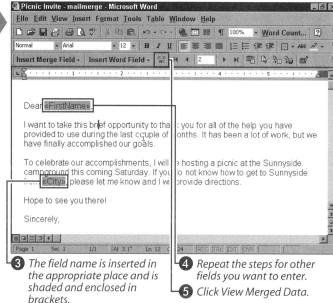

③ The field name is inserted in the appropriate place and is shaded and enclosed in brackets.

④ Repeat the steps for other fields you want to enter.

⑤ Click View Merged Data.

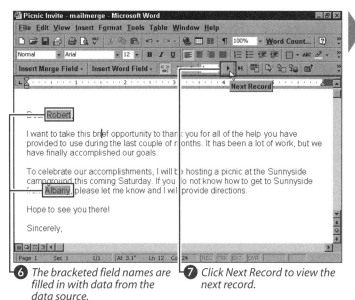

⑥ The bracketed field names are filled in with data from the data source.

⑦ Click Next Record to view the next record.

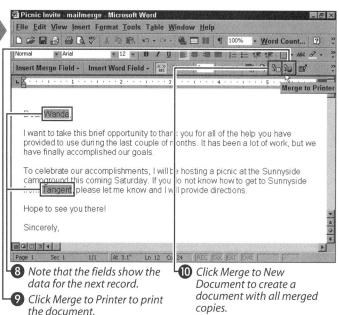

⑧ Note that the fields show the data for the next record.

⑨ Click Merge to Printer to print the document.

⑩ Click Merge to New Document to create a document with all merged copies.

Using a Microsoft Access File as Your Data Source

Word 2000 contains all of the tools you need to create and publish form letters. Word even enables you to create a data source, a function not normally associated with a word processing program. Maintaining data records is normally the function of a database program such as Microsoft Access. Access 2000 comes with the both the Standard Edition and Premium Edition of Office 2000, or you can purchase it separately just like Word.

As the name implies, a database program is designed to store and manage pieces of data. Databases are often used to store information about customers and other data. Each customer has a separate record in a database file, and each record can contain a variety of data fields. As you can see, this is similar to the data source function that is available within Word.

If you are merging records that you create yourself, and don't use the records for anything but mail merge actions, it's fine to stick with a Word data source. But if many other people also need to use the data, or if the data needs to be used in other programs, a real database program such as Access is probably the best way to go. In fact, many companies already make it a practice to store important information in a database, so there is a good chance that a data source already exists that you could use.

The database ensures that information is maintained centrally, so that it has a better chance of being up to date when you need to use it. It also makes more efficient use of everyone's time, because each department doesn't need to spend a lot of time creating redundant data records. Data in Access might be used in Excel spreadsheets, Word mail merges, and various other programs.

The figures on the facing page show you how to use a Microsoft Access data source. Although this procedure is performed in Access, the technique can be used to obtain records from other sources as well.

TAKE NOTE

▶ USING DATA FROM AN ADDRESS BOOK

In addition to a database like Access, you can use an address book such as the one in Microsoft Outlook as a data source. This also prevents you from duplicating effort by using existing resources for names, addresses, and other information you might have recorded there.

▶ SELECTING DATA FROM A QUERY OR TABLE

When you use Access as a data source, you must select the data from a table or query in Access. When you use a query, it is linked by default so that each time you retrieve the same instructions it makes a new query. You can clear the Link to Query check box to always use the original data you selected.

CROSS-REFERENCE

To learn more about using Access, see *Teach Yourself Microsoft Access 2000* by Charles Siegel.

FIND IT ONLINE

Find some great online tips for using Access at http://www.bpro.com/.

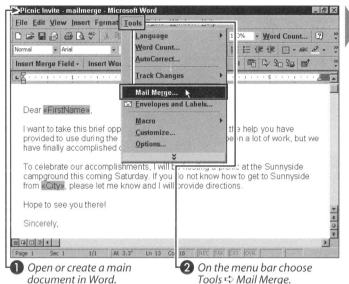

1 Open or create a main document in Word.

2 On the menu bar choose Tools ➪ Mail Merge.

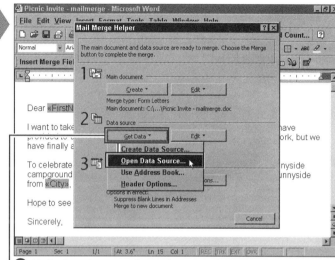

3 Under Data Source in the Mail Merge Helper, click Get Data ➪ Open Data Source.

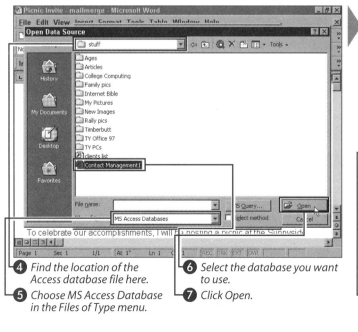

4 Find the location of the Access database file here.

5 Choose MS Access Database in the Files of Type menu.

6 Select the database you want to use.

7 Click Open.

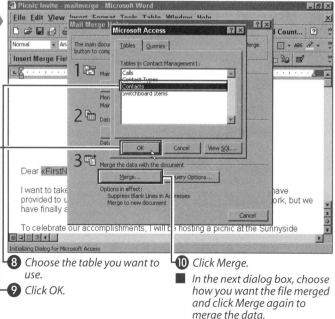

8 Choose the table you want to use.

9 Click OK.

10 Click Merge.

■ In the next dialog box, choose how you want the file merged and click Merge again to merge the data.

Personal Workbook

Q&A

1 What two document elements do you need to perform a mail merge?

_____

_____

_____

2 Which element would contain the body of a form letter?

_____

_____

_____

3 What are three possible sources of data for a mail merge?

_____

_____

_____

4 In a Word data source, can you create your own fields?

_____

_____

_____

5 Can you limit the records merged from the data source?

_____

_____

_____

6 What will the merge fields look like in the main document?

_____

_____

_____

7 How can you preview a merged document?

_____

_____

8 In what situation is it better to use an Access database rather than a Word document as your data source?

_____

_____

_____

ANSWERS: PAGE 372

EXTRA PRACTICE

1 Create a main document to invite members of your family to a reunion.

2 Create a data source and a custom field called "Cook."

3 Create data records for your family members. In the "Cook" field, type **Yes** if the person enjoys cooking, or **No** if the person doesn't enjoy cooking.

4 Preview the merged document.

5 Create another main document that describes a baking contest to be held at your family reunion.

6 Merge the document with your family data source, but filter it so that only people with a "Yes" in the Cook field receive the letter.

REAL-WORLD APPLICATIONS

✔ Use customer feedback or registration cards to get important marketing information from your customers. Include fields for their favorite activities, the type of computer they own, etc. You can then use this information in Mail Merge to direct advertising letters to likely markets.

✔ A school could create a data source that lists all students in the school. If one of the data fields lists the grade level of each student, you can use this to send mail-merged form letters to all parents of children in a certain grade.

✔ Create a data source that lists parts in your inventory. You can use Mail Merge to produce inventory lists for stock on hand, including part or serial numbers.

Visual Quiz

Which portions of this document are merge fields? Can you change the merge fields so that they show the actual data inserted into them? How? How would you switch to another copy of the document with the next data record in it?

_____

_____

_____

_____

CHAPTER **18**

MASTER THESE SKILLS

▶ **Creating a Numbered or Bulleted List**

▶ **Formatting a Numbered or Bulleted List**

▶ **Using Headers and Footers**

▶ **Using Borders and Shading**

▶ **Working with Columns**

▶ **Creating Outlines**

▶ **Using Footnotes**

▶ **Counting Words**

▶ **Tracking Changes**

Using Advanced Formatting

Throughout this book, I demonstrate how to take advantage of some of Word's best features for helping you publish high-quality, professional-looking documents. If you've followed along thus far, you have learned how to manipulate the look and shape of your pages; how to apply special formatting to your text; how to add graphics and other distinct elements to your documents; and how to publish your documents on paper and on the World Wide Web.

As useful and versatile as these features are, there are still many more tools that Word 2000 can offer you to give your documents a custom touch. This chapter introduces you to some advanced formatting tools that have not been previously discussed. Most of the tools described here apply to page and paragraph formatting, and many of them expand on skills you have already learned. Numbered and bulleted lists are a good example of this, because they expand on the AutoFormat feature discussed in Chapter 12. You explore the ins and outs of working with these lists in the first two tasks of this chapter.

Many other page layout tools await you here as well. Here you learn how to insert headers and footers into your documents, and you work with borders and shading to give documents a more exotic and finished look. You format a page with columns, similar to what newspapers and magazines use. Word makes it easy to create outlines, which is often the first step in composing a large document. You discover how to include footnotes in your documents, a feature normally associated with more advanced publications but still very useful to you.

The last two tasks in this chapter don't necessarily apply to formatting, but they do describe a couple of Word's most advanced editing tools. One task shows you how to count the words, lines, and paragraphs in your document, an especially important tool for professional or freelance writers. Finally, you learn how Word can help you keep track of changes as you edit, making it easier for you to see what has been changed, who changed it, and when. Once you have mastered the basics and moved on to these more advanced skills, you can truly be considered a Word 2000 pro!

Creating a Numbered or Bulleted List

Not surprisingly, most of the text you type into a document will be in the form of sentences and paragraphs. These are the most basic forms of text, and constitute the body of most documents. That said, garden-variety sentences and paragraphs are not the only forms of text you can use in a Word 2000 document. Many other document elements consist of text: headings, subheadings, image captions, and so on.

Another format for text in a document is a list. You can use lists for a wide variety of things. For instance, you could use a list as a table of contents at the beginning of a document, or you can list items in a row. You can even type whole paragraphs in lists if you wish.

Word lets you create lists in your document in a couple of different ways. The simplest way is to autoformat a list. If you seem to be typing a list in your document, Word automatically applies formatting to it. If you have the AutoFormat feature disabled, you can manually format the list by selecting the list and clicking the appropriate list button on the toolbar. Alternatively, you can select the list and format it using the Bullets and Numbering dialog box in the Format menu. When Word automatically formats a list, the list items are indented and a number or bullet is placed next to each item.

The first type of list you practice creating here is a bulleted list. A bulleted list usually has bullets next to each list item. A bulleted list includes items that don't necessarily have to be in a certain order, such as a grocery list. The figures on the facing page show you how to create a bulleted list using AutoFormat. Pay special attention to the last two figures, which show you how to end the list just as quickly as you created it.

Continued

TAKE NOTE

▶ WHAT IS A BULLET?

A bullet is a small graphic element that provides a visual key for readers to focus on. Bullets are often nothing more than small dots, but they can be other symbols as well, such as asterisks. You can even choose to have no symbol at all in your "bulleted" list. You should use the same bullet symbol for each item in the list.

▶ BULLETED LISTS IN WEB DOCUMENTS

Bulleted lists work well in Web documents if you need to list links to other sites. On your main Web page, use a bulleted list to display the contents of the various pages of your Web site. Make the first word or two of each bulleted item a hyperlink to the page it describes.

CROSS-REFERENCE

If you have disabled autoformatting for bulleted lists, see "Using AutoFormat" in Chapter 12 to enable it.

FIND IT ONLINE

Visit Free Gifs & Animations, at **http://www.fg-a.com/**, to find GIF images you can use as bullets in a list.

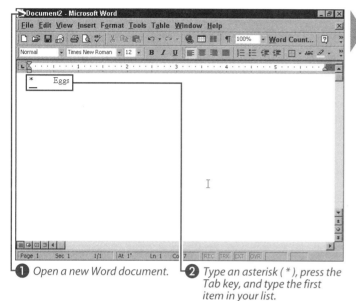

① Open a new Word document.

② Type an asterisk (*), press the Tab key, and type the first item in your list.

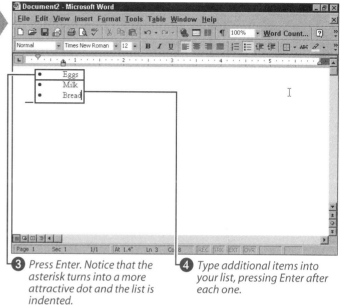

③ Press Enter. Notice that the asterisk turns into a more attractive dot and the list is indented.

④ Type additional items into your list, pressing Enter after each one.

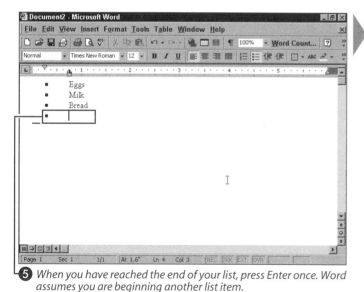

⑤ When you have reached the end of your list, press Enter once. Word assumes you are beginning another list item.

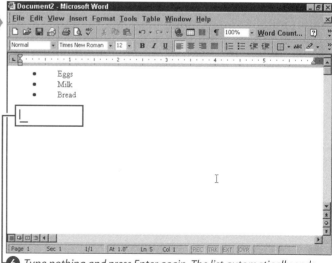

⑥ Type nothing and press Enter again. The list automatically ends.

303

Creating a Numbered or Bulleted List *Continued*

The previous page illustrates how to create a bulleted list in a Word document. Specifically, an asterisk and a tab character are placed at the beginning of each line of the list, and AutoFormat then formats the entries. This is not the only way to create such a list; you can still create a list even if the AutoFormat feature is disabled.

To create a list without AutoFormat, simply type the lines of the list and press Enter (or Shift+Enter) at the end of each line. But in this case, don't type an asterisk or press the Tab key at the beginning of each line. When the list is finished, select it and press the Bullets button on the Formatting toolbar (press the Numbering button for a numbered list). If you want more formatting options, you can also choose the Bullets and Numbering dialog box from the Format menu (which is discussed further in the next task).

You can create a numbered list in Word just as easily as you can create a bulleted list. A numbered list works better than a bulleted list for items that should be in a certain order, such as a set of instructions for assembling a tent. The sequential series of numbers for the items is the only difference between a numbered and a bulleted list.

Numbered lists don't have to use numbers. You can create a "numbered" list that uses letters instead of numbers, or even Roman numerals. When you start to type such a list, Word recognizes common list numbering schemes and automatically formats the rest of the list accordingly. In addition, you do not need to start your list with 1, A, I, or i. If you start a list with the letter *j*, the second list item begins with *k*. Also, if you insert a new item into the middle of a numbered list, Word automatically renumbers the rest of the list.

The figures on the facing page show you how to create numbered lists in Word using AutoFormat. First create a list with standard numerals, and then create another list using Roman numerals.

TAKE NOTE

▶ NUMBERED LISTS IN TEXT DOCUMENTS

If your document is (or will be converted to) a text document, you should not use autoformatted lists. Numbered lists cause formatting problems when they become plain text because the numbers are incorrect or missing altogether.

▶ CREATING OUTLINES

If you create a numbered list, and then create another list immediately under it with a different numbering scheme (such as letters), Word automatically indents the second list, as in an outline.

CROSS-REFERENCE

See "Creating Outlines" later in this chapter to learn how to use autoformatted lists in outlines.

FIND IT ONLINE

Learn how making lists can help you be more organized with tips from **http://www.organizenow.com/**.

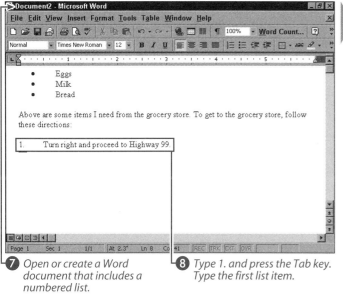

7 Open or create a Word document that includes a numbered list.

8 Type 1. and press the Tab key. Type the first list item.

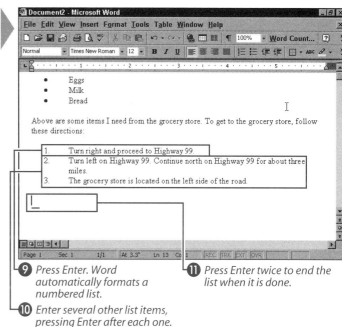

9 Press Enter. Word automatically formats a numbered list.

10 Enter several other list items, pressing Enter after each one.

11 Press Enter twice to end the list when it is done.

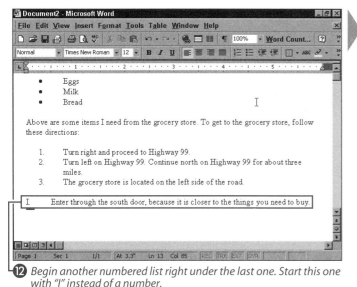

12 Begin another numbered list right under the last one. Start this one with "I" instead of a number.

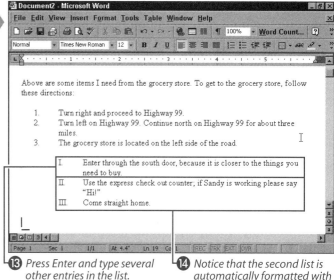

13 Press Enter and type several other entries in the list.

14 Notice that the second list is automatically formatted with Roman numerals instead of regular numbers. Also, notice that the second list is indented.

305

Formatting a Numbered or Bulleted List

Numbered and bulleted lists are useful and offer many possibilities for the creative PC user. With AutoFormat, creating these lists takes very little extra time or effort. However, as with anything that happens quickly and easily in Word, you might find the final look of the list a little plain or generic.

The solution to ordinary lists is to apply extraordinary formatting to them. Actually, applying custom formatting to lists is quite simple, but it does require a concerted effort on your part. Adjusting the formatting of a list takes a bit more time, but it might be the only way to make your documents conform to your exact standards.

When formatting your lists, you can adjust many of the same characteristics that you can also adjust for regular text. You can change the font, size, color, or any other aspect of the appearance of text in a list, and you can also apply paragraph formatting standards such as increased line spacing. You apply these formatting changes to lists in the same way as you would to any other kind of paragraph.

However, there are other issues to consider when you are formatting a list. In the case of a bulleted list, the first change you make will probably be to the bullet itself. Word has numerous types and styles of bullets available for you to choose from, and you can browse through them in the Bullets and Numbering dialog box. You can choose from different bullets, arrows, boxes, check marks, and more.

The figures on the facing page show you how to customize the bullets used in the list you created earlier. Once you have completed these steps, you can move on to the next two pages, which discuss other list-formatting issues you can control.

Continued

TAKE NOTE

▶ USING SPECIAL FONT CHARACTERS FOR BULLETS

Word comes with a number of fonts that contain nothing but unusual characters. These fonts include Almanac MT, Bon Apetit MT, Webdings, and many others. Most fonts with "MT" at the end of their name contain these special characters, and you might want to browse them when you are looking for a custom bullet for your list. Just make sure that the font you use is installed on the computer you plan to print from.

▶ USING PICTURES FOR BULLETS

In addition to special font characters, Word also provides some simple GIF images that work well for bullets. These are available by clicking the Pictures button in the Bullets and Numbering dialog box. Because they are small (1–2K) GIF images, these pictures work especially well in Web documents. However, depending on your printer, they might not look very good on paper. Make sure that the image file for the bullet is copied into the folder for your Web documents.

CROSS-REFERENCE

To learn more about viewing fonts, see "Working with Fonts" in Chapter 7.

SHORTCUT

Quickly open the Bullets and Numbering dialog box by right-clicking the list and choosing Bullets and Numbering from the shortcut menu.

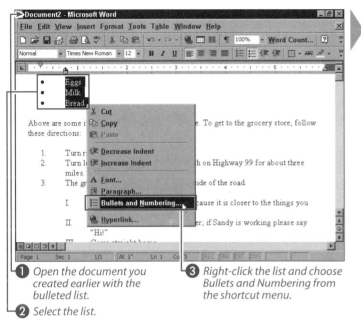

1 Open the document you created earlier with the bulleted list.

2 Select the list.

3 Right-click the list and choose Bullets and Numbering from the shortcut menu.

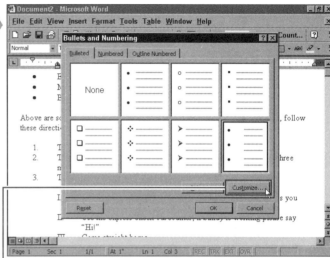

4 Choose a different bullet style or click Customize.

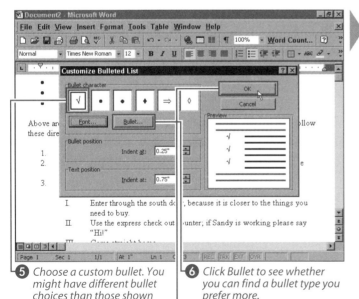

5 Choose a custom bullet. You might have different bullet choices than those shown here.

6 Click Bullet to see whether you can find a bullet type you prefer more.

7 Click OK.

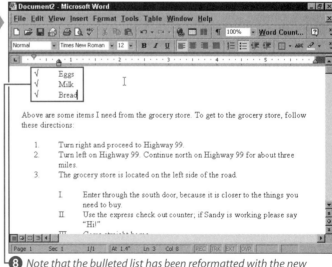

8 Note that the bulleted list has been reformatted with the new bullet style.

Formatting a Numbered or Bulleted List *Continued*

Modifying the appearance of the bullet used in a bulleted list is a great way to improve the look of that list. You can modify the appearance and numbering scheme of numbered lists as well. Even if you used AutoFormat to create a numbering scheme, you can still choose a different numbering option from the Bullets and Numbering dialog box. Not only can you modify the numbering scheme, but you can also choose the starting number or letter for a list, and you can adjust the positioning of that number or letter.

The appearance of bullets or numbers in lists is not the only aspect of list formatting that you can modify. There are also some important alignment issues for the list itself that you should address. First you must decide where the bullet or number should appear. You can choose whether you want the bullet or number aligned left, right, or centered, but more importantly, you need to decide how far the list should be indented from the page margin.

Once you have selected the position of the bullet or number, you must decide how far the list text itself should be indented. Obviously, the first line of a list item is indented after the number or bullet, but if the text of a list item runs longer than a single line, you have to decide how far it should be indented. If you choose zero, the text lines up on the left margin, which might look strange. Generally speaking, the text should be indented more than the bullet or number itself.

The figures on the facing page show you how to adjust the alignment of numbers and text in a numbered list. Notice the difference in list layout from the first figure to the last. Also, keep in mind that although this example uses a numbered list, the same techniques work for bulleted lists as well.

TAKE NOTE

▶ PICKING UP WHERE THE LAST LIST LEFT OFF

If your document contains more than one numbered list, you have some additional options to select in the Bullets and Numbering dialog box. The default setting is Restart Numbering, which means that the numbering starts over at 1 with each new list. However, if you choose Continue Previous List, the numbering picks up where the last list left off. If the last number in the previous list was 5, the first number in the next list will be 6.

▶ PREVIEWING LIST FORMATTING CHANGES

The Preview window in the Customize List dialog box may or may not provide an accurate preview of what your list looks like. For best results, just apply the formatting changes and see how they look in your document. If you don't like the changes, they can be easily undone.

CROSS-REFERENCE

See "Formatting Paragraphs" in Chapter 7 to learn more about indenting text.

FIND IT ONLINE

Another great source of free bullet GIFs is available at http://thepage.simplenet.com/gif-bull.htm.

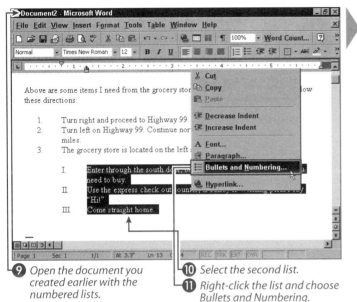

⑨ Open the document you created earlier with the numbered lists.

⑩ Select the second list.

⑪ Right-click the list and choose Bullets and Numbering.

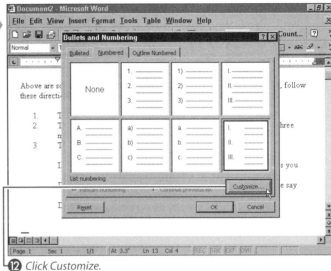

⑫ Click Customize.

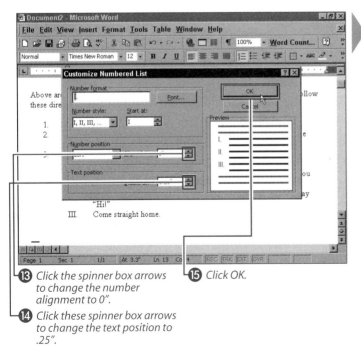

⑬ Click the spinner box arrows to change the number alignment to 0".

⑭ Click these spinner box arrows to change the text position to .25".

⑮ Click OK.

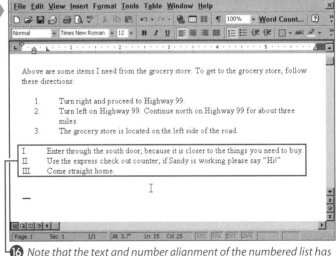

⑯ Note that the text and number alignment of the numbered list has been changed.

Using Headers and Footers

Word provides you with many interesting and useful tools to help you improve the quality and overall appearance of your documents. One fascinating thing you can do with Word documents is to add headers and footers to your pages. A header is a line or two of text that appears at the top of every page in your document. Usually it remains constant throughout the document, although there are some elements that can change. A footer is just like a header, except that it resides at the bottom (foot) of the page rather than the top (head).

Headers and footers are normally invisible when you are editing a document, but they are in view if you are using Print Preview. You should also be able to see these elements when you are using Print Layout View, but they appear in a lighter color and act as if they are in the background or not there at all. Still, viewing them in this manner can help you to be sure that the overall page layout looks the way you want it.

Many different kinds of information can be placed in headers or footers, but there are some typical uses for these tools. Most books, for instance, have headers and/or footers on the pages to tell you the title of the book, the author's name, and often the page or chapter number. Magazines, too, use footers to show the name of the magazine and the date, volume number, or even the article name.

The figures on the facing page show you how to insert a header into a document. The steps are roughly the same for inserting a footer. You can type almost anything you want into a header or footer, but in the interest of maintaining a professional appearance overall, you should keep header and footer text to a minimum. Once you have inserted a header or footer, move on to the next two pages. There you will learn how to edit and change the look of your headers and footers.

Continued

TAKE NOTE

HEADERS, FOOTERS, AND REAL ESTATE

Whenever you insert a header or footer into a document, it takes up space on the page just like any other line or paragraph would. If space is limited on your pages, it is better to stick with one or the other, but not both.

PAGE NUMBERS IN HEADERS AND FOOTERS

If you have applied page numbers to your document, the numbers appear as part of the header or footer itself. You can edit them at the same time you edit other header and footer information. See the next section to learn more about inserting page numbers in footers.

CROSS-REFERENCE

See "Changing the View" in Chapter 2 to learn more about controlling what you see in Word.

FIND IT ONLINE

Fancy yourself an electronic publisher? Visit desktopPublishing.com at **http://www. desktoppublishing.com/**.

USING ADVANCED FORMATTING

Using Headers and Footers

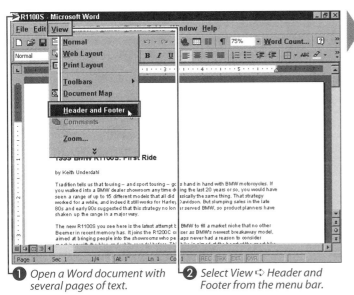

1 Open a Word document with several pages of text.

2 Select View ➪ Header and Footer from the menu bar.

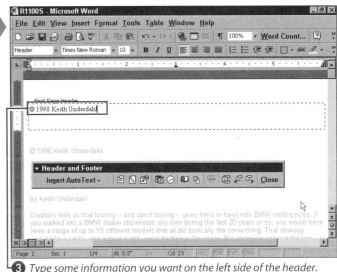

3 Type some information you want on the left side of the header.

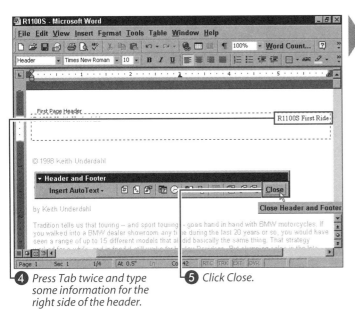

4 Press Tab twice and type some information for the right side of the header.

5 Click Close.

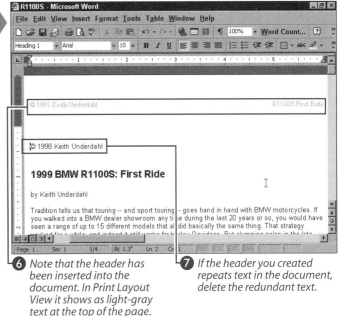

6 Note that the header has been inserted into the document. In Print Layout View it shows as light-gray text at the top of the page.

7 If the header you created repeats text in the document, delete the redundant text.

Using Headers and Footers

Continued

You can use a header or footer to convey a wide variety of information. As mentioned earlier, a header or footer is a good place to provide information about the document itself. This can include the name of the document, or the name of a particular page's section, chapter, or part. One option you should consider is to place different information on facing pages. For instance, on even-numbered pages (which appear on the left side when you bind your document) you could place a book title, and on the odd-numbered pages (which appear on the right) you could insert the chapter number.

Headers and footers can also provide specific information about your editing. You can include the current date and time and choose to have this information updated automatically every time you edit the document. This approach might be useful for memos and other documents of a timely nature, but for a project like a book, this information is probably less useful.

Perhaps the most common type of information to include in a footer or header is a page number. You can insert just a page number, or you can insert a page number and the number of pages in the document. For example, if the reader is looking at the second page of a five-page document, she would see "Page 2 of 5" or something like that. This can be useful if you are sending the document in the mail or via facsimile, because the reader can easily determine if pages are missing.

The figures on the facing page show you how to insert a page number and some AutoText information into a footer. The techniques described here work on both header and footers.

TAKE NOTE

▶ SWITCHING BETWEEN HEADERS AND FOOTERS

If you are in the header but want to place information in the footer of a document, click the Switch Between Header and Footer button on the Header and Footer toolbar. This button acts as a toggle between the two elements.

▶ CREATE A FOOTER OR HEADER ONLY ONCE

No matter how many pages are in your document, you only have to create a header or footer once. As you type or insert information into a header or footer, it is automatically inserted into headers and footers on other pages as well. You can change this by clicking the Page Setup button on the Headers and Footers toolbar. There you can choose to have different headers or footers on even and odd pages, or you can use a different one on just the first page (such as none at all).

CROSS-REFERENCE

To get more information on page numbering, see "Numbering Your Pages" in Chapter 5.

FIND IT ONLINE

Need an idea for your document? Visit **http://www.ideasiteforbusiness.com/** for some creative tips.

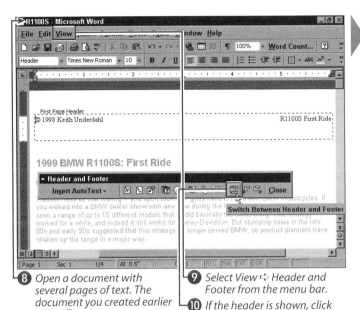

8 *Open a document with several pages of text. The document you created earlier will suffice.*

9 *Select View ⇨ Header and Footer from the menu bar.*

10 *If the header is shown, click the Switch Between Header and Footer button.*

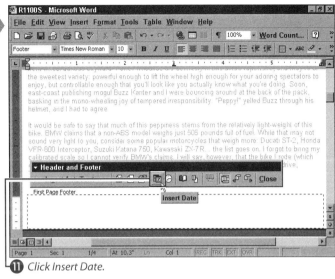

11 *Click Insert Date.*

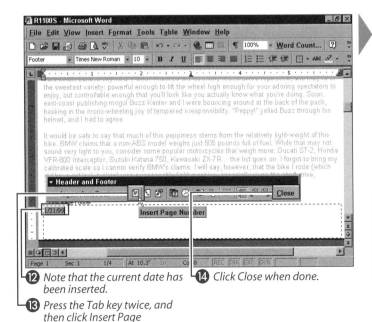

12 *Note that the current date has been inserted.*

13 *Press the Tab key twice, and then click Insert Page Number.*

14 *Click Close when done.*

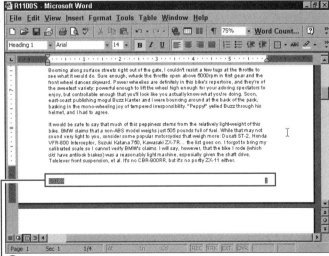

15 *Note that the current date and page number are now part of the footer. In the Word document window, they will probably appear as gray blocks because they can be automatically updated.*

Using Borders and Shading

Most of the documents you have created have been on standard-sized, plain white pages. But Word, being the all-purpose publishing tool that it is, lets you change the appearance of your pages by adding borders to your text or by applying shading to the page.

Borders and shading work well together, but they do not necessarily have to be used together. A shaded area often looks good with some sort of border to separate it from the rest of the document, but "unfenced" shading has its own special appeal. You can apply borders or shading to an entire document, or you can just apply it to paragraphs or small bits of text. For instance, suppose you are creating a document that lists a recipe. You could use a bulleted list for the ingredients, and then shade that list slightly. This gives your document a unique look that has a significantly greater impact than a plain old white page would.

When you apply borders or shading to an entire page, pay special attention to how this design choice affects the overall appearance. Having an entire page shaded can be a bit much for most readers, and can actually turn them off rather than draw their attention. Also, keep in mind that printing large shaded areas uses up a lot of toner. If you are printing completely shaded pages — especially those with color shading — you might find your toner and ink bills

astonishing, to say the least. On the other hand, a border around your entire page could have a nice effect. When doing this, double-check what is selected in the Apply to box. You can apply these borders to your entire document, or just to specific pages.

The figures on the facing page show you how to apply borders and shading to an area of a document. Although this task only demonstrates how to apply the elements to a few paragraphs, you can apply borders to an entire page by clicking the Page Borders tab in the Borders and Shading dialog box.

TAKE NOTE

► KNOW YOUR PRINTER'S LIMITATIONS

Shading that looks nice on your computer screen may look entirely different once printed on paper. Some lower-resolution printers don't do a very good job at printing these design elements, and the result may be that your nice, even shading is blocky or grainy on paper. If it is very dark, it can also make text difficult or impossible to read.

► APPLYING PARTIAL BORDERS

If you do not want to apply a border to all four sides of a paragraph or page, you can click the appropriate border in the Preview section of the Borders and Shading dialog box. Only the borders you click will be applied.

CROSS-REFERENCE
To learn more about controlling table borders, see "Formatting Tables" in Chapter 8.

FIND IT ONLINE
SOHO America, at **http://www.soho.org/**, is a great resource for small-business owners.

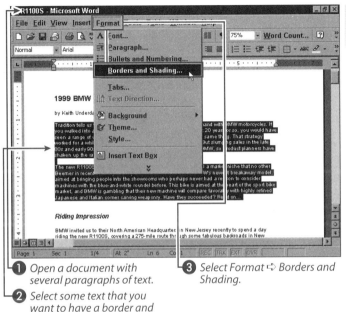

1 Open a document with several paragraphs of text.

2 Select some text that you want to have a border and shading.

3 Select Format ⇨ Borders and Shading.

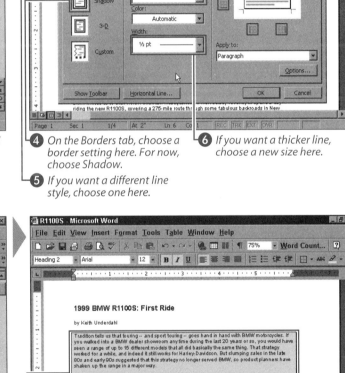

4 On the Borders tab, choose a border setting here. For now, choose Shadow.

5 If you want a different line style, choose one here.

6 If you want a thicker line, choose a new size here.

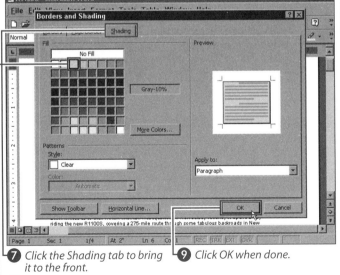

7 Click the Shading tab to bring it to the front.

8 Select a level of shading you want by choosing a color here. For now, choose Gray-10%.

9 Click OK when done.

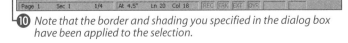

10 Note that the border and shading you specified in the dialog box have been applied to the selection.

Working with Columns

You have probably noticed that not all publications use the same general page layout. One of the greatest variances comes in the form of columns on a page. Books often use a single column when displaying print, as do memos and most other publications that you produce with Word. But many other types of publications—especially newspapers and magazines—lay out their text in multiple columns on the page.

How many columns are used depends on the size of the page, but most publications use between two and four. Using more than four columns can result in inefficient use of the page, because the white area between columns is essentially wasted space. If you are working with standard 8.5" by 11" pages, two columns is sufficient for most needs.

Whether you decide to use columns depends entirely on the kind of document you are producing. Columns typically appear in publications that must use small typeface to fit more words into a limited space. If the text is very small, it is easy to "get lost" as your eyes move across a wide page; columns help eliminate this problem. You can use columns in any document in which ease of reading is a serious concern.

The best place to use columns in your own documents is in a newsletter or any document that you want to have a magazine-style look and feel. Columns can be especially useful if you have several different elements that must fit on a single page. For

instance, if you are producing a flyer for your company picnic, you could include a numbered list in one of the columns that provides directions to the picnic area. Enclose the directions in a border, or even shade them somewhat, to visually separate this element from the rest of the document.

The figures on the facing page show you how to use columns in a document. The first three figures show you how to format thc columns, and the last figure shows you how to change your view of the columns.

TAKE NOTE

▶ VIEWING YOUR COLUMNS

When you are working with columns, Word automatically switches to Print Layout View. This is because if you work in Normal View the columns do not appear side by side, as they do on paper. In Normal View, the contents of a column are displayed in one continuous column until a page has been filled. If you want to see what the columns will look like printed, you should work in Print Layout View.

▶ ENDING A COLUMN

If you want to end a column and move to the next one, insert a column break by selecting Insert ⇨ Break and choosing Column Break from the Break dialog box.

CROSS-REFERENCE
To learn about working with section breaks, see "Inserting Breaks" in Chapter 5.

SHORTCUT
You can quickly insert a column break by pressing Ctrl+Shift+Enter.

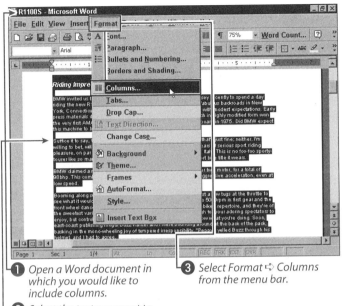

① Open a Word document in which you would like to include columns.

② Select the text you want to format into columns.

③ Select Format ⟶ Columns from the menu bar.

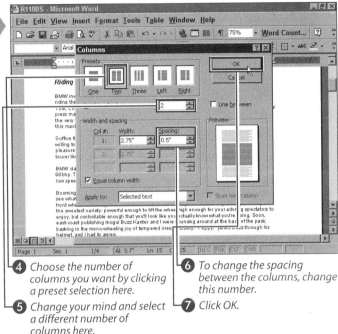

④ Choose the number of columns you want by clicking a preset selection here.

⑤ Change your mind and select a different number of columns here.

⑥ To change the spacing between the columns, change this number.

⑦ Click OK.

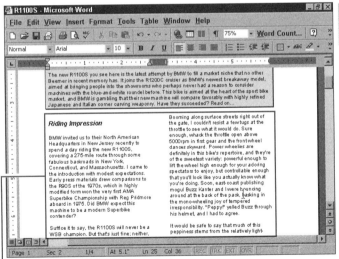

⑧ Note that the selection has been formatted into the columns you specified. Print Layout View shows you how the printed document will appear.

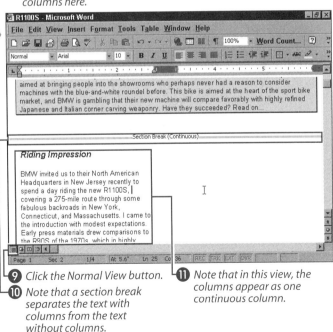

⑨ Click the Normal View button.

⑩ Note that a section break separates the text with columns from the text without columns.

⑪ Note that in this view, the columns appear as one continuous column.

Creating Outlines

One of the most versatile yet simple types of documents you can create with Word is an outline. An outline can serve many purposes. If you are a student, you might be required to create an outline for a paper or report that you have to write. In this case, you use the outline to help you plan the contents of the paper to ensure the document follows a logical order.

One nice feature of Word is that you can turn this outline into the actual document, ensuring that you stick to your original plan. You can convert outline entries directly into headings in your document, and then you simply type the text you want under each heading. If you don't want the headings to remain in the final draft, you can delete them after the appropriate text has been typed.

Outlines can serve many other purposes as well. An outline is very well suited for preparing notes for a meeting or seminar you need to conduct. If you want, you can set up your page and printer to print the outline onto notecards, though the heading styles used by Word in outlines should be changed to a smaller font size to ensure they fit on the cards. But in general, regular sheets of paper are easier to deal with. You can easily staple pages together, for example, which means you are less likely to be embarrassed because the cards got out of order or one got lost. Most professional instructors use large binders to hold their presentations, not notecards.

The figures on the facing page show you how to begin creating an outline in Word. Once you have started your outline as described here, move on to the next couple of pages. There you learn more about controlling the appearance of your outline, and learn how to move around within a large outline more effectively.

Continued

TAKE NOTE

PREPARING NOTES FOR A MEETING

If you are preparing notes for a meeting, you might find that regular letter-sized sheets of paper are easier to work with and read when you are up in front of a group. Tiny notecards used in presentations are usually just a paradigm left over from grade-school speech classes, and are generally more trouble than they are worth. For best results, use landscape orientation for your pages when the notes are printed.

PLANNING IS EVERYTHING

Many people have a general idea of what they want to say in a document, but putting those thoughts on paper can be a little tough. The best way to make sure what you write reflects what you want to say is to plan your document with an outline. Plan out each paragraph to ensure all your important points are covered.

CROSS-REFERENCE

If you want to change the layout of your page, see "Setting Up the Page" in Chapter 5.

FIND IT ONLINE

Need more technical advice for your publications? Try developer.com at **http://www.developer.com/**.

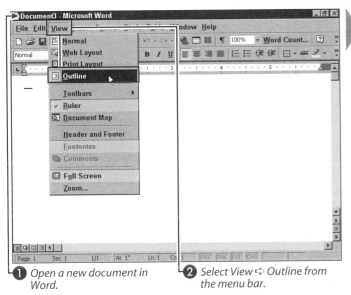

1 Open a new document in Word.

2 Select View ➪ Outline from the menu bar.

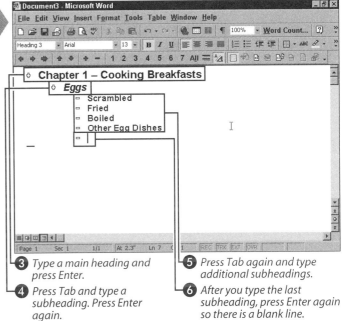

3 Type a main heading and press Enter.

4 Press Tab and type a subheading. Press Enter again.

5 Press Tab again and type additional subheadings.

6 After you type the last subheading, press Enter again so there is a blank line.

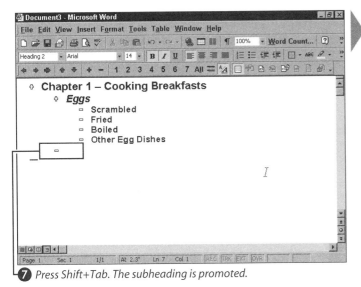

7 Press Shift+Tab. The subheading is promoted.

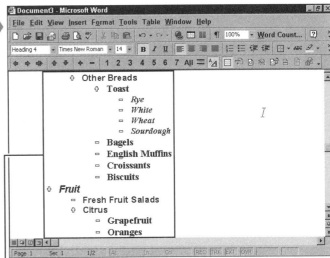

8 Type additional headings and subheadings, as shown. Continue to use Tab and Shift+Tab to create different heading levels.

Creating Outlines

Continued

When you do start creating larger outlines, you need to learn more about controlling the way they are displayed. For example, suppose you are writing a technical manual for one of your company's products. The first level of headings will probably represent chapters, with subheadings for parts or sections within each chapter. The outline might continue down to the point where each paragraph is planned out in the outline.

In this case, the outline might be many pages long. If you want to review the chapters or perhaps the chapters and the major topics within each chapter, you can "collapse" the outline so that only the heading levels you want to see are displayed. You can then expand individual headings to see what is contained in each one, or you can expand the entire outline. Collapsing the outline can also provide a quicker way of moving around in the outline. If you need to move from an early heading down to a much later one, consider collapsing the outline, selecting the later heading from the shorter list, and then expanding the outline once more.

In many respects, an outline structure in Word works a lot like the folder structure for files on your hard drive. In Windows Explorer, you can expand or collapse the folder structure by clicking plus and minus signs next to each folder. The only real difference here is that the plus and minus signs don't change in your outline when you click them. A plus sign in an outline simply indicates that subheadings exist under a heading, and a minus sign tells you that there are no more subheadings.

The figures on the facing page show you how to expand and collapse an outline in Word. You also learn how to change the view with some of the other buttons available on the Outlining toolbar.

TAKE NOTE

▶ MORE SPEECH ADVICE

If you are outlining a speech or presentation, avoid using whole sentences or paragraphs in the outline. Long sentences cause you to spend more time reading verbatim from the outline and less time providing your audience with eye contact and a personalized presentation. Instead, use words or short sentence fragments to help trigger your memory as you present the information.

▶ SHOWING AND HIDING FORMATTING

Outline headings usually contain special formatting, such as boldface, italics, and larger point sizes for fonts. As attractive as this may be, it ultimately results in more space being consumed by the outline. If you want a no-frills outline that takes up as little space as possible, click the Show Formatting button on the Outlining toolbar. This button acts as a toggle, so you can click it again the restore the special formatting. Experiment with the button to see which view you prefer.

CROSS-REFERENCE

See "Applying Styles" in Chapter 7 to learn more about heading styles in your outline.

FIND IT ONLINE

Need more practice speaking in public? Visit Toastmasters International at **http://www. toastmasters.org/**.

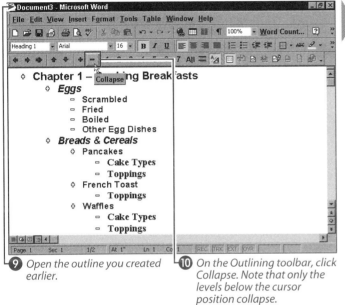

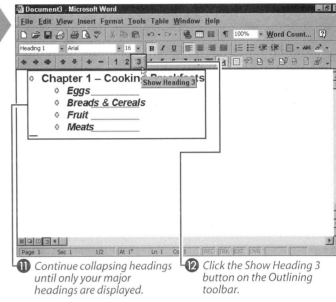

9 Open the outline you created earlier.

10 On the Outlining toolbar, click Collapse. Note that only the levels below the cursor position collapse.

11 Continue collapsing headings until only your major headings are displayed.

12 Click the Show Heading 3 button on the Outlining toolbar.

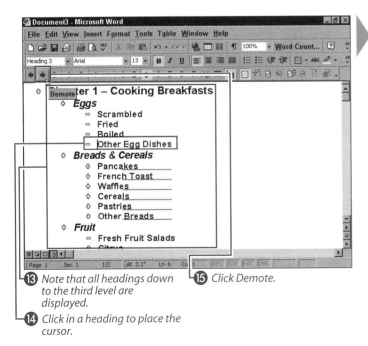

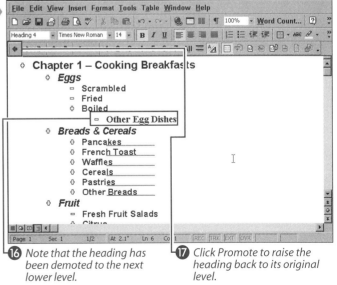

13 Note that all headings down to the third level are displayed.

14 Click in a heading to place the cursor.

15 Click Demote.

16 Note that the heading has been demoted to the next lower level.

17 Click Promote to raise the heading back to its original level.

Using Footnotes

Often, items in a book or paper require some explanatory information above and beyond what is included in the text. For instance, a paper that discusses the practice of whale hunting might mention some Native American tribes such as the Makahs, who practice traditional, subsistence hunts. In this case, if you simply mention the name *Makah*, the reader must assume a lot about those people. It could be useful to let the reader know that the Makah Nation lives on the Olympic Peninsula of Washington State; but because that fact has little or nothing to do with the topic of whaling, it might not be appropriate to provide that detail in the body of your text.

The best solution in this case is to include a *footnote*. As the name suggests, a footnote provides a brief note or some explanatory information about something in the text, and usually resides at the bottom of a page. In the report on whaling, a small, superscripted number or symbol would be shown next to the word *Makah* that corresponds to a note at the foot of the page.

As with any other element you add to the pages of your documents, you must keep in mind that footnotes reduce the amount of space available for other text on the page. However, unlike headers and footers, you do not necessarily need to be limited to one line in a footnote; in fact, some footnotes in academic texts can go on for pages all by themselves!

Fortunately, you are helped by the fact that footnotes can use relatively small text. By default, Word formats footnotes as 10-point Times New Roman; but if you have a high-resolution printer and your readers have glasses, you can reduce the point size even further. Try not to make footnotes smaller than 8 or 9 points, however, because they could become unreadable.

The figures on the facing page show you how to insert a footnote into a document. Notice that the document must be in Print Layout View to see the footnotes.

TAKE NOTE

▶ USING ENDNOTES

If you would prefer that notes be placed at the end of your document rather than at the bottom of each page, choose the Endnotes option in the Footnote and Endnote dialog box. This option might be preferable if your document has fewer than ten pages.

▶ USING SYMBOLS FOR FOOTNOTES

Footnotes have been common in traditional, academic works for centuries. However, in years past, footnotes were usually numbered with a series of symbols instead of actual numbers. These symbols included asterisks, daggers, double daggers, and so on. You can specify this or some other custom numbering scheme by clicking the Options button in the Footnote and Endnote dialog box.

CROSS-REFERENCE

See "Changing Character Sizes" in Chapter 7 to learn more about modifying text size.

SHORTCUT

You can jump quickly between a reference and a footnote by double-clicking the number.

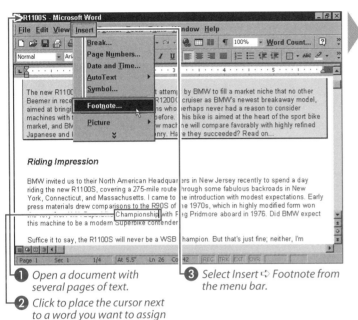

1 Open a document with several pages of text.

2 Click to place the cursor next to a word you want to assign a footnote to.

3 Select Insert ⇨ Footnote from the menu bar.

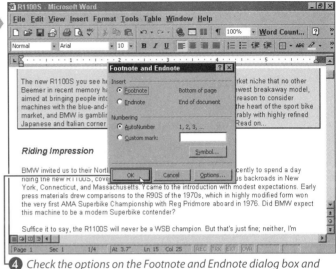

4 Check the options on the Footnote and Endnote dialog box and click OK.

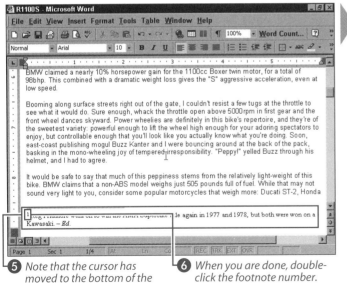

5 Note that the cursor has moved to the bottom of the page, where a footnote number appears. Type the text of the footnote.

6 When you are done, double-click the footnote number.

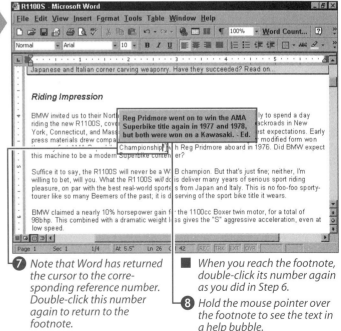

7 Note that Word has returned the cursor to the corresponding reference number. Double-click this number again to return to the footnote.

■ When you reach the footnote, double-click its number again as you did in Step 6.

8 Hold the mouse pointer over the footnote to see the text in a help bubble.

Counting Words

Engineers, politicians, and sociologists aren't the only people concerned with abstract statistics. Writers and publishers also spend a lot of time tracking numbers and statistics of a very different nature. Specifically, they are concerned about word counts in articles and other written documents that they must work with every day.

This is nothing new. For years, magazine and newspaper writers have had to track how many words were used in their documents, because editors and publishers usually have very specific requirements for article length. Articles have traditionally been assigned by word count, and turning in work that was significantly above or below the specified count would be unacceptable. So, writers were forced into the menial and time-consuming task of counting each and every word they typed or wrote, or they used imprecise estimation techniques to guess how many words were on a page or in a line.

Word eliminates the need to perform this chore by keeping track of word counts for you. In fact, Word even goes so far as to count pages, words, paragraphs, lines, and individual characters. This includes things you might usually ignore such as spaces and punctuation. Counting characters in a long document would be virtually impossible to do by hand.

Teachers and instructors have traditionally asked for specific page counts when assigning writing work. But with the proliferation of computers and advanced word processing programs like Word 2000,

the number of words on a page can vary greatly between students. In the interest of fairness, some teachers are now assigning work by word count instead of pages. If you receive such an assignment, Word's counting feature really comes in handy because you can spend more time writing a quality report and less time counting words.

The figures on the facing page show you how to count the words in your documents. Notice that the dialog box displays other statistics about your document as well. In the last two figures, you count the words in a selected paragraph rather than the entire document.

CROSS-REFERENCE
To learn how to add a Word Count button to your toolbar, see "Adding New Toolbar Buttons" in Chapter 2.

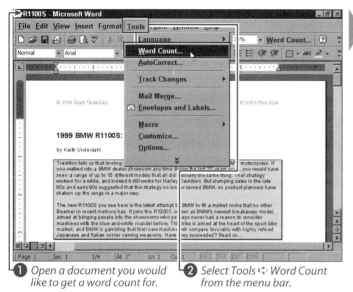

1 Open a document you would like to get a word count for.

2 Select Tools ➪ Word Count from the menu bar.

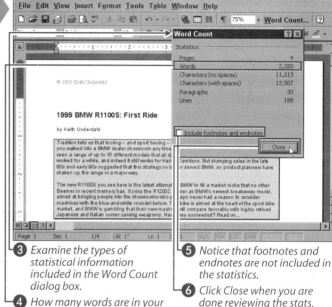

3 Examine the types of statistical information included in the Word Count dialog box.

4 How many words are in your document?

5 Notice that footnotes and endnotes are not included in the statistics.

6 Click Close when you are done reviewing the stats.

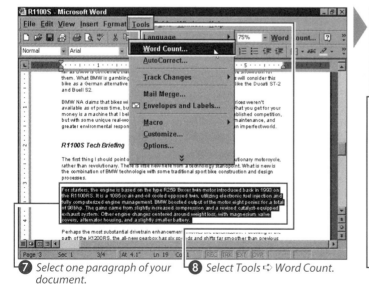

7 Select one paragraph of your document.

8 Select Tools ➪ Word Count.

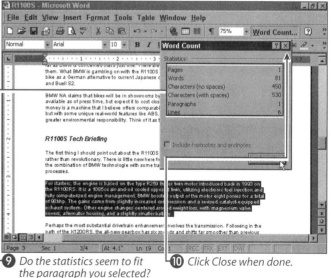

9 Do the statistics seem to fit the paragraph you selected?

10 Click Close when done.

Tracking Changes

Perhaps the most significant way in which a personal computer helps you produce better printed documents is that you have far greater flexibility in editing than you do using any other writing method. If you do not like something you see while proofreading a document, modifying it could not be easier. Furthermore, you can make all your changes without having to reprint the document over and over again.

In addition, other people can edit your document easily using a computer as well. You may not be the only person who works on a specific document; your boss, editor, or some other person may have the responsibility for reviewing it. If you are an editor by profession, you routinely edit documents created by someone else. Having an electronic version of a document simplifies the review and editing process, particularly if multiple people are involved.

Unfortunately, as with many other advances, this one has its drawbacks. Contrary to the popular cliche, change is not always good. You may find that some of the editing you do to a document makes it worse, not better. Add other people into the editing process, and the potential for bad editing multiplies. Furthermore, even if the edits are good, there may be a difference in opinion or judgement about how the final document should look.

With this problem in mind, Word's creators have incorporated a feature that helps you keep track of changes made by you and by others. With the Track Changes feature enabled, changes you make are tracked, and replaced or deleted items are not truly deleted. The feature tracks each and every edit, showing not only what was done but who did it.

The first figure on the facing page shows you how to enable the Track Changes feature in Word. The remaining three figures demonstrate how to edit a document with the feature enabled, and shows how those edits will look. Pay special attention to what happens when you delete something.

Continued

Continued

TAKE NOTE

▶ REVISION MARKS AND CHANGE TRACKING

If you are familiar with older versions of Word, such as Word 95, you know about revision marks. The Track Changes feature in Word 2000 serves the same purpose as revision marks, but the name is new and some of the options are a little different.

▶ WHERE DOES DELETED TEXT GO?

With Track Changes enabled, deleted text remains in the document. However, deleted text is displayed with a line struck through the middle of it to indicate the deletion. If you copy a paragraph that contains deleted text to a new location, the struck-through text will not be copied with it. However, if you try to count the words in a document with struck-through changes, the word count reflects the deleted words.

CROSS-REFERENCE

To learn some editing basics, see "Editing Text" in Chapter 10.

FIND IT ONLINE

Visit DesignSphere Online, at **http://www.dsphere. net/**, for some great desktop publishing tips.

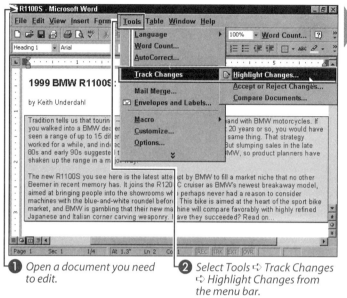

1 Open a document you need to edit.

2 Select Tools ➪ Track Changes ➪ Highlight Changes from the menu bar.

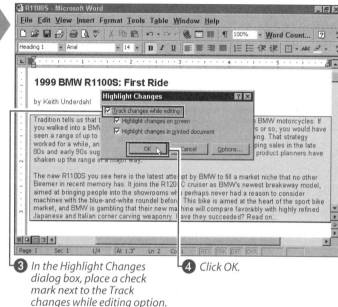

3 In the Highlight Changes dialog box, place a check mark next to the Track changes while editing option.

4 Click OK.

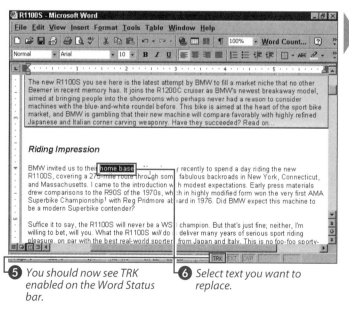

5 You should now see TRK enabled on the Word Status bar.

6 Select text you want to replace.

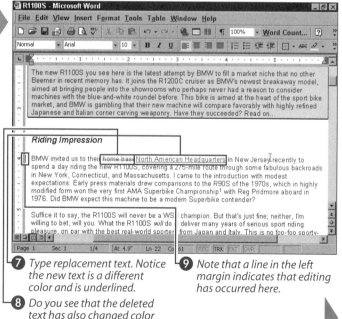

7 Type replacement text. Notice the new text is a different color and is underlined.

8 Do you see that the deleted text has also changed color and has been struck through?

9 Note that a line in the left margin indicates that editing has occurred here.

327

Tracking Changes

Continued

As you can see, monitoring your edits with the Track Changes feature can be valuable as you prepare your document for publication. Using this tool gives whomever has responsibility for the document the greatest amount of control over the final product.

If you are that person, you need to know how to deal with the revised text when you are ready to publish it. In the past, simply turning off the Revision Marks feature was enough to accept all changes and get rid of the revision marks. However, disabling the Track Changes feature in Word 2000 does not have the same effect. If you disable this feature, no further revisions will be tracked, but existing revision marks will remain. This ensures that each revision is reviewed at the end of the editing process.

To address the highlighted changes, you must either accept or reject them. You can do this in one of two ways; each method works better in different situations. The first method enables you to address changes one at a time by using a shortcut menu. Right-click a change and choose to either accept or reject it. If you accept a change, the highlighting is removed and the change is permanently incorporated into the document. If you reject it, the change is undone. For instance, if a sentence has been deleted but you feel it should remain, just right-click it and choose Reject Change. If you reject a change in this manner, make sure that other edits — such as text that replaced a deleted sentence — still make sense.

The other method is to open the Accept or Reject Changes dialog box. This dialog box takes you through each revision in the document, telling you who made each change and when they did it. You can use this dialog box to accept or reject changes with a single mouse click. The figures on the facing page show you how to accept and reject changes. The first figures demonstrate how to do this using a shortcut menu, and the remaining figures show how to use the Accept or Reject Changes dialog box.

TAKE NOTE

▶ WHO MADE THAT CHANGE?

If many different people worked on a document, it might be useful to know who made each change and when they did it. Although each user's changes should be in a unique color, you can get more information by simply pausing the mouse pointer over a change. After a second or two, a help bubble appears telling you exactly who made the change, when they did it, and what exactly they did.

▶ MAKE IT QUICK

If you have already reviewed the document and want to accept or reject all of the changes that have been made, click the Accept All or Reject All button (as appropriate) in the Accept or Reject Changes dialog box.

CROSS-REFERENCE

Word must know who you are to track changes. See "Setting Key Options" in Chapter 2 to learn how.

FIND IT ONLINE

You can ask questions and discuss desktop publishing at the following newsgroup: **news:comp.text.desktop**.

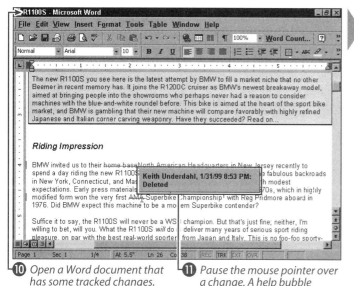

⑩ *Open a Word document that has some tracked changes. The document you edited on the last two pages will suffice.*

⑪ *Pause the mouse pointer over a change. A help bubble appears, telling you who made the change and when.*

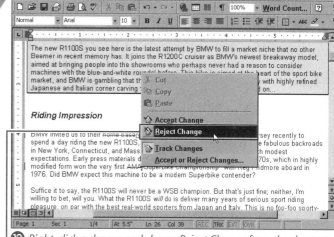

⑫ *Right-click a change and choose Reject Change from the shortcut menu.*

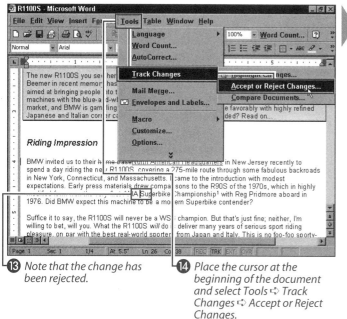

⑬ *Note that the change has been rejected.*

⑭ *Place the cursor at the beginning of the document and select Tools ⇨ Track Changes ⇨ Accept or Reject Changes.*

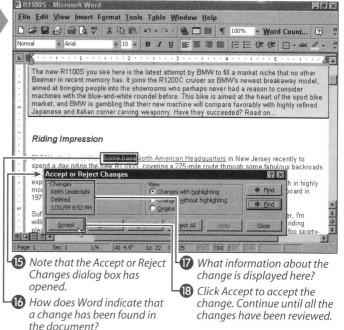

⑮ *Note that the Accept or Reject Changes dialog box has opened.*

⑯ *How does Word indicate that a change has been found in the document?*

⑰ *What information about the change is displayed here?*

⑱ *Click Accept to accept the change. Continue until all the changes have been reviewed.*

Personal Workbook

Q&A

1 How do you start creating a bulleted list using AutoFormat?

_____

_____

_____

2 Can you use something other than regular numbers in a numbered list?

_____

_____

3 When inserting a header, do you have to create a separate header for each page?

_____

_____

4 Will borders and shading have the same appearance on paper that they do on the screen?

_____

_____

_____

5 What is the purpose of columns?

_____

_____

_____

6 Once you have created an outline, can you change the position of headings? How?

_____

_____

_____

7 What kind of information does Word Count provide other than the number of words?

_____

_____

_____

8 If you delete some text with the Track Changes feature enabled, what happens to that deleted text?

_____

_____

_____

ANSWERS: PAGE 373

EXTRA PRACTICE

1 Create an outline for an article you would like to write about participating in your favorite pastime.

2 Using the outline, write your article. At the bottom of the article, create a bulleted list of items the reader should obtain to participate in the pastime.

3 Insert a header into the article with your name and the title of the article.

4 Format several paragraphs of the article into columns.

5 Count the words in your document.

6 Edit your document with the Track Changes feature enabled. When you are done editing, review your changes and accept or reject each one.

REAL-WORLD APPLICATIONS

✔ If you are creating a document to help your kids and a club they belong to plan for a camping trip, you can created a bulleted list of the things that each kid should bring. Use large, hollow squares for the bullets to serve as check boxes so that items can actually be checked off as they are packed.

✔ Columns could be useful if you are producing a document that might include some advertising. This way, the advertisement will be visually closer to the text, and more people will actually read it.

✔ If you are writing a paper or article where technical accuracy is extremely important, you might want to have a subject matter expert review the document. If so, tell the reviewer to use the Track Changes feature so that you can review the changes.

Visual Quiz

The first couple of paragraphs are darker than the rest of the document. Why? What is unique about the paragraphs under it? What does the crossed-out heading mean? Why are the words next to it underlined?

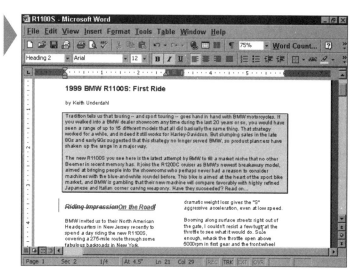

CHAPTER **19**

MASTER
THESE
SKILLS

▶ **Linking Objects**

▶ **Linking an Excel Worksheet**

▶ **Updating Linked Objects**

▶ **Embedding Objects**

▶ **Editing Embedded Objects**

Linking and Embedding Objects

I t would be safe to say that the personal computer has truly come of age. This could easily be evidenced by the way in which so many PC-related technologies are now taken for granted. Perhaps one of the most important of these is the way in which different programs can work together by sharing data and other program resources.

Software programs can work together at the same time, or be integrated, primarily due to the multitasking capability of modern processors. *Multitasking* means that more than one program can use the processor at once. It wasn't long after this capability was introduced before software engineers took full advantage of it by changing the way in which programs were written. Now, different functions of a program are created as smaller components called *objects*. In theory, an object can be opened at any time, even if the program that object is normally associated with is not. This technology is called Object Linking and Embedding (OLE), and it has been refined significantly over the last couple of years.

What does this mean to you? Simply stated, OLE lets you link your programs and share items (or objects, if you prefer) between them. For instance, suppose you are producing a promotional brochure for your real estate office. To demonstrate how effective your sales team is, you may want to show some specific sales numbers in the brochure. If you track that information in an Excel worksheet, you can simply link a worksheet right to the brochure in Word. This has the added benefit of making it easy for you to keep the worksheet in the brochure up to date as well.

Linking and embedding can come in many forms. In fact, even inserting graphics files in Web documents is a form of OLE. This chapter explores the concept of OLE and how you can make it work for you. You begin by learning how to link objects, with special emphasis on how to link an Excel worksheet. Linked objects maintain a link to the document they were copied from and are updated whenever the source is. You then learn about embedding objects. Embedding differs from linking in that an embedded object does not remain linked to a document in its native program. You also practice editing embedded objects within the document.

Linking Objects

As detailed in Chapter 10, blocks of text, pictures, and other kinds of objects can be copied back and forth within Word, and even copied from one program to another. Copying objects in this manner is an extremely valuable skill, and once you learn it, you'll probably use it all the time.

Copying items from one program to another can have its drawbacks, however. For instance, suppose you are publishing a financial report for your company. Such a report will include data from a variety of sources outside of Word. The most important information will probably take the form of statistics and specific data developed in another program, such as Excel. If the data is simply copied from Excel into Word, the information in your report will become outdated as soon as the Excel data is changed. But if you link the data, the report will be updated whenever the Excel data is modified.

In addition, you may have to include other kinds of information, such as a statement or article from your company's president. Because the article would probably be stored in another Word document, you may think that the easiest way to incorporate it is to simply copy in the text. However, the text of this article could easily change before the report you are working on is published.

The best solution to this problem is to link the data rather than just copy and paste it. When an object is linked into a document, it retains a connection to the original source. If the original document is changed, the linked object is automatically updated. So in the case of the article you are thinking about incorporating, any changes made to the source file you linked into your Word document will be incorporated automatically. The figures on the facing page show you how to link text into another Word document.

TAKE NOTE

CONSERVE RESOURCES BY LINKING

If the size of your Word document is a concern, you can save space by linking an object rather than copying it into the document. If you copy an object, it becomes a permanent part of that file, which can significantly impact the number of kilobytes it uses.

CHOOSING WHAT TO LINK THE OBJECT AS

When you are creating a link in the Paste Special dialog box, you will be asked what kind of object you want to paste it as. A list of choices will appear under "As." When you click an item in this list, a description of it will appear at the bottom of the dialog box under "Result." Click each option and read its result before you make a choice.

CROSS-REFERENCE
Links are not always updated automatically. See "Updating Linked Objects" later in this chapter.

FIND IT ONLINE
Learn more about OLE at **http://www.microsoft.com/oledev/olecom/aboutole.htm**.

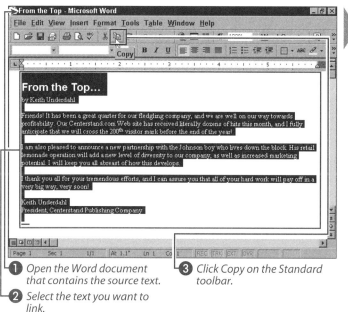

① Open the Word document that contains the source text.

② Select the text you want to link.

③ Click Copy on the Standard toolbar.

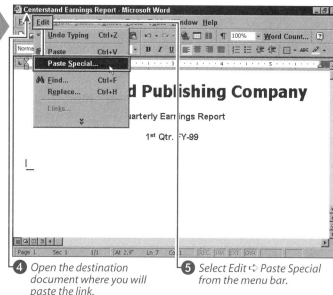

④ Open the destination document where you will paste the link.

⑤ Select Edit ➪ Paste Special from the menu bar.

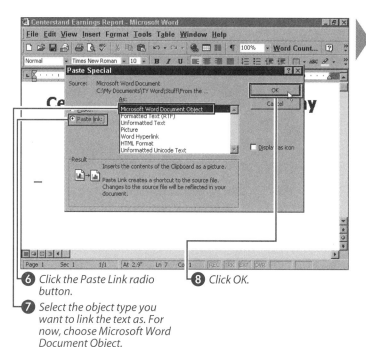

⑥ Click the Paste Link radio button.

⑦ Select the object type you want to link the text as. For now, choose Microsoft Word Document Object.

⑧ Click OK.

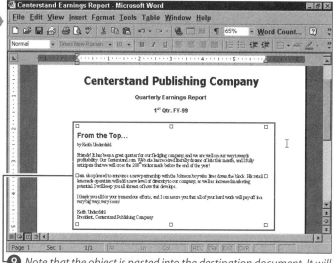

⑨ Note that the object is pasted into the destination document. It will remain linked to the source document.

Linking an Excel Worksheet

You can use linking for many purposes. The preceding task demonstrated how to link one Word document into another. Many other kinds of objects can be linked into a document, including images, sound objects, and other multimedia elements. But without a doubt, one of the most common types of linking operations is the linking of an Excel worksheet into a Word document.

In an earlier example, I suggested a scenario in which you were producing a financial report for your company. You linked an image into the document to ensure you always have the current version of your company logo. In such a report, you would almost certainly need to include financial data. Your company probably manages this type of data in a spreadsheet program such as Excel or Quattro Pro. It would be simple to put the data into the report by copying it from the spreadsheet program, but this approach creates a significant problem. What if the numbers in the spreadsheet change before you have a chance to publish the report?

In this type of situation, linking is the only reasonable solution. Linking spreadsheet data to a report in Word provides exactly the kind of automation most people envisioned when the personal computer revolution first took hold. Surprisingly, however, few people take advantage of it.

The figures on the facing page show you how to link an Excel worksheet into a Word document. To practice these steps exactly as they are shown, you must have Excel installed on your computer. If you do not, check to see whether you have another Windows spreadsheet program installed. If you do, you can practice linking spreadsheet data using that program.

The first figure shows a Microsoft Excel window, and demonstrates the technique for selecting and copying the data to be linked. This technique should be similar in other spreadsheets, as well as older versions of Excel. The remaining figures demonstrate how to paste the data into a Word document so that it is linked rather than simply copied.

TAKE NOTE

► USING THE INSERT MICROSOFT EXCEL WORKSHEET BUTTON

You may have noticed a button on the standard toolbar called Insert Microsoft Excel Worksheet. Clicking this button embeds a worksheet into your document. This is a useful option if you just need a very basic spreadsheet in your document. This feature works only if Excel is installed on your computer. Learn more about embedded objects later in this chapter.

► LINKING CHARTS

You can link charts from Excel as well as other kinds of data into your Word documents. As a result, you can include graphs, pie charts, and other visual aids in a Word document and still be assured that the information contained in them is up to date.

CROSS-REFERENCE

See "Selecting Cells" in Chapter 8 to learn how to select cells in a spreadsheet or table.

FIND IT ONLINE

Learn more about Microsoft Excel at **http://www. microsoft.com/excel/default.htm**.

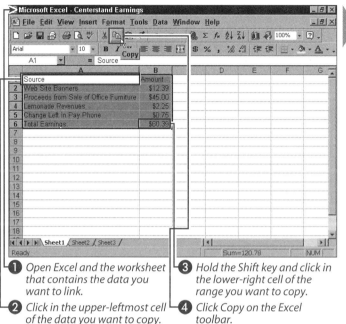

1 Open Excel and the worksheet that contains the data you want to link.

2 Click in the upper-leftmost cell of the data you want to copy.

3 Hold the Shift key and click in the lower-right cell of the range you want to copy.

4 Click Copy on the Excel toolbar.

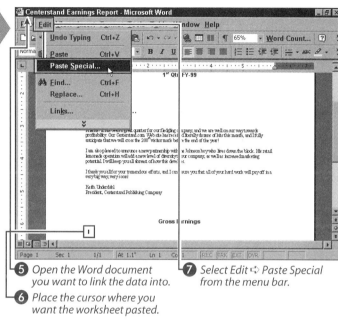

5 Open the Word document you want to link the data into.

6 Place the cursor where you want the worksheet pasted.

7 Select Edit ➪ Paste Special from the menu bar.

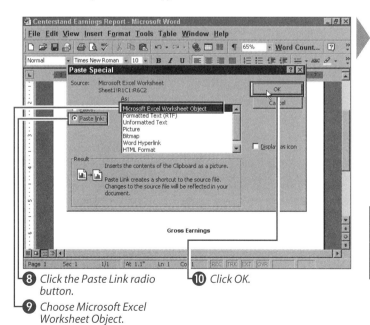

8 Click the Paste Link radio button.

9 Choose Microsoft Excel Worksheet Object.

10 Click OK.

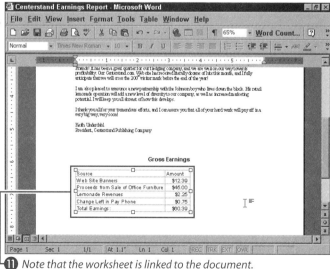

11 Note that the worksheet is linked to the document.

Updating Linked Objects

As you have learned, there is a huge difference between copying data and linking data. Linking is a far more advanced way to share information between documents and programs, because it synchronizes the data between the two files.

The term *synchronize* implies that linked objects are updated constantly, which isn't entirely true. Updates happen at specific intervals, and it is important for you to understand exactly when it happens. You can then ensure that your documents are truly up to date.

Some updates happen automatically. For instance, by default Word updates links every time you open a file. If there have been changes to the source document, linked items should be updated as the file is opened. This process makes the file open just a bit more slowly, but that is the price of automation. You can also choose to have linked objects updated before you print a file. To do this, select Tools ⇨ Options from the menu bar and click the Print tab. Place a check mark next to the Update links option to ensure links are automatically updated whenever the file is printed.

Linked objects can also be linked manually. In fact, you may prefer to handle this task manually, especially if the link to the source file is not always reliable (such as a link to a networked file). If you do prefer to do your updates manually, you can select that option in the Links dialog box. Select Edit ⇨

Links and look for the Automatic and Manual radio buttons near the bottom of the dialog box. Once you have chosen this option, updating links is still quite simple. You update them from the Links dialog box, and you can choose to update one, some, or all of your links within the document.

The first two figures on the facing page show you how to open the Links dialog box and set some important options. The last two figures demonstrate how to update the links in a document.

TAKE NOTE

► LINKING FILES OVER A NETWORK

You can link objects over a network; but if the network connection is broken, the object may not be updated when it is supposed to. In this case, you also need to make sure the file on the network is not moved or deleted by someone else, because this will sever the link.

► LINKS VS. HYPERLINKS

It is easy to get confused by hyperlinks, such as those used on Web pages, and the kinds of object links discussed here. They both link to information outside of Word, but an object link shows information from the source document in your Word document, whereas a hyperlink is simply a word, phrase, or picture that you click to visit some other kind of Web document.

CROSS-REFERENCE

Still don't know what hyperlinks are for? See "Creating Links" in Chapter 16 to learn more.

FIND IT ONLINE

Check out a PC Magazine series covering OLE at http://www.zdnet.com/pcmag/issues/1419/pcm001 18.htm.

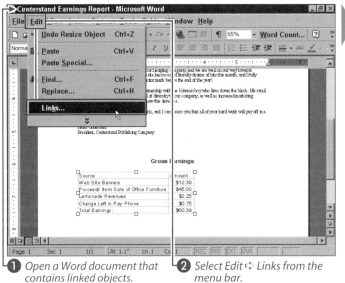

① *Open a Word document that contains linked objects.*

② *Select Edit ▷ Links from the menu bar.*

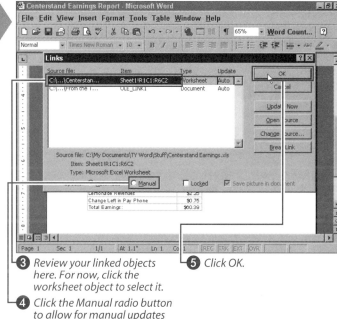

③ *Review your linked objects here. For now, click the worksheet object to select it.*

④ *Click the Manual radio button to allow for manual updates of the link.*

⑤ *Click OK.*

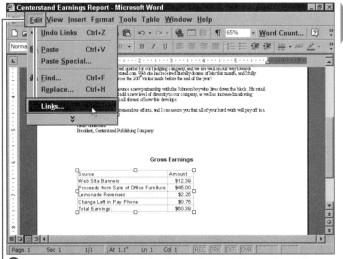

⑥ *To manually update a link for the worksheet object, select Edit ▷ Links from the menu bar.*

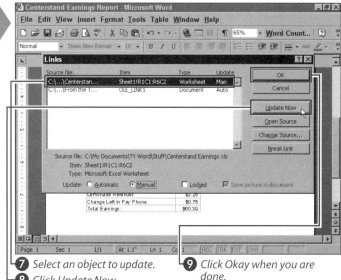

⑦ *Select an object to update.*

⑧ *Click Update Now.*

⑨ *Click Okay when you are done.*

Embedding Objects

Embedding objects is different from linking them. An embedded object does not retain a link to the original source document. You can still copy an object from another program and embed it in a Word document, but changes made to the original source document will not be reflected in the embedded object.

At first introduction, an embedded object looks a lot like it was just copied and pasted into the document. However, embedding is very different, primarily in that it brings with it software elements from the source program. For example, if you simply copy a picture from a graphics program and paste it into Word, the image becomes a rigid part of the page, almost as if it were part of the background. If you need to change the picture, you will not be able to do it from within Word. Instead, you would have to delete the image from Word, open the original graphics program, edit the picture, and recopy it to Word. Suffice it to say, this is not the most efficient way to edit an object that you are using in Word.

A better solution is to embed the object. When an object is embedded, it retains its original format and acts like a linked object, but without the link. You can still edit the object using its original program by simply double-clicking it. This opens tools from the program that the object was created in so you can perform the editing. Depending on the software in question, the entire program may or may not open.

The figures on the facing page show you how to embed an object in Word. Here, you embed an Excel worksheet from an existing Excel document. If you do not have Excel, you can still embed a worksheet using the Insert Microsoft Excel Worksheet button on the Standard toolbar. Once you have embedded an object, move on to the next task to learn more about editing embedded objects.

TAKE NOTE

▶ EMBEDDING EXCEL WORKSHEETS

You can embed an Excel worksheet in a Word document, just as you can with many others. With an embedded Excel object, information is not automatically updated by the original source, but it is still very easy to edit. An easy way to embed a new Excel document would be to click the Insert Microsoft Excel Worksheet. This opens a new Excel worksheet.

▶ EMBEDDING NEW OBJECTS

You can embed a wide variety of objects in a Word document by simply selecting Insert ⇨ Object. The dialog box will display a selection of objects that are installed on your computer and can be set up. Select an object and click OK to embed it.

CROSS-REFERENCE

To learn more about dealing with images, see "Inserting Graphics" in Chapter 9.

FIND IT ONLINE

For more on using embedded objects, see **http://www.microsoft.com/win32dev/uiguide/uigui291.htm**.

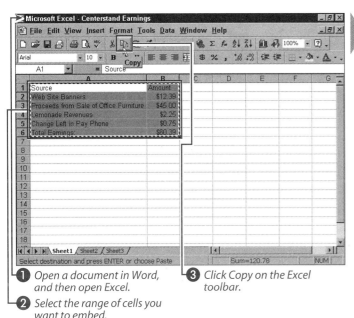

① *Open a document in Word, and then open Excel.*

② *Select the range of cells you want to embed.*

③ *Click Copy on the Excel toolbar.*

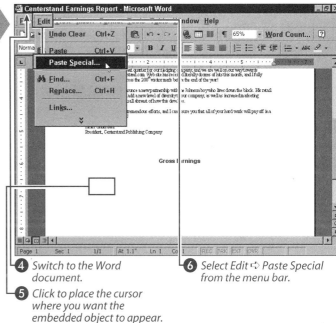

④ *Switch to the Word document.*

⑤ *Click to place the cursor where you want the embedded object to appear.*

⑥ *Select Edit ➪ Paste Special from the menu bar.*

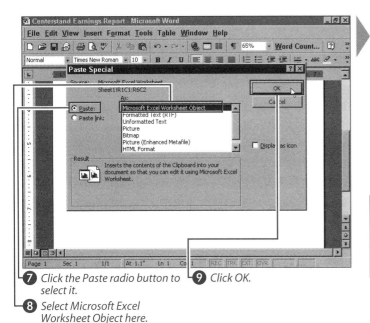

⑦ *Click the Paste radio button to select it.*

⑧ *Select Microsoft Excel Worksheet Object here.*

⑨ *Click OK.*

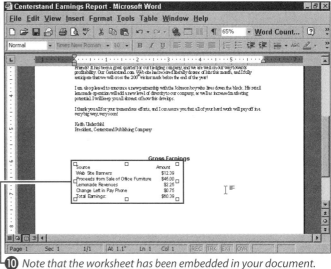

⑩ *Note that the worksheet has been embedded in your document.*

Editing Embedded Objects

As you learned in the previous task, embedded objects differ from linked objects. They do not maintain a link to the source document. If you embed data from an Excel worksheet into a Word document, and the data in the original worksheet is modified later, the embedded data will not be updated to reflect those changes.

Although no link is maintained with the source document, embedded objects still retain a link to the source *program*. As a result, you can easily edit the object from within Word. Double-clicking the object opens editing tools from the source program (see some exceptions to this in the "Take Note" section). This editing capability is important, and can save you a great deal of time and heartache later on.

For instance, suppose you have inserted (but not linked) an image of your company logo into a Word document. If you find that you need to change the logo slightly to conform with other elements of the document, this could present some interesting challenges. Without OLE, you would have to delete the logo from your Word document, and then go back to the original graphics program and create a new one. But because Word enables you to embed these objects into a document rather than just paste a rigid, unchangeable snapshot, quick modifications are just a double-click away.

The figures on the facing page show you how to edit the object you embedded in the previous task.

In this case, you change some data in the Excel worksheet, but the basic technique works with virtually all embedded objects. Keep in mind that just as changes to the original source document have no effect on embedded objects, changes you make to an embedded object will not impact the original source document. If you find that you routinely need to make the same edits in multiple locations, consider linking the object rather than embedding it.

TAKE NOTE

▶ DOUBLE-CLICKING DOESN'T ALWAYS WORK

Although you can edit most embedded objects by double-clicking them, this technique does not work on all object types. For instance, many audio and video objects play when you double-click them, rather than open for editing. If you need to edit one of these as an embedded object, first select the object and then select Edit ⇨ Object or choose the name of the object from the edit menu.

▶ EXITING THE EDIT MODE

When you are done editing an embedded object, how you exit the editing mode depends on how it is being edited. If the object opened in its own window with the source program, select File ⇨ Exit on the menu bar for that program. If the object opened in a small window within Word, click anywhere outside of the object window.

CROSS-REFERENCE

Are you making duplicate edits? See "Linking Objects" earlier in this chapter to learn an easier way.

FIND IT ONLINE

Get more Word help at **http://www.peninsula.wednet.edu/help_word.htm**.

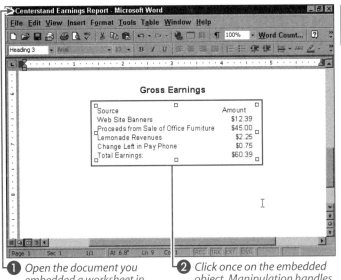

1 Open the document you embedded a worksheet in earlier.

2 Click once on the embedded object. Manipulation handles appear around the border, and you can move or resize the object as if it were a graphic.

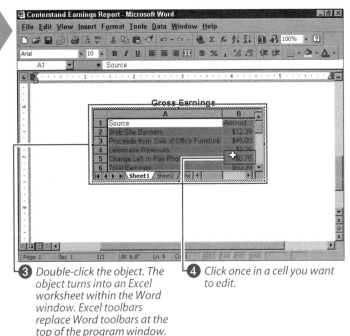

3 Double-click the object. The object turns into an Excel worksheet within the Word window. Excel toolbars replace Word toolbars at the top of the program window.

4 Click once in a cell you want to edit.

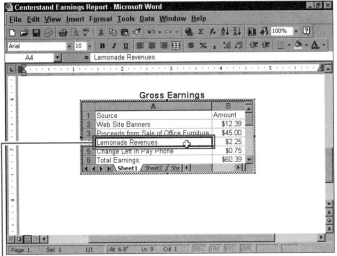

5 Type some new data. Click in another cell for your edits to take effect.

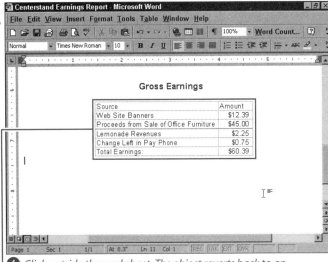

6 Click outside the worksheet. The object reverts back to an embedded object, and you are returned to Word.

Personal Workbook

Q&A

1 What is the difference between linking and embedding?

_____

_____

_____

_____

2 Can you link any kind of object you want into Word?

_____

_____

3 Can linked objects be updated automatically?

_____

_____

_____

4 How do you manually update a linked object?

_____

_____

_____

5 Why would you want to link text from another Word document rather than just copy and paste it?

_____

_____

_____

6 If you change the source document of an embedded object, will the object be updated?

_____

_____

_____

7 Can you edit embedded objects from within Word?

_____

_____

8 Give an example of when an embedded object would be more useful than a linked object.

_____

_____

_____

_____

ANSWERS: PAGE 374

EXTRA PRACTICE

1 Create a new Word document and type several paragraphs of text.

2 Copy one paragraph of text.

3 Create another Word document, and link the copied text from the first document into it.

4 Return to the source document and edit the text that you linked earlier.

5 Check the destination file to make sure the link was updated. If not, update it manually.

6 Use the Links dialog box to sever the link between the two documents.

REAL-WORLD APPLICATIONS

✔ It is not uncommon to have similar information published on a company Web site as well as internal reports. For instance, if you publish meeting schedules on your company's intranet, you can link that schedule to a printed version of the schedule that you produce in Word.

✔ If you work in advertising, you will probably end up working with a new company jingle. You can propose versions of the jingle to company executives by embedding or linking a sound file into a Word document. Then all they have to do is read your text and double-click the sound object to hear it. If the sound object is linked, changes to the jingle could be automatically updated in linked proposal letters across a company network.

Visual Quiz

The table in this document has been linked here from Excel. Can you be sure it is current? If not, how can it be updated? If you change a number in the source document, will this be affected? How?

_____

_____

_____

_____

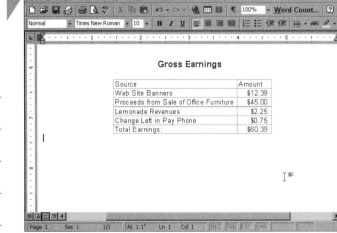

CHAPTER 20

MASTER THESE SKILLS

▶ Creating New Macros

▶ Running a Macro

▶ Managing Your Macros

▶ Editing a Macro

Using Macros

Word 2000 contains many features, ranging from simple text editing and formatting tools up to advanced software integration features such as OLE and mail merging. A few pundits have criticized Word 2000 and other modern word processing programs for being too complicated, but that's probably because they've never tried to take advantage of these advanced features to see what they are capable of.

Among the most underrated features offered by Word are *macros*. Word offers many different automation tools, and you have learned about them throughout this book. Macros can be thought of as the ultimate automation tool in Word, because you can program them to perform virtually any task.

Do you find yourself performing the same repetitive task over and over on your documents? If so, you could probably save some time by writing a macro for that task. For instance, suppose you work for a company called NorthWestern Communications, and you are regularly asked to edit and review a variety of documents. With a name like NorthWestern, it is entirely foreseeable that there will be some common spelling errors in the documents you review. "North Western" might appear in some documents, whereas "Northwestern" may appear in others. You could spend a lot of time correcting the same errors over and over again.

An excellent time-saving solution would be to create a macro that checks for and corrects these common spelling errors before you even start your review. You can run this spelling macro on every document you get, thereby correcting these errors with a single mouse click. You could use the same macro to perform other tasks as well, such as attaching a special letterhead to the beginning and end of each document.

Few Word users take advantage of macros. But if you find yourself doing the same task over and over again, there is a good chance that a macro could save you a great deal of time. The tasks in this chapter introduce you to macros by showing you how to create and edit a basic macro. You also learn how to manage your macros once you have created a number of them.

Creating New Macros

Word offers many automation tools, and among the most versatile are macros. A macro can be used to perform a wide variety of procedures in Word, from simply applying some styles and inserting text to more advanced Find and Replace actions. Whatever you use macros for, you will probably find that it's important to understand how Word's Find and Replace features work. If you haven't done so already, now would be a good time to review Chapter 13 to learn more about using Find and Replace.

Macros provide a set of instructions for Word using the Visual Basic programming language. This doesn't mean you need to learn about programming to take advantage of macros. Creating a macro requires no programming experience whatsoever. The easiest way to create a macro of your own is to *record* it. You simply start recording the macro, follow the steps you want the macro to perform, and then stop the recording process. While you are recording a macro, a small cassette tape icon appears next to the mouse pointer to remind you that you are recording. A Record macro toolbar has buttons to stop or pause the recording process.

The first step in recording a macro is to decide if you want to launch the macro from the toolbar or keyboard. If you choose *toolbar*, a toolbar button will be created for that macro. If you choose *keyboard*,

you will create a keyboard shortcut for the macro. If you choose neither, the macro can still be run from within the Macros dialog box. The figures on the facing page show you how to start the recording process. In the example shown here, you create a macro that is launched by a toolbar button.

Continued

TAKE NOTE

▶ MACROS AND PREVIOUS VERSIONS OF WORD

Macros are recorded in whatever template you happen to be using at the time (probably the Normal template). If you are using a template created with an older version of Word, Word 2000 will still be able to use the macros from it. However, if the template is from Word 95 (7.0) or older, the macro is converted from Word Basic to Visual Basic, and can no longer be used in the older version.

▶ BEWARE OF MACRO VIRUSES

Word documents from other computers can sometimes become infected by macro viruses, which can impact your copy of Word in a variety of ways. Be sure to scan all incoming files with some virus-checking software, such as PandaVirus or McAfee VirusScan. Some virus-scanning software (such as Norton AntiVirus) does not automatically review Word documents, so make sure you have your virus program set to look for this kind of hazard.

CROSS-REFERENCE

See "Adding New Toolbar Buttons" in Chapter 2 to learn more about custom toolbar buttons.

FIND IT ONLINE

Visit The Macro Virus Help Center to learn more about this hazard at **http://training.csd.sc.edu/virus/macro.htm**.

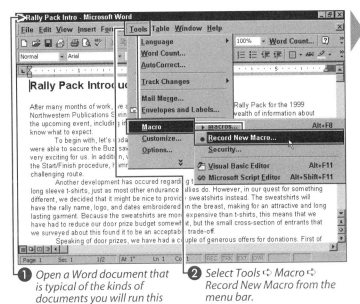

1 Open a Word document that is typical of the kinds of documents you will run this macro on.

2 Select Tools ➪ Macro ➪ Record New Macro from the menu bar.

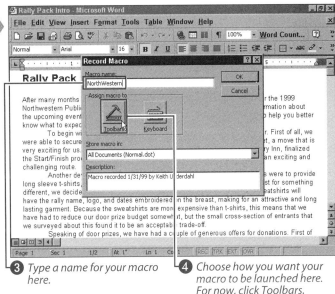

3 Type a name for your macro here.

4 Choose how you want your macro to be launched here. For now, click Toolbars.

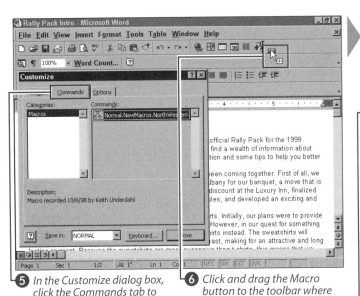

5 In the Customize dialog box, click the Commands tab to bring it to the front.

6 Click and drag the Macro button to the toolbar where you want the button located.

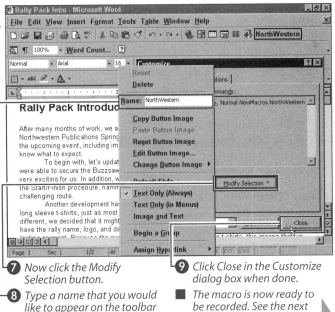

7 Now click the Modify Selection button.

8 Type a name that you would like to appear on the toolbar button here.

9 Click Close in the Customize dialog box when done.

■ The macro is now ready to be recorded. See the next two pages to learn how.

Creating New Macros

Continued

Once you have completed the process of deciding whether to have the macro launched with a toolbar button, keyboard shortcut, or the Macros dialog box, you are ready to start recording the macro. From the time you start recording, every action you perform will become part of that macro. This includes mistakes, even if you undo them. If you do make a mistake that you have to undo, that doesn't mean you have to start all over. You can edit the macro later and manually remove the mistakes. You learn how to do that in the last task in this chapter, "Editing a Macro."

Before you start recording the macro, you should have a solid plan of exactly what the macro will include. As mentioned before, you can do almost anything in a macro. This includes finding and replacing text, adding some formatting, adding text and tables, and more. You can even perform commands like saving and closing a document or printing it.

Macros can range from extremely simple to extremely complex. For instance, suppose you frequently need to enclose certain words or phrases in parentheses. You could create a macro that places parentheses around a selection, so all you have to do is make your selection and click the button to run the macro. At the other extreme, some macros are so large that they could run for several hours on a single file. For instance, in one example I have worked with, a macro searches a Bible commentary and spells out abbreviated names of books of the Bible. Because there are numerous books and many possible abbreviations for each, this macro can run for hours before it is complete.

In the example shown on the opposite page, you create a macro that looks for certain misspellings of a company name and corrects them. If you make a mistake while recording your own macro, don't worry about it right now. You can edit it later in this chapter. You can continue adding as many tasks to the macro as you want, but don't forget to stop recording when you are done.

TAKE NOTE

▶ CLOSING FILES WITH A MACRO

You can close a document file with a macro, but it might be interrupted if the changes aren't saved first. To avoid this problem, click the Save button immediately before closing the document when you are recording the macro.

▶ USING FIND AND REPLACE IN MACROS

If you are using Find or Replace in a macro, make sure that the correct search pattern is selected. For instance, if you want the macro to search the entire document for a word, but the Search Down search pattern is set, any text above the cursor will be ignored by the macro.

CROSS-REFERENCE

To learn how to use Find and Replace, see "Replacing Text" in Chapter 13.

FIND IT ONLINE

Visit Advanced Visual Basic for live chat and how-to articles at **http://vb.duke.net/**.

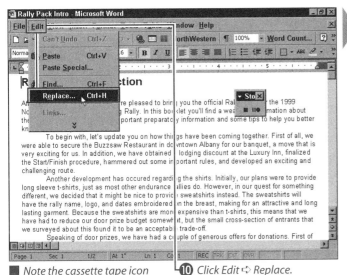

■ Note the cassette tape icon next to the mouse pointer, which indicates that your actions are being recorded into the macro.

⑩ Click Edit ➪ Replace.

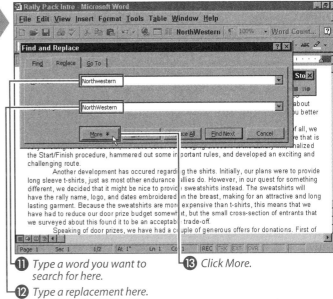

⑪ Type a word you want to search for here.

⑫ Type a replacement here.

⑬ Click More.

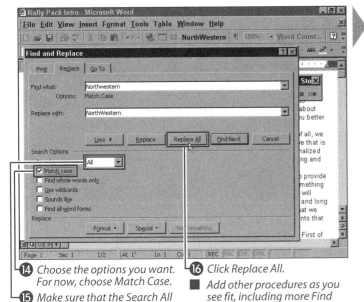

⑭ Choose the options you want. For now, choose Match Case.

⑮ Make sure that the Search All option is chosen here.

⑯ Click Replace All.

■ Add other procedures as you see fit, including more Find and Replace actions for additional misspellings.

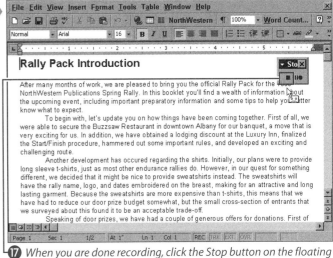

⑰ When you are done recording, click the Stop button on the floating Stop toolbar.

Running a Macro

Obviously, one of the first things you probably want to do after you create a macro is run it. Although macros are all about automation, you have to manually start the macro before it will perform its work. Fortunately, running a macro is quite easy. If you chose to create a toolbar button or keyboard shortcut for the macro, running it is a simple matter of clicking that button or pressing the appropriate shortcut.

Macros can be run at any time while you edit a document. Most macros are designed to be run when you first start editing a document. For instance, suppose you are the editor of a club newsletter and you are using Word to prepare articles that other people submit. You probably want the articles to conform to a certain appearance, so you could create a macro that automatically changes text to a certain font and applies specific format to headings. It might also apply some default header and footer information to the articles to save you some time. The logical time to run a macro like this would be when you first receive an article.

Running macros before you perform other editing has other benefits as well. For instance, consider the macro you created earlier that corrects common misspellings of an unusual company name. This is definitely the kind of thing you would want to run before performing other editing. That way you have a better chance of catching things that somehow slip past the macro by going through the document after it has been run.

The figures on the facing page show you how to run a macro. Although this example uses a macro created earlier that has a toolbar button, it shows you how to open the Macros dialog box and run it from there. The third figure shows what your screen should look like while the macro is running, and the last figure shows the results.

TAKE NOTE

▶ STOPPING A MACRO

You can stop a macro from running in process by pressing the Esc key on your keyboard. If the macro runs to completion before you have a chance to stop it, you can undo it by clicking the Undo button on the Standard toolbar. You might have to press Undo more than once if the macro performed many different tasks. If you aren't sure, click the drop-down arrow next to the Undo button to see which actions have been performed.

▶ RUNNING MACROS ON SELECTED TEXT

Macros can also be run in process while editing or composing a document. For instance, you might design a macro to perform some tasks on a selection. You could create a macro that replaces a word you select, or one that formats a word or phrase you select in boldfaced magenta with marching red ants around it.

CROSS-REFERENCE
See the next task, "Managing Your Macros," to learn more about managing your macros.

FIND IT ONLINE
Microsoft has Visual Basic information online at **http://msdn.microsoft.com/vbasic/**.

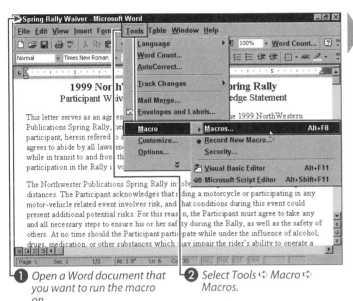

1 Open a Word document that you want to run the macro on.

2 Select Tools ➪ Macro ➪ Macros.

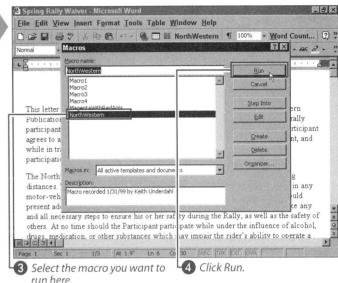

3 Select the macro you want to run here.

4 Click Run.

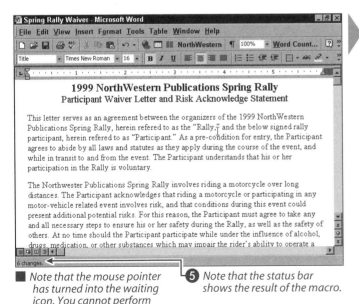

■ Note that the mouse pointer has turned into the waiting icon. You cannot perform other work in Word while the macro is running

5 Note that the status bar shows the result of the macro.

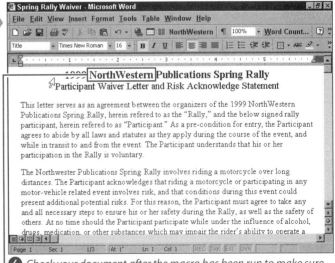

6 Check your document after the macro has been run to make sure the changes are to your satisfaction.

Managing Your Macros

When you create a macro in Word, it becomes part of whatever template happens to be loaded at the time. Unless you have specifically chosen another template, this is probably going to be Word's Normal template. If you have created a number of different macros, you can easily lose track of them, so being able to manage them is important.

The Macros dialog box is your best source for managing macros. It is your first stop for performing many macro-related tasks. In fact, you already used this dialog box to run a macro in the previous task. This dialog box will also be your first stop if you want to edit a macro, and you can delete macros from here as well.

Managing macros from this dialog box is fairly straightforward. Select a macro from the Macro Name list, and click one of the buttons on the right side of the dialog box to perform an action. From here you can run, edit, or delete a macro, or you can begin creating a new one. If you click the Create button here to create a new macro, keep in mind that it will simply open the Microsoft Visual Basic Editor for you to manually create the macro. At this point, you will need some level of Visual Basic programming ability to do anything. Unless you are an experienced programmer, the far easier way to create a macro is to simply record it as outlined in the first task in this chapter.

The figures on the facing page show you how to open and use the Macros dialog box. Once the dialog box is open, you can choose to run, delete, or edit macros as you choose. Just remember that once a macro is deleted, you won't be able to restore it.

TAKE NOTE

GET RID OF UNUSED MACROS

If you have a lot of macros that you never use listed in the Macros dialog box, you should consider getting rid of them. Most of your macros are probably part of the Normal template, and each macro adds to the size of that template. Because the template requires more memory, Word will load much more slowly. I have seen a Normal template that was over 18 *megabytes* (the standard Normal template is just 36 *kilobytes*) simply because it contained a number of very large macros!

CHANGING TEMPLATES

In the Macros dialog box, you can choose other locations to look for and manage macros. Choose another template in the Macros In menu to see what is available in other templates. By doing this, you can use macros from other templates in the document you are currently working in. You can also review the list of Word Commands to see macros that are built into Word.

CROSS-REFERENCE

To learn more about using dialog boxes, see "Using Dialog Boxes" in Chapter 1.

FIND IT ONLINE

For more on macros, visit **http://www.itis.gatech.edu/security/wordmacro/**.

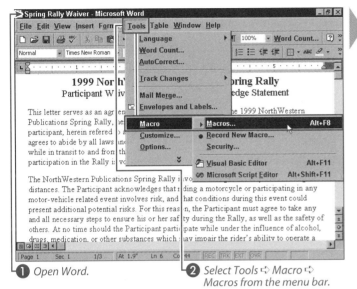

1 Open Word.

2 Select Tools ➪ Macro ➪ Macros from the menu bar.

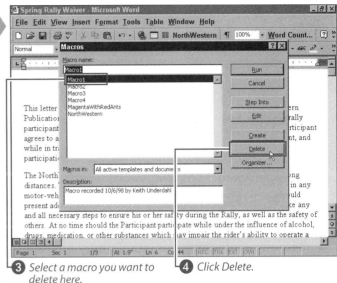

3 Select a macro you want to delete here.

4 Click Delete.

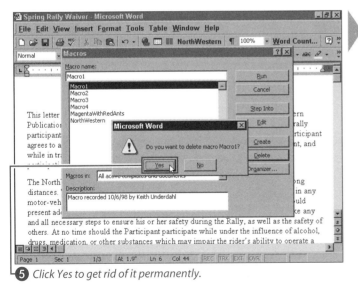

5 Click Yes to get rid of it permanently.

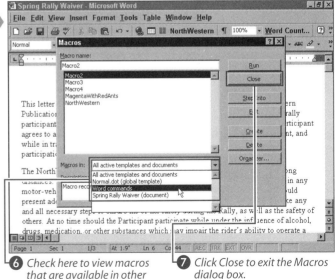

6 Check here to view macros that are available in other templates.

7 Click Close to exit the Macros dialog box.

Editing a Macro

In all likelihood, you will have to make changes to macros you have created. Fortunately, making modifications is possible because a macro is nothing more than a simple program that runs inside Word. You change a macro by simply editing the Visual Basic programming code that it uses.

At this point, you might be taking a step back from the proposition of messing with program code. Fear not; editing macros is much easier than you think. Most of the code used in macros is self-explanatory, although you should be careful about what changes you do make. If there is any doubt in your mind, you might find it easier to just record a new macro to replace your old one. You begin by opening the Microsoft Visual Basic Editor (it launches automatically when you choose to edit a macro).

Lines of code in a macro are arranged in an outline-like format without line numbers. Indentation controls the hierarchy in Visual Basic. If you are familiar with the macro, you should be able to identify the purpose of each part by simply looking at the text of each item.

Many items in the macro will have a value. This value could be a name, such as "Times New Roman" to describe a particular font. The value could also be a number, such as a specific point size for the text. Other items may simply have a true or false value. For instance, if you are formatting characters and you want the characters to be bold, the Bold value in the macro will be *true*. If the characters are not bold, the Bold value will be *false*.

The figures on the facing page show you how to open and edit the Visual Basic code for a macro you created in Word. Changes will be saved automatically as you incorporate them, so simply click the editor's Close (X) button when you are done.

TAKE NOTE

▶ UNDOING CHANGES

You can undo changes that you make in the Visual Basic Editor; however, once you exit a macro, the changes are incorporated automatically. You cannot, for instance, close a macro without saving to reject all the changes you have made, because changes are incorporated into the Normal template the moment you type them.

▶ ADDING TASKS TO A MACRO

If you know how to program with Visual Basic, you can add tasks by typing them in with the VB Editor. Otherwise, the easiest way to add a procedure would be to record a new macro containing only the new procedure. Next, open the new macro in the editor and copy the code lines for the task. Open the macro to which you want to add the procedure. Choose an appropriate location and paste the lines of code in from the new macro you just recorded.

CROSS-REFERENCE

See the first task in this chapter, "Creating New Macros," to learn about recording macros in Word.

FIND IT ONLINE

Visit Carl & Gary's Visual Basic Home Page for some tremendous VB resources at **http://www.cgvb.com/**.

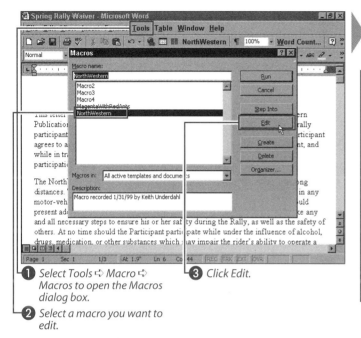

① Select Tools ➪ Macro ➪ Macros to open the Macros dialog box.

② Select a macro you want to edit.

③ Click Edit.

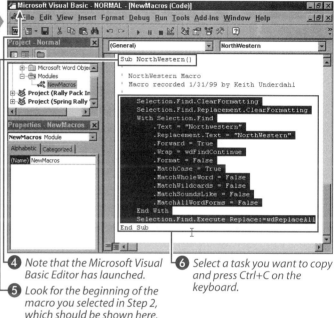

④ Note that the Microsoft Visual Basic Editor has launched.

⑤ Look for the beginning of the macro you selected in Step 2, which should be shown here.

⑥ Select a task you want to copy and press Ctrl+C on the keyboard.

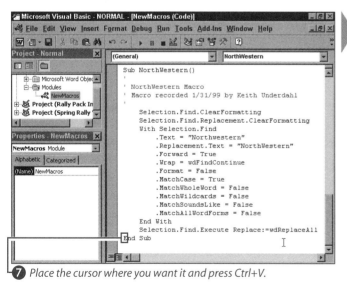

⑦ Place the cursor where you want it and press Ctrl+V.

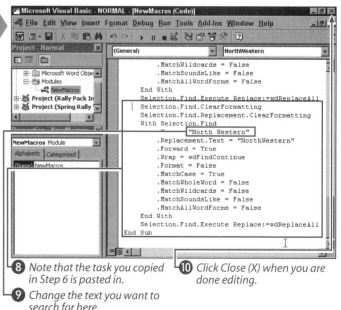

⑧ Note that the task you copied in Step 6 is pasted in.

⑨ Change the text you want to search for here.

⑩ Click Close (X) when you are done editing.

Personal Workbook

Q&A

1 What is the easiest way to create a macro?

_____

_____

_____

2 What programming language do macros use?

_____

_____

_____

3 Can a macro be used to print a document? How?

_____

_____

_____

4 Why should you delete unneeded macros?

_____

_____

_____

5 How can you access the macros built into Word 2000?

_____

_____

_____

6 Can you perform other work in Word when a macro is running?

_____

_____

_____

7 How do you open the Microsoft Visual Basic Editor to modify a macro?

_____

_____

8 Can you close the Visual Basic Editor without saving the changes you make?

_____

_____

_____

ANSWERS: 374

EXTRA PRACTICE

1. Open a Word document with several pages of text.

2. Create a new macro called Head&Foot and begin recording.

3. Create a header and footer for your document that contains standard information for all your documents.

4. Stop recording the macro.

5. Open the macro in the Visual Basic Editor and delete any mistakes you might have made.

6. Run the macro on another document and view the result.

REAL-WORLD APPLICATIONS

✔ If you are using Word to create Web pages, you probably spend a lot of time inserting and formatting graphics and tables. If all the graphics and tables you use have similar formatting, create a macro to apply that formatting to each one.

✔ Another Web application of macros involves hyperlinks. Create a hyperlink that looks for every occurrence of a certain name or phrase. Every time the macro finds an occurrence of the name, it could be formatted as a hyperlink.

✔ Depending on your profession, you may encounter a lot of common acronyms and jargon that apply to your job. Create a macro that looks for and either spells out or explains this jargon. Run that macro on any document that must be read by laypeople.

Visual Quiz

Can you record a new macro from this dialog box? How do you run the second macro listed here? Can it be modified? How? How would you delete one of these macros? Could it be undeleted?

_____

_____

_____

_____

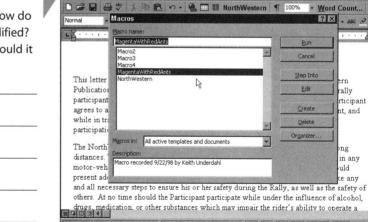

Personal Workbook
Answers

Chapter 1

see page 4

1 **How do you open Word without using a desktop icon?**

A: You can open Word by clicking the Windows Start button and choosing Programs ⇨ Microsoft Word. You can also open Word by first selecting a Word document from the Windows Documents menu.

2 **Why do menus show only the most commonly used items at first?**

A: Word's menus show only the most commonly used items so that they can be found more efficiently.

3 **How can you view additional menu items?**

A: If a menu does not display all the options you want, click the down arrow at the bottom of the menu to display more options.

4 **When does a shortcut menu appear?**

A: Shortcut menus appear when you click an item with the right mouse button.

5 **How can you tell whether selecting a menu item will open a dialog box?**

A: Menu items that open dialog boxes have an ellipsis (. . .) after them.

6 **Can you hide or minimize the Word window without closing the program? How?**

A: You can minimize the Word window by clicking the Minimize button on the title bar. The program remains open, but hidden down on the Windows taskbar.

7 **What is the difference between a screen page and a print page?**

A: A screen page is everything that can be seen on your computer's monitor at once, and a print page is everything that is printed on one piece of paper. Usually, one print page is equal to about two screen pages.

8 **What kind of information does the Document Map display?**

A: The Document Map lists the major headings of your document. If you click one of the headings, the screen moves to that heading.

Visual Quiz

Q: **Does the Document Map shown here reflect all the headings in the document? How can you tell? What are two ways to scroll down to the end of this document? How can you quickly view some commands for an area of text in this document?**

A: A plus sign next to the one heading shown here indicates that other headings are not currently displayed. To scroll down the document, you can press the down arrow keys, click in the scroll bar, drag the scroll bar slider to the bottom of the bar, or press Ctrl+End. To quickly view some commands for an area of text, select some text and right click it to show a shortcut menu.

Chapter 2

see page 24

❶ What should you do if a Word feature you want to use is unavailable?

A: If a Word feature is unavailable, open the Word program setup utility and find the feature in question. You can make it available and install it from there.

❷ How do you change the default location for saving your documents?

A: You can change your default location for saving files on the File Locations tab of the Options dialog box.

❸ Can the automatic spelling checker be disabled? How?

A: On the Spelling and Grammar tab of the Options dialog box, you can disable the automatic spelling checker by deselecting the option Check spelling as you type.

❹ What does Print Layout View represent?

A: Print Layout View closely represents what your document will look like once printed on paper.

❺ What do page breaks look like in Normal View?

A: In Normal View, page breaks are indicated by a dotted line across the page.

❻ Can you add a single button to an existing toolbar?

A: Yes. You can place one or more buttons on any toolbar.

❼ What dialog box must you open to create custom toolbars, toolbar buttons, or shortcut keys?

A: You can add buttons to existing toolbars or create new toolbars in the Customize dialog box. Click the Keyboard button in this dialog box to open the Customize Keyboard dialog box, and use this to create new shortcut keys.

❽ When creating a new shortcut key, how do you know if the key combination is not already assigned?

A: When you create a new shortcut key, the Customize Keyboard dialog box tells you if the combination you tried is already assigned to another command.

Visual Quiz

Q: What view mode is this document currently being viewed in? Why does the document appear so small? What is the free-floating object on the right side of the screen? How was it created?

A: The document shown here is being viewed in Print Layout View. It appears smaller than normal because it is set at 50 percent zoom. The free-floating object on the screen is a custom toolbar that was created in the Customize dialog box.

Chapter 3

see page 42

❶ Can you close a Word document without also closing Word?

A: Yes. Documents can be closed independently of the Word program.

❷ How do you know if more than one Word document is open?

A: Multiple open Word documents have individual buttons on the Windows taskbar.

Personal Workbook Answers

③ What are two ways to switch between open Word documents?

A: You can switch between open documents by clicking the appropriate button on the Windows taskbar, selecting a document from the Window menu, or pressing Alt+Tab.

④ Should you do anything different when saving a file that will need to be used in Word 6.0 later?

A: Documents that will be used in older versions of Word — such as Word 95 or Word 6.0 — must be saved in a special format for that version.

⑤ Can Word read document files that were created with WordPerfect?

A: Word can convert and open documents created in WordPerfect. This might require you to install a converter from the Word program disk.

⑥ What kind of formatting can you include in text files?

A: Text only (ASCII) files cannot contain any character formatting.

⑦ What are text files often used for on program disks?

A: Many program disks include text files that have important installation, compatibility, and setup information about the software.

⑧ What are two ways to change the name of a document file?

A: You can change the name of a document by clicking File Save As and choosing a different file name to save it as, or you can launch the Open dialog box, right-click a filename, and choose Rename from the shortcut menu.

Visual Quiz

Q: Are there any text-only documents shown here? How was the folder named "Rally Pack Stuff" created? Can you rename the file shown here? How?

A: The Open dialog box shown here does not display any text-only files. To create a new folder, click the New Folder button near the top of the Open dialog box. To rename the file shown here, right-click it, choose Rename from the shortcut menu, and then type a new name for the file.

Chapter 4

see page 60

① What does the Office Assistant usually look like?

A: The default appearance of the Office Assistant is a dog named Rocky.

② By default, what does the Office Assistant do every time you open Word?

A: By default, the Office Assistant displays a tip of the day every time you start Word.

③ How do you use the Assistant to obtain help on a particular topic?

A: To gain help from the Office Assistant, click him and type a question in the text box that appears. Click Search.

④ How do you disable the Assistant?

A: You can disable the Office Assistant by clicking Options, and then deselect the option Use the Office Assistant.

⑤ Can you produce a printed copy of help topics? How?

A: If you want to print a help topic you are reading, click Print in the Help window.

6 **What is the quickest way to search for help in the Microsoft Word Help window?**

A: You can quickly search for help in the Help window using the Answer Wizard.

7 **Where are most wizards located?**

A: Most wizards are located in the New dialog box, which can be accessed from the File menu.

8 **What kind of information does Microsoft provide for you on the Internet?**

A: Microsoft includes free software add-ins, online tips, upgrades, and product news on the Office on the Web site.

Visual Quiz

Q: What is the quickest way to produce a fax cover sheet, as shown here? What does the cartoon dog in the lower-right corner represent? What will happen if you click some of the text in the dialog bubble coming from the dog? Can you disable this feature? How?

A: This fax cover sheet was produced using the Fax Wizard. The dog shown here is the Office Assistant. The dialog bubble coming from him lists help topics, and if you click one, you will be able to read it. You can disable the Office Assistant by clicking Options.

Chapter 5

see page 78

1 **How do you insert a line break?**

A: You can insert a manual line break by pressing Shift+Enter. Automatic line breaks are created at the end of every line.

2 **How do you view the exact locations of line and paragraph breaks?**

A: You can view the exact location of line and paragraph breaks by clicking the Show/Hide button on the toolbar.

3 **What must you do to select text using only the keyboard?**

A: You can select text using the keyboard by holding down the Shift key as you move the cursor with the arrow keys.

4 **What are two ways to insert a page break?**

A: You can insert a page break by clicking Insert ➪ Break on the menu bar and choosing Page Break in the dialog box. An easier way is to simply press Ctrl+Enter on the keyboard.

5 **How do you adjust margins on the page?**

A: You can adjust page margins from within the Page Setup dialog box in the File menu.

6 **What does the term landscape mean when referring to page layout?**

A: A landscape page is oriented so that the long side of the page is horizontal rather than vertical.

7 **How do you insert a special character that is not on the keyboard?**

A: You can insert special characters by clicking Insert ➪ Symbol on the menu bar and choosing a character from the Symbol dialog box.

8 **Does Word automatically number pages in your documents? How do you change page numbering options?**

A: Pages are not numbered by default. You can change this and other page numbering options by clicking Insert ➪ Page Numbers on the menu bar.

Personal Workbook Answers

Visual Quiz

Q: How was the shape and size of this page modified? Is the layout oriented in landscape or portrait? Is the page numbered? How was the special copyright symbol inserted?

A: The shape of this page was modified by adjusting measurements in the Page Layout dialog box. This particular page is oriented in landscape format. Copyright symbols can be inserted from the Symbols dialog box or by typing (c).

Chapter 6

see page 98

1 How do you begin creating a new document using a template?

A: You can use a template to create a new document by selecting File ⇨ New on the menu bar and then choosing a template to use.

2 Will only those templates actually installed on your computer be displayed in the New dialog box?

A: The New dialog box displays all templates available to Word, whether they are currently installed or not.

3 Can you use templates from older versions of Word with Word 2000?

A: You can use templates from previous versions of Word with Word 2000.

4 What kind of information can be stored in a template?

A: Templates can store styles, page layout information, macros, and even text.

5 Why is using a template to create a new document often preferable to simply copying an existing document?

A: Templates can include explanatory information about the document you are to create and ensure a standardized format.

6 Can you create your own templates?

A: You can create your own custom templates in Word.

7 What kinds of text should you include in templates?

A: If you create a new template, include some text that provides instructions and helpful tips to the user.

8 Can you modify templates that come with Word?

A: You can modify any template, whether it is one you made yourself or one that came with Word.

Visual Quiz

Q: How do you open this dialog box? Can you view templates other than what are shown here? How? How can you begin creating your own template? Can these templates be modified? How?

A: You can open this dialog box by clicking File ⇨ New on the menu bar. Click the tabs in this dialog box to view other templates. If you want to create a new template, click the template radio button before you click OK. You can modify a template by first opening it as you would a regular document, and then making modifications.

Chapter 7

see page 114

1 What is a font?

A: A font is a typeface used for text in Word. Different fonts provide different appearances for text.

② **Can you change the size of a font? How?**

A: Fonts can be resized by clicking a different point size in the Font Size drop-down menu.

③ **How do you make text bold?**

A: Select some text and click the Bold button on the formatting toolbar to make it bold.

④ **Does animated character formatting work for all documents?**

A: Animated character formatting does not work in Web documents, text only documents, or those that will be used with Word 95 or earlier.

⑤ **How do you center a paragraph?**

A: To center a paragraph, place the cursor in the paragraph and click the Center button on the formatting toolbar.

⑥ **What does the term justify mean in relation to paragraph formatting?**

A: Justified text stretches to fill the entire width of the page (minus margins, of course).

⑦ **What kind of information can a style contain?**

A: A style can contain information about character and paragraph formatting.

⑧ **How do you apply a style?**

A: To apply a style, click in a paragraph and choose a style from the Style drop-down menu.

Visual Quiz

Q: **How do you change the font in the title of the document shown here? Based on the style displayed on the Formatting toolbar, where do you suppose the cursor is currently located? How is that paragraph aligned on the page? Is there any other special formatting applied to the characters in that paragraph that you can see?**

A: You can change font by selecting the appropriate text and choosing a new one in the Font drop-down menu. Based on the style shown in the drop-down menu, the cursor must be in the line that says, "by Keith Underdahl." That paragraph is centered on the page, and the characters are italicized.

Chapter 8

see page 136

① **How do you insert a table?**

A: You can insert a table by placing the cursor where you want the table to go and clicking the Insert Table button on the Standard toolbar.

② **What is the difference between a column and a row?**

A: A column runs vertically in a table, and a row runs horizontally.

③ **What is the quickest way to format a table?**

A: You can quickly format a table by selecting it and clicking Table ⇨ Table AutoFormat on the menu bar.

④ **Can you change the size of just one cell in a row without affecting the other cells?**

A: If you resize a cell, all other cells in that row or column will be similarly affected. All cells in a row must have the same height, and all cells in a column must have the same width.

Personal Workbook Answers

5 **How do you change text direction in a cell?**

A: You can change the direction of text in a table by right-clicking in a cell and choosing Text Direction from the shortcut menu.

6 **What kind of information can you put in a table?**

A: Tables can include text, numbers, graphics, and almost anything else that can be inserted into a Word document.

7 **Do table borders have to be visible on your printed document?**

A: Table borders can be invisible, if you want.

8 **Once a table is created, is it too late to change the number of columns or rows?**

A: You can always add or delete rows and columns in a table using the shortcut menus.

Visual Quiz

Q: **This for-sale brochure contains a table. Where is it? Why is it difficult to detect? How is the text in that table oriented? How would you reproduce this effect? If there is room on the page, how could you insert more columns?**

A: The table is located at the bottom of this page, but is difficult to notice because the borders are invisible. The text in the table is oriented vertically on the page. You can perform this action using options in the table shortcut menus. If you wanted to insert more columns into this table, you could simply select a column, right-click it, and choose Insert Column from the shortcut menu.

Chapter 9

see page 152

1 **How do you insert a graphic into a document?**

A: You can insert a graphic from a file on disk by clicking Insert ➪ Picture ➪ From file on the menu bar. Locate the graphic file and insert it.

2 **What is the name of the clipart collection Microsoft provides with Word?**

A: Microsoft provides the clipart gallery, a collection of free clipart that you can use in Word documents.

3 **Is all of this art installed on your hard drive?**

A: Most of this art remains on the Word 2000 program CD, and will not be installed until you choose to actually use it.

4 **What is the quickest way to resize a graphic?**

A: You can resize a graphic by clicking it and dragging the manipulation handles that appear.

5 **How can you ensure the proportions of the graphic are not changed when you resize the graphic?**

A: Maintain a picture's proportions by right-clicking it and choosing Format Picture from the shortcut menu. Click the Size tab, and make sure the Lock aspect ratio option is selected.

6 **How do you begin drawing shapes in your document?**

A: Begin drawing shapes by clicking Insert ➪ Picture ➪ AutoShapes on the menu bar.

7 **Can your shapes be resized after they are created?**

A: You can move and resize shapes just as you would other graphics in Word.

8 **What program must be installed on your computer to use charts?**

A: You must have Microsoft Excel to use the Charts tool.

Visual Quiz

Q: **Can the picture shown here be moved? How? If you drag the bottom manipulation handle down, how will the graphic be affected? How was the arrow created? How can you resize it?**

A: You can move the picture shown here by clicking it. Move the mouse pointer over the picture until it becomes a four-headed arrow, and then click and drag the image to a new location. If you drag just the bottom manipulation handle down, the picture will take on a stretched look. The arrow was created using the Word drawing objects. It can also be resized by clicking and dragging manipulation handles at each end of it.

Chapter 10

see page 172

1 **When should you edit text?**

A: You can edit text both during your initial composition, as well as after you have completed a first draft. Basically, you can edit constantly and whenever you want.

2 **What kind of actions are involved in editing?**

A: Editing might involve adding, deleting, moving, or copying text or other objects.

3 **What is the easiest way to replace text in a document?**

A: The easiest way to replace text is to select it and begin typing the replacement text.

4 **What does OVR on the Word status bar mean?**

A: OVR means that you are in type-over mode.

5 **How do you delete an object from Word?**

A: To delete an object, just click it and then press the Delete key on your keyboard.

6 **What is the difference between deleting text and deleting images?**

A: Text and images are deleted in exactly the same way.

7 **How is moving an object different from copying?**

A: When you move something, it is removed from the original location and put in a new one. When you copy it, the original stays put and the copy is saved elsewhere.

8 **How do you restore something you deleted by accident?**

A: You can restore an accidental deletion by pressing the Undo button on the toolbar.

Visual Quiz

Q: **The figure shows four copies of the same picture. What is the easiest way to create this effect? Can the figures be copied to another document? How? Can you insert more text into the middle of the sentence near the bottom? How? How do you delete the images? How can you restore them again after deletion?**

A: The easiest way to create this effect is to simply copy and paste the image. These images can also be copied individually into other programs. To insert text into the middle of a sentence, click to place the cursor and begin typing. Make sure that OVR does not appear on the taskbar. You can delete an image just as you would any other object by selecting it and pressing Delete on the keyboard. It can be restored again by clicking Undo.

Personal Workbook Answers

Chapter 11

see page 186

1 **How does Word indicate a spelling error?**

A: Incorrectly spelled words are indicated by a red wavy underline.

2 **Does this mark always indicate that a word is misspelled?**

A: In addition to spelling errors, red wavy underlines are also placed under words that aren't in the Word spelling dictionary or under words that are repeated.

3 **How can you avoid having to always spell check your own name?**

A: You can avoid getting a spelling error for your own name by adding it to the custom spelling dictionary.

4 **Can you remove words from your custom dictionary? How?**

A: You can remove words from the custom dictionary by opening it as a text file and deleting words you don't want.

5 **Name at least three kinds of errors that the grammar checker will identify.**

A: The grammar checker looks for improper punctuation, capitalization, tense errors, passive sentences, incorrect use of similar words, and more.

6 **How does Word identify grammatical errors in your document?**

A: Grammatical errors are identified by a green wavy underline.

7 **How do you disable the grammar and spelling checkers?**

A: You can disable the grammar and spelling checkers through options available on the Spelling and Grammar tab of the Options dialog box.

8 **What does the Word Thesaurus do?**

A: The thesaurus suggests synonyms for selected words or phrases.

Visual Quiz

Q: **Is the dialog box identifying a spelling or grammar error? Is the word misspelled? Could you tell Word never to call this a spelling error again? How? If it is an error, how would you correct it?**

A: The dialog box has identified a word that is not in the dictionary. However, in this case it appears to be a company name rather than a misspelling. You can click Add to add this word to your custom dictionary so that Word does not identify it as an error again. If this were indeed a spelling error, the easiest way to fix it would be to pick a selection from the Suggestions list and click Change.

Chapter 12

see page 200

1 **If you accidentally type "teh" instead of "the," what do you have to do to correct the error?**

A: This error is corrected automatically by AutoCorrect.

2 **What is the quickest way to enter a copyright symbol (©) into your document?**

A: You can quickly enter a copyright symbol by typing (c).

3 Can you create a shortcut to enter a long company name? How?

A: You can create a shortcut for a long name by creating a new AutoCorrect entry for it in the AutoCorrect dialog box.

4 How do you delete an AutoCorrect entry?

A: In the AutoCorrect dialog box, select the entry you want to delete and press the Delete button.

5 What is one way to access AutoText entries?

A: You can access AutoText items by clicking Insert ⇨ AutoText on the menu bar, or press Tab or Enter when an AutoComplete tip appears.

6 How do you enter text from an AutoComplete tip into your document?

A: To enter text from an AutoComplete tip, just press Tab or Enter when it appears.

7 If you insert the current date into your document, can it be updated automatically? How?

A: If you insert the date with the Update Automatically option set, it will be replaced by the current date whenever you open or print the document.

8 Web site URLs are automatically formatted as hyperlinks. How can you disable this feature?

A: You can disable automatic formatting of URLs by deselecting the "Internet and network paths with hyperlinks" option on the AutoFormat tab of the AutoCorrect dialog box.

Visual Quiz

Q: Is there a quick way to enter the company name at the top of this document? How can the special formatting used in the fraction and ordinal in the address be applied quickly? What is the quickest way to enter the date shown here? Can it be updated automatically? What about the time? What kind of quotation marks are used around the quote?

A: You can quickly enter a company name using AutoText, or by creating an AutoCorrect entry for it. Special items such as fractions and ordinals are automatically formatted using AutoFormat options. You can quickly enter the date by clicking Insert ⇨ Date and Time on the menu bar. It will be updated automatically whenever the file is opened or printed. The current time could be entered in a similar way. The quote shown here is enclosed in smart quotes.

Chapter 13

see page 216

1 When you use Find, does Word ignore extra spaces you type at the end of the word?

A: No. Find looks for the exact search string you type in, including spaces.

2 Can you make more than one replacement at a time?

A: You can replace every occurrence of a "Find what" search string by clicking Replace All instead of Replace.

3 What is a wildcard?

A: A wildcard acts as a variable in a search string. For instance, ^# is a wildcard for any number.

4 What is the wildcard for any letter?

A: The wildcard for any letter is ^$.

Personal Workbook Answers

⑤ What is the wildcard for a paragraph mark?

A: The wildcard for a paragraph mark is ^p.

⑥ What kinds of changes can you make with Find and Replace?

A: You can replace text directly, or you can use it to apply special formatting.

⑦ Can you edit your document while the Find and Replace dialog box is open?

A: You can edit your document while the Find and Replace dialog box is open.

⑧ Does Find and Replace have a wildcard for a whole word?

A: Find and Replace does not have a wildcard that searches for a whole word.

Visual Quiz

Q: In this Find and Replace dialog box, what is the text that will be replaced? How will the replacement text differ from the text that was found? Are more options available? How do you see them? Without using a formatting menu, how was the formatting for this item changed?

A: Any occurrence of (XS-P) will be replaced. In this case, it will be replaced by the search result, but will be italicized. More Find and Replace options are available by clicking the More button. Almost any kind of character formatting can be applied using Find and Replace.

Chapter 14

see page 234

① How do you open the Print dialog box?

A: You can open the Print dialog box by pressing Ctrl+P on your keyboard or by clicking File ⇨ Print on the menu bar.

② Why would you want to open the Print dialog box before printing?

A: The Print dialog box enables you to set important printing options before the document is actually printed.

③ Can you preview more than one page at a time in Print Preview?

A: You can preview multiple pages at once in Print Preview.

④ What are some printer settings you should check before printing?

A: You can often change the quality and speed settings of your printer. If you have a color printer, you can usually choose to print either in color or black ink only.

⑤ How do you print three pages of a five-page document?

A: You can print only a few pages of a multipage document by choosing the Pages radio button in the Print dialog box and typing the page numbers you want to print.

⑥ How do you print more than one copy of a document at a time?

A: You can print multiple copies of a document by choosing a different number next to "Number of copies" in the Print dialog box.

⑦ What does the Collate option do?

A: The Collate option prints one complete copy of the document in page order before moving on to the next copy.

⑧ Can you print using a printer that is not connected to your computer?

A: You can print to other printers by printing your document to a file.

Personal Workbook Answers

Visual Quiz

Q: The document in the figure is in Print Preview. How do you close the Preview? How can you quickly control the zoom in Preview? How many copies of this document will be printed? Will every page be printed? Will the pages be collated or printed consecutively?

A: You can close Print Preview by clicking Close on the toolbar or by pressing Esc on your keyboard. You can change the zoom level by choosing a different number in the zoom level drop-down menu. With the current settings, only one copy of pages 1, 3, 4, and 5 will be printed. The pages will be printed separately because the collate option is disabled.

Chapter 15

see page 250

❶ Do you have to manually measure the size of any label you want to print?

A: No. Most labels come in standard sizes, and Word contains formatting information for labels from many different label manufacturers.

❷ Can you use any kind of graphic you want on a label?

A: You can use any graphic on a label you want, but it's best to use something with only one or two colors.

❸ What should you do before printing labels?

A: You should test print the labels on a plain sheet of paper before printing the actual labels.

❹ What should you do if the labels are misaligned?

A: You can adjust the page margins to help labels line up properly.

❺ Can you feed a sheet of labels through your printer more than once?

A: Label sheets should never be fed through a printer more than once, as printer damage could result.

❻ What is the best way to address a single item?

A: If you only need to address one item, it's best to print an envelope instead of a label.

❼ What additional postal information besides the address can Word print on an envelope?

A: In addition to an address, Word can automatically generate and print a postal bar code on your envelopes.

❽ What is the best type of printer to use when printing envelopes?

A: Laser printers usually work better than ink-jet printers for printing envelopes.

Visual Quiz

Q: How were these labels created? What kind of label is this? Does the label format have to be manually created? Why or why not? How was the graphic added to the labels? Will it appear on the printed labels? If you only need to print one address, what would be a more efficient way to do that?

A: These labels were created from within the Envelopes and Labels dialog box in the Tools menu. These particular labels appear to be floppy disk labels. The label format can be created automatically by choosing the correct product code in the Envelopes and Labels dialog box. Graphics can be added to labels just as they are to any other document. In this case, the graphic was copied to each label and will appear when the labels are printed. If you needed to print only one address, the best way to do that is to print it directly on an envelope.

Personal Workbook Answers

Chapter 16

see page 264

❶ What is the difference between the Web toolbar and Web Tools toolbar?

A: The Web toolbar provides tools to help you navigate Web pages, and the Web Tools toolbar contains tools for creating some advanced Web page elements.

❷ If you have a Web browser installed on your computer, will Web documents open in Word?

A: If you have a Web browser installed on your computer, Web pages will probably open in it instead of Word.

❸ What file format must you use when you save a file as a Web document?

A: Web documents must be saved in HTML format.

❹ What is the easiest way to align a picture and some text alongside each other in a Web document?

A: An easy way to align text and graphics alongside each other in a Web document is to place them in a table.

❺ What is a hyperlink?

A: A hyperlink is text or a graphic that, when clicked, leads to another Web document.

❻ Can you create a link that makes it easier for people to contact you?

A: An e-mail link that makes it easier for people to contact you.

❼ What must you do before others can view your Web pages?

A: If you want other people to view your Web pages, they must be published on a Web server.

❽ Where should your Web files be located before your publish?

A: For best results, you should locate all your Web files in a single folder before publication.

Visual Quiz

Q: The Web document shown here has a picture alongside some text. What is an easy way to create this setup? Are there any hyperlinks on this page? What does a hyperlink look like?

A: A table was used here to align the text and graphic alongside each other. There are no hyperlinks apparent here. A hyperlink would appear as blue or purple underlined text.

Chapter 17

see page 288

❶ What two document elements do you need to perform a mail merge?

A: You must have a main document and data source to perform a mail merge.

❷ Which element would contain the body of a form letter?

A: The main document would include the body of a form letter.

❸ What are three possible sources of data for a mail merge?

A: Mail Merge can obtain data from a Word data source, an Outlook personal address book, or an Access table or query.

❹ In a Word data source, can you create your own fields?

A: Yes, you can create your own fields in a Word data source.

⑤ Can you limit which records are merged from the data source?

A: Yes, you can filter data records that will be merged by comparing them to specific criteria.

⑥ What will the merge fields look like in the main document?

A: Merge fields will appear as gray blocks with the field name in your main document.

⑦ How can you preview a merged document?

A: You can preview merged documents by clicking the View Merged Data button on the Mail Merge toolbar.

⑧ In what situation would it be better to use an Access database rather than a Word document as your data source?

A: If your company already uses Access to track customer information, it would be better to use it as a data source rather than create your own.

Visual Quiz

Q: Which portions of this document are merge fields? Can you change the merge fields so that they show the actual data that will be inserted into them? How? How would you switch to another copy of the document with the next data record in it?

A: The gray blocks called "FirstName" and "City" are merge fields. You can preview actual data in these fields by clicking the View Merged Data button. You can then click the Next Record button to view the next data record merged into the form letter.

Chapter 18

see page 300

① How do you create a bulleted list using AutoFormat?

A: You can automatically create a bulleted list by typing an asterisk (*) in front of each line of the list.

② Can you use something other than regular numbers in a numbered list?

A: Numbered lists can use numbers, roman numerals, letters, and other numbering formats.

③ When inserting a header, do you have to create a separate header for each page?

A: Normally you only create one header, which will be used on every page of the document.

④ Will borders and shading have the same appearance on paper that they do on the screen?

A: Borders and shading will have roughly the same appearance on screen that they do on paper, but keep in mind that your printer might not be able to print them as nicely as they appear on your monitor.

⑤ What is the purpose of columns?

A: Columns provide a visual break in long magazine or newspaper articles and make them easier to read.

⑥ Once you have created an outline, can you change the position of headings? How?

A: You can move headings up and down, or demote or promote them using buttons on the outlining toolbar.

⑦ What kind of information does Word Count provide other than the number of words?

A: Word count also counts pages, characters, paragraphs, and lines.

⑧ If you delete some text with the Track Changes feature enabled, what happens to that deleted text?

A: It is struck through with a line but remains on screen.

Personal Workbook Answers

Visual Quiz

Q: The first couple of paragraphs are darker than the rest of the document. Why? What is unique about the paragraphs under it? What does the crossed-out heading mean? Why are the words next to it underlined?

A: Some shading has been applied to the first couple of paragraphs of this document. The paragraphs underneath are arranged in newspaper columns. The crossed-out heading has been deleted, but is still displayed because the Track Changes feature is enabled. The underlined words have been added in place of the deleted words.

Chapter 19

see page 332

1 What is the difference between linking and embedding?

A: Linked objects maintain a link to the source document and are updated whenever the source is. Embedded objects do not maintain such a link, and the data is actually saved in the Word document.

2 Can you link any kind of object you want into Word?

A: You can link any kind of object that can be edited or created with software on your computer.

3 Can linked objects be updated automatically?

A: Linked objects are updated automatically every time the document is opened or printed.

4 How do you manually update a linked object?

A: You can manually update a linked object by clicking Edit ➪ Links on the menu bar and then choose which objects to update from the Links dialog box.

5 Why would you want to link text from another Word document rather than just copy and paste it?

A: You might want to link text from another Word document that you think might be updated before your final document is published.

6 If you change the source document of an embedded object, is the object updated?

A: Changes to the source document of an embedded object do not affect the embedded object.

7 Can you edit embedded objects from within Word?

A: You can edit embedded objects by clicking them. Tools then appear to facilitate editing.

8 Give an example of when an embedded object would be more useful than a linked object.

A: Embedding is a better option for files that exist on other computers over an unreliable network connection, or for source files that you think might be deleted or archived soon.

Visual Quiz

Q: The table in this document has been linked here from Excel. Can you be sure it is current? If not, how can it be updated? If you change a number in the source document, will this table be affected? How?

A: The data should have been updated when the document was opened. You can update it manually from the Links dialog box in the Edit menu. Changes in the source document are reflected automatically here.

Chapter 20

see page 346

1 What is the easiest way to create a macro?

A: The easiest way to create a macro is to record it.

2 **What programming language do macros use?**

A: Macros use the Visual Basic programming language.

3 **Can a macro be used to print a document? How?**

A: A macro can perform many functions, including printing. Simply print the document while you record the macro.

4 **Why should you delete unneeded macros?**

A: You should delete unneeded macros because they take up space in your templates.

5 **How can you access the macros that are built into Word 2000?**

A: In the Macros dialog box, choose Word Commands from the Macros in drop-down menu.

6 **Can you perform other work in Word when a macro is running?**

A: You cannot perform other work in Word while a macro is running.

7 **How do you open the Microsoft Visual Basic Editor to modify a macro?**

A: You can open the Visual Basic Editor by clicking Edit in the Macros dialog box.

8 **Can you close the Visual Basic Editor without saving the changes you make?**

A: You cannot reject changes you make in the Visual Basic Editor by closing it without saving. Changes are automatically incorporated into the template when you close the Editor.

Visual Quiz

Q: **Can you record a new macro from this dialog box? How do you run the second macro listed here? Can it be modified? How? How would you delete one of these macros? Could it be undeleted?**

A: You cannot begin the recording process from this dialog box. To run a macro, select it in the Macro name list and click Run. You can modify a macro by selecting it and clicking Edit. If you click Delete, a selected macro is deleted. Once a macro is deleted, it cannot be recovered.

Index

INDEX

Continued

INDEX

document(s) *(continued)*

inserting breaks in, 88–89

inserting header or footer into, 310

linking a Microsoft Excel worksheet into, 336–337

main. *See* main document

merging, 294–295

moving around in, 18–19

multicolor, 240

new, using a template to create, 100–101

numbering pages in, 94–95

open, switching between, 52–53

printing, 235–249. *See also* printing

saving as a templates, 110

searching, 222

selecting text for, 86–87

setting up the page in, 82–85

text, numbered lists in, 304

using special characters and symbols in, 90–93

viewing, 32–33

wavy green line in, 192

wavy red line in, 188, 190

Web. *See* Web document(s)

document Close button, 44

Document Map, 20–21

document scraps, 180

document template. *See* template(s)

Dolphin.exe, 70

dot-matrix printers, 254

double-clicking, 342

double-spacing, 126

drawing objects

defined, 160

making transparent, 160

using, 160–163

drivers, for printers, 240

E

e-mail, using Word to compose, 206

e-mail links, 278

Earthlink, 268

editing

documents, 173

embedded objects, 342–343

exiting from, 342

in insert mode, 174

a macro, 356–357

text, 174–175

in type-over mode, 174, 176

using Undo and Redo, 182–183

WordArt text, 158

embedded object(s)

moving, 164

resizing, 164

embedding

linking versus, 333

Microsoft Excel Worksheets, 340

objects, 340–341

editing embedded objects and, 342–343

new, 340

Emboss, Character formatting, 120

endnotes, 322

entering

graphics on labels, 254–255

envelope(s)

addresses on, 251, 258

barcodes on, 258, 260

formatting, 258–259

printing, 84, 251, 260–261

envelope size and, 258

printer compatibility and, 260

size of, 258

Index

Index

L

label(s)
designed for your printer, 256
entering graphics on, 254–255
formatting, 252–253
number of colors on, 254
preformatted, 252
printing, 251, 256–257
printing addresses on, 252
product codes and, 252
uses for, 252, 254
using entire sheet of at one time, 256
Label Options dialog box, 252
landscape orientation, 84
Las Vegas Lights, 122, 123
laser printers
envelopes and, 260
moisture problems and, 244
quality of, 254
left alignment, 124
legal paper, 84
line break, 88
line spacing, 126
line styles, choosing, 160
link(s) hyperlinks versus, 338
linking
charts, 336
embedding versus, 333
Microsoft Excel worksheet, 336–337
objects, 334–335
over a network, 338
updating linked objects and, 338–339
saving space by, 334
synchronization and, 338
Links dialog box, 338

list(s)
bulleted
creating, 302–305
formatting, 306–309
in Web documents, 302
numbered
creating, 302–305
formatting, 306–309
restarting numbering and, 308
in text documents, 304

M

macro(s)
adding tasks to, 356
closing files with, 350
creating, 348–351
defined, 347
from earlier versions of Word, 348
editing, 356–357
undoing changes and, 356
Macros dialog box, 354
managing, 354–355
running, 352–353
stopping, 352
unused, getting rid of, 354
using, 347–359
viruses and, 348
Macros dialog box, 348, 350, 352
Mail Merge
data source and. *See* data source
filtering and, 294
main document and. *See* main document
merging documents and, 294–295
using, 289–299
Mail Merge dialog box, 290

Index

T

Index